The Copernican Revolution:

Putting the Earth into Motion

Anthony Millevolte

The Copernican Revolution: Putting the Earth into Motion
Anthony Millevolte
Tuscobia Press
August 2014

Theano Old Style font courtesy of fontsquirrel.com

ISBN-13: 978-1500433765
ISBN-10: 1500433764

[The cover image is a medieval miniature of clerk, an astronomer, and a mathematician in an illuminated early 13th century psalter. It is the first image that appears in a prayer book from the library of Charles V and Family. Image courtesy of Bibliothèque Nationale, Paris and the Europeana Regia project.]

To Laura

Preface and Acknowledgements

This textbook was the product of necessity since I was unable to find materials adequate for teaching an introductory course on the Copernican Revolution. While there exist excellent historical surveys of astronomy that offer more astronomical detail than what you will find here, they tend not to emphasize the historical, philosophical, and religious contexts in which the different astronomical traditions were practiced. Histories of astronomy tend to focus on what astronomers were doing. This text is designed to give a greater emphasis on why astronomers were doing what they were doing and to also examine how their activities were related to the society of which they were a part.

The need for up-to-date textbooks is underscored by the fact that Kuhn's famous book, *The Copernican Revolution*, is still assigned in colleges today – even though it was first published in 1957. As well written as it is, the obviously unavoidable weakness of Kuhn's text is that it doesn't reflect over a half century of active scholarship in the field. Indeed, historians of science view the Copernican Revolution in a considerably different light than they did fifty years ago. Thus, it strikes me as most remarkable that there are so few contemporary introductions devoted to one of the most important intellectual transitions in history – and, as far as I know, none that also underscore the cultural elements of the story.

Having grown impatient with waiting for someone more obviously qualified to do it, I began writing this textbook about ten years ago. At the outset, I naively supposed that all I would have to do is carefully examine what the experts have said, identify what the consensus opinions were, and then synthesize these views into a coherent narrative that would be accessible to freshmen and sophomore university students. The historiography of the episode is very rich, and the quality of the scholarship is truly impressive. Scores of monographs have been published over the last fifty years on a wide range of topics relevant to the Copernican Revolution – from ancient Greek science all the way up through early eighteenth century physics and astronomy. By their nature, these books are written by specialists and are narrowly focused on particular issues, works, and/or biographies – thus, they are not very accessible to introductory students.

In retrospect, I now understand why no one has tried to write a "Copernican Revolution" since Kuhn: It turns out that the experts disagree on a good many of the central elements of the story – so much so that it is sometimes challenging to identify an acceptable narrative. The canonical account that I had hoped to capture and present here doesn't quite seem to exist. In spite of this, I believe that most of what I've provided in this text reflects the mainstream views of historians of science. At those points where the absence of a consensus view challenged my goal to provide a coherent narrative, I pushed through as best I could and provided endnotes and references that can serve as points of departure for the interested reader. If I've said anything novel or that would inspire criticism, it is most likely to be found in the final chapter.

I would like to thank Oscar Chamberlain in particular for helping me get this project off the ground, as well as Drs. Sue Patrick and Paul Chase who also provided important encouragement and advice all along the way. I would also like to acknowledge the University of Wisconsin Colleges, which supported a sabbatical program during difficult times and the chairs of the UW Colleges History Department – David Huehner, Michael Thorn, and Dan Kallgren for their support and willingness to include a scientist among them. Important critical comments on some of the chapters and passages were provided by Christopher Graney, Michael H. Shank, Alistair Kwan, and Thony Christie as well as members of the HASTRO-L listserv. I would also like to thank Kerry Magruder and the University of Oklahoma History of Science Collections for several of the images. Finally, I owe a great deal of gratitude to Jayant Anand, Jui Gadade, Sheena Fallon, Alyssa Pelish, Amanda Kupsch, and Rhonda Dietrich for important editorial and proof reading assistance.

Finally, the most important contributors to the text were my history of science students who held my feet to the fire regarding those passages in earlier versions that either lacked clarity or completeness. This book was written for them.

Anthony Millevolte
University of Wisconsin Colleges

CONTENTS

Chapter One – Introduction and Early Western Astronomy: Prehistory, Egyptians and Babylonians

Introduction

We all learned this as schoolchildren: the apparently solid ground on which we stand is, in reality, the surface of a large spinning ball that orbits the sun. While this isn't at all obvious to our senses, we've accepted the idea of a moving earth for so long that we no longer give it a second thought. This wasn't always the case – the well-known story of Galileo (1564-1642) and the great troubles he experienced with the Roman Catholic Church when he publicly advocated for the moving earth illustrates the strong resistance the idea first encountered. Given our matter-of-fact belief in the earth's motion today, we might ask: *Why was it so difficult for people to accept the idea that the earth moves?* We intend to address this question by developing an appreciation for the struggles of those who first experienced this new way of thinking. This is a challenging undertaking, and to be successful at it we need to be sympathetic to the people who held earlier beliefs about the earth and the cosmos – even if *we* now consider these beliefs to be "wrong." Moreover, in order to fully-appreciate the efforts of the scientists, their followers, *and* their detractors we'll need to carefully consider the societies and cultures in which they lived.

Before we begin, it is important to first recognize that the idea of a moving earth is not the product of common sense – if it were, it would have caught on much earlier, and Galileo would never have gotten himself into hot water. Instead, it was the unexpected outcome of a two-thousand-year-long effort to develop an accurate mathematical description for the motions of heavenly bodies. In the following pages, we will consider the beliefs of many early astronomers in order to learn how their collective effort eventually led to a surprising conclusion. In considering their work, we will also need to appreciate that these early astronomers cared about much more than just technical astronomy – they had values, expectations, and intellectual habits that reflected the cultures

1

they were a part of and that strongly influenced their thoughts about the nature of the heavens. Their "commonsense" beliefs about the world and God's creation were similar to those held by their parents, their friends, and their neighbors. When they found it necessary to diverge from these widely-held beliefs, they found themselves in the uncomfortable position of disagreeing with nearly everyone around them.

To understand why some scientists[1] persisted in holding these new ideas in the face of intense criticism, we'll need to closely examine the unusual reasoning that led them down their difficult paths. Indeed, in this context it may be useful to turn the central question of the book on its head and instead ask: *"Why would it have occurred to anyone that the earth could be in motion?"* That is, perhaps we shouldn't be surprised that people found it difficult to accept the idea of a moving earth, but should instead be amazed that it ever entered anyone's mind in the first place.

For our purposes, it is necessary to focus our attention on the astronomical practices that existed in the area encompassing the Mediterranean basin, the Middle East, and Europe. As we will see, within this greater region and over many centuries, the astronomical and scientific practices of one cultural group often strongly influenced the astronomical and scientific traditions in another. We will refer to the collective product of all of these interacting astronomical traditions as "Western Astronomy," and we will greatly limit our study of astronomical practices to those that took place in this part of the world. There is no evidence that these Western astronomers were influenced by astronomical knowledge that had developed elsewhere. On the other hand, if we completely neglected to consider other astronomical traditions, it would be impossible to fully appreciate what would later become special to Western astronomy.

Early Astronomy and Cosmology: Western and non-Western
Life is, and always has been, an unpredictable affair. Good times can come to an abrupt end. Disease, war, or famine might be just around the corner. The world is constantly in flux. Depending very much on the time and place, our ancestors' worlds were at least as unpredictable as our own – often much more so. In contrast to the uncertainties surrounding

their life on earth, our ancestors found themselves beneath a predictable and unchanging realm in the heavens above. Knowledge of the regular patterns and positions of the stars was common to people who lived at a time when the only sources of light at night, besides an occasional fire or lamp, were the stars, the planets, and the moon.

The vast majority of the visible celestial objects are stars, which have a fixed and unchanging appearance as they rise in the east and set in the west. Their relative positions remain forever fixed upon the dark canvas of the night sky as they move across it in unison. Given the eternal presence of the stars, it shouldn't be surprising that people imagined them to be the home of immortal gods. People also understood that particular celestial events affected their lives and their livelihood. The most profound physical correlation between the celestial realm and the earth, and the one that was most widely-appreciated across world cultures, is the connection between the annual path of the sun through the sky and the seasons. Some peoples living in coastal areas also recognized an association between the phases of the moon and the height of the ocean tides. And in Egypt, astronomer-priests watched for the first appearance of the star Sirius in the early morning sky – an event that anticipated the annual flood of the Nile River.

The existence of such celestial influences on the earth led many people to believe that the heavens could have a direct effect on kingdoms and on men as well. This expectation, the basis of astrology, served as a powerful impulse for gaining more knowledge of the heavens, because such knowledge could be used to anticipate the future and guide one's life on earth. Until recently, the desire for improved astrological forecasting helped inspire the development of Western mathematical astronomy.

Celestial Observing Across Cultures
Early cultures left a broad assortment of physical structures as evidence of their interest in the heavens. The orientation and design of the structures often reveals the identity of the astronomical bodies that their owners observed. The Egyptian, Chinese, Mayan, Incan, and Anasazi are only a few of the cultures that have left behind such evidence. Because of the

importance of the sun and its connection to the daily and annual cycles of life, structures devoted to its observation are particularly common.[2]

[Figure 1.1. 10th century Mayan pyramid at Chichèn Itzá. It is remarkable for its "descending serpent," which is visible on the west-facing side of north stairway during the last hour before sunset on the spring equinox. Public domain, Wikimedia Commons.]

The images of two examples are displayed in the figures – one from 10th century Mesoamerica and one from 13th century China.

In light of the great many astronomical traditions that have existed across the world, we can identify several reasons for choosing to focus our attention on Western astronomy: (1) it was the only one that put the earth into motion and displaced its believers from the center of things, (2) its conclusions have since been adopted by most other cultural groups and, (3) it helped catalyze progress in other disciplines of science – particularly in physics. In Chapter Ten, we will get a brief glimpse of how this new cosmological viewpoint helped to inspire the development of the other sciences and led to a broader cultural phenomenon referred to as the "Scientific Revolution" and, later still, to the "Enlightenment."

[Figure 1.2. 13th century Chinese solar observatory of Guo Shou jing looking due south. A horizontal bar at the gap in the top of the tower casts a shadow onto the long low "shadow measuring wall" on the ground. The design of this structure allowed for an exact determination of summer and winter solstice dates. Photo courtesy Robin Rector Krupp. See E.C. Krupp, 1983, for more detail.]

To understand why these developments ultimately unfolded in Europe, we'll need to go back to the very beginning – the dawn of civilization. And before we begin that story, it is worthwhile to consider some thoughts on the subject of history itself.

History and the History of Science

One of the major challenges in studying any episode in history is to mentally transport oneself back in time. This is particularly difficult when we are primarily interested in learning about the *beliefs* of people who lived long ago. Our success at learning what our predecessors believed and why they believed it will largely be determined by our ability to check our modern thinking at the door. This is easier said than done. We aren't always aware of our modern ways of thinking and usually take for granted the expectations we have about the world – nor are we typically aware of the extent to which we have learned our ideas from others. In this book, we will consider how our collective beliefs have been derived from an intellectual ancestry that extends back many thousands of years. If we know more about the natural world than our intellectual ancestors did, it is because they helped teach us what we know.

Stone Age Cultures and Early Civilizations

Evidence for modern humans is dated to approximately 100,000 years ago – a blink of the eye compared to the 4 billion-year-old history of the earth. Settled agricultural practices developed even more recently – beginning roughly 12,000 years ago. Before this time, humans won their livelihood solely through hunting and gathering. Large-scale civilizations began to emerge 5,500 years ago, and the "Early Modern" period in European history began only 400-500 years ago.[3]

By 13,000 years ago, humans had occupied all of the continents except Antarctica. They inhabited a tremendous variety of ecological niches and had out-competed other hominids like the Neanderthals. How and why they were able to do this is still a matter of conjecture – but *that* they did it is quite evident. Like the hominids before them, humans used tools, and with accessible materials they fashioned an impressive array of weapons, clothing, shelter, and other implements. Cultures of humans using tools of this type and engaging in hunter-gatherer lifestyles are referred to as Paleolithic or "Old Stone Age" cultures.

Approximately 12,000 years ago, a major change in the habits of humans began to emerge independently in a number of locations around the world: the development of settled agricultural practices. The production of food through the cultivation of plants and/or the domestication of animals dramatically changed the relationship of people to the land *and* to each other. Cultural groups that adopted such agricultural practices are referred to as Neolithic or "New Stone Age" cultures. What anthropologists and archeologists know about Paleolithic and Neolithic cultures has been learned from studying both the archeological evidence and by considering the habits of such groups that are still in existence today.

6

Settled agricultural practices first emerged in the Middle East, where the development of cities soon followed. These cities were a secondary development of agriculture – they were created by groups of people who began to organize themselves into larger units in order to store their food and to protect themselves and the products of their labor from raiding neighbors. The ancient Walls of Jericho and Damascus, the earliest archeological evidence of agricultural villages, are over 9,000 years old.

Later, the first large-scale civilization emerged in Mesopotamia ("the land between the two rivers": the Tigris and Euphrates), in what is modern day Iraq. Much of the land in the lower reaches of these rivers was agriculturally productive only when water was diverted from the rivers to irrigate crops. The scale of cooperation necessary to maintain such an extensive irrigation system favored the development of a large government and bureaucracy. In addition to engineering needs, there were also agricultural surpluses to be stored and an army mustered to protect the kingdom. This required an extensive bureaucracy of engineers, bookkeepers, astronomer-priests, and royal aides to administer the day-to-day business.

The complexity of managing such a large bureaucracy would have been difficult, if not impossible, without permanent aids to memory. It is no coincidence that the earliest written language emerged first in Mesopotamia about 3,400 BCE,[4] and that it was first used to keep track of warehouse inventories, lists of laborers, tax rolls, and public works projects. This early writing system, called cuneiform, was based on a series of triangular impressions made on soft clay tablets, which were later baked in order to preserve them. Cuneiform was difficult to learn and schools were founded for passing on the technique to new scribes. Indeed, many of the surviving cuneiform tablets appear to be examples of student exercises.

The appearance of similar "hydraulic civilizations" (civilizations based on water-control projects) occurred independently in other parts of the world. About 3,200 BCE the Egyptian civilization emerged and was centered on engineering projects associated with the annual flooding of the Nile. Likely inspired by the Mesopotamians, the Egyptians developed a script that differed dramatically from cuneiform, but which served a similar function.[5] These Egyptian hieroglyphics were both carved in stone and recorded onto papyrus.

Similar stories are repeated in the Indus Valley (Harrapan, 2,500 BCE), in China (Yellow River, 1,800 BCE), in Mesoamerica (Mayan, 500 BCE), and in the Andes (Incan, 300 BCE). All of these civilizations were associated with large-scale water control projects. Likewise, they all had sophisticated bureaucracies that required a permanent record-keeping method in order to function.[6] These original "hydrologic cultures" are also referred to as the "pristine civilizations" by anthropologists and linguists because they each independently developed their own writing systems without borrowing from another culture.[7]

Early Western Intellectuals: The Mesopotamians (Babylonians) and Egyptians

We will focus our attention on the accomplishments of the Babylonian and Egyptian civilizations because they had an important influence on Greek thought. Greek civilization, in turn, had a major influence on subsequent Islamic and European Christian cultures. Thus, with the benefit of hindsight, we can follow the lineage of modern science and Western culture all the way back to the Babylonians and Egyptians.

Though many standard histories take Greece as the starting point for Western Civilization (with good reason, as we will see), we need to acknowledge that Greek civilization didn't start from scratch, but was itself a culture that borrowed heavily from preexisting Mediterranean and Middle Eastern civilizations. If the Greeks managed to do something new and different, it was because they had so much to work with.

Language, Literacy, and Thought

We will consider in this section the new activities that a written language made possible. Social scientists have debated whether or not there are fundamental differences between cultures that possess the ability to permanently record language and those that do not. These debates can become heated because of a concern that some people might conclude that some cultures are more "advanced" or "highly developed" than other cultures. Thus, we will avoid contentious questions such as: "Which is *better* – an oral culture or a literate culture?" Instead, we'll ask a more productive one: "What sort of activities do we find in literate cultures that are *different* from those that we find in non-literate cultures?" In considering the ramifications of literacy, it is important to first recognize that all groups of people possess oral languages of comparable sophistication. Linguists have concluded that, except for minor differences in specialized vocabularies and number systems, all spoken languages can express the full range and nuance of human ideas and experiences.[8]

Writing

The earliest permanent records were not complete writing systems, but were instead pictograms and/or tally marks that were incapable of fully expressing the spoken languages of their users. Pictograms were pictures that represented objects or events. Since not all words can be represented with a simple picture, an oral language cannot be recorded using these symbols alone. A complete written language system that has the capacity to fully record oral speech can take a variety of forms. Some are easier to master than others.

The advantages of having a permanent written record in a sophisticated bureaucracy should be obvious: the vast numbers of items in inventories and lists would be impossible to maintain without memory aids. These written records were also supported by number systems that made accounting and calculations possible. Later, number systems were also applied to the recording of astronomical observations. Without permanent records, there was a practical limit to the amount of information a society could maintain and manipulate.

This is not to say that oral traditions are incapable of maintaining long-term records. They can keep fairly accurate accounts of selected events, traditions, histories, medicines, and other cultural practices over many generations. But such knowledge has to be highly valued by many individuals in the group – and over many generations. And even in these cases, the amount of information that can be passed from one generation to the next is limited by the capacity of human memory and by how much time is needed to tell the stories many times over so they can be remembered by the entire group.

In a written tradition, even the mundane act of creating and examining a list of things can open up intellectual vistas that don't exist in oral traditions. In addition to the vast quantities of information that can be easily recorded (inventories of food, records of solar and lunar eclipses, floods, calendars, payment records, worker lists, monthly brick and beer production, etc.), the very process of compiling lists allows for new ways of thinking about the objects themselves. One can consider the items independently of their original meaning or context. The items can be classified and grouped by quantity, color, relative value, age, size or weight, origin and so on. This process of "decontextualizing" objects can provide new perspectives and reveal previously undetected patterns.

Moreover, writing and speaking serve different functions: "writing employs only a single channel....and is usually aimed at a wider, more distant, and more impersonal audience."[9] Indeed, the author of a work can reach an audience that was born long after the writer has died. Furthermore, with writing it is possible to easily maintain more than one account of the same event or subject matter and then to later compare the different written accounts – whereas, in an oral tradition, it would be very difficult, if not impossible, to maintain conflicting accounts of a single event. Oral histories are inherently conservative because the continued existence of an oral account depends on a strong group consensus – any challenge to an oral account would be a challenge to the consensus required to maintain it.

Writing can lead to an extended critical tradition that is unlike those found in oral cultures. For example, in the Western intellectual tradition, there has been a practice of critical analysis and written commentary on the works of previous authors. These commentaries have in turn become the object of additional commentaries, and so on.... It is a practice which has continued over the last 2,500 years right up to the present. This property of the written word was eloquently captured by Umberto Eco in *The Name of the Rose*:

Now, I realized that not infrequently books speak of books: it is as if they spoke among themselves. In light of this reflection, the library seemed all the more disturbing to me. It was then the place of long, centuries-old murmuring, an imperceptible dialogue between one parchment and another, a living thing, a receptacle of powers not to be ruled by a human mind, a treasure of secrets emanated by many minds, surviving the death of those who had produced them or had been their conveyors.

Mathematics and Astronomy in Antiquity

Among the needs of early civilizations was the development of number systems capable of supporting the activities of engineers, bookkeepers, managers, and brewers. These systems developed alongside written languages and, as we will see, the different number systems were not of equal utility.[10]

For example, the Egyptian number system, which was similar to the Roman number system that we still occasionally use, had symbols that represented *some* of the numbers. Any whole number could be expressed by stringing the appropriate symbols together. The Roman and Egyptian systems are both examples of aggregated number systems (called "sign-value" notation). Consider the Roman number system:

<u>Values of Roman Numerals</u>
I = 1
V = 5
X = 10
L = 50
C = 100
D = 500
M = 1000

Roman numerals are grouped and added together to express a particular number. In cases where a smaller numerical symbol appears to the left of a larger one, it is subtracted from the larger symbol:

III = 3
IV = 4

VI = 6
VIII = 8
IX = 9
XXXIV = 34
XLII = 42
XC = 90
CDXXI = 421
MCMLXII=1962
MMIV=2004

To represent larger numbers in a reasonable amount of space, additional symbols were invented. These include "bar X", an "X" written with a horizontal line over it that represented the number ten thousand; "bar C" for one hundred thousand, and "bar M" for the number one million.

People who used the Egyptian and Roman systems encountered a number of difficulties when carrying out calculations. As an example, consider the act of multiplying the Roman numbers XXIV and XVIX without the benefit of using our Hindu-Arabic numerals (0, 1, 2, 3, 4, 5, 6, 7, 8, and 9). While multiplication and division can be performed within the Roman number system, the operations are more awkward and present problems that we don't encounter in our Hindu-Arabic number system.[11] A second drawback to the Roman and Egyptian systems is that in order to express larger and larger numbers, more and more symbols needed to be created (whereas our Hindu-Arabic system can express any size number using only ten symbols). Another major limitation of the Roman and Egyptian number systems was their cumbersome and limited methods for expressing fractions. Some fractions were easily expressible, whereas other fractions were not. Often, fractional values needed to be expressed as the sum of two or more fractions – for example, an Egyptian mathematician could express 7/10 as "1/2 + 1/5" (though, of course, using Egyptian symbols).

Whatever limitations these systems may have had relative to the Hindu-Arabic system we use today, the Egyptians and Romans found them to be adequate for the management of their empires and for the design of massive engineering projects. As but one example, the pyramid of Khufu

(Cheops) is 476 ft tall and deviates from a perfect square by no more than seven inches on a side.

Most Europeans used the Roman number system until the 1400s. Exceptions to this were astronomers and mathematicians who adopted the Hindu-Arabic system much earlier and who also continued to use the much older Babylonian number system, which developed in Mesopotamia and gets its name by association with the city of Babylon. The Babylonian number system was a base sixty, or sexagesimal, system that was originally expressed in cuneiform. It was similar in some respects to the Roman and Egyptian systems in that the symbols were aggregated until the number 59 was reached.

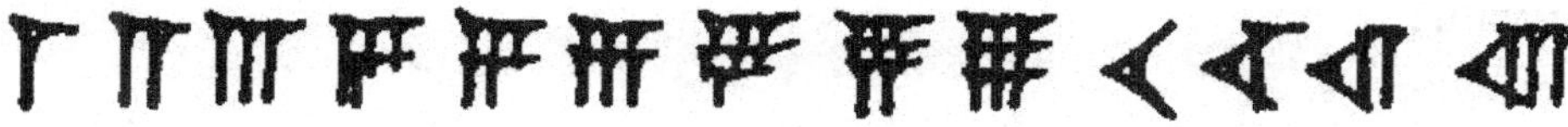

[Figure 1.3. The Babylonian numbers 1-13.]

[Figure 1.4. The Babylonian numbers 10-50.]

However, for the expression of numbers greater than 59, the Babylonian differs greatly from the other number systems. The Babylonian symbol for "one" can also represent the number "sixty" – only the context or position of the symbol helps to distinguish its actual value. This is very much in the same way that our Hindu-Arabic symbol "1" can also represent the number ten when it is followed by a zero. Though the Babylonians didn't have a zero to use for this purpose, they did use the relative positions of the symbols to determine their value.

In the following series, the original context in which these symbols appeared made it clear to the reader that they represented the numbers 60, 70, 80, ... 120, 130.

[Figure 1.5. The Babylonian numbers 60-130. Figures from Otto Neugebauer, *The Exact Sciences in Antiquity*, 2nd Edition, 1969. Figures 1.3-1.5 courtesy Dover Publications.]

As odd as such a system may seem to us, it was far easier to carry out complex calculations with it than it was with either the Egyptian or Roman systems. In fact, it offers the mathematician all of the possibilities that the Hindu-Arabic system does. For instance, in contrast to the Egyptian and Roman systems and similar to the Hindu-Arabic system, Babylonian fractional notation was capable of easily expressing fractions of *any* value.

The "positional" or "place-value" notation of the Babylonian system allowed for the efficient writing of very large numbers by simply adding more columns. The first column represents "the ones" place – up to the number 59. The column to the left of the first column represents the "sixties" place, the next column represents the 3600ths place (60^2), the column after that multiples of 60^3, and so on. This is directly analogous to the placeholder system we use in our Hindu-Arabic number system today, except that ours is a base 10 system instead of a base 60 system. Also, in parallel with our own fractional decimal system, the Babylonian system had a "1/60th place" instead of a "tenths" place, a "1/3,600th place" ($1/60^2$) instead of a "hundredths" place, and so on.

Many centuries later, we continue to retain vestiges of the Babylonian number system in our methods of measuring angles and in keeping time. In measuring angles, we define a circle as having 360 degrees (6 x 60). Fractions of a degree are measured in minutes (1/60th of a degree), and fractions of minutes are measured as seconds (1/60th of a minute). In reckoning time we divide up an hour into 60 minutes and a minute into 60 seconds (so that there are 3600 seconds in an hour). For instance, 2 minutes, 16 seconds can be converted fully into the decimal Hindu/Arabic system: $(2 \times 60^1) + 16 = (2 \times 60) + 16 = 136$ seconds.

YBC 4607

[Figure 1.6. A mathematical cuneiform text approximately 1700 BCE, YBC 4607. The scale to the left is in centimeters. The text deals with problems in calculating areas and volumes of bricks of various dimensions. See O Neugebauer and A Sachs, 1945, pp. 91-97 for more detail. Image courtesy of the Yale Babylonian Collection and Christine Proust.]

However, we rarely bother to convert the Babylonian style of hours and minutes into the Hindu-Arabic equivalent of seconds. For example, because of our familiarity with reporting time using a Babylonian format, it is easier for us to picture how long 1 hour, 47 minutes, and 18 seconds is than it is for us to picture the Hindu-Arabic equivalent of it: 6438 seconds. We seem to be content using a Babylonian system to describe time with very little trouble or awareness that we are doing so.

The Hindu-Arabic system eventually prevailed over the Babylonian system because it was easier to use and because it eventually included an important practical innovation – the number "zero." The symbol for the number zero served as a place holder, eliminated ambiguities, and facilitated calculations – in this capacity, it reduced the number of mistakes that might be made (for example, it could be quite easy to confuse the number "one" with the number "sixty" in the Babylonian system – but it is not so easy to confuse the number "one" with the number "ten," in the Hindu-Arabic system). In the Hindu-Arabic system it is possible to memorize the entire multiplication table for all number combinations up to its base number (10 x 10). In contrast to this, the Babylonian system required knowledge of multiplication tables up to 60 x 60! However, since Babylonian mathematicians used written tables to aid them in their calculations, it was not a serious barrier to using the system efficiently.

The Babylonians expanded existing mathematical knowledge beyond anything that had existed before them. They were able to calculate square and cube roots, had methods for solving what we would call quadratic equations, and had compiled a long list of special right triangles where all three sides had whole number lengths. Babylonian mathematicians also worked at solving other problems and puzzles that appear to have had no practical applications. In other words, they seem to have engaged in fundamental mathematical research in 1700 BCE – many centuries before the Greeks began their work in mathematics.

Babylonian Astronomy
Like people in most other cultures, the Mesopotamians (Babylonians) were interested in knowing as much about future events as they could. A product of this interest was a vast "omen literature" that was based on the examination of sheep livers, birth defects in newborn children, and the positions of celestial bodies in the sky. This motivation, along with the

16

practical need for agricultural and legal calendars, helped drive the development of increasingly sophisticated astronomical practices. With these ends in mind, they directed their considerable mathematical talents toward making predictions of the future positions of the sun, moon, and planets. As surprising as it might seem to us now, they didn't provide geometric explanations for the celestial motions that they observed, but used only numerical extrapolations for determining where and when these objects would be found in the sky.[12] And at this, they were quite successful. Greek astronomers would later inherit many of these Babylonian observational records and calculating tables, which they then used in the development their own astronomy.[13]

---

[1] My use of the words "science" and "scientist" in this text is not technically or historically accurate. In fact, in English the word "scientist" was not coined until well into the nineteenth century. However, lacking an alternative I've chosen to use the word "scientist" in the broadest possible sense to include anyone who was interested in the study of nature – including natural philosophers, natural theologians, mathematicians, astrologers, alchemists, and astronomers, among others. The modern definition of a "scientist" has a special connotation, as will be discussed in the final chapter.

[2] For an excellent account of ancient astronomical activity across cultures, consult *Echoes of the Ancient Skies: The Astronomy of Lost Civilizations* by E. C. Krupp, 1983.

[3] Note the vastly different usages of the term "modern" by anthropologists and historians. Anthropologists use it as a biological term, historians as a cultural one.

[4] Dates in this text are often identified by the use of BCE and CE rather than the older style BC (before Christ) or AD (Anno Domini – "In the year of our Lord"). Both BC and AD designations imply that the author and readers are all of the Christian faith.

BCE stands for "before the common era" or alternatively, "before Christian era" and CE stands for "common era" or "Christian era." Thus, in using "CE" or "BCE" it is unclear whether the term "common" or "Christian" is implied by the author. While the use of "common" may be more appealing to some historians, it does not reveal the Christian origins of our convention for numbering the years. I leave it to the reader to decide.

[5] If the Egyptians were aware of the existence of Babylonian cuneiform, which they likely were, they didn't borrow from it to express their own language.

[6] Note that the Incans had a very different record keeping tradition of elaborate strings of knots call quipu, which, at the very least, appears to have been a sophisticated method of bookkeeping, but that likely recorded other information as well. To date, much of it has defied analysis.

[7] McClellan and Dorn, *Science and Technology in World History—An Introduction*, 1999.

[8] Pinker, Steven, *The Language Instinct*, 1994.

[9] Goody, Jack. *The Power of the Written Tradition*, 2000.

[10] See Aaboe, Asger. *Episodes from the Early History of Mathematics*, 1997, for an introduction.

[11] The modern base ten number system is commonly referred to as the "Arabic" number system. However, this designation doesn't reveal its true origins. Indian mathematicians had used base ten number systems for centuries and its use eventually spread west into Persia and the Islamic world. The script was substantially modified by Islamic mathematicians before it was adopted by their European neighbors. Thus the number system, as Europeans encountered it, is best described as the Hindu-Arabic system.

[12] Early Babylonian astronomical observers, like those in many other cultures, were primarily concerned with measuring and predicting the changing locations and times that the sun and moon rise and set on the horizon and tying those phenomena to a calendric system. A particularly important goal for the Babylonians was to predict the first visibility of the moon following a new moon (when it appears as a barely visible thin crescent) – a task that is more complex than one might think. See O. Neugebauer, *The Exact Sciences in Antiquity*, 1969, pp. 106-122 for a more detailed description.

[13] See Alexander Jones, 1991 for more detail.

Chapter Two – Early Greek Thought

Greek civilization emerged from very different physical and economic circumstances than had the Egyptian and Mesopotamian civilizations. The cultivation of land in the Greek-speaking world didn't depend on the existence of large-scale water projects, and the geography of the region favored the formation of many independent Greek city-states. These city-states, called *poleis*, (singular: *polis*) were spread across islands and harbors from the Ionian Coast on the western edge of Asia Minor (modern-day Turkey) to the southern Italian peninsula and Sicily. While these poleis were politically independent, they shared a common language and culture.

[Figure 2.1. A map showing the ancient-Greek regions in the Mediterranean. These include the territories of modern-day Greece, the west coast of modern-day Turkey, and extensive Greek colonies in the southern Italian peninsula and Sicily. Public domain.]

The Greeks relied on a vibrant trading economy that placed them into contact with other civilizations in the Mediterranean basin and beyond. Over the course of several centuries, these cross-cultural interactions proved to be enriching for the Greeks. They borrowed actively from their neighbors – adapting a writing system from the Phoenicians and incorporating mathematical and astronomical knowledge from the Egyptians and Babylonians. Although they clearly benefited from this contact, Greek thinkers soon produced their own intellectual innovations in a remarkably competitive social environment.

Greek society was affluent enough to support a sizable upper class with enough political power and leisure time to be engaged in governing the oligarchies and democracies that existed across the Greek world. In Athens, participation in its democratic government was *expected* of all free men; it was considered a responsibility as much as it was a right. In these highly politicized environments, those with good speaking and reasoning skills were held in high esteem. A few of these thinkers turned their attention towards philosophical, mathematical, and scientific questions with the same degree of interest and skepticism that they brought to the political realm. It was in this dynamic social context that the struggle to understand nature on its own terms began.

Why science and philosophy developed in the ancient Greek world has been the subject of much speculation. It is a difficult question to address – especially since there was no single aspect of Greek culture that was unique to it. There were, however, several elements that appeared to have collectively contributed to the phenomenon:

1) A high degree of wealth, which provided essential leisure time for many members of Greek society.
2) The possession of relatively advanced technologies in agriculture, seafaring and navigation, pottery and textile manufacturing, and metallurgy.
3) An understanding of many other cultures as a consequence of Greek geography and trade.
4) A high literacy rate.
5) The development of democratic and oligarchic city-states, which fostered a high regard for reasoning and rhetoric among citizens.

These were the notable features of Greek Civilization that, taken together, helped fuel its dynamic intellectual life.[1]

Politics and Religion

A few Greeks even expanded their inquiries to include religion as an object of study. An early philosopher, Xenophanes (ca. 570-475 BCE) drew attention to the anthropomorphic nature of gods: "men think that gods are born and that they have clothes and voices and shapes like their own," he observed. Xenophanes' view was inspired by a multi-cultural comparison: "Ethiopians say their own gods are flat-nosed and dark, the Thracians say theirs are blue-eyed and red-haired." He then went on to satirize these beliefs with an analogy: "If oxen and horses and lions had hands and could draw with their hands and produce works of art like men, horses would draw the forms of the gods like horses, and oxen like oxen, and they would make their bodies such as each of them had themselves." But Xenophanes was no atheist; rather, he believed in "one god, greatest among gods and human beings, not like mortals in body and form." To Xenophanes, this god was all-encompassing and perhaps even "identical with the world."[2]

The expression of such opinions should not be taken as evidence that many Greeks ceased to believe in their traditional gods – nor does it mean that Greek philosophers could criticize the religious beliefs of their neighbors without consequence (criticism of religious beliefs by philosophers often provoked a great deal of anger from their fellow citizens). However, the interest and willingness to subject religious thought to analysis underscores the breadth of the topics that Greek thinkers considered. Some historians have speculated that Greek familiarity with the numerous religious beliefs in the Mediterranean region caused some thinkers to be skeptical of *any* religious explanation for the natural world. Whatever its origin, non-religious explanations of nature became increasingly valued. Greeks began to view the events and objects in the natural world more and more as manifestations of a coherent and rationally-structured universe – and less and less as the result of capriciously acting gods. The new belief that the universe was well-ordered was an assumption that motivated natural philosophers for centuries to follow. The quest to understand the natural world became a struggle to uncover the structure of nature itself. The philosopher Heraclitus put this succinctly in his maxim: "Nature loves to hide."

Greek Mathematics

The Greeks inherited a great deal of mathematical knowledge from both the Babylonians and the Egyptians.[3] As we've seen in these earlier civilizations, mathematics originally developed in the service of commerce, government, astronomy, and engineering. While it provided these functions in Greek society as well, Greek intellectuals took existing mathematical knowledge and uncovered broader patterns and made well-grounded generalizations. In doing so, they rendered mathematics more theoretical. Through the development of logic, they established "mathematical proofs" – mathematical lines of reasoning so tightly argued that no reasonable person could disagree with the conclusions. Such careful analyses provided Greek mathematicians with confidence in their far-reaching and often counter-intuitive results.

Logical reasoning and its application in mathematics, philosophy, and science is taken for granted today – as though it has always existed. But logic was an innovation whose origins aren't as pure as today's enthusiasts of logic would wish to believe: in reality, it was yet another product of the Greek fondness for debate and rhetoric.[4]

An early example of what Greeks accomplished in mathematics can be found in their study of right triangles. They had inherited from the Babylonians knowledge of a special group of right triangles where all three sides were of integer lengths. Moreover, it was always the case that when the lengths of the two shorter sides were squared and added together, they equaled the square of the longest side ($a^2 + b^2 = c^2$, in modern notation – see figure 2.2.). Interested in this phenomenon, the Babylonians had already produced extensive lists of these triangles to a degree that exceeded any practical usefulness.

Greek mathematicians exploited this existing knowledge and used it to take mathematics in a more abstract direction. The Greek mathematician Pythagoras showed that there were not only *a large number* of special triangles that satisfied the relationship $a^2 + b^2 = c^2$; he proved, using a rigorous geometric argument, that it had to be true for *all* right triangles – whether or not the lengths of the sides were whole numbers.

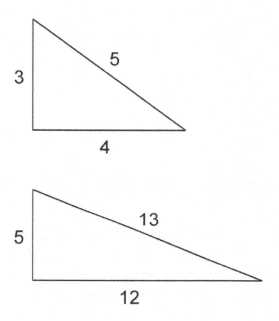

[Figure 2.2. Triangles that possess whole number solutions to the Pythagorian theorem (now known as "Pythagorian triples.") In the first example above, $3^2 + 4^2 = 5^2$ $(9 + 16 = 25)$. Figure courtesy Danica Oudeans.]

The starting point of a logical or mathematical proof is dependent on a handful of facts whose truth is unquestioned, or "self-evident." We can see one example of the kind of statement that constitutes a "self-evident truth" in the following postulate taken from Euclidian geometry: "two parallel lines never meet." By taking such a postulate as a starting point and following accepted rules of argumentation, one can arrive at a "new truth." The process ends up sounding like: "...if you believe "A" and you believe "B," I can show you that "C" must also be true."[5]

For example, Pythagoras[6] examined the ratio of the length of the side of a square to the diagonal line that bisected it (figure 2.3). He found that he could not express the ratio of the lengths using ordinary numbers. For example, if the sides of a square are of length one, then the length of the diagonal is equal to a number, n, since $1^2 + 1^2 = n^2$. Here, "n" is the

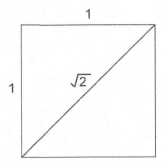

[Figure 2.3. Incommensurability of the sides and the diagonal of a square. Figure courtesy Danica Oudeans.]

"square root" of two, which is the number that, when multiplied by itself, equals two. But such a number "n" could not be expressed as a fraction of two whole numbers. In its decimal form the square root of two *begins* as 1.414213562373095... and continues on forever without any repeating pattern – unlike the ratio of two whole numbers, which *can* be expressed in a simple decimal form, as in the first two examples below, or in a regular repeating pattern of decimals, as in the second two examples:

2/5 = 0.4
7/10 = 0.7
1/3 = 0.333333...
9/11 = 0.818181...

What is remarkable and, indeed, characteristic of the Greek mathematicians is that they were able to *prove*, using logic, that the "square root of two," and other numbers like it, *could not be expressed as the ratio of two whole numbers*.[7] The discovery of these "irrational numbers" was surprising to early mathematicians because until this time they had always conceptualized mathematical and physical relationships in terms of ratios of whole numbers. Suddenly, geometry had presented mathematicians with numbers that were unrelated to the normal numbers they had used for counting, measuring, and calculating.

Mathematics in Nature

Early Greek thinkers recognized that there were many close correspondences between the abstract patterns in mathematics and the natural phenomena found in the world around them. In particular, they discovered that mathematical relationships could sometimes be used to describe or explain aspects of music and astronomy. Especially captivating was the discovery that two strings, when vibrated in unison, sounded in harmony when the ratio of the string lengths corresponded to special whole number ratios. Thus, the emotionally charged experience of harmony could be correlated with the intellectually satisfying numerical relationships of the strings' lengths. These uncanny connections, between the purely mathematical and the real, led to the development of a deep intuition among some thinkers that the natural world was fundamentally organized on mathematical foundations. Indeed, Pythagoreans were so convinced of this that they proclaimed that "everything is number." As extreme as this statement might seem to us, this intuition about the natural world reappeared over the centuries to follow in the development of Western Science. Indeed, it remains alive and well today in some of the sciences – physics in particular.

These early developments in Greek mathematics were followed with the systematic formalization of geometry by Euclid (fl. 300 BCE)[8] who logically organized and extended the existing knowledge of geometry. Euclid began his geometry with a handful of postulates and then carefully elaborated on these in a work that proved to be the most successful textbook ever. Though it's no longer written in ancient Greek, modern high school geometry textbooks continue to present Euclid's work in much its original form. Other Greek mathematicians followed with their own investigations: Apollonius of Perga (ca. 262–ca. 190 BCE) made important mathematical contributions to theoretical astronomy and investigated the properties of conic sections (circles, parabolas, ellipses, and hyperbolas). And Archimedes (fl. 240 BCE), one of the greatest mathematical minds ever, produced a number of important innovations in pure mathematics. He also used his talents in solving problems of applied mathematics – from determining whether his king had been duped by a goldsmith, to inventing and engineering useful military hardware for defending his native Sicily from the Romans.

Early Greek Natural Philosophy: The Milesians

The Milesian Philosophers were named for their home city of Miletus on the Ionian coast. Thales (fl. 585 BCE) was considered to be the first of these early philosophers. Among his many views on nature was his idea that "everything is water." That is, he believed that the different objects we find in the natural world are all composed of a primary elemental substance.

Knowing what we know about physics and chemistry today, Thales' explanation may seem rather fanciful to us. But if we consider the *kind* of explanation he was offering, and then contrast it with the explanations of nature that had circulated before his time, we can appreciate that his innovation shares a fundamental feature with modern scientific explanations offered today: Thales provided accounts of natural phenomena that were based on nature itself (rather than viewing events in nature as the separate acts of external and independent gods). He believed that there existed hidden features of nature that were responsible for its superficial appearance. It was this fundamentally new perspective that Thales had in common with modern scientists.

In addition to his idea about the nature of matter, Thales also postulated that the earth was a disk that floated on water. He then used this idea to explain the underlying cause of earthquakes – that waves of water shook the floating earth. Again, our modern explanation for an earthquake seems not to have much in common with Thales' explanation until we compare it to the popular one his contemporaries offered: namely, that earthquakes were caused by the activity of the god Poseidon.[9]

Milesian philosophers following Thales offered explanations for natural phenomena that differed from those that he had proposed. But even though they disagreed with the details of Thales' explanations, they continued to offer the same *kind* of explanations. For example, Anaximander (fl. 555 BCE) believed that everything was composed of an indefinite substance he called the "Boundless." He also posited that the cause of thunderbolts was the wind and that lightning was the result of clouds breaking in two. Later, Anaximines (fl. 535 BCE) proposed that the fundamental basis of matter was "air." In Greek science, as in politics, there was a great diversity of opinion – and although natural philosophers disagreed over whose explanations were correct, they did agree on the *kind* of explanation that should be offered.

It is important to keep in mind that Greek natural philosophers weren't employees of the government as the astronomer-priests of Babylonia or Egypt had been. Instead, they were either independently wealthy or made their way through life as freelance teachers. A philosopher's success was determined by the number of students he had; thus, philosophers competed with each other in the "intellectual free market" to gain followers and promote their ideas. They criticized one another's views and adopted new and striking intellectual positions in order to enhance their reputation. During this period, these thinkers contemplated a vast range of subject matter and produced a stunning diversity of ideas. Over the centuries that followed, much of this diversity was lost or nearly lost when it became obscured by the successes of just a few philosophers. Two men who particularly dominated later conceptions of Greek thought were Plato and Aristotle.[10]

Plato and Socrates

The philosopher Socrates (469-399 BCE) never recorded his own thoughts in writing – instead, what we know of his beliefs was passed on to us through the words of his pupil, Plato (429-347 BCE). Plato portrayed Socrates as a person who was appalled by the intellectual excesses of the philosophers of his day. The philosophers with whom Socrates took exception were called "sophists" – men who gained their reputation largely through their ability to win arguments in public forums. As time went on, the sophists came to be judged less on the quality of their ideas and more by their ability to argue successfully from any side of an issue. Socrates believed that this sort of activity was mere gamesmanship and that sophists had little or no regard for uncovering the "Truth." Socrates publically challenged them through a strategy of critically questioning. In doing so, he dismissed the sophists' claims of knowledge and even called into question the value of their profession. His clever arguments and rhetorical strategies dazzled people and gained him followers – and, not surprisingly, detractors.

Philosophers and orators had a great deal of intellectual freedom in ancient Greece, but freedom in any society has its limits. Some of Socrates' activities upset the authorities of Athens, who charged him with impiety, corrupting the youth, and for not believing in the gods of the city. He was not the only philosopher to make such transgressions, but instead of accepting the traditional option of going into exile, he held his ground and refused to submit. The local authorities sentenced him to death (though they appear to have given him an opportunity to avoid the sentence by fleeing). Socrates stood firm and accepted his drink of poison hemlock. Much of what we know of Socrates is through the writings of Plato, who portrayed Socrates as a martyr for the Truth because of Socrates' unwillingness to compromise his beliefs.

Plato

In addition to informing us about the life of Socrates, Plato wrote extensively on many aspects of philosophy, politics, and to a lesser extent, natural philosophy. The vast majority of his writings have survived intact; in fact, he is the earliest philosopher whose major works we can read directly. Inspired by his mentor and hero, Plato sought to apply his intellect toward developing a philosophy that would reveal the ultimate nature of reality. After a great deal of thought, Plato eventually concluded that the superficial world in which we live is but a pale shadow of true reality. The realm where Truth can be found is not in the imperfect, impure, corrupt world that exists immediately around us but in a transcendental realm – a realm of pure reason and flawlessness. It is in this ideal realm that the "Forms" of objects and ideas reside. These Forms are abstract idealizations that are theoretically related to the real objects in the world around us – in a sense, they serve as "ethereal templates" for the structure of the world and the objects that are in it.

Plato believed that knowledge of the Forms was not to be acquired by being overly concerned with the details of the confused and imperfect world around us but by careful contemplation. His epistemology, or theory of knowledge, was based on his belief that we had once been granted full knowledge of this transcendental realm prior to our birth but had then since forgotten most of it. According to Plato, only through focused and sustained reflection could we hope to re-acquire our lost knowledge and gain access to the "Truth."

Plato's epistemology accounted for how we are able to easily classify different objects into groups and how we are able to make generalizations from particulars. For example, we are able to classify certain kinds of animals as dogs, whether they are poodles, Great Danes, Chihuahuas, or wolves. Not only can we do this quickly and without dispute (no one ever classifies a Chihuahua as a cat), but we are also capable of picturing a generalized image of a dog without needing to picture any one dog in particular. These indistinct, mental images helped inspire Plato's intuition about the realm of the Forms. Indeed, in Plato's way of thinking, it is the non-specific image in our mind's eye that is the essence of a dog. By contemplating a "dog," we get a mere shadow of the "Form of the Dog."

Plato described his notion of the "forms" through his famous analogy, "The Allegory of the Cave"[11]

> BOOK VII. And now I will describe in a figure the enlightenment or unenlightenment of our nature:--Imagine human beings living in an underground den which is open towards the light; they have been there from childhood, having their necks and legs chained, and can only see into the den. At a distance there is a fire, and between the fire and the prisoners a raised way, and a low wall is built along the way, like the screen over which marionette players show their puppets. Behind the wall appear moving figures, who hold in their hands various works of art, and among them images of men and animals, wood and stone, and some of the passers-by are talking and others silent.
>
> 'A strange parable,' he said, 'and strange captives.'
> They are ourselves, I replied; and they see only the shadows
> of the images which the fire throws on the wall of the den;
> to these they give names, and if we add an echo which returns
> from the wall, the voices of the passengers will seem to proceed from
> the shadows.
>
> Suppose now that you suddenly turn them round and make them
> look with pain and grief to themselves at the real images; will they

29

believe them to be real? Will not their eyes be dazzled, and will they
not try to get away from the light to something which they are able to
behold without blinking? And suppose further, that they are dragged
up a steep and rugged ascent into the presence of the sun himself, will
not their sight be darkened with the excess of light? Some time will
pass before they get the habit of perceiving at all; and at first they will
be able to perceive only shadows and reflections in the water; then they
will recognize the moon and the stars, and will at length behold the sun
in his own proper place as he is.

Plato's concept of Forms extended into the realm of ethics as well and
included Plato's extensive discussions of the "Form of the Good." His
theory of knowledge is what historians and philosophers refer to when
they use the terms "Platonic" or "Platonism" in discussions of philosophy
or scientific thought.

While Plato wasn't as prolific in science and mathematics as he was in
philosophy and politics, he surely appreciated them as worthy of study. In
fact, he thought so highly of mathematics that he had engraved over the
entryway to his institution, The Academy,[12] "Let no one enter here who is
ignorant of mathematics." Although Plato's writings on science and
mathematics were quite modest, his opinions on how to properly study
them were influential to natural philosophers who followed. In the shorter
term, Plato managed to bring together some very talented people at his
school – many of whom were more interested in studying the natural
world than he had been.

Plato and Aristotle

Aristotle (384-322 BCE) was from Macedonia, a northern region of the
Greek world where his father served as a court physician to the local king.
As a young man, Aristotle traveled to Athens to study under Plato at the
Academy, and he remained there until Plato's death. Undoubtedly,
Aristotle was greatly influenced by Plato's thought – but even so, he far
from accepted all of Plato's ideas. In particular, Aristotle didn't believe
that the "Forms" were otherworldly. He believed that a dog was a dog –
and that the configuration it took and the purpose it served did not
depend on an external "form of the dog." For Aristotle, just because all
dogs have some features in common does not mean that there exists some

independent, transcendent form of dog. Instead, he believed that the notion of the "form of the dog" was merely an idealization that was produced in one's mind. Aristotle explained the similarity of dogs, or the similarity of any other set of objects belonging to the same class, by postulating the existence of internal forces or "causes" that shaped the material. According to Aristotle, what caused one hunk of matter to be a dog and another one a rock were the different types of causes that were associated with each material. We don't have the room here to consider Aristotle's elaborate and difficult-to-grasp theory of causes, which he used to explain everything from inanimate objects, to biology, to human actions. To make a long story short, we can crudely say that Aristotle took the Platonic forms out of the transcendental realm and put them into the very material that made up an object or a living thing.

[Figure 2.4. Detailed inset from Rafael's much larger painting "The School of Athens" (1509-1511) at the Vatican. 1509, Fresco, Stanza della Segnatura, Palazzi Pontifici, Vatican.]

The picture (figure 2.4) is the center section of a large painting by Rafael (1483-1520 CE). It depicts Aristotle and Plato walking side by side with Plato motioning to the sky as he explains the Forms and the Truth to Aristotle. For Plato, Truth was to be found by looking beyond the superficial sensations of the immediate world. Aristotle disagrees and instead motions to the ground as if he were saying, "No, no, no – it's all down here – right around us!"

Both men greatly influenced later Western thought. In the early European Middle Ages, the Christian worldview incorporated many elements of Platonic idealism into its theology and philosophy. Later, in the High Middle Ages, when Aristotle's works were recovered and studied by European scholars, Aristotelian natural philosophy became very prominent in Western thought.

Aristotle

Aristotle's life coincided with important changes that occurred in the Greek world. He was associated with the court of King Philip of Macedonia and became the tutor of the king's son, Alexander. After Philip's death, Alexander quickly took control of his father's kingdom and began a conquest of the entire Greek world.

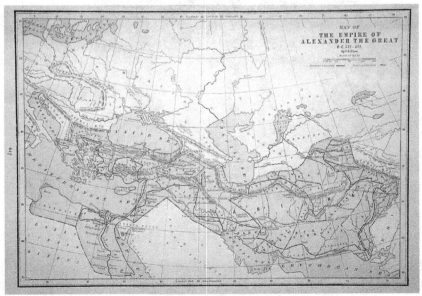

[Figure 2.5. Empire of Alexander the Great. Public domain.]

Alexander's military successes marked the end of the independence of the Greek Poleis and the beginning of the "Hellenistic" period in the Mediterranean and the Near East. His realm stretched beyond the limits of the Greek-speaking world – south into Egypt, eastward through Persia, into Afghanistan, and to the very edge of the Indian subcontinent.

At the same time Alexander was unifying and expanding the Greek world, Aristotle was unifying and expanding many of the existing Greek beliefs about the natural world. The result of Aristotle's efforts was a grand and coherent philosophy that encompassed a vast range of human thought and experience – from logic and science to ethics.

Aristotle's Science
The topics that Aristotle addressed were far-reaching. Using modern categories, we might say that Aristotle was a philosopher, a logician, a biologist, a physicist, and a cosmologist. He was a particularly keen observer of the biological world – so much so that many of his descriptions have withstood the scrutiny of modern biology. For our purposes, we will focus most of our attention on Aristotle's cosmology, physics, and theory of matter. We will then see how his ideas were unified into a single, coherent system and how it came to be adopted by later cultures – first in the Islamic world, and then later in Europe. We will start by considering some of the ideas that Aristotle borrowed from earlier Greek philosopher-scientists – in particular, Empedocles and Eudoxus.

Empedocles (fl. 445 BCE) developed a theory that could be used to explain the nature of matter *and* its transformations. He proposed that not one, but four different elements composed the fundamental stuff of all matter: fire, air, water, and earth. Using this scheme, he explained the tremendous diversity of materials found in the world (i.e. wood, rocks, soil, wine, bread, olive oil, glass, copper, feathers, etc.) as a combination of just four basic elements in fixed ratios. For instance, Empedocles proposed that bone was composed of fire, water, and earth in a 4:2:2 ratio. Empedocles' scheme was an improvement over earlier single-element theories because it could more readily account for the variety of properties that different materials possessed. Plato and Aristotle later modified

Empedocles' theory so that it could better explain changes that took place when one kind of matter transformed into another.

Aristotle believed that each element resulted from the combination of two qualities (Figure 2.6). The evaporation of boiling water is just one example of how changes in matter could be explained with this scheme: the element water was believed to be a combination of the qualities "wet" and "cold." The action of heating the water caused the "cold" of the water to be transformed into the quality "hot." The new qualities that resulted are "wet" and "hot" – which corresponded to the element "air." Thus, the scheme could successfully explain the evaporation of water, as it could many other transformations.

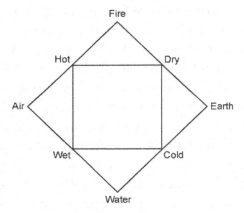

[Figure 2.6. The "Greek" Elements. Figure courtesy Danica Oudeans.]

This conceptual scheme would be used, with some modifications and elaborations, as a central organizing principle by natural philosophers, alchemists, and physicians for two thousand years.

The Round Earth and the Two-sphere Model
We know that during Plato's time, the concept of a spherical earth was still new. However, we don't know who first proposed the idea – their identity having been obscured by the loss of many pre-Platonic writings. But considering the Greeks' interest in geometry, perhaps it isn't surprising that *someone* found the symmetry of a spherical earth appealing. This notion appears to have emerged along with the idea that

the Universe, which contains the earth, is also spherical and shares its center. This is the Greek "two-sphere" model. It is difficult to over-emphasize the importance of this uniquely Greek view of the cosmos to the development of later Western science – even if we are unable to provide the names of the people who were first responsible for developing it.

The Aristotelian Universe

Aristotle's conception of the universe combined Empedocles' theory of matter with the Greek Two-Sphere Model of the cosmos. Aristotle envisioned each of the four elements as adopting its natural location in the spherical universe (see Figure 2.7). The element "earth" had its normal position at the center of the Universe; surrounding the sphere of earth was the sphere of water, then the sphere of air, and then, fire. In the absence of any disturbances, all of the elements would be expected to take on this symmetric arrangement around the center of the universe.

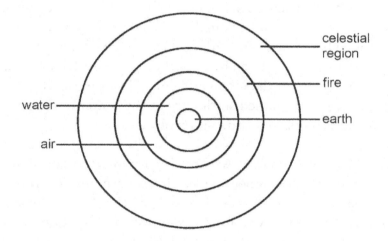

[Figure 2.7. The Aristotelian cosmos. Figure courtesy Danica Oudeans.]

In this view, Aristotle developed a successful framework for understanding common physical phenomena. For example, if someone picked a rock up off the ground and then let it go, the rock fell. Aristotle explained that the rock, because it was composed of the element earth, sought its natural position in the universe – at the center. Likewise, an

Aristotelian watching the action of a fire would interpret the upward motion of a flame through air as the motion of the flame toward its natural position in the sphere of fire. Bubbles of air rising upward through water to reach the sphere of air would be similarly understood. In contrast to our modern conception of the universe, the Aristotelian universe was a universe of *place* rather than space.

Aristotle envisioned a fifth celestial element, which was different from the four elements that existed in the terrestrial realm. This fifth element is often called "quintessence" (sometimes also called "aether" or "ether"). He believed that the celestial realm was made out of this fifth element because the heavens possessed properties very different from anything found on earth. The celestial realm was unchanging and perfect, and the motions of the stars and planets were circular and unending. In contrast to the regular and unchanging nature of the celestial region, the terrestrial realm was a place of constant change and gross imperfection, of growth and decay, and of imperfect motion that had a beginning and an end. Rocks might fall when released, but their motion stopped when they hit the ground. Carts could be pulled by oxen but came to a rest when they were pulled no more. Everything located below the orbit (sphere) of the moon was considered to be part of the terrestrial realm; everything from the sphere of the moon and beyond was in the celestial realm. Finally, the earth remained stationary at the center of the cosmos while the sun, moon, planets, and stars all revolved around it.

It may be challenging for us to take Aristotle's cosmology seriously today because we've been taught fundamental ideas in modern physics from a very young age – that there is a "solar system," and that "space" has no boundaries. But if we instead try to forget what we've been taught and look at the world with our senses, we find that Aristotle and Greek astronomers had a point: it certainly *appears* as though the earth is in the center of things and that the sun is in motion as it rises and sets during the course of a day. And, if we watch the night sky from one evening to the next, we see the same collection of stars – their relative positions forever unchanging as they appear to move around us. In fact, it is not at all uncommon to hear modern astronomers describe the sky as though they still believe this motion is occurring. In normal speech, we say that

"The sun rose this morning," rather than the very awkward "The sun became visible to us as our location on the earth's surface rotated so that we were now on the side of the earth that faced the sun..." The bottom line is that it doesn't *look* like the earth is moving and it doesn't *feel* like it is moving – not in Aristotle's day, and not in our own.

Aristotle's Ideas on Motion
Aristotle's ideas about motion also relied on other common sense explanations. He believed that there were two types of motion on earth: natural motion and violent motion. Natural motion was the motion that took place as an object moved toward its proper location in the universe – like a flame rising up through the air to reach the sphere of fire, or a rock falling so that it can reach the sphere of earth. In Aristotle's scheme, these motions took place *naturally* in that they required no external force or agent. A different kind of natural motion was found in the celestial realm: uniform circular motion, which continued on forever without slowing down or speeding up – a natural and essential property of the quintessence of which it was composed.

"Violent" motions, on the other hand, were those earthly motions that were caused by an active agent. An example of this is the motion of a wheeled cart, which results from the effort of a person pushing on it. Motion of this type will occur only as long as the active agent is in contact with the moving object – thus, when a person stops pushing a cart, it slows down and comes to a halt. It is important to realize that, given normal experiences of motion, Aristotle's view seems more sensible than the modern Newtonian view that "everything in motion remains in motion."[13] In fact, in most cases, the modern view doesn't seem to correspond well to very many of our ordinary experiences.

Aristotle's Influence
Aristotle's ideas about the physical world dominated the Western intellectual tradition for the better part of two thousand years. His ideas were handed down through the centuries and were later assimilated by Hellenistic, Islamic, and Christian cultures. The power and scope of Aristotelian natural philosophy didn't begin to lose its influence on European thought until the seventeenth century. In many historical

accounts, people living during the Middle Ages have been criticized for having needlessly adhered to the "authority of Aristotle." While it is true that his beliefs commanded much respect and served as a starting point for thinking about the natural world, the appeal and the usefulness of his philosophy accounted for its long-term success at least as much as any blind submission to his authority. In any case, it would be a gross misrepresentation to say that later "Aristotelians" accepted everything he had said. The Aristotelian viewpoint was modified in significant ways at different times and in different places. For example, Aristotelian belief in sixteenth-century Europe was different from Aristotelian belief in second-century Alexandria, which in turn differed from what Aristotle himself had conceived.[14] Indeed, even thinkers who lived at the same time and place didn't necessarily agree on all aspects of Aristotelian natural philosophy. There was a diversity of opinion on the details of scientific matters then, just as there is now.

Greek Astronomy

Like people in other cultures, the Greeks used the sky for reckoning time. The daily rising and setting of the sun, the monthly cycle of the moon through its phases, and the annual path of the sun through the zodiac were all ways people across the world kept time. In some cultures, astronomers made attempts to coordinate the annual cycle of the sun with the monthly lunar cycle of the moon's phases. However, the desire to create a calendar that could effectively incorporate both solar and lunar cycles was nearly impossible to satisfy, because the length of the solar year is not an integer multiple of a lunar month. One "lunar month" is the length of time it takes for the moon to complete a cycle of its phases.[15] A "solar year"[16] is the length of time it takes for the sun to return to an original equinox or solstice position in the sky – for example, the time it takes for the sun to go from one spring equinox to the next spring equinox. There are more than twelve lunar months in one solar year, but less than thirteen. Thus, a calendar year containing only twelve lunar months (of approximately 29 days) will end before the sun returns to its original position in the sky, and the calendar will be too short to represent a full solar year. With thirteen lunar months, the solar calendar would be too long.

Knowledge of lunar and solar cycles was applied to calendar-making by providing most years with twelve lunar months and then adding a thirteenth month (a "leap month") as local rulers saw fit. After grappling with this problem for centuries, the Babylonians and Greeks partially solved it by estimating that in 19 solar years there are 235 lunar months. This 19-year solar/lunar cycle is called the Metonic cycle after Meton (fl. 425 BCE), who is often credited with developing it.[17]

There was fundamental awareness of the nature of the motions of the sun, the moon, and the planets in Aristotle's time – though much more astronomical detail was yet to be appreciated. Greek astronomers continued to contribute to their traditional goal of describing all motions in the heavens, including some apparently irregular ones, as the result of some combination of uniform circular motions. Before we consider their contributions, however, we need to consider how earlier Greeks used the "Greek two-sphere model" to explain the most basic celestial motions (see figure 2.8).

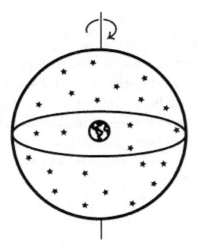

[Figure 2.8. The Greek two sphere model. Figure courtesy Sarah Caldwell.]

Let's begin by considering the two spheres individually:

The Earth Consider the small circle in the middle of the diagram, which depicts the spherical earth as the Greeks had imagined it: at the center of the universe and unmoving. This representation of the earth shows its north pole pointed upward.

The Celestial Sphere The larger outer circle represents the celestial sphere, which shares its center with the sphere of the earth. The celestial sphere encloses the outermost boundary of the entire universe – nothing exists beyond it. The interior surface of the celestial sphere is where the sun, the stars, the moon, and the planets are found and where they can be seen from the centrally-located earth. Unlike the stationary earth, the celestial sphere rotates daily from east to west (or clockwise, when viewed from above the North Pole). It is this motion that accounts for the nearly daily appearance of the stars, sun, moon and planets rising in the east and setting in the west that we observe from the earth's surface. The North Star is located at the top of this celestial sphere and is on the north-south axis that includes the North Pole and the center of the earth. This position, on the axis of the celestial sphere, is the reason that the North Star doesn't appear to move in the sky as the celestial sphere turns on its axis.

By Aristotle's day, Greeks were well aware that as they travelled north or south different groups of stars were visible. Indeed, this fact helped lead them to accept the idea of a spherical earth and a spherical cosmos in the first place. We will consider here what observers at different locations on the earth's surface could expect to see using the Greek two-sphere model. Let's first consider what observers standing at the North Pole on the earth's surface would see as they looked directly overhead at the top of the celestial sphere: they would find the stationary pole star, or "North Star," unmoving at the zenith (the highest point in the sky) as all of the other visible stars rotated around it in a counterclockwise direction. These stars, which appear to rotate around the pole star and never dip below the horizon, are called "circumpolar stars." Thus, in this location on the earth's surface, the Greek two-sphere model predicted that no stars would rise or set on the horizon as the celestial sphere turned on its axis.

Although no ancient Greeks ever traveled this far north, this is precisely what was seen by later observers at the North Pole. Much farther to the south, at the earth's equator, the Greek two-sphere model predicted something much different: all of the stars would appear to rise along the eastern horizon and set along the western horizon – and none of them would be circumpolar. Once again, this prediction proved to be accurate; it is what was observed by the early Spanish and Portuguese explorers who were the first Westerners to reach the equator – two thousand years after the two-sphere model was first developed!

At intermediate positions on the earth's surface, in the northern mid-latitudes (North America, Europe and Asia), the two sphere model is equally successful at explaining what is seen in the sky. Consider what is actually observed as one travels northward on the earth's surface from the equator: more and more stars remain above the horizon circling the North Star, and fewer and fewer stars rise and set on the horizon.

[Figure 2.9. Time-elapsed photo of circumpolar stars viewed from a northern mid-latitude (photo taken facing northward). The stellar motion is in the counterclockwise direction. From *A Text-Book of Astronomy* by George C. Comstock, 1903.]

Thus, the Greek two-sphere model explained why circumpolar stars exist *and* why more of them are visible as one travels north. Furthermore, the model also provided a theoretical foundation for a mathematical geography of the earth's surface. From their experience in applying trigonometry to astronomy, Greek astronomers and geographers realized that each location on the earth could be specified by assigning it angular values of latitude and longitude (see figure 2.10).

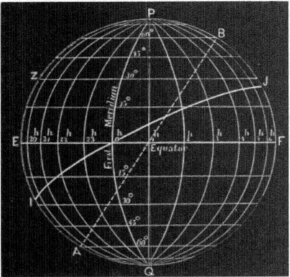

[Figure 2.10. Sphere of the earth with lines of latitude and longitude. From *Astronomy*, Newcomb and Holden, 1892. Public domain, archive.org]

Navigators could use the two-sphere model to determine how far north or south they were (their latitude) on the earth's surface by measuring the angle between the horizon and the North Star. Determining longitude was a much more difficult problem and it was not solved conveniently and generally until the eighteenth century.[18]

It is difficult to exaggerate the importance of the two-sphere model to the development of Western science – though it can be challenging to imagine that such a long-standing (and now erroneous) model was once a path-breaking innovation. The importance of the two-sphere model is not sufficiently appreciated in most accounts of the history of science – perhaps because no one can be credited with its development, or perhaps because it would threaten to detract from the importance of the later Western European Scientific Revolution. Regardless of the reason, if one of our motivations is to identify aspects of Western thought that were essential to the development of modern astronomy, we have to appreciate the two-sphere model for what it was: the key innovation that made possible all of the subsequent developments in Western theoretical astronomy. No other culture in the world had taken this step; from this point on, Western astronomy was on a unique path. And even if it could be somehow stripped of this greater historical role, the two-sphere model remains a remarkable accomplishment: it was the source of several important and successful predictions about the geography of the earth. For example, although the ancient Greeks had never been to the North Pole, they knew that such a location existed on the surface of the earth and they knew what the sky would have looked like to people who were located there. They also knew that the earth must possess a Southern Hemisphere even though it too was a region otherwise unknown to them. Indeed, their confidence in the reality of the spherical earth allowed them to seriously speculate about whether the Southern Hemisphere had habitable land and, if so, whether there could be people populating it (whom they referred to hypothetically as the "antipodes"). Once again, Greek scientists were able to predict what the sky would look like in this unknown land: they knew it would appear to be similar to what is seen in the Northern Hemisphere with stars and planets rising daily in the east and setting in the west and circumpolar stars moving around the southern pole, but in a *clockwise* direction.[19]

It is frequently surprising to modern-day Americans that the idea that the earth was round and that one could sail westward from Europe in order to get to Asia was far older than Christopher Columbus. According to Aristotle, "Those who imagine that the region around the Pillars of Heracles [the Strait of Gibraltar] joins on to the regions of India, and that in this way the ocean is one, are not, it would seem, suggesting anything utterly incredible" *(On the Heavens)*. It is simply a gross historical misconception that Columbus struggled against a prevailing European view that the earth was flat. This erroneous idea has been perpetuated by school teachers and even some historians for many generations.[20]

It would be easy, and misguided, for us to remain unimpressed by this early Greek understanding of geography and astronomy. For although this knowledge might seem trivial today, the two-sphere model was the source of our current geographic knowledge of the earth. There is no evidence that any other culture had developed a similar understanding of spherical geometry, geography, and astronomy. The Greek's successful prediction of locations on the earth that were otherwise unknown (the North Pole, the South Pole, the equator, and the southern hemisphere with its hypothetical antipodes) was a remarkable accomplishment in the history of science and in human understanding.

Elaborations on the Two-Sphere Model
The two-sphere model wouldn't have needed to be any more complicated than this if Greek astronomers had remained interested only in the motion of the stars. But of course, they also sought explanations for the motions of the sun, moon, and planets. Let's first consider the motion of the sun as it actually appears above the earth's surface:

In the northern mid-latitudes at summer solstice (in Wisconsin, for example), the sun rises in the northeast and sets in the northwest at the most northerly points on the horizon; the sun is high in the sky at noon, the days are long, and the nights are short. At both spring and fall equinox, the sun rises in the east and sets in the west and the days and nights are of equal length. At winter solstice, the sun rises in the southeast and sets in the southwest at its most southerly points on the horizon; the sun is low in the sky at noon, the days are short, and the nights are long.

The Motion of the Sun in the Two-Sphere Model
As described earlier, the celestial sphere turns from east to west carrying the stars, the sun, the moon, and the planets around the earth once a day – more or less. It is this rapid daily motion that explains why the sun, moon, planets, and stars appear to rise in the east and set in the west. But, of all the celestial objects, only the stars are permanently fixed to positions on the inner surface of the sphere. Together, they make a complete circuit around the earth every 23 hours, 56 minutes. The sun, on the other hand, lags slightly behind the stars and completes its circuit in 24 hours – the amount of time that we call "a day." Thus, the sun is *not* fixed to the celestial sphere, but instead is slowly drifting "backwards" in a *west-to-east* direction across the interior surface of the celestial sphere as the celestial sphere itself rotates rapidly in the other direction. It takes one year for the sun to complete its backwards circuit against the fixed

background of stars before returning to its original position. The path
that the sun takes is called the ecliptic (see figure 2.11). Keep in mind
that while the sun follows its slow annual west-to-east motion along the
ecliptic, the rapid daily east-to-west motion of the entire celestial sphere
continues to take place. So while it takes an entire year for the sun to
drift backwards along the ecliptic, the celestial sphere rotates 366 times in
the east-to-west direction – causing the sun to rise and set 365 times.

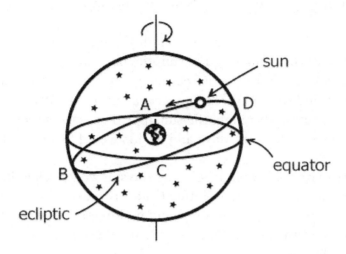

[Figure 2.11. The Greek two sphere model. Figure courtesy Sarah Caldwell.]

To picture the motion in this view of the cosmos (which can be difficult to
do) it is customary to simplify the situation by ignoring the rapid daily
motion of the celestial sphere. Instead, we traditionally reference the
motions of the sun, the moon, and the planets to the background of fixed
stars on the inside of the sphere and, while doing so, imagine that the
sphere itself is stationary. The rate at which the sun, moon, and planets
move on the interior surface of the celestial sphere is on the order of
weeks, months, and years – much slower than the rapid daily motion of
the sphere itself.

Let's first consider the annual motion of the sun along the ecliptic, which
is a circular path tilted by 23° from the celestial equator, and which shares
its center. This feature of the two-sphere model allowed astronomers to
account for the changing position of the sun in the sky throughout the

year. When the sun is at its most northerly point on the ecliptic (the Tropic of Cancer), it is at the Summer Solstice position (point "D" in the upper right-hand part of figure 2.11). This yielded the prediction that for observers in a region near the North Pole, the sun would not set during this time of year. Instead, they would find the sun running its daily circuit high in the sky around them – never setting below the horizon. This feature also explained the observed path the sun takes through the sky at the northern midlatitudes during Summer solstice.

Approximately three months later, at Fall Equinox (point "A"), the slow annual motion of the sun along the ecliptic has taken the sun to the celestial equator. At this time of year, people located at the earth's equator would find the sun directly overhead at noon. When at this position on the celestial sphere, the sun appears to rise directly in the east and set in the west; thus, the days and nights would be of equal length.

Three months later, at Winter Solstice, the sun would reach its southernmost journey on the ecliptic at the Tropic of Capricorn (point "B"). At this time of year, the sun would no longer rise above the horizon in the region near the North Pole. At the northern mid-latitudes the sun would rise in the southeast, set in the southwest, and remain low on the southern horizon during the day. The days would be short and the nights long.

In this model, the sun then continues its travels to the Spring Equinox position (point "C) and finally back again to Summer Solstice (point "D") over the course of the remaining six months. Keep in mind that while the sun is traveling slowly along the ecliptic on the inner surface of the celestial sphere, it is still being carried rapidly around the earth by the celestial sphere once a day. It is the rapid daily motion of the celestial sphere that accounts for the daily rising and setting of the sun and it is the very slow motion (only ~1° per day) of the sun around the ecliptic that accounts for the sun's changing height in the sky and the seasons.

Motion of the Moon and Planets According to the Two-sphere Model

Though the sun lags slightly behind the stars as they travel in their daily east-to-west motion, the moon lags behind them even more. Like the sun, the moon follows a well-defined circular path, which is very close to the path of the sun – though it is tilted slightly to it (5°) crossing the ecliptic at two points (the "nodes" where solar or lunar eclipses are possible). The planets also have paths slightly inclined to the ecliptic – though the length of time that the different planets take to complete their circuits varies greatly. The narrow band of stars in the celestial sphere where the motions of the sun, moon, and planets take place is called the zodiac.

It is important to note that in this early Western astronomical tradition, the sun and the moon were classified as planets because they wandered among the stars along with the other planets (the word "planet" has its origins in the Greek word for "wanderer").

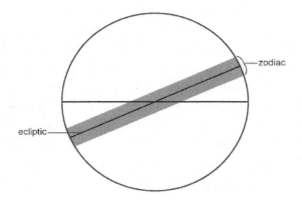

[Figure 2.12. The ecliptic (path of the sun) and the zodiac (which is the region on the celestial sphere that includes the paths of all the other Planets). The horizontal line marks the "celestial equator" which is in the same plane as the equator of the earth. Figure courtesy Danica Oudeans.]

Details of Planetary Motion
The length of time that the known planets (Mercury, Venus, Mars, Jupiter, and Saturn) take to complete their circuit through the zodiac varies widely: from an average of one year for Mercury and Venus, to twenty-nine years for Saturn. Planetary motions can be explained only crudely using the two-sphere model because the planets exhibit extremely irregular motions on their travels across the zodiac. Indeed, upon closer inspection, even the motions of the sun and moon are not quite as regular

as was first thought. An irregularity in the motion of the sun was uncovered after amassing centuries' worth of astronomical observations, first in Babylonia and then in Greece: it turns out that the four seasons are not of perfectly equal length. Indeed, in the Northern Hemisphere it takes more time for the sun to move from spring equinox to fall equinox than it takes to go from fall equinox to spring equinox – that is, summer is longer than winter. A simple, unadorned two-sphere model cannot account for this fact. Similarly, a careful consideration of the moon's motion revealed that it is even more irregular than that of the sun – a lunar month can vary in length by as much as 7 hours from one cycle to the next (about a 1% variation). Later ancient Greek astronomers developed new models to more accurately account for lunar and solar positions in the sky.

The other planets exhibit a far greater irregularity in their motions compared to those of the moon and the sun. Although much of the time the five planets are moving slowly in a west-to-east direction through the zodiac, they occasionally slow down, come to a halt, reverse their direction, and move in an east-to-west direction for a short period of time before reversing their direction once again back to the normal west-to-east motion (see figure 2.13). This reversal in planetary motion is called "retrograde motion." Finally, in addition to these anomalies of motion,[21] the planets exhibit corresponding changes in brightness as they move through the zodiac.

"Saving the Appearances"

As we have seen, the Greek natural philosophers believed that a hidden, orderly structure underlay nature's superficial appearances. They simply could not accept that nature was as "messy" as it appeared to be, and they instead confidently assumed that it was more rational than that. Their oft-stated goal was to "save the appearances," which in a sense was to save nature from appearing to be incoherent and nonsensical. Greek astronomers did not believe that the wild loops that the planets took in the sky represented what nature was actually doing – instead, they believed that there was a rational symmetry and perfection behind the apparent disorder. It was an intuition which they held to doggedly and that had profound implications for the future of understanding nature.

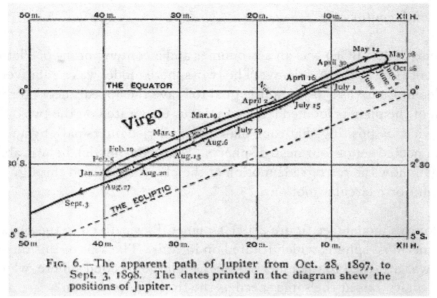

FIG. 6.—The apparent path of Jupiter from Oct. 28, 1897, to Sept. 3, 1898. The dates printed in the diagram shew the positions of Jupiter.

[Figure 2.13. A record of retrograde motion of Jupiter from the northern midlatitudes. Since at these latitudes the zodiac is found high in the southern sky, this diagram represents what a northern observer would see facing south. Thus, east is to the left side of the diagram and west is to the right. From *A Short History of Astronomy*, Arthur Berry, 1899. Public domain, archive.org]

The Greek astronomers and mathematicians worked to satisfy their intuition by assuming that the motion of the planets was the result of perfect circular motion or some combination of perfect circular motions. They settled on the use of circles and spheres in their explanations – probably for two reasons: (1) The two-sphere model had already employed circles and spheres, so it would have been natural to elaborate on an already fruitful strategy.[22]   That is, since the motion of the vast majority of objects in the heavens (stars) was perfectly circular, it would have been reasonable to presume that the planets would have possessed underlying circular motions as well. (2) Of all the possible geometric figures, the simplicity and symmetry of the sphere and the circle best satisfied the intuition that the heavens were orderly in structure and perfect and immutable in content.[23]   Plato had suggested that only the simplest forms could account for motion in the heavens – in his view, the creator (the Demiurge) would not have constructed the universe with anything less worthy. This fundamental assumption about the circular-spherical structure of planetary motion persisted until the early seventeenth century CE.

Eudoxus (fl. 365 BCE) was an astronomer and a contemporary of Plato's who spent time at the Academy. The two-sphere model was a relatively new idea in Eudoxus's day, and the goal to "save the appearances" for the motion of the planets loomed large. Eudoxus elaborated on the two-sphere view by positing that each planet was carried on its path by an interconnected set of four nested spheres. Using this model, he was able to explain how the retrograde motion of the planets occurred through simple uniform circular motion.

In Eudoxus's model (see figure 2.14), a planet, P, was fixed to the surface of its innermost sphere, which rotated on its axis. The axis of this inner sphere was attached to the inner surface of a larger second sphere, which rotated on its axis at the same speed as the first sphere, but on a differently inclined axis and in the opposite direction. This second sphere was attached to the interior of a third one, which was moving at a different speed. All together there were four spheres rotating with different orientations. It is difficult to appreciate how the combined motions of the Eudoxean spheres could explain the motion of a planet, so modern animations are helpful.[24]

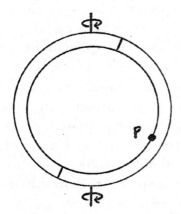

[Figure 2.14. The two innermost spheres in the Eudoxean model.]

Careful analysis of the two innermost spheres shows that a planet located on the innermost sphere of the two counter-rotating spheres traces out a figure-eight diagram (called a hippopede). If these two inner spheres are then carried around the zodiac by the third sphere, retrograde motion can be accounted for.

It is important to remember that models of planetary motion relate the motion of the planets to the fixed sphere of stars, since the location of a planet in the sky is specified by describing its location in the zodiac (the collections of stars that the planet could appear in front of – i.e. Sagittarius, Libra, Cancer, etc.). The fourth Eudoxean sphere accounts for the daily rising and setting of the planet. A later effort by Callippus (fl. 330 BCE) appears to be an attempt to improve upon Eudoxus's system so that it was more accurate (though not enough details remain in the historical record to draw solid conclusions about the precise nature of Eudoxus or Callippus's work).

Aristotle later elaborated on the Eudoxan/Callippean planetary models[25] with the goal of explaining the motions of the planets with a single unified device (rather than treating each planet's motion independently, as had Eudoxus and Callippus had done). Aristotle's desire to understand nature as a coherent system led him to propose that all of the planetary motions were caused by 55 interconnected concentric spheres. In this scheme, the motion of the outermost sphere was passed down to the sphere below, and that sphere transmitted some of its motion to the sphere below it, and so on, until the motion of all the planets could be accounted for. This complex scheme included some spheres that merely "unrolled" the motion of the planetary spheres above and below it, much like an idler gear. We are uncertain about how confident or serious Aristotle was with his model, nor do we know what his contemporaries thought about it, but we do learn from his effort what he and his contemporaries thought a good explanation of nature *should* look like.

---

[1] Lloyd, G.E.R., *Magic, Reason and Experience: Studies in the Origins and Development of Greek Science*, 1979.

[2] Roochnick, David, *Retrieving the Ancients*, 2004.

[3] While the Greeks undoubtedly inherited a great deal of mathematical and astronomical knowledge from their neighbors and modified and used that knowledge to their own ends over many centuries, they most often expressed numerical values in mathematics using their own number system. The Greek number system employed the Greek alphabet. The first letter alpha, α, represented the number one; the second letter beta, β, represented the number two; and so on... Additional symbols and rules were employed to accommodate for larger numbers and fractions. Other languages, like Hebrew, have also employed letters in their alphabet to represent numbers.

[4] DeLong has described the function of logic in *A Profile of Mathematical Logic*, 1970: "There would be no need to state logical principles if either there were no disagreements or only a small number of them (since in the latter case each could be considered individually)... ...For the value of a proof is to convince a person of something about which he is not initially convinced. For example, it is perfectly possible for someone to simultaneously accept the common notions and postulates of Euclidean geometry and yet doubt the Pythagorean Theorem. The purpose of the proof is to show that the doubt is unjustified." DeLong then adds, "...logic is vastly more comprehensive and useful than merely a device which may be used to show that an opponent is wrong. Yet, *we should not overlook the egoism and spirit of competitiveness which marked its origin*." (my emphasis).

[5] A simple example of this method is the statement that the number 0.999... (where the number 9 repeats forever) is in reality, the same as the number "1.000... An informal proof of this statement goes along the lines of the following:

Since the fraction $1/3 = 0.333...$
And since $1/3 + 1/3 + 1/3 = 1$ therefore,
$0.333... + 0.333... + 0.333... = 0.999...$ and since it is also true that, $0.333... = 1/3$
then it must be true that, $0.999... = 1$

[6] The historical record isn't complete enough to conclude with certainty whether the man, Pythagoras, was responsible for a particular mathematical or philosophical conclusion or whether it was one of his followers.

[7] This relationship is general and holds for other right triangles that are not "Pythagorean triples." For example, if one bisected a rectangle that has one side equal to 1 and the other side equal to 2, it results in a diagonal that is equal to $1^2 + 2^2$

$= c^2$, where c is equal to the square root of 5, also an irrational number. The following version of the proof is taken from Lloyd, G.E.R., 1970:

> Let AC be the diagonal of the square, AB its side
> Suppose AC is commensurable with AB, and let a:b be their ratio expressed in the lowest terms. Since AC > AB, a > 1.
> Then AC:AB = a:b
> So, $AC^2:AB^2 = a^2:b^2$
> But (by Pythagoras's theorem) $AC^2 = 2AB^2$
> Therefore $a^2 = 2b^2$
> So a^2, and therefore a, is even, and since a:b is in its lowest terms, b is odd.
> Since a is even, let a = 2c
> So $4c^2 = 2b^2$
> So $2c^2 = b^2$
> From which it follows that b is even.

Since the assumption that AC is commensurable with AB leads to the impossible consequence that the same number, b, is both odd and even, the assumption must be false.

[8] Often times the birth and death dates for a historical figure are unknown. However, from their written works we know when they were active. The abbreviation fl. stands for flourit, which is the approximate period in which a figure was active working or "flourishing." Thus in the case of Euclid, we know he was actively working and writing in the years roughly centered on 300 BCE.

[9] Lloyd, G.E.R., *Early Greek Science: Thales to Aristotle*, 1970.

[10] Much of what we know about these early philosophers we know through the writings of Plato, Aristotle, and other commentators. The works of later Greek thinkers also went in and out of fashion over the ages and were lost or nearly lost.

[11] From Plato's *Republic* (Trans. Benjamin Jowett, 1894). Public domain, accessed from Project Gutenberg.

[12] The Academy was an informal school-like institution where scholars, philosophers, and disciples could come to study and discuss a variety of subjects. Aristotle would later found a similar institution called the "Lyceum."

[13] The one important exception to this was Aristotle's explanation for projectile motion, which was not well-received by subsequent thinkers and which generated a great deal of criticism and commentary from later philosophers.

[14] For example, the strong distinction between the celestial and terrestrial realm was an important one for many "Aristotelians" – though it is not at all clear that

Aristotle himself would have seen it in such black and white terms. When we refer to "Aristotelian" ideas in this text, we are most often referring to the beliefs of people who understood themselves to be followers of Aristotle – with their ideas being, more or less, related to those that Aristotle held.

[15] This is often measured from one new moon to the next.

[16] There are slightly different definitions for a "solar year." A solar year that maintains a fixed period for the seasons (from vernal equinox to vernal equinox, for example) is properly referred to as a "tropical year." A "sidereal year" is the length of time that it takes for the sun to return to the same position against the background of the stars in the ecliptic. The slight difference between the two was first noted by Hipparchus (second century BCE). This phenomenon is now explained by the slow precession of the earth's axis.

[17] The Mesopotamians, who were contemporaries of Meton, were called Chaldeans by the Greeks. The "Metonic" 19-year solar cycle appears in Chaldean astronomical records at approximately the same time as it appears in the Greek records, and it seems very likely that the innovation was originally a Babylonian one.

[18] Although it was much more difficult and less accurate than latitude determination, occasions early geographers could use eclipse records in combination with local times to determine the relative longitude of locations on land. However, the accuracy of these early longitude determinations was poor.

[19] Eighteen hundred years later, western navigators discovered the "Southern Cross" – the four stars that are grouped around the southern pole.

[20] See note 14 in Chapter 4 for a lengthy discussion.

[21] The variation in the speed of the planets, as they move in their normal west-to-east motion, was often referred to as "the first anomaly." The qualitatively distinctive feature of retrograde motion was referred to as "the second anomaly."

[22] Lloyd, G.E.R., *Magic, Reason and Experience: Studies in the Origins and Development of Greek Science*, 1979.

[23] The sphere (and in a similar way, the circle) can be seen as "perfect" because of its infinite symmetry and because it contains the greatest volume to surface ratio of any solid body (Taub, 1993). Also, the circle and sphere were also considered to be ideal for perpetual circular motion because there is no beginning or end at any point on a circular path.

[24] For an excellent animation of the motions, see the video of the Eudoxean spheres by Museo Galileo:
http://catalogue.museogalileo.it/multimedia/EudoxussSystem.html

[25] See North, 1995. These astronomical systems are also referred to as "homocentric" or "concentric" sphere models.

Chapter Three – Hipparchus and Ptolemy: Hellenistic Planetary Astronomy in Greek, Roman, Islamic, and European Civilizations

The high point of later Greek or "Hellenistic" astronomy was marked by the work of Ptolemy of Alexandria (fl. 150 CE) who lived and worked five centuries after Aristotle. During the intervening period, the record of astronomical observations had greatly improved and Greek astronomers had developed an appreciation for existing Babylonian astronomical knowledge.[1]

Prior to Ptolemy, the most important Hellenistic astronomer was Hipparchus (fl. 135 BCE) whose pioneering mathematical astronomy combined the Greek desire to provide a geometric/physical explanation for celestial motion with the Babylonian desire to provide numerically accurate astronomical prognostications. Hipparchus used geometric models to produce quantitative predictions for the future positions of the sun and the moon. He also created a stellar atlas that described the location of over one thousand stars. With this knowledge, and with access to centuries of Babylonian astronomical records, he discovered the very subtle "precession of the equinoxes."[2] Indeed, Hipparchus made such extensive use of Babylonian astronomical data in his work that it appears likely he learned of it by working directly with Babylonian astronomers.[3]

Three centuries later, Ptolemy offered a greatly elaborated and improved version of Hipparchian astronomy. He benefited from the additional astronomical data that had accumulated since Hipparchus's time. Ptolemy also made some of his own astronomical observations and added an important theoretical innovation. His major astronomical work is most commonly referred to as the *Almagest*.[4] Because of Ptolemy's great success, his works superseded Hipparchus's – and for this reason, very little of Hipparchus's work has survived. In fact, much of what we know about Hipparchus's astronomy is through Ptolemy's account of it.[5] Perhaps it would be most fair to label the resulting astronomical system "Hipparchian-Ptolemaic Astronomy," but following well-established practice in the history of science, we will refer to it simply as "Ptolemaic Astronomy."

Ptolemaic Astronomy – the Eccentric

The "eccentric" was a model frequently used to explain the motion of the sun and moon in Hellenistic astronomy. In this model, the sun or moon possesses uniform circular motion around a circle with center C (that is, it moves at a constant rate around its circular path). The key feature of the eccentric is that its center is displaced slightly from the center of the universe (such that it is not directly centered on the earth). If the sun or moon were viewed from the earth, "E", it would *appear* to slow down as it got farther from E, and speed up as it got closer – even though it would actually be moving at a constant speed on its circular path.

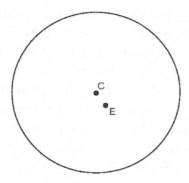

[Figure 3.1. Eccentric model. Figure courtesy Danica Oudeans.]

From the vantage point of the earth, the apparent speed of the sun or moon through the sky would be relatively slow when it was on the other side of the circle from E and it would appear faster when it was near E (in the same way that cars on a highway *seem* to be moving faster when one observes them standing close to a highway rather than from a greater distance).

While the eccentric alone couldn't account for retrograde motion, it *could* be used to explain the changing rate that the planets exhibited as they moved through the zodiac. This model was most frequently applied to the motion of the sun in order to explain the unequal lengths of the seasons.[6]

The Epicycle-on-Deferent

One of the fundamental elements of Ptolemaic astronomical theory was the "epicycle-on-deferent model" of planetary motion through the zodiac. Consider the following figures depicting the motion of a planet "P." P revolves in a counterclockwise direction around a small circle called the *epicycle*, which is centered on the empty point "A." At the same time that P is revolving counterclockwise around point A, point A is revolving counterclockwise around E (the earth) on the larger circle, called the *deferent.*

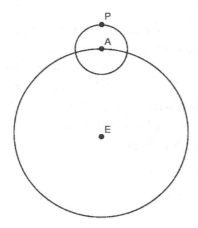

[Figure 3.2a. Epicycle-on-deferent model. Figure courtesy of Danica Oudeans.]

In the first diagram (Figure 3.2a), planet P is situated at its greatest possible distance from the earth. In this configuration, P will appear to be moving rapidly in its normal west-to-east direction against the background of stars because it is being carried by both the epicycle *and* the deferent in the same direction. At this position, because of its distance from earth, planet P should also appear to be relatively faint in the sky. Consider a later position of planet P (Figure 3.2b) after it has moved on its epicycle while the center of the epicycle has also moved on its deferent (Figure 3.2b).

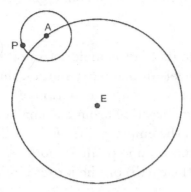

[Figure 3.2b. Epicycle-on-deferent model. Figure courtesy Danica Oudeans.]

To reach this second position, P had revolved counterclockwise around the center of its epicycle while the center of its epicycle had revolved counterclockwise around the center of its deferent. Because of P's new position on the epicycle (and its motion *toward* the earth), it no longer appears to move as quickly in a west-to-east motion through the zodiac when viewed from E. Later still, the planet P has arrived at a position that is now much closer to the earth (Figure 3.2c).

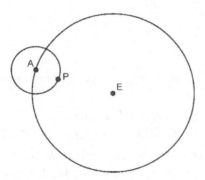

[Figure 3.2c. Epicycle-on-deferent model. Figure courtesy Danica Oudeans.]

In this configuration, the planet is moving around on its epicycle in a direction *opposite* to the motion of the epicycle around the deferent. This counter-directional motion, when viewed from the earth, results in the appearance of P moving backwards (in an east-to-west motion) against the field of stars. (Remember: motion in these planetary models is referenced to the fixed sphere of stars while neglecting the superimposed daily motion.[7]) Furthermore, during this period of retrograde motion, the planet P would necessarily appear brighter in the sky than it had in its earlier positions because it would be physically closer to the earth. A modified epicycle-on-deferent model could also be used to explain the motion of the sun and the moon (even though they do not display retrograde motion).[8]

It is well worth noting that this model of planetary motion was successful at accounting for an otherwise unexplained and striking coincidence: planets undergoing retrograde motion are also at their brightest state. This was a phenomenon that the concentric shell theories of Eudoxus, Callippus, and Aristotle could simply not account for. But even the epicycle-on-deferent model had its limitations: when it was used without additional modifications, it failed to give quantitative predictions as accurate as astronomers had hoped for.

The Equant

The careful application of the eccentric and epicycle-on-deferent models of planetary motion, first by Hipparchus and then by Ptolemy, was very fruitful. However, attempts to develop increasingly accurate accounts of planetary motion were limited if only these two models were used. It became apparent to Ptolemy that something new was needed in order to improve the correspondence between theory and observation.[9] This need led him to propose his own innovation – the **equant** model of planetary motion.

Consider the following diagram of the equant. The path of the planet, P, is described by the solid circle centered on point C. The equant point, Q, and the Earth, E, are equidistant from and on opposite sides of C. In the equant model, the speed of the planet on its circular path is *not* constant. Instead, the planet speeds up and slows down on its path in a very well defined manner – in such a way that if the planet were viewed from Equant point Q it would appear as though it was moving at a constant rate around the imaginary dashed circle center on it.[10] For the planets that underwent retrograde motion, Ptolemy used the equant model to drive the center of the epicycle around the deferent.

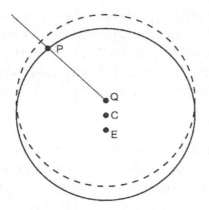

[Figure 3.3. Equant model of planetary motion. Figure courtesy Danica Oudeans.]

Ptolemy was very successful in accounting for the details of planetary motion. However, his equant model demanded that much of the observed variation in planetary speed was due to a real variation in the speed of the planet on its path around the earth and not due solely to an apparent variation (as in the case of an eccentric). For example, in the equant model as a planet gets closer to the earth on its eccentric path, it doesn't just *appear* to speed up; it actually *does* speed up. Thus, the equant violated the accepted maxim of uniform circular motion. Because of this, there were many early astronomers and philosophers who cast great doubt on the physical plausibility of Ptolemy's equant – even in the face of its great success. Ptolemy's justification for using the equant was that if it worked so well (which it did), there must have been an underlying logic that supported it – even if it wasn't apparent to him, or anyone else, what that logic was.

Ptolemy's Cosmology
Ptolemy fashioned eccentrics, equants, and/or epicycles to successfully describe the motion of each planet. But Ptolemy was interested in far more than predictive astronomy – he was also motivated by a strong commitment to astrology. He believed, as others before him had, that the

heavenly bodies could directly affect events on the earth and on its inhabitants. Ptolemy wrote a major work on astrology, the *Tetrabiblos*, in which he outlined his astrological beliefs and the wonderful benefits of being able to predict the future. Moreover, for Ptolemy, the study of the heavens was an ethical pursuit – in his mind, the heavenly bodies were perfect and contemplation of them could lead to "virtuous conduct."[11] He believed that any credible study of astrology or meteorology required detailed and accurate knowledge of the planetary motions that caused the effects he was interested in. These were some of his underlying motivations for creating an accurate theoretical account of planetary motions.

It was also important to Ptolemy to know more than where a planet *appeared* in the sky – he also wanted to know how it was physically positioned relative to the other heavenly bodies. This was yet another interest of Ptolemy's that went beyond the narrow pursuit of predictive mathematical astronomy. Such broadly encompassing views of the universe often include considerations of how the heavenly bodies and the earth are physically related and how and why planets move, as well as specific astrological practices and religious beliefs. The collection of beliefs that people possess about the universe is called a *cosmology*. While a predictive astronomical theory might be *part* of a cosmology, it is not the whole thing. As we will see, people can have many different reasons to accept or refute certain views of the cosmos.

Ptolemy had accepted the long-standing view that the earth was unmoving in the middle of the cosmos. As an astronomer and geometer, he also understood that the earth was very small compared to the size of the celestial sphere.[12] Like earlier astronomers, Ptolemy located the planets between the earth and the sphere of stars. He was not entirely certain about the order of the planets, but after a great deal of consideration he adopted the view that the moon was the closest to the earth, followed by Mercury, Venus, the sun, Mars, Jupiter, and Saturn. Since a particular planet was sometimes closer and sometimes farther away from the earth (because of the epicycle and/or eccentric paths they took), they were each assigned shells of varying thicknesses to move within. The actual size of each planet's shell, or sphere, was partially determined by the amount of room it needed to accommodate its eccentric, equant, and/or epicycle[13] (See figure 3.4).

[Figure 3.4. From the work of a later Ptolemaic astronomer in Europe, Georg von Peuerbach, *Theoricae novae planetarum*, 1474. The outer surface of a planet's sphere is represented by the outer boundary of the black area, and the inner surface of its sphere is the inner boundary of the black area. Note that the planet's sphere is centered on the earth (mundi) but that the center of the planet's motion is instead located at "deferetil" (This eccentric also has an equant point (labeled "equatil"). Public domain image, Wikimedia Commons.]

The second medieval cosmological diagram (figure 3.5) shows the Ptolemaic ordering of the planets (though necessarily simplified and not drawn to scale so that all of the planets' shells can be shown on the diagram).

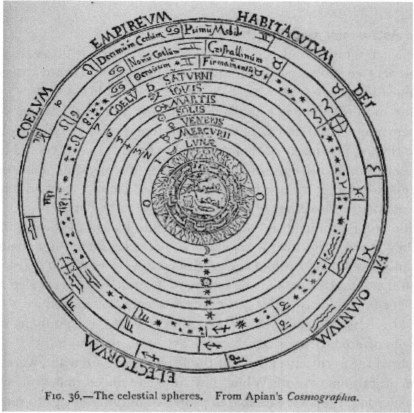

FIG. 36.—The celestial spheres. From Apian's *Cosmographia*.

[Figure 3.5. A Renaissance depiction of the Ptolemaic cosmos. Note the additional spheres beyond the sphere of stars (Firmamentum). From *A Short History of Astronomy* (Arthur Berry, 1899).]

Ptolemy defended his ordering of the planets, in part, on the assumption that the more slowly a planet appears to move through the zodiac, the more distant it must be from earth. Since Saturn has the longest period, it was assumed to be the farthest away; Jupiter, with the second longest period, was presumed to be the next planet in, and following it, Mars. The moon makes the quickest pass through the zodiac, so it was placed closest to earth. The sun, Mercury, and Venus presented a problem,

65

however, because they all take an average of one year to complete their circuits. Astronomers had traditionally disagreed over the ordering of these three planets. Ptolemy provided several reasons for arriving at his arrangement of planets, which was accepted, more often than not, for centuries to follow.[14]

Ptolemaic Astronomy after Ptolemy

Ptolemaic astronomy dominated Western astronomy for 1400 years. Astronomers after Ptolemy offered their own changes and innovations but continued to operate well within the theoretical tradition that Hipparchus and Ptolemy had established. However, several Islamic astronomers and natural philosophers offered remarkable criticisms of Ptolemaic theory, and many of them refused to believe that it could be the correct description of the cosmos. Some doubted the physical plausibility of epicycle-on-deferent motion because it deviated from perfect circular motion around a single center of the cosmos, as occurred in the Aristotelian and Platonic ideal. Many objected to his use of the equant because they found it physically implausible that celestial motion could speed up and slow down. Both of these criticisms were based on fundamental assumptions about the nature of motion, which revealed a preference or faithfulness to the earlier ideas of celestial motion as envisioned by Aristotle and others. What is so striking is that many of the men who offered these criticisms were astronomers who fully acknowledged the predictive power of the Ptolemaic system and were often even practitioners of it! While they were convinced that Ptolemaic theory was wrong, they were unable to propose anything better to replace it.[15]

A successful alternative theory would have to wait for a very different time and place: the 1500s and Northern Europe. Why a Northern European in the sixteenth century might have had the motivation and insight to challenge the well-established Ptolemaic view is a question we will consider in the next chapter. But, before we can address the question of "Why Europe?" a consideration of the medieval Mediterranean world is in order.

The Greek, Roman, Islamic, and Medieval European Worlds
This is a very brief sketch of Western thought from the end of the ancient, classical world to the beginning of the 1500s. The purpose of providing this historical background is to reveal the origins of later European thought about the natural world. It is important to appreciate the nature of these beliefs in order to understand how European thinkers responded to the changes that were, unbeknownst to them, just around the corner.

We will begin this story in the Hellenistic World, which stretched from modern-day Afghanistan to Egypt and Greece (see figure 3.6). These Greek occupied lands were made Greek or "Hellenized" after their conquest by Alexander the Great and the military and political dominance of their later Greek rulers. During this period, Greek architecture, art, politics, philosophy, and science were introduced to these regions. While Hellenization did not completely replace existing cultural traditions, it did have a particularly strong influence in the cities and created cultural amalgams that survived long after Greek rule ended.

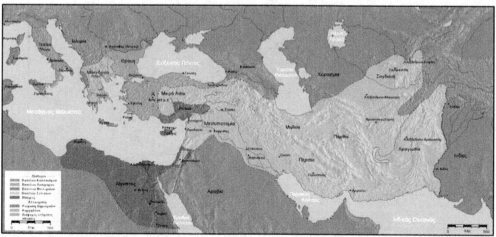

[Figure 3.6. The Hellenistic Kingdoms after the death of Alexander the Great ~300 BCE. Image courtesy Alexikoua, Wikimedia Commons.]

Immediately following the end of Alexander's conquests, Alexander fell ill and died in Babylon, and the conquered territory was divided among his principal lieutenants. These separate Hellenistic empires continued to compete with each other and thrived for over two centuries until the Roman Empire began to encroach upon them.

Hellenistic culture did not disappear with the military and political conquest of these areas by the Romans, but it continued to flourish within the Roman Empire. Trade in the eastern Mediterranean provided most of the Empire's wealth. The Greeks were known as the scholars and teachers in that society, even if they were slaves to their Roman masters. Many Romans readily acknowledged the superiority of Greek learning as well as its tremendous influence on their culture: "Captive Greece," said the Roman author Horace, "took captive her conqueror."

[Figure 3.7. The Roman Empire in the second century CE. Public domain image.]

Before the final "fall of Rome" in the 400s CE,[16] the Roman Empire had split into the Western Roman Empire, with Rome as its capital, and the Eastern Roman Empire, with Constantinople as its capital. Standard accounts of European history often fail to underscore the fact that the

Eastern Roman Empire continued to exist for centuries after the demise of the Western Empire – indeed, it didn't fall entirely until 1453.

Historians refer to the later Eastern Roman Empire as the "Byzantine Empire" because its capital, Constantinople, was built on the site of a town originally known as Byzantium. The Byzantine Empire comprised much of the former Hellenistic world and, at its core, remained culturally and linguistically Greek even though it had been subsumed into the Roman Empire for several centuries. It was here in the east that Christianity got its start. When the eastern half of the Roman Empire finally went its own way, the Latin that had been used for administrative purposes all across the Roman Empire had lost this function in the east and fell into disuse.

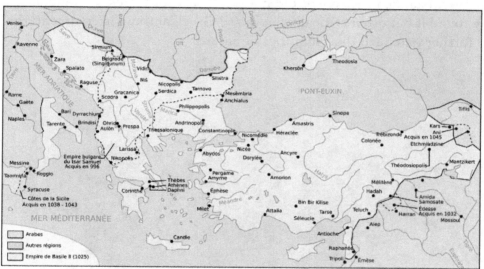

[Figure 3.8. The Byzantine Empire in 1025 (Empire of Basile II). Image courtesy Nécropotame, Wikimedia Commons.]

The Rise of Islam

In the early 600s CE, to the southeast of the Byzantine Empire in the Arabian Peninsula, Mohamed and his followers founded a new religion – Islam. The rapid spread of this religion through the military prowess of its Arab adherents soon encroached on the Byzantine Empire, reducing its size and influence in the region.

In time, the Islamic world began to assimilate classical learning from the Hellenistic world that it had conquered – this included works in medicine, mathematics, science, and philosophy. Important intermediaries of this knowledge were Nestorian Christians who had fled eastward out of the Byzantine Empire as heretics in 450s CE.[17] Their new Persian hosts were interested in their knowledge of Greek learning and provided a favorable environment for the practice of Nestorian medicine and the translation of Greek texts. In the beginning, many translations were from Greek into Syriac (the language the Nestorians taught in) and Persian. When Islamic armies conquered Persia, the Nestorians retained their role as teachers and scholars, and Greek texts were translated into Arabic by Nestorian and Islamic scholars. By the tenth century, many of the Greek texts that we have available to us today had been rendered into Arabic.[18] However, Islamic intellectuals did not simply accept Greek learning as they found it but often critically appraised Greek authors in commentaries and further extended their inquiries of nature.

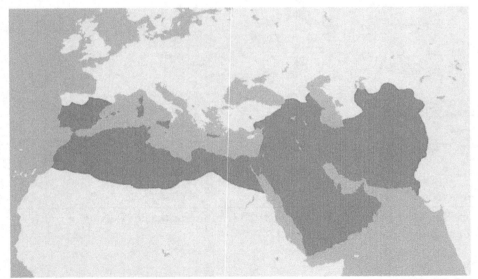

[Figure 3.9. Map of the Arab/Islamic world at its greatest extent, c. 850 CE. Image courtesy Gabagool Wikimedia Commons.]

Islamic Astronomy in the Middle Ages
Islamic scientists[19] made important contributions to theoretical and observational astronomy. They also worked to provide two particularly important services for the Islamic faith: the local determination of the

direction to the city of Mecca (for prayers), and the prediction of the first day of lunar visibility following a new moon.

Mohamed, the founder of Islam, had decreed that the first day of the month in the Islamic calendar was the day on which the new crescent moon was first observable[20] – an event that turns out to be far more difficult to predict than one might think: For starters, the length of time it takes for the moon to complete an orbit around the earth is approximately twenty-nine and a half days (a lunar month), but can vary by as much as 7 hours from one cycle to the next. Furthermore, knowing whether a crescent moon will be visible on a particular day also depends on knowing where and when the sun sets on the horizon (the angle that the ecliptic makes with the horizon at a particular time of year for a given location), on the angle between the moon's path and the horizon, and on the moon's position above or below the ecliptic.

Also important in Islam is determining the direction to Mecca for prayers, the Qibla, which required sophisticated knowledge of spherical geometry in order to properly relate the prayer location and Mecca. Geography problems like this were understood to be solvable by applying the geographical and astronomical ideas of Ptolemy. Islamic astronomers rose to these challenges. They designed and constructed observing instruments, such as the astrolabe, and found new ways of conceptualizing problems they wanted to solve.

Over several centuries, Islamic scientists and scholars also made important contributions to alchemy, optics, and mathematics. In addition to the Hindu-Arabic number system, other vestiges of our Islamic scientific heritage can be found in English words of Arabic origin such as *azimuth, alchemy, algorithm, alcohol, algebra, cipher, zero,* and others. By the tenth century, the Islamic world's European neighbors to the north became increasingly self-confident and outward-looking after enduring a challenging period in their history. Western European scholars also became more and more interested in the vibrant and sophisticated Islamic culture that existed just south of them in Moorish Spain. Here, they discovered the accomplishments of Islamic scientists and the "lost Greek knowledge" that the Islamic world possessed. These Europeans were very impressed – and envious. But before we can move forward and complete the telling of this story, we should first take a brief step backwards in time to examine how the cultural and intellectual disparity between Islamic and Western Christian worlds developed in the first place.

[Figure 3.10. Astrolabes were used for observing and for making computations and were originally a Greek invention, but they later became very common in the Islamic World. This example is a planispheric astrolabe from Al-Andalus (Islamic Iberia), made in Toledo (Spain). Photo courtesy Photo: Luis García, Wikimedia Commons. The astrolabe is in the collection of the National Archaeological Museum of Spain, Madrid.]

Greek Knowledge in the Roman World

As described earlier, the Romans had subsumed Hellenistic lands into the Roman Empire through conquest. Having done so, they recognized the value of Greek culture and treated it as another spoil of war. Greek scholars and tutors found ready employment in the households of the Roman aristocracy – quite often as slaves. An education in the Greek language and classics quickly became an important part of the development of young Roman aristocrats. Ironically, this knowledge of Greek by upper class Romans meant there was little need for Romans to translate Greek texts into their native Latin. The small amount of Greek learning that had been rendered into Latin was largely limited to encyclopedias and books written for a popular audience.

This was the state of affairs in the Western Roman Empire in the 400s CE when economic, demographic, and political instabilities left it vulnerable to repeated raids by its neighbors. In this environment, it was difficult or impossible for upper class Romans to continue the luxury of providing their children with a classical Greek education. By the early 500s, the military and political landscape had deteriorated to the point that the Italian peninsula was ruled by a non-Roman king, Theodoric the Ostrogoth. Theodoric had an aide named Boethius (480-534 CE), who was a Roman from the aristocratic class. Boethius, and a few of his other highly educated contemporaries, realized that the kind of education that they received in *their* youth would no longer be available to the generation following them. They also recognized that Western knowledge of Greek learning would be lost unless it was quickly translated into Latin. Boethius resolved to translate as many Greek works as he was able to.

Unfortunately, before he got very far he fell out of favor with Theodoric and was imprisoned and then executed. In spite of this, Boethius, and a few others, managed to save a glimpse of the Greek Tradition for later Western scholars.

In the politically fragmented post-Roman Middle Ages, the early Latin translations survived mainly in monasteries.[21] While these non-religious texts were often considered important enough to maintain and to occasionally copy, far less attention was paid to them than to the Bible and theological works. This would be all that remained of Greek learning in Europe for the next 500 years – from the Early Medieval period (once known as the "Dark Ages") until the High Middle Ages. There were isolated examples of original European works in philosophy and science during this period, but as a whole, it was not a very impressive time for learning in Europe – especially when compared to the activity of their Islamic neighbors to the south. For instance, the Caliph of Alexandria (in present-day Egypt) had a library of 10,000 books at the same time the European Emperor Charlemagne (742-814 CE) was struggling to write his name as a full-grown adult. Although Charlemagne probably never achieved literacy in his lifetime, the educational and religious reforms he promoted helped expand literacy and learning in Europe at a time when they were a rarity.

The Medieval Christian World in the High Middle Ages (1000-1300)

By the early eleventh century, Europe had stabilized politically and was growing economically. Proximity and occasional diplomatic relations with Moorish Spain led some Europeans to conclude that there were features of Islamic civilization worth knowing more about. An increasing European interest in Greek science and philosophy, and an awareness that the Greek intellectual tradition had been maintained in the Islamic world helped create a new market for Latin editions of Greek and Arabic works. A vigorous translating industry arose in Spain and was carried out by Moorish Muslims, resident Christians (Mozarabs), and Jews – as well as occasional itinerant European scholars who were willing to relocate to Spain and learn a new language so that they could produce their own translations.

In this way, Arabic texts were translated into Latin just as Greek texts had been translated into Arabic several centuries earlier. A person who translated a text directly from Arabic into Latin obviously needed to be fluent in both Arabic *and* Latin, but quite often that facility did not exist in a single person. For this reason, texts were sometimes translated into an intermediate language through the collective effort of two translators. One person translated the Arabic into a vernacular language (i.e. Castillian) while the other translated it from the vernacular into Latin. There also existed Moorish texts in Hebrew – the product of Islam's Jewish intellectual tradition. These Hebrew texts served as additional source materials for the new Latin translations.

European scholars were aware that they were receiving second-, third-, or possibly even fourth-hand translations of Greek texts. For example, the possibility existed that a Latin text might be the product of a Greek-to-Syriac-to-Arabic-to-Castillian-to-Latin translation. The questionable quality of these texts created a perpetual demand for more reliable translations directly from Greek (for those texts that still existed in their original Greek).[22] Some of these early direct Greek-to-Latin translations took place in Sicily and southern Italy where Greek-speaking communities still existed and contact with Byzantium continued.

Christian Europe—The Roman Catholic Church
In the Latin West, Christianity had been unified under the Roman Catholic Church. The Church provided theological stability for the salvation and comfort of its adherents. It was more than just a religion as we might think of one today; but was a major cultural, moral, and political presence. It tied together a Europe that was otherwise divided by language and political boundaries. To a large extent, Christianity, under the banner of the Catholic Church, is what made Europe identifiably Europe.

The Pope was the religious and political leader of the Catholic Church and could realize his full power by threatening a king with excommunication and by denying Holy Communion to both him and his subjects – an action that could threaten their eternal salvation. On the other hand, the popes were sometimes limited in their actions by powerful kings, Church tradition, and even local politics. There were powerful Cardinals who advised popes and an elaborate Church bureaucracy (the papal curia) that existed for carrying out Church policy.

Aristotle and Universities in the High Middle Ages
By the 1000s, a relatively stable and economically dynamic Europe had created the need for a larger educated class that could work in business, government, and the Church. The demand for more education led to the expansion of the traditional "Cathedral Schools," some of which gained independence and became the first universities. It was in these early universities that students and scholars shared, discussed, and criticized the recently rediscovered Greek knowledge.

Before this time, Europeans knew very little about Aristotle beyond his works on logic. Upon exposure to his previously unknown works, many European scholars found Aristotle's views to be intellectually refreshing and intriguing. Most of them seemed willing to overlook or side-step some of the apparent incompatibilities of Aristotelian thought with Christian theology. However, some Christian theologians saw the new knowledge as a worrisome challenge to religious belief. One example of the potential problem that Aristotle presented to Christianity was his view that the earth and the Universe were of an infinite age – a belief that was clearly contrary to scripture.

There was an intense and extended struggle over the value of these new ideas. For a time, some of Aristotle's works were even banned at the University of Paris. After a long and vigorous debate among theologians and scholars, the study of Aristotelian philosophy and science was legitimized through the efforts of St. Thomas Aquinas (1225-1274) and others, who amalgamated Christianity and Aristotelian thought. In doing so, they changed both Catholic theology and Aristotelian natural philosophy. The creation of European Universities and the synthesis of Aquinas created a legitimate and supportive social space for science and philosophy, which began to be studied along with theology. Indeed, they were even viewed as "handmaidens" to Christianity. As just one example, Aquinas's "proof" for the existence of God was inspired by Aristotelian logic.

It is worth noting that this dynamic period of European history, "The High Middle Ages," included many cultural elements in art, music, and science that are sometimes associated with the later Renaissance period. Without the social discontinuity caused by the "Black Plague" in the 1300s, some features of the High Middle Ages might now be interpreted as belonging to an earlier phase of the Renaissance.

Early Christianity and Platonism

The incorporation of Aristotelianism into Medieval Catholic Christian culture contrasted significantly with the neo-Platonic ideas that characterized early Christianity. Indeed, looking all the way back into antiquity, it appears as though Plato's idealistic views and the views of

late Greek neo-Platonic philosophers, such as Platonius, were proto-
Christian in their outlook – even though they were not Christian
themselves. Recall Rafael's portrait of Plato and Aristotle: Plato
motioned to the heavens while Aristotle motioned to the earth. This is
important, because right from the beginning Christian theologians have
been interested in using Greek philosophy to help them make sense of
their faith.

The Bishop St. Augustine of Hippo (354-430 CE), was a particularly
important figure in the early Church. He began his career as a professor
of rhetoric in a Greek-speaking region of North Africa and was well
versed in the Greek intellectual tradition. Augustine witnessed the demise
of the Western Roman Empire and eventually converted to Christianity.
As an intellectual, and as a Christian, he relied heavily on his Platonic
philosophical outlook to understand his newly revealed faith. In doing so,
he helped establish the early theological foundations of Christianity. It
was, in part, this Platonic intuition that some later medieval theologians
had tried to protect when the Latin West was exposed to the natural
philosophy of Aristotle in the High Middle Ages. The significance of
Aquinas's success in legitimizing Aristotle cannot be overestimated, for
he and others managed to allow this second strand of Greek thought to
establish itself in Europe.

Athens and Jerusalem

The early Christian theologian Tertullian (160-225 CE) once posed the
rhetorical question: "What has Athens to do with Jerusalem?" Historians
and philosophers still use the phrase "Athens and Jerusalem" as a
reference for these two distinct and important influences on European
thought: its Greek intellectual heritage and its Judeo-Christian outlook.
Both of these traditions were maintained, to a greater or lesser extent,
throughout the history of Western Christianity. This is a remarkable
accomplishment, given that they were potentially incompatible ways of
seeing the world. Greek skepticism and inquiry existed with the goal of
understanding the natural world through rational thought alone.
Christian belief was the product of revelation and faith in a Christian God
for salvation in a life hereafter. Christian theology and Greek thought
would each be constrained and defined by people who wished to believe in

both. The nature of the compromise depended on the place, the time, and the people.

---

[1]For a description of the transmittance of Babylonian astronomical knowledge to the Greek world, see Jones, 1991. For an excellent primer on the details of Babylonian and Greek astronomy, see Aaboe, 2001

[2] Precession of the equinoxes is a phenomenon where the sun, on its annual path around the ecliptic, doesn't quite end up at the same place on the stellar sphere as it crosses the celestial equator. This phenomenon is now explained in the modern heliocentric system as being due to a very slow reorientation of the earth's axis with a period of 26,000 years (like a slowly wobbling top). Geocentric astronomers first explained the cause of precession by adding another slow moving sphere beyond the sphere of stars.

[3] See Toomer, G.J., 1988. The Hellenization of Mesopotamia would have made it relatively easy for Hipparchus to visit Babylonian (Chaldean) astronomers or for Babylonian astronomers to travel to Greek lands so that Hipparchus could gain access to the astronomical data that did not exist in Greece.

[4] The title the *Almagest* is an Arabic corruption of the Greek word "The Greatest." Its original title in Greek was the *Mathematical Syntaxis*, which some historians argue should be used today. I choose to use "*Almagest*" in this text because it continues to reflect the most common usage among historians of science and because it is the title that would have been recognized by the European astronomers we will be studying later.

[5] Before the printing press, written works were considerably more expensive because they were hand copied. Ptolemy's success at improving upon Hipparchus's work made it less appealing for people to reproduce old copies of Hipparchus's work when they could find the new and improved version in Ptolemy. This scenario, where a successful work superseded and replaced an earlier one, is common in antiquity.

[6] In the simplest model of solar motion, the sun travels with uniform motion on a circle with the earth at its center. In this case, the equinoxes and solstices would be separated by the same distance on the circle and the seasons would be the same length.

However, it was known even before Hipparchus's time that the seasons were of unequal length; therefore, such a simple circular model would not suffice. In our era, the lengths of the seasons in the northern hemisphere are approximately (Evans, 1998):

Spring   93 days
Summer   93

Autumn   90
Winter   89

Because of precession of the equinoxes, these seasonal lengths will change over the course of centuries.

[7] These planetary models ignore the daily rising and setting of the stars, moon, sun, and planets but instead explain how the positions of the sun, moon, and planets change against the background of stars from one night to the next. For example, if you observed the sky at 10:00 PM one day and then again at approximately the same time the next night (9:56 PM) the stars would appear in the same location as they had the day before, However, the moon's position would have changed dramatically and the planets' positions slightly. The point is, these planetary models described how the positions of the sun, moon, and planets changed <u>relative to the stars</u> from one night to the next.

[8] The eccentric motion of lunar and solar positions could be reproduced using an epicycle-on-deferent model. In these cases, the epicycle size was very small and the object rotated in a *clockwise* direction around the epicycle at precisely the same rate that the center of the epicycle rotated around the deferent in a *counterclockwise* direction. The path the body would trace out in such a model is an eccentric. The exact equivalence of the two models raised questions early on about the physical reality of astronomical models – it was a topic that was revisited by astronomers and philosophers many times in the centuries that followed.

[9] One problem that mathematical astronomers needed to address, and which Ptolemy could account for by using his equant in combination with the epicycle-on-deferent, was that a planet would not undergo its retrograde motion in a consistent way. Sometimes, a planet's observed retrograde loop is large; at other times it is small. Moreover, the length of time between a planet's successive retrograde periods varied as well. These were the challenges that drove Ptolemy to invent the equant.

[10] Ptolemy stated that a planet must *appear* to be moving at a constant speed when viewed from the geometric point, Q, so that when the planet is far away from Q (i.e. when it is on the other side of the earth) it must actually be moving faster on its path so that it doesn't *appear* to slow down when viewed from Q. Likewise, when the planet approaches nearer to Q on its path, it must actually move more slowly (so that it doesn't appear to be speeding up when viewed from Q). Since we actually observe the planet from the earth, E, Ptolemy was able to use his device to make the angular motion of a planet in the sky speed up and slow down to a greater extent than was possible in a simple eccentric model.

[11] For a more detailed discussion see Taub, 1993.

[12] Ptolemy argued in the Syntaxis that "the earth has sensibly the ratio of a point to its distance from the sphere of the so-called unwandering stars" (Taub, 1993, pp. 82). He explained that only if the sphere of the earth is very small compared to the outer sphere would we be able to see half of the stars in the heavens at one time (which is, in fact, what we can observe). Consider the opposite case: if the earth's diameter was significant in comparison to that of the celestial sphere then fewer than half the stars would be observable from the earth's surface at any one time.

[13] The terms "sphere" or "orb" of a planet are most frequently used to refer to the region between the surface of its inner and outer shells. These "spheres" or "orbs" needed to have a great enough thickness to accommodate the planets' epicycle and/or eccentric.

[14] He placed Mercury closest to the moon because both the moon and Mercury possessed unusual motions that required the use of similar geometric devices in his planetary theory. He placed Venus next to Mercury because both Venus and Mercury appeared to be always close to the sun in the sky – as though they were tethered to it. He placed the sun next because its motion was tied to that of Mercury and Venus. After that, Ptolemy could rely solely on the periods of the planets.

[15] Some Aristotelian philosophers objected to epicycle-on-deferent motion so strongly that they made periodic attempts to resurrect the "concentric" or "homocentric" sphere models of Eudoxus and Callippus. These thinkers believed that all celestial motions should take place around a single center. However, the failure of the concentric shell models to adequately address the changing brightness of a planet during its passage through the zodiac kept the models from gaining wider acceptance. In spite of the problem, however, concentric sphere models continued to attract a handful of enthusiastic followers throughout the Islamic Middle Ages and into the European Renaissance.

[16] If there is a date that can be given to the "fall" of the Roman Empire, it is 476 CE when the last Roman Emperor was deposed by a Germanic leader. However, it is better to describe the end of the Roman Empire as a long decline that began well before this date, and which continued afterwards as well since non-Roman leaders considered themselves rulers of the remaining Empire as it continued to fragment. This long decline marks the Early Middle Ages. So, in a very real sense, the Middle Ages had begun before Rome had fallen entirely.

[17] Their exile followed the official Christian church Councils of Nicaea and Chalcedon where politically dominant Christians condemned Nestorian religious beliefs – in particular the Nestorian conception of the nature of Jesus Christ, which

was in opposition to the emerging Catholic view of the Trinity and the divinity of Christ.

[18] Lindberg, David C. *The Transmission of Greek and Arabic Learning to the West*, in *Science in the Middle Ages.* Edited by David C. Lindberg, 1978, pp. 52-90.

[19] I've chosen to refer to this intellectual culture and tradition as "Islamic" even though there were significant contributions to it by Christians and Jews who lived in the Islamic World. Some historians of science instead use the term "Arabic" to denote the same culture and tradition – even though languages other than Arabic were used (Persian, Hebrew, Syriac, and Castellan, for example). Thus, both terms are problematic, though "Islamic" seems to have a greater usage in the history of science community, so I will use it consistently here with the understanding that not all "Islamic" scholars were in fact Muslim.

[20] This Islamic calendric tradition is related to the much older Babylonian astronomical tradition. See Neugebauer, O., 1969 for details concerning the difficulty of predicting the moon's first appearance following a new moon.

[21] Cassiodorous, a contemporary and friend of Boethius, collected scholarly works in his personal library. Because of the instability in Rome, he traveled south into the Italian peninsula and founded a monastery where he began the tradition of preserving and copying books (Lindberg in Lindberg, 1978).

[22] Finding a text in its original Greek was no guarantee that it was mistake-free – simple transcription errors could accumulate over the centuries. For this reason, careful translators sometimes sought as many as three unrelated copies of the same text to compare them for consistency.

Chapter Four – Renaissance Astronomy and Copernicus

European Renaissance Astronomy

Nicholas Copernicus (1473-1543) was born at a time when European astronomers were mastering Greek and Islamic astronomy. From the late Middle Ages (1300-1500) onward, they had acquired Greek and Islamic texts and astronomical tables[1] and were manufacturing their own instruments for making observations and calculations. A popularized introduction to astronomy written by Sacrobosco in the 1200s was used to introduce the subject to beginning students right up through Galileo's day.[2] However, an *advanced* European understanding of mathematical astronomy was slower to develop because of problems in producing good translations of Ptolemy's *Almagest*. Its highly technical subject matter made the going difficult – even for translators who were well-versed in Greek.

The problem was finally addressed through the sustained efforts of Georg Peurbach (1423-1461), a professor at the University of Vienna, and Regiomontanus (1436-1476), his pupil.[3] These German astronomers received essential help from Cardinal Bessarion, an émigré from the Greek-speaking Byzantine Empire. Bessarion had converted to Catholicism from Eastern Orthodox Christianity and traveled to Vienna to try to convince the Holy Roman Emperor to fight a crusade against the Turks, who had conquered his homeland. Bessarion was concerned that the loss of the Byzantine Empire would also lead to the loss of Greek culture. He was dismayed by the limited understanding of Greek knowledge he found in Europe and invited Peurbach and Regiomontanus to stay with him in Italy where they could study his extensive library of Greek manuscripts.

But Peurbach soon fell ill and died. On his death bed, he begged Regiomontanus to complete their goal of creating a high quality work on Ptolemaic astronomy in Latin. To aid Regiomontanus in his task, Cardinal Bessarion provided Regiomontanus with Greek manuscripts and introduced him to a social network that included Greek-speaking exiles who had fled to Italy after the fall of Constantinople.[4] With this material and moral support, Regiomontanus was able to finish the manuscript, which he presented and dedicated to the Cardinal. However, neither Bessarion nor Regiomontanus published the manuscript before their deaths, and it wasn't until 1496 that the *Epitome of the Almagest* finally appeared in print.[5]

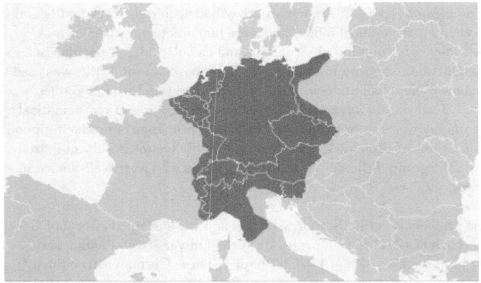

[Figure 4.1. Approximate extent of The Holy Roman Empire[6] in 1600 shown over a current map of Europe (its territorial extent varied over time). This singular "Empire" was, in reality, a loose confederation of hundreds of free cities, principalities, and states that had varying degrees of independence from the Emperor. Note that the Empire didn't include the city of Rome. Figure courtesy of Ssolbergj, Wikimedia Commons.]

Regiomontanus had made the details of advanced Ptolemaic astronomy accessible to European scholars for the first time. Moreover, he had grappled with unresolved problems in astronomy and developed an important alternative model for the motions of the planets that Ptolemy himself had overlooked.[7] The *Epitome* served as a major intellectual resource for European astronomers – in particular, it gave Copernicus access to state-of-the-art Ptolemaic theory from the very beginning and Regiomontanus's innovation likely provided him with "a crucial stepping stone" for his work.[8]

Cosmology and Religion in Renaissance Europe

By the High Middle Ages (about 1000-1300 CE), Europeans had adopted a cosmology that was a synthesis of Aristotelian physics, Ptolemaic astronomy, and Christian theology. This view was colorfully portrayed in Dante's *Divine Comedy* (see figure 4.2).

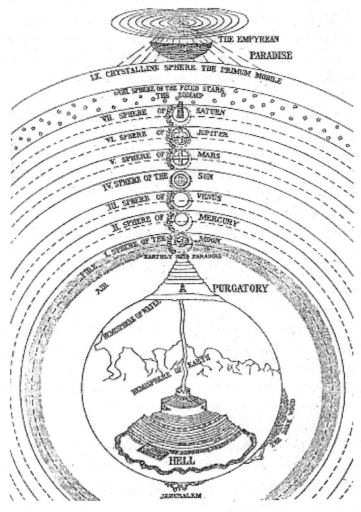

[Figure 4.2. From the description in Dante's (1265-1321) "The Divine Comedy," Image from "La Materia della Dvina Comedia di Dante Alighieri," Michelangelo Cactani (1855). Public domain.]

The European conception of the cosmos retained the fundamental features of Aristotelian physics and its four terrestrial elements.[9] The terrestrial/celestial boundary was located at the outer surface of the sphere of fire, which coincided with the sphere of the moon. From the sphere of the moon and beyond was the celestial region, which was composed of quintessence and included, in order: the spheres of Mercury, Venus, the sun, Mars, Jupiter, Saturn, and the fixed stars. The planetary "spheres" contained enough space for the Ptolemaic mechanisms for each planet.[10] Beyond the last astronomical sphere was the unmoving Empyrean Heaven – God's realm. Additional spheres were often believed to exist between the sphere of stars and the Empyrean Heaven to serve specific astronomical, physical, and/or theological functions.[11]

This Christianized cosmology included geographic features as well: Europe, Africa and Asia were on the same side of the earth, with their collective geographic center located at Jerusalem. In some versions, the rest of the earth's surface was covered by a giant ocean with the Garden of Eden ("Earthly Paradise") in the middle. This paradise was inaccessible to man, who had been cast out of it. Finally, Hell was located at the center of the earth – as far away as possible from Heaven. There were many minor variations on this basic cosmology. One common addition included angels turning the spheres in order to keep them in motion like giant clockwork.

In Dante's fictional account, the particular level of Hell a person's soul was assigned depended on the seriousness of his worldly transgressions – the punishments ranged from the mildly tedious to the most severe. Interestingly, at the lowest level of Hell, which was occupied by the worst sort of people, the eternal punishment he envisioned was immersion in ice.

A Changing World: The Renaissance and Reformation
In Copernicus's day, Europe was in the midst of a period that historians now refer to as the "Renaissance." As frequently as the term is used, there remains some debate among historians as to precisely what the Renaissance was and when it began and ended. For our purposes, we will use the term to refer to the dynamic period in European history between 1400 and 1600 CE that was characterized by intellectual and artistic

innovation as well as great religious upheaval and reform. Here, we will consider four features of the Renaissance period that in different ways and to different degrees influenced the development of European astronomy and cosmology.

Humanism

This was an intellectual movement whose members sought a fuller understanding of ancient classical texts. Their efforts went far beyond the limited and largely second- and third-hand knowledge of Greek works that had been circulating in Europe since the High Middle Ages. Renaissance humanist scholars attained a mastery of the ancient Greek language and began working directly from Greek sources[12] – many of the Greek works were completely new to European scholars and were transmitted to Europe from the declining Byzantine Empire. These new sources exposed the scholars to a vast range of thought beyond the standard works of Aristotle, Plato, and Ptolemy. Unlike their medieval scholastic predecessors who tended to focus on detailed arguments about specific propositions, humanist scholars sought to understand these Greek literary and philosophical works in their original cultural and historical contexts. In short, they tried to understand what the ancient authors were trying to say and why. Ironically, this old knowledge opened up new vistas of thought and possibility to European thinkers. The recovery of classical philosophy, literature, and art during this period is where the term "Renaissance," or "rebirth," arises.

For our purposes, and to make a long story short, the impact of Renaissance Humanism on astronomy and physics was to weaken the authority of Medieval Aristotelian thought and to legitimize a wider range of alternative ideas about the natural world. Many of these ideas either hadn't been considered by European thinkers or had been considered out-of-bounds for serious scholars. In this way, the humanists' deliberate look into the past created a fresh intellectual environment where old problems could be considered in a new light.

The Reformation

By 1500 many worshipers, humanists, and even clergy had become dissatisfied with the Roman Catholic Church. The Church was increasingly viewed as corrupt, worldly, and dissociated from the needs of its flock. It had an effective monopoly on the salvation of souls and used the position to great political and financial advantage. Many disaffected Catholic humanists and clergy worked hard to reform the Catholic Church from within, but in Wittenberg in 1517 an Augustinian monk named Martin Luther finally lost his patience. He wrote a document highly critical of Catholic Church practices – a work that is now known as his *Ninety-Five Theses*. Over the following years, Luther's widely known writings and sermons became increasingly confrontational, and the Catholic Church responded in kind. Soon, he was excommunicated, labeled a dangerous heretic, and subject to arrest by agents of the Holy Roman Emperor. Fortunately for Luther, he was protected from the wrath of the Emperor and the Church through the active political and military support of sympathetic German princes.

To make yet another long and interesting story short, Luther's actions initiated a wider movement in Europe that resulted in the fragmentation of the Catholic Church into a number of new Christian sects – most prominently Lutheranism, Calvinism, and the independent Church of England. Attempts by all of the sects to establish "proper" religious belief led to painful personal and political struggles across Europe for more than a century. This turmoil culminated in the catastrophic Thirty Years' War, which began in 1618 and laid waste to much of the Holy Roman Empire.

The Printing Press
In the mid-1400s, Johannes Gutenberg created a movable type printing press that made possible the mass production of books, calendars, pamphlets, and almanacs. Before this time, texts like Aristotle's *On the Heavens* or Ptolemy's *Almagest* had to be hand copied by transcriptionists and were expensive and limited in availability. With the printing press, books could be produced by the thousands. Thus, the new ideas that were generated in the Renaissance, whether they were scientific, literary, or theological in nature, could be printed and distributed to a mass audience across Europe in a relatively short period of time. Books were no longer an expensive or rare commodity.

Discovery of New Worlds

The voyages of discovery by seafaring explorers shattered existing beliefs about geography and terrestrial cosmology. In the fifteenth-century, Portuguese navigators traveled farther and farther south along the coast of Africa in their attempts to reach the Far East. During these expeditions, they discovered that not only was there land south of the equator but that there were people there as well (the "antipodes"). Both of these facts had remained in question for thousands of years. Most philosophers and theologians had believed that it was impossible for people to exist near or south of the equator – for physical and theological reasons. In the end, the philosophically unsophisticated but determined voyagers had proven the great thinkers wrong.[13]

The discovery of the Americas by Christopher Columbus,[14] Amerigo Vespucci, and others was plainly announced to the world when the continents of North and South America first appeared on the famous Waldseemüller map of 1507.[15] It is important to appreciate that the discovery of the Americas was the discovery of a realm whose existence had not at all been anticipated. The New World did not have a place in

[Figure 4.3. Waldseemüller map of 1507. Library of Congress. Note the previously unknown continents of the Americas on the left side of the map. Public domain image courtesy Library of Congress.]

European cosmology – it was unknown to the Greeks and had not been described in the Bible.

The discovery of the Americas raised theological issues. For one, the people who populated these continents could not possibly have had access to the word of God and would have had no chance for salvation prior to the arrival of Europeans. Furthermore, the New World was the home to plants and animals that were different from anything that was found in Europe, Africa, or Asia. These facts, along with the presence of people, raised questions about biblical creation and the account of Noah's ark. It was an astonishing development that, at the very least, required Europeans to make minor modifications to their existing cosmology – and it may have inspired some thinkers to contemplate even more radical ideas.

Copernicus

Copernicus was born into this changing world in 1473 and was only ten years old when his father died. Fortunately, Copernicus was adopted by his uncle, Lucas Watzenrode, who later became the Catholic bishop of a Prussian province in northern Poland.[16] This uncle provided for Copernicus's education and later guaranteed him employment within the Catholic Church.

Copernicus attended the University of Cracow in 1491 and left it a few years later without a degree. He then traveled to Italy where he attended the Universities of Bologna, Padua, and Ferrara to study law and medicine in preparation for a position as a church canon, an administrative position within the Catholic Church hierarchy. After he received his doctoral degree in canon law, he returned home and performed administrative duties for the Church in his uncle's cathedral. By all accounts, it was a job that Copernicus did exceedingly well. Because of his good reputation, Copernicus was often asked to help solve difficult problems and was urged to take on leadership roles in the Church. He was also strongly encouraged by his mentors and friends to become ordained as a priest – a step necessary to advance upward in the Church hierarchy. But in spite of his abilities and his highly favorable personal connections, Copernicus chose not to become ordained. Many historians have speculated that at this point he was protecting his leisure time so that he could pursue his new ideas in astronomy.[17] An ordained priest would have too many demands to be able to do what Copernicus appears to have set out to do.

Copernicus and His Astronomy

Copernicus's training in astronomy most likely began at the University of Cracow, where Ptolemaic theory was taught. Later, when Copernicus studied in Italy in preparation for his future position in the Church, he worked with the astronomer Domenico Maria Novara – a former student of Regiomontanus. Novara had taken in Copernicus as a boarder and as an assistant for making astronomical observations. Novara himself had proposed original ideas in astronomy that went against prevailing opinion – an activity that may not have been lost on a young Copernicus. Before Copernicus left Italy for good, he is reported to have given a public lecture on astronomy in Rome. In any case, he must have developed a good reputation as an astronomer because he was later asked by Vatican officials to assist them in reforming the calendar. Copernicus declined the request and politely responded that astronomy itself would need to be reformed before the calendar could be.[18]

Copernicus returned from Italy and began working at the cathedral as a canon for his Uncle Lucas, The Bishop of Ermland. After several years at the busy palace, Copernicus moved to Frauenburg[19] in 1510 – a place that he would later refer to as "this remote corner of the earth." He appears to have intentionally isolated himself there so that he could work out his new astronomy in relative peace.[20] From the castle tower in which he lived, Copernicus could see the Baltic Sea to the north and enjoyed a full panorama of the sky.

At about the time he moved to Frauenburg, Copernicus wrote and distributed a short description of his new astronomical theory in which the earth is in motion around the sun as it spins on its axis. He distributed this in the form of a letter, which is now referred to as the *Commentariolus*, or "Little Commentary."[21] The letter was copied and circulated widely enough that his ideas were known among other scholars in his lifetime. Copernicus stated in the *Commentariolus* that a larger work was forthcoming, but he was later hesitant to make good on the promise. It is likely that he struggled with theoretical problems he hadn't anticipated and was probably reluctant to publish what he considered to be an incomplete work – especially in the face of the sharp criticism he could expect for making such a radical proposal.

Although Copernicus is not known as an observational astronomer, he did take observations with measuring instruments so that he could match his theory to recent planetary positions.[22] One of Copernicus's most difficult and important tasks, and one that he wasn't entirely successful at, was to select the best data from existing astronomical records – some of which were well over a thousand years old.[23]

His Theory
Copernicus placed the sun at the center of the universe and set all of the planets, including the earth, into motion around it. The earth completed its circuit around the sun once a year while it rotated on its axis daily. The moon revolved around the earth once a month as they both traveled together around the sun. The other planets revolved around the sun in the same direction and in nearly the same plane as the earth. The interior planets completed their revolutions more quickly than the outer planets, with Mercury having a period of 88 days; Venus, 225 days; the earth, 365 days; Mars, 687 days; Jupiter, 12 years; and Saturn, 29 years.

Copernicus believed that the apparent motion of heavenly bodies was essentially an illusion that was the result of viewing the objects from a moving earth. According to Copernicus, *the sun and the stars were stationary – not the earth.* The rapid daily east-to-west motion of the sun, the moon, the planets, and the stars across the sky was an impression that was caused by the rotation of the earth in the opposite direction. In this view, the sun doesn't really rise in the east – rather, it only *appears* to rise as we rotate towards it on the surface of a spinning earth. Copernicus also explained the slower and irregular motions of the planets – an appearance that resulted from viewing the moving planets from an earth that was in motion around the sun.

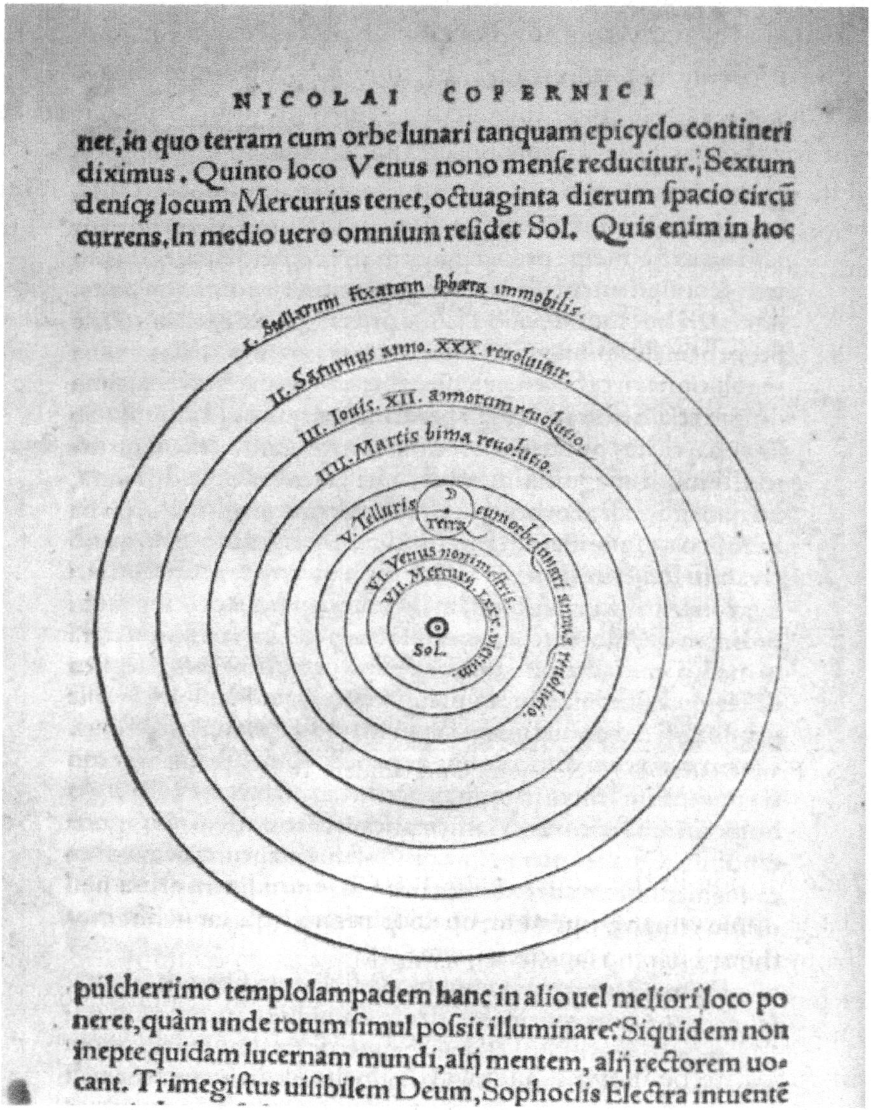

NICOLAI COPERNICI

net, in quo terram cum orbe lunari tanquam epicyclo contineri
diximus. Quinto loco Venus nono menfe reducitur. Sextum
deniq; locum Mercurius tenet, octuaginta dierum fpacio circu
currens. In medio uero omnium refidet Sol. Quis enim in hoc

I. Stellarum fixarum fphæra immobilis.
II. Saturnus anno. XXX. reuoluitur.
III. Iouis. XII. annorum reuolutio.
IIII. Martis bima reuolutio.
V. Telluris cum orbe lunari annua reuolutio.
VI. Venus nono menfis.
VII. Mercurii 88 dierum.
Sol.

pulcherrimo templolampadem hanc in alio uel meliori loco po
neret, quàm unde totum fimul pofsit illuminare? Siquidem non
inepte quidam lucernam mundi, alij mentem, alij rectorem uo=
cant. Trimegiftus uifibilem Deum, Sophoclis Electra intuente

[Figure 4.4. Diagram of Copernicus's planetary scheme in the original Latin text, *De Revolutionibus*. The sun (Sol) is in the middle of the diagram and the planets revolve around it. Mercury is the closest to the sun, followed by Venus, the earth (with its moon), Mars, Jupiter, and Saturn. Photographic Image from *De Revolutionibus* courtesy History of Science Collections, University of Oklahoma Libraries.]

93

Thus far, we've considered two of the three motions that Copernicus gave to the earth: (1) the daily spinning motion about its own axis, and (2) the annual revolution on its path around the sun. In addition to these motions, Copernicus also gave the earth a "third motion," which he used to account for the seasons: He proposed that the earth's spin axis changed its orientation to the sun during the year and instead maintained its direction fixed relative to the stars. Because Copernicus continued to hold traditional ideas about physics, he believed that as the earth revolved around the sun, it was necessary for the earth's axis to "move" in order to keep it directed at the North Star.[24]

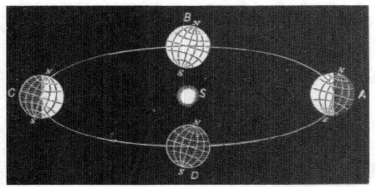

[Figure 4.5. From *Astronomy*, Newcomb and Holden, 1892. Public domain, archive.org.]

Retrograde Motion in the Copernican System

Consider the apparent motion of a superior planet (a planet located farther from the sun than the earth), using Mars as an example. Because the inner planets orbit the sun more frequently than outer planets do, the earth will periodically overtake Mars (see figure 4.6). When this occurs, Mars will *appear* to be moving backwards in the sky. This is similar to the way a slower moving car *appears* to be moving backwards when it is viewed from a car passing it on a highway.

The earth and a superior planet are shown in six different positions in their orbit around the sun. At the start, the earth is at A and the planet is at H. Viewing the planet from A, one would find it located at point O in the field of fixed stars. When the earth and planet have moved to B and I respectively, the planet appears at point P in the sphere of stars – and thus, it appears to have moved eastward through the zodiac for this period of time. This continues until the earth begins to overtake the planet – when the earth is at C and the planet is at K, the planet appears in between P and Q on the sphere of stars and now appears to be moving retrograde relative to its former position (and now possesses a westward motion through the zodiac). Note the physical proximity of the earth to the planet at this point – thus, the model also explains why superior planets are brighter during their periods of retrograde motion.

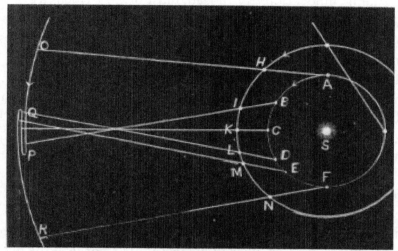

[Figure 4.6. From *Astronomy* (1892) Newcomb and Holden, 1892. Public domain, archive.org]

A similar analysis accounts for the retrograde motion of the inferior planets (Mercury and Venus).[25]

Copernican Cosmology and Copernican Mathematical Astronomy

The preceding description of Copernicus's system is the non-mathematical version of his theory. It is the basic "solar system" that most of us first learned about as school children. In this view, the planets are on circular paths around the sun – free from all the complex mechanisms of epicycles, eccentrics, or equants found in traditional Ptolemaic theory. In this form, Copernican astronomy explains the retrograde motion of the planets using a very simple model. I will refer to this basic arrangement as the *Copernican cosmology*. However, there is a problem with this bare bones version of the Copernican system: Beyond accounting for the existence of retrograde motion, it provided only a crude approximation of planetary motion.

The fully mathematical version of the Copernican system was much more elaborate than the Copernican cosmology I've presented here. Most people are surprised when they learn that the original and complete version of Copernicus's theory included a complex combination of eccentrics, small epicycles, and other geometric devices – some of which appear to be Islamic innovations.[26] Indeed, most of Copernicus's effort was directed toward fine-tuning these geometric models and making sure that they corresponded closely to the actual appearances in the heavens. Thus, the unabridged version of Copernicus's theory was very complicated and very different from the simple diagrams that are presented in history or science textbooks. Indeed, he employed so many geometric devices that some historians of science consider Copernicus to be the last great Ptolemaic astronomer.[27] I will refer to the highly technical, mathematical aspect of Copernicus's system as *Copernican astronomy*. It may seem ironic that the initiator of the most radical change to European cosmology was very conservative in his mathematical astronomy, but that is a puzzle we can't resolve with the benefit of hindsight. It will have to be enough for us to accept that, like all innovative thinkers, Copernicus had his feet in two worlds – the old and the new.

Problems with Copernican Cosmology

There were three key problems with Copernican cosmology that emerged immediately and that led most people to reject it: (1) it required that one accept the notion of a physically moving earth, (2) it led to the prediction of "stellar parallax," an astronomical phenomenon that was not observed, and finally, (3) it appeared to be incompatible with several passages in the Bible.

A Moving Earth

The absurdity of a moving earth was probably the most compelling reason for people to dismiss Copernican cosmology out of hand. People who relied on their senses didn't need to contemplate their surroundings for long in order to conclude that the earth is not in motion. Thus, the

Copernican belief – that the earth rotated on its axis at nearly a thousand miles an hour while it simultaneously revolved around the sun at an even faster rate – is far from commonsensible. Wouldn't such fantastic motions be perceptible? Wouldn't birds and the wind blow strongly in the direction opposite to the earth's motion? How could anything stay in its place?

These physical questions would not be resolved for more than one hundred years after Copernicus's major work was published. We will take these up again when we discuss the work of Galileo Galilei, and we will not find a truly satisfying answer until we consider the work of Isaac Newton. In the meantime, early Copernicans managed to convince themselves that the stability of the earth was yet another "appearance" or "illusion." It was a tremendous leap of imagination for the handful of early converts to have taken.

Stellar Parallax Problem

The second of the three problems, which we will consider in some detail here, was the absence of an observable "stellar parallax." In short, if Copernicus was correct and the earth made a large annual circuit around the stationary sun over the course of a year, there should appear a noticeable variation in the positions of the fixed stars relative to each other. This effect is called "stellar parallax" and ought to occur if the Copernican system is true because individual stars would necessarily be viewed from different positions throughout the year.[28] The following diagram illustrates why the relative positions of stars above the plane of the earth's orbit would appear to change.[29]

Stellar parallax was a problem for Copernicans, because during the thousands of years of observing the sky, no one had ever noted any annual variation in the positions of the stars. The only explanation that Copernicus could offer was that these changes took place, but were too small to detect because the sphere of stars was much, much farther away than anyone had ever imagined.[30] In this greatly expanded Copernican universe, the annual path of the earth around the sun, however great it might be, was insignificantly small compared to the vast distance to the stars.[31]

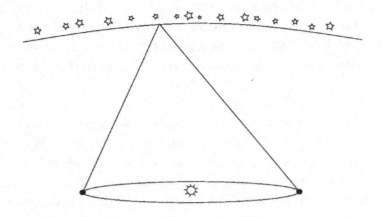

[Figure 4.7. Stellar Parallax. Diagram showing earth's orbit around the sun and its position six months apart. The angular direction to a particular star would change over the course of a year. Figure courtesy Danica Oudeans.]

Thus, Copernican theory yielded a prediction that was not observable and Copernicus had attempted to explain it away by proposing that the Universe was unimaginably vast. No doubt to his opponents, this would have seemed like a quick and convenient fix to a very serious problem. Many people rejected the idea of a greatly expanded universe – primarily for two reasons: (1) it meant that most of God's creation served no function, and (2) it displaced Heaven to a distant, unknown location. Recall that the traditional cosmological location for heaven was just beyond the sphere of stars. Now Copernicus proposed that the minimum distance to the stars was much farther than anyone had ever imagined; and even worse – he seemed to suggest that exactly how far away the stars were was anyone's guess. There was no longer a certain place for heaven in Copernican cosmology.

Scriptural Problems
The last type of objection to the Copernican cosmology was scriptural. Reading the Bible confirmed what common sense had already dictated: The earth was stationary. There are many biblical passages that support this view; three of the most explicit are provided here:

- The earth abideth forever. The sun also riseth, and the sun goeth down and hasteth to his place where he arose. The wind goeth toward the south and turneth about unto the north. (Ecclesiastes 1:4-6)

- The world also is stablished that it cannot be moved. (Psalm 93: 1)

- Who laid the foundation of the earth, that it should not be removed forever. (Psalm 104:5)

We will take up this issue in much more detail in later chapters, but before that a caveat: while the religious element in the Copernican controversy was very real, it is also important not to exaggerate it. The writings of many anti-Copernicans reveal that they were not necessarily relying on scripture to decide what to believe in the first place, but were instead using scripture to confirm what they had already concluded on rational grounds.

The Development of the Copernican System and its Advantages

Copernicus and his followers had such great enthusiasm for his system because it really was a *system* – the positions and motions of the planets were inescapably bound to each other like tightly fitting pieces of a puzzle. The relative distances of the planets from the sun were all interdependent, well-defined, and could not be changed in any way without the entire system unraveling. Indeed, the Copernican system was the first astronomical system that was capable of assigning unambiguous positions for the planets. In the Copernican view, the planets all had specific distances from the sun and specific rates of revolution around it, with the most rapidly moving planets closest to the sun and the slower moving planets increasingly distant from it. The sun, exceptionally large and luminous, seemed well-suited as the unique center of the universe (at least to Copernicans), and there was no need for epicycles to explain the retrograde motion of the planets. Copernicus and subsequent Copernicans would refer again and again to the coherence or "harmony" of the system as evidence that it must be true.[32]

In contrast to harmony of the Copernican system, the Ptolemaic system really wasn't a system at all. In the geocentric Ptolemaic model, each planet's position and motion could be treated independently and without regard to any of the other planets. Indeed, even the ordering of the planets could be changed in the Ptolemaic system as long as the sizes and speeds of each planet's epicycle and deferent were properly adjusted.

Ptolemy determined the order of the planets using physical arguments that had little to do with pure astronomy. While the superior planets, Mars, Jupiter, and Saturn, were assigned positions based on the relative rates at which they travelled through the zodiac, this criterion failed to work with Mercury, Venus, and the sun, all of which passed through the zodiac an average of once every year. Thus, the order and distances of the planets from the earth were somewhat arbitrary:[33] Each planet could be treated as an independent problem. It wasn't so much that the individual puzzle pieces didn't fit together in the Ptolemaic model – it's that they weren't puzzle pieces at all. Copernicus strongly criticized the disconnected nature of the Ptolemaic system. In his preface and dedication to Pope Paul III he compared it to assembling the body parts of different people in order to create a single person – however well-proportioned they may be individually, the body parts would not fit well together and would better approximate a monster than a man.

Interestingly, Copernicus tended to stress that the great advantage to his system was the absence of Ptolemy's equant. Like many other astronomers before and after him, Copernicus found the non-uniform planetary motion of the equant in Ptolemy's system to be abhorrent. Copernicus believed that only uniform circular motion could serve as the basis for motion in the heavens. It may seem ironic that Copernicus's conservative view on uniform circular motion, inspired by ancient Platonic idealism and Aristotelian mechanics, helped him make a radical break from the cosmology of his day.

Although Copernicus's distaste for the equant was his most prominently stated motivation, he offered other strong arguments for the superiority of his system. Indeed, historians of science have called into question Copernicus's claim that the elimination of the equant was the central reason that he adopted his new astronomy, since he could have gotten rid of the equant and still have maintained the earth as the center of the cosmos. We will not take the time necessary to speculate on the train of thought that Copernicus may have followed to develop his system, but it is worth acknowledging that historians of science have proposed some reasonable hunches as to how and why he did it.[34]

Coincidences that Remained Unexplained in the Ptolemaic System Are Explained by the Copernican System

Another advantage of the Copernican model was that it explained some apparently unrelated coincidences that existed in the Ptolemaic system. For example, in the Ptolemaic model the inferior planets, Mercury and Venus, appear to be tethered to the sun.

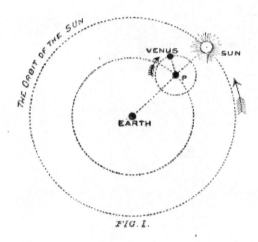

[Figure 4.8. Ptolemaic diagram of the epicycle of Venus, whose deferent always follows the sun. From *Great Astronomers*, Ball, 1895. Public domain, archive.org]

Stated in geometric terms, the centers of the epicycles of Mercury and Venus are *always* lined up directly with the sun instead of moving independently of it (see figure 4.8). This is the Ptolemaic account for why Venus and Mercury appear either as a "morning star" or as an "evening star" but never high in the nighttime sky.

In the Ptolemaic system, an element of the sun's motion also appears in the motion of the superior planets (Mars, Jupiter, and Saturn), but in a different way. Here, the center of each superior planet's epicycle is free to move around the sun on its deferent independently. However, the motion of each superior planet around the center of its epicycle *is* tied to the motion of the sun. Figure 4.9 shows how Mars and the sun revolve around their centers of rotation at the same rate and in the same direction, so that a line drawn between a superior planet and the center of its epicycle remains parallel to the line drawn between the earth and the sun. This is also true for Jupiter and Saturn.

Thus, in the Ptolemaic system, the motion of all of the planets, in one way or another, parallel the motion of the sun. Ptolemaic astronomers could not explain why this was the case in purely astronomical terms, but they

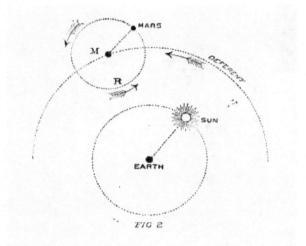

[Figure 4.9. Ptolemaic diagram of the epicycle of Mars. Note that, in the diagram, the earth-sun line and the deferent-Mars line are parallel to each other. This is always the case, as they move around their centers with the same frequency. From *Great Astronomers*, Ball, 1895. Public domain, archive.org]

did offer *ad hoc* reasons, which more or less amounted to stating that it was the planets' nature to move in these ways. Copernicus saw this as a critical failure of the Ptolemaic system. To him and other Copernicans, the solar motion reflected in each planet's motion was simply a consequence of the mistaken belief that the sun revolved around the earth rather than the other way around.

Copernicus: Developing and Sharing His Ideas

Copernicus remained quiet for three decades after writing and distributing the *Commentariolus*, his early unpublished letter that announced his new system of the world. He may have remained quiet forever if it hadn't been for the enthusiastic support and encouragement of a young Lutheran astronomy professor from the University of Wittenberg, Georg Joachim Rheticus (1514-1574). Rheticus had heard reports of Copernicus's work and was intrigued enough to travel hundreds of miles (and into Catholic territory) to meet with Copernicus and learn about his astronomical system.

Rheticus arrived at Copernicus's doorstep quite sick. Copernicus and a friend nursed him back to health, and he stayed with Copernicus for more than two years, studying his system intensely. Soon, Rheticus and others were begging Copernicus to publish his theory.[35] After only a few months studying with Copernicus, Rheticus wrote a description of the astronomical system of "his teacher" and travelled to Danzig to have it printed. In 1540, the *First Account,* or *Narratio prima,* of the Copernican system was published by Rheticus. The *Narratio prima* was a well-written and remarkably clear introduction to the Copernican system; it generated a great deal of interest and helped convince Copernicus that he should finally publish his work.[36] Later, Rheticus personally oversaw the initial effort to print Copernicus's major work, *On the Revolutions of Heavenly Spheres* – a work most frequently referred to by historians by the shortened Latin title *De revolutionibus* or, in English, *On Revolutions.* Copernicus dedicated his work to Pope Paul III. He also acknowledged in his work that the idea of a moving earth had been proposed in antiquity, so that he wasn't suggesting something completely radical and new.[37]

Rheticus left Prussia and "his teacher" in order to oversee the printing *De Revolutionibus* in Nuremberg. But it wasn't long before he needed to leave Nuremberg in order to accept a teaching position at the University of Leipzig. The task of overseeing the printing was transferred to a Lutheran theologian named Andreas Osiander, who was also enthusiastic about seeing Copernicus's work appear in print. However, unlike Rheticus and Copernicus, Osiander felt strongly that the work should be presented only as a mathematical hypothesis rather than as an actual description of reality. Without consulting either Rheticus or Copernicus, Osiander took it upon himself to write an anonymous preface to *De Revolutionibus*. In it, he appealed to the reader that the theory presented in the text was merely one possible hypothesis among many and could not be proven as fact.[38] Osiander's preface created some confusion among the readers of *De Revolutionibus*, because it seemed to be at odds with the main text, which was written by an author who appeared to whole-heartedly believe in the reality of his sun-centered system. Copernicus was presented with a copy of his printed text on the day of his death, but it seems unlikely that he was aware of it.[39]

Reception of Copernican Theory

Copernican cosmology, the belief that the earth and the planets actually moved around the sun as it spun on its axis, was accepted by only a handful of people prior to 1610.[40] In contrast, the *mathematical* aspect of Copernicus's work, Copernican *astronomy*, was immediately held in high regard among professional astronomers – particularly those in Northern Europe. This intriguing contrast between the welcome reception of Copernican mathematical astronomy and the rejection of the basic *physical* features of the Copernican cosmology has been referred to as the "Wittenberg Interpretation."[41]

Before we continue and describe the reception of Copernicus's work, we should make it clear that Copernicus's system was no more accurate at describing the motions of the planets than the Ptolemaic system had been. The Copernican cosmology was a striking alternative to the existing cosmology and, as such, it had different internal strengths and weaknesses. However, the closeness of its fit to the astronomical observations alone didn't provide a clear reason for someone to choose it over the Ptolemaic system – the two systems were, for the most part, equally successful in predicting planetary positions. In spite of this, Copernicus's astronomical work managed to provide many practical advantages to practicing astronomers – even for astronomers who didn't believe it was true!

Since Copernicus began his work from scratch, he had the opportunity to select a new set of observational data on which to base his theory. He critically considered the preexisting astronomical data, some of it centuries old, and made new observations himself so that he could have confidence that his theory "fit" the data. In doing so, Copernicus provided an updated and valuable resource that other astronomers could draw upon. Furthermore, Copernicus provided a significantly improved description of the motion and appearance of the moon, which solved a serious problem that existed in Ptolemaic theory.[42] And in the case of the moon, it really didn't matter whether an astronomer believed in a geocentric or heliocentric cosmos; either way, the moon's motion was referred to the earth.

The prototypical adherent to the "Wittenberg Interpretation" of Copernican theory was Erasmus Reinhold, who was a professor of astronomy at the University of Wittenberg. He rejected Copernicus's cosmology, but remained a great admirer of Copernicus and his mathematical astronomy. Reinhold relied on Copernicus's work to produce the new *Prutenic Tables*, which served as a popular alternative to the older astronomical tables that had been used in Europe until that time.[43] For these and other reasons, the work of Copernicus began to successfully compete with the traditional works based on Ptolemy – even for astronomers who refused to believe that the earth moved. It was largely in this way that Copernican astronomy was kept alive during the several decades before more people began to believe that it might be true.

Early Opposition to Copernican Cosmology

Hardly anyone considered Copernican cosmology to be a threat, because so few people believed that it was true. However, there were a few early criticisms of Copernicus. There was the famously recorded rant of Martin Luther who called Copernicus a "fool" during one of his dinner time conversations – although, considering the extent to which Copernican astronomy was popular in Luther's own Wittenberg, it is unlikely that his words resonated far beyond his dining room walls. It seems likely that Luther had far more pressing issues to deal with at the time. A more determined opposition to Copernicus's work appeared briefly in the Catholic world, but then ended quickly with the death of its first antagonist.[44] Strong opposition to Copernican cosmology would not arise for many decades – and then only when its advocates began to muster a serious threat to existing cosmological belief.

Early Copernicans

Consider the diagram of Englishman Thomas Diggs (figure 4.12), one of the few early scholars who accepted Copernicus's cosmology[45] as a description of reality, and who popularized Copernicus's work in the English language.

[Figure 4.10. Diagram of the Copernican System by the English Thomas Diggs (1546-1595) from *A Perfit Description of the Caelestiall Orbes* (1576). His endorsement of the Copernican Universe with the added feature of a field of stars with no apparent boundary, suggesting the conception of an infinite universe, or, at the very least, the ambiguity of their vastly distant locations. Public domain.]

As we will see, although the "Copernican Revolution" started with Copernicus, it took other astronomers and scientists over a hundred years to complete it. Copernicus managed only to get his foot in the door. It would be another sixty years before Kepler would radically transform Copernican astronomy so that its predictive power was unprecedented. And Galileo, working at the same time as Kepler but untroubled by the details of mathematical astronomy, used his telescopic discoveries and his studies on motion to offer potent physical arguments for a heliocentric Universe – arguments that even non-experts could understand. But the world would have to wait even longer for an Isaac Newton to explain how it all worked.

One Last Thought...

Copernicus is often credited with transforming the earth into a planet. And although this is true, the earth continued to retain a special standing among the celestial bodies in his system. In Copernican cosmology, the earth remained special among the planets, because it was the only one that possessed its own satellite (at least as it was known at the time). In Copernican astronomy, the earth remained unique because the other planets' motions were all tied theoretically to the motion of the earth.[46] The scientific world would have to wait for the contributions of both Galileo *and* Kepler before the earth would finally lose its special standing and become a planet like any other.[47]

[1] Astronomical tables (called "zīj" in the Arabic-speaking world) are essentially mathematical recipes for generating predictions of planetary positions. These tables are based on theory (whether Ptolemaic or otherwise) and are used to produce ephemerides (singular: ephemeris), calendars, almanacs, and astrological charts that describe where and when celestial objects appear in the sky.

[2] Sacrobosco is also known as "John of Holywood." Multiple editions of Sacrobosco's *Tractatus de Sphaera* and related commentaries circulated in Europe for more than four centuries. See Lattis, 1994, for examples.

[3] His given name was Johannes Müller von Königsberg. Regiomontanus was a Latinized pseudonym based upon the region in which he was born, which was a popular practice among Renaissance scholars.

[4] The city of Constantinople was the last vestige of the Byzantine Empire. It was a well-defended trading city, but advances in military hardware, along with the tenacity of the opposing Turkish forces, led to its fall in 1453.

[5] Regiomontanus's *Epitome of the Almagest* was not a simple translation of Ptolemy; it was an extended commentary designed to explain Ptolemaic astronomy and the contributions of later Ptolemaic astronomers to interested readers in an understandable way. It also drew attention to unresolved problems and questions regarding Ptolemaic astronomy.

[6] Voltaire later quipped: "The Holy Roman Empire was neither holy, nor Roman, nor an empire."

[7] Ptolemy had developed an alternative to the epicycle-on-deferent model for the motion of the outer planets. This model, often confusingly referred to as the "eccentric" model, is similar to the epicycle-on-deferent model, except that the epicycle and deferent have changed places so that the deferent has become the size of the epicycle, and the epicycle the size of the deferent. Ptolemy had proposed this model only for the superior planets, suggesting by omission that it would not work for the inferior planets. Regiomontanus showed that it also worked for Mercury and Venus – and thus, for all of the planets.

[8] See Swerdlow, 1973, for an account of how Regiomontanus's application of the eccentric to all of the planets may have paved the way for the later Copernican and Tychonic planetary systems (see note 7). For an excellent overview of this topic see Shank, 2002.

[9] If we look at the diagram more closely, we find a problem with the ideal Aristotelian scheme: the positions of the earth and water appear to be slightly removed from their ideal positions so that dry land exists above the surface of the ocean. There were a number of different explanations for this – one common variation was that the centers for the sphere of water and for the sphere of the earth had been slightly offset from each other. This explained why there was one great ocean on one side of the earth and a single expanse of land (the three interconnected continents) on the other. However, not everyone agreed with this conception. Copernicus argued early in Book One of *De revolutionibus* that this could not be true – for if it was, the ocean would be too deep for islands to exist far from shore and the continents too high for there to be bays or inlets. Furthermore, by Copernicus's day, the Americas were known to exist and could not be explained if the centers of the spheres of the earth and water had been offset.

[10] It can be seen in this diagram that each planet's "sphere" was not a single geometric sphere, but rather defined a volume that was bounded by the surfaces of an inner sphere and an outer sphere. Thus the use of the term "sphere" in this context might better be described as a "shell" of definite thicknesses like the layers in an onion. These "spheres" allowed space for the insertion of the epicycle, eccentric, and equant mechanisms that were necessary for Ptolemaic astronomy. The planetary spheres in the diagram are not drawn to scale in the way that a Ptolemaic astronomer would have designed them.

[11] Many astronomers proposed the existence of these additional spheres beyond the stellar sphere in order to explain the precession of the equinoxes, a phenomenon that is understood quite differently today.

[12] There were also successful efforts to translate Hebrew works, including the Old Testament and works of medieval Jewish scholars.

[13] See Hookaas, 1984.

[14] There is a persistent misconception that before Columbus, Europeans believed the earth was flat. This is completely untrue – there are no written records from the period that mention the roundness of the earth as being any matter of debate – not in Columbus's own writings nor in anyone else's. The real reason that Columbus had difficulty gaining support for his venture to Asia was that he had vastly underestimated the earth's circumference, and the court mathematicians of Spain and Portugal knew it. They were not concerned that Columbus's ships might fall off the edge of the earth, but that he and his sailors would die from lack of food and water in the midst of the giant ocean that separated the west coast of Europe from the eastern shores of Asia. It turns out that the actual distance between the Canary Islands and Japan is over 13,000 miles – Columbus estimated this distance to be less

than 3,000 miles (Russell, 2001). The experts, who were advising the Spanish Crown, provided estimates closer to the modern value. Even so, after Columbus persisted and repeatedly requested support for the venture, the Spanish, who were behind in their race with Portugal to reach the Indies, decide to bet on him as a long shot. As it turns out, Columbus's otherwise doomed expedition was rescued only through the intervention of a vast expanse of land – the Americas. Even so, there was nothing about Columbus's voyage that provided proof that the earth was round – only the successful circumnavigation of the entire earth by Magellan's crew thirty years later would accomplish that.

The falsehood, that medieval Europeans believed that the earth was flat, continues to be repeated by school teachers to this day. The source of the error has been traced, in part, to the American author Washington Irving who popularized the myth in his fanciful book *A History of the Life and Voyages of Christopher Columbus, 1828.* Other writers and even professional historians in the early 1800s contributed to the error.

Indeed, with only a handful of identifiable exceptions, the reality of the spherical earth was accepted by all educated people from the 5th century BCE in Greece onward through the Islamic and Christian Middle Ages and up to the present time. The interesting question is how the historical error that Medieval Europeans believed the earth was flat ever came into existence. The historiography of this "Error" is addressed thoroughly in Russell, 1997 and placed into a greater historical context in Grant, 2001.

To make a long story short, Renaissance humanists, in their effort to place themselves in the best possible light, resorted to minimizing and criticizing the European thinkers who had come before them. As Russell so aptly put it, "The Renaissance Humanists did not merely attack the Middle Ages; they invented them." The Humanists unmercifully mischaracterized their creation and portrayed medieval learning as sparse, unimaginative, and pointless. But even with that ax to grind, it would never have occurred to the Humanists to invent a flat-earth myth in their day, because they believed that the earth was a sphere in the middle of a spherical cosmos.

By the early 1800s, historical awareness of earlier European thought had somehow gotten misplaced and several influential writers, including Washington Irving, created the myth. The two medieval examples that historians relied on to maintain the Error was Lactantius (ca. 245-325 CE) and Cosmas Indicopleustes (fl. 550 CE). These two men were held up again and again as evidence that all Medieval thinkers believed that the earth was flat (and not minding that Lactantius lived in Late Antiquity and Cosmas in the earliest part of the Middle Ages). Authors who promoted the Error then began referencing each other's works, making it seem to readers as though the weight of the historical evidence for the medieval belief in a flat earth was overwhelming. But the fact remained that Lactantius and Cosmas were glaring historical exceptions to the otherwise unanimous belief that the earth was spherical.

By the mid-1800s, the Error was well-established and it soon proved to be useful in attacks on the Catholic Church – both in Europe and in the United States. These attacks were inspired by very different motivations – in the United States it was inspired by an anti-immigration movement, in Europe the Catholic Church presented a barrier to the popular unification of Italy. In both cases, the Error could be invoked to underscore just how absurdly backward and out-of-touch the Catholic Church had been.

Soon, the utility of the Error was wielded again in a very different confrontation: in the debate over Darwinism. In their attempts to defend evolution against a religious backlash, supporters of evolution used the Error to illustrate the great harm that comes to science when it is circumscribed by traditional religious belief. This time, the criticism wasn't limited to the Catholic Church, but against all Christians who would dare place limits on science for religious reasons. This was particularly important to influential writers like John Draper and Andrew Dickson White who had announced in the last half of the 1800s that a war between science and religion was occurring and that the ensuing battles would determine the direction that civilization would take. This is the modern origin of the "warfare thesis" of science and religion, which has been severely criticized by subsequent historians, but continues to remain in circulation today.

[15] This is the first map that features the name "America." The only complete copy of the map was recently purchased by the United States and now resides in the Library of Congress.

[16] Prussia was a northern German-speaking region on the Baltic Sea. Warmia, the Prussian province in which Copernicus spent most of his adult life in, was a protectorate of the Polish crown in his day. Thus, it is not surprising that modern Germany and Poland each lay claim to Copernicus as one of their own. This modern sense of nationalism did not exist in Copernicus's day, so the argument is somewhat anachronistic. The evidence suggests that Copernicus's native language was German, but it seems likely that he also spoke Polish reasonably well – he did some bureaucratic work for the Polish Crown and had attended a Polish university in his youth (although the classes would have been conducted in Latin). Of course, Copernicus's scientific work was written in Latin – the language that he shared with scholars all across Europe.

[17] See Rosen (1960) and Rosen (1984).

[18] See Rheticus, 1540 (trans. Rosen, 1939). Also, Rosen, 1984 and Swerdlow and Neugebauer, 1984.

[19] Frauenberg was also known as Frombork (as it is today) – now part of Poland. The dual German/Polish heritage of Eastern Prussia has resulted in multiple proper names and alternative spellings for the people and places referred to in this episode.

[20] Copernicus's relocation to Frauenberg was anything but a career move. Indeed, he was foregoing additional church offices and a pay raise that he had been offered if he stayed on at the cathedral. Instead, he appears to have intentionally avoided the demanding bureaucratic work of administering the diocese. In Frauenberg, with no family to support and a comfortable salary, Copernicus would have the time and means to create a new astronomical system. It seems likely that this was his aim when he left the cathedral.

[21] It is known with certainty that the *Commentariolus* was written between 1508 and 1514. Neugebauer and Swerdlow believe that 1510 is a likely date. The letter became known as the *Commentariolus* long after Copernicus had written it. The writing of such letters was one of the main methods of communicating scientific information in Copernicus's day when there were no scientific journals for publishing short or preliminary accounts of work. These letters were sent to interested colleagues and correspondents who often made copies and distributed them to others. In this way, letters like the *Commentariolus* could become reasonably well-known (even if occasional mistakes might arise in the process of copying them).

[22] Swerdlow and Neugebauer (1984), pp. 64.

[23] The amount of astronomical data that was available to Copernicus was large, but it wasn't always good. Copernicus worked hard to select the best possible data from the historical record, but ultimately, some of the observations that he used were incorrect. Thus, Copernicus attempted to fashion a set of astronomical models that would account for both the bad data as well as the good – a problem for which there is no good solution. The data problem would be alleviated by the extensive and careful astronomical observations of Tycho Brahe several decades later.

[24] It is important to appreciate that Copernicus's conception of motion was not that of Newtonian inertial physics with which we are familiar today. Copernicus believed that in order for the earth's axis to remain fixed with respect to a single point in the stationary celestial sphere (the North Star), its axis would need to be slowly moving backwards against its motion of revolution. This was the "third motion" – the motion of the inclination. Put a different way, Copernicus believed that without the third motion the earth's axis would remain in a fixed position relative to the sun. To keep this from happening, he found it necessary to have the earth's axis "move"

relative to the position of the sun. The advantage to using this mechanism was that with a slight modification of the rate of the third motion he could also explain the more subtle and long-term phenomenon of the precession of the equinoxes.

[25] In the Copernican system, inferior planets (Mercury and Venus) are those that are closer to the sun than the earth is; the superior planets (Mars, Jupiter, and Saturn) are those that are further from the earth than the sun than the earth is. The classification scheme is the same in the geocentric view point, but for different reasons – in the Ptolemaic, for example, the inferior planets (Mercury and Venus) are closer to the earth than the sun is, and the superior planets are farther from the earth than the sun is. In the Copernican view, retrograde motion for the inferior planets occurs as the planets pass in front of the sun – thus, they are not visible for the duration of retrograde motion as the superior planets are. Explanations of brightness for the inferior planets are also not as straightforward, since the inferior planets express a full range of phases (as would later be described by Castelli and Galileo).

[26] Like many other astronomers, Copernicus abhorred Ptolemy's use of the equant. He instead used "minor epicycles" or "epicyclets" that are very small epicycles that accounted for minor variation in the rate of a planet's motion through the zodiac – essentially replacing the function of Ptolemy's equant. Copernicus also used an interesting mathematical device now called the "Tusi-couple" after its inventor the great Persian scientist/astronomer Nasir al-Din al-Tusi (1201-1274). It seems most likely that Copernicus learned of this mathematical device while he resided in Italy. Although the possibility that he discovered it independently cannot be absolutely excluded (Blåsjö, 2014), it is known that there was an important Jewish scientific emissary from the Ottoman Empire at Padua during the time that Copernicus lived there. See Morrison, 2014 for an account and for a description of other possible sources of transmission of astronomical knowledge from the Islamic world to Europe during the Renaissance.

[27] Swerdlow and Neugebauer (1984).

[28] "Parallax" is a phenomenon that occurs in a situation where an object can be observed from more than one location. A common example of this can be observed by holding one's arm outward steadily and extending the index finger upward in front of something. If a person opens only one eye and notes the background beyond their finger, and then closes that eye and opens the other, they will note that the background beyond their finger appears to shift from side-to-side. "Stellar Parallax" is the same phenomenon on a very large scale. In the Copernican system, stellar parallax ought to occur at different times of the year because the stars are being viewed from different positions. And instead of the small difference in position

between one eye and the other, the difference in the position of the earth from one half of the year to the next is enormous.

[29] The diagram depicted in the text is designed to illustrate stellar parallax as most of Copernicus's contemporaries would have envisioned it: with all of the fixed stars equidistant from the center of the universe. Later astronomers imagined a three-dimensional *field* of stars with some stars closer and some farther away from the sun and the earth. Although Copernicus discussed the size of the Universe and the possibility of its infinite extent in *De revolutionibus*, he didn't commit himself to one view or another.

[30] Copernicus in *De revolutionibus*: "So it is as regards the place of the earth; for although it is not at the centre of the world, nevertheless the distance is as nothing, particularly in comparison with the sphere of the fixed stars" (Trans. Wallis, pp. 15). Thus, Copernicus employed the same kind of reasoning that Ptolemy used in arguing that the size of the earth is as a point to the sphere of stars, except that Copernicus argued that the size of the *earth's orbit* was as a point to the sphere of stars. This is stated most clearly in Rheticus's *Narratio prima* (pp. 145, trans. Rosen): "Consequently it is quite clear that the sphere of the stars is, to the highest degree, similar to the infinite, since by comparison with it the great circle vanishes, and all the phenomena are observed exactly as if the earth were at rest in the center of the universe." And once again in Copernicus's *De revolutionibus* (Trans. Wallis, Book 1, Chapter 7): "But let us leave to the philosophers of nature the dispute as to whether the world is finite or infinite..."

[31] It wasn't until 300 years later, in 1838, that astronomers managed to observe stellar parallax telescopically. Sirius, the closest star visible from the northern hemisphere, is approximately 75,000 times farther from the sun than is Saturn. Even today, astronomers can observe stellar parallax for only a limited number of stars: those that are relatively close to us (which is, in fact, how we *know* these stars are close to us).

[32] Another way in which the "puzzle pieces" fit together so neatly in the Copernican system was its ability to explain why the different planets exhibited the particular forms of retrograde motion that they did – including the frequency with which retrograde motion occurred and the relative lengths of the retrograde arcs that each planet made. Any change to the relative distances between the planets and their periods of revolution around the sun would have destroyed the Copernican system's capacity to account for these patterns of retrograde motion.

[33] However, recall from Chapter 3 that Ptolemaic astronomers believed that there was no empty space between the outer reaches of one planet's motion and the inner reaches of the next one. This is a physical criterion that Ptolemaic astronomers

could use to help determine the size of each planet's sphere – though it wasn't a criterion needed to make the mathematical astronomy work.

[34] There appear to be several influences that may have inspired Copernicus to imagine his system: (1) The alternative astronomical mechanism, the eccentric, that Regiomontantus presented in the *Epitome of the Almagest*, see Swerdlow (1973) and Shank (2002) and end notes 7 and 8 in this chapter. (2) Peurbach had pointed out that in the Ptolemaic system, the motion of all of the planets was, in some way, tied to the motion of the sun: "It is evident that each of the six planets shares something with the sun in their motions and that the motion of the sun is like some common mirror and rule of measurement to their motions." For a discussion of how this may have caused Copernicus to conclude the sun was the center of the planetary system, see Westman (2011). (3) For the first time, Copernicus was able to establish an unambiguous ordering for the planets – this was based on the relationship between the period of a planet (the length of time it took to orbit the sun) and its distance from the sun. In the Copernican system, the planets closest to the sun have the shortest periods (88 days for Mercury, 225 days for Venus, 365 days for earth, etc.). This is in great contrast to the Ptolemaic system where planetary ordering was ambiguous – while, the *superior* planets followed a distance period relationship in the Ptolemaic system based on their distance from the earth, Mercury, Venus, and the sun did not – they all had the same period: one year. Thus, the planetary order for Mercury, Venus, and the sun remained uncertain in the Ptolemaic view. This is why other astronomers before and after Ptolemy were able to reasonably propose alternative geocentric orderings for Mercury, Venus, and the sun (Goldstein, 2002 and Westman, 2011, pp. 58). (4) Copernicus's knowledge and contemplation of the "Capellan" system – an ancient geocentric system similar to the Ptolemaic system, but with Mercury and Venus orbiting the sun as the sun orbits the earth, Goldstein (2002). While the earth remains the major center of motion in the Capellan system, the sun is a secondary center of planetary motion.

[35] Earlier, in 1536, Cardinal Nicholas Schonberg offered to finance the publication of Copernicus's work, but Copernicus did not take him up on it (Rosen, 1984). Copernicus's friend, Bishop Tiedeman Giese, along with Rheticus, continued to encourage Copernicus to publish his work.

[36] The *Narratio prima* was popular enough that a second edition was published in Basel in 1541. It was so well-written and easy to understand that it was re-published even after Copernicus's major work was published. The third time the *Narratio* was printed it appeared as part of the second edition of Copernicus's *De revolutionibus* in 1566. As the Copernican scholars Swerdlow and Neugebauer (1984) describe it: "If the purpose of the *Narratio* was to inform the learned world and create a greater interest in Copernicus's work, it succeeded splendidly. It is brilliantly written— eloquent, learned, quite detailed and clear—above all enthusiastic, and even after four

hundred years the most informative popularization of Copernicus's more difficult book."

[37] In the Renaissance it was customary to legitimize one's work and views by citing ancient authors. The ancient geokinetic and heliocentric thinkers Copernicus was able rely upon to support his cause were the Pythagoreans and Aristarchus (310-230 BCE). Of the two, the Pythagoreans were much better known in Copernicus's day and he a makes reference to their geokinetic beliefs in his text *De revolutionibus*. Aristarchus was less well-known at the time and references to his beliefs hadn't yet been published in Europe. Nonetheless, Copernicus became aware of the heliocentric system of Aristarchus (probably while studying in Italy) and referenced it in an early manuscript edition of *De revolutionibus*. However, the reference to Aristarchus did not appear in the final print version of his text. It is worth taking the time to discuss the two ancient systems further.

Aristarchus's geokinetic system was fundamentally the same as the Copernican system. We know of Aristarchus's heliocentric views primarily through Archimedes (287-212 BCE), who described it in his *Sand Reckoner*. Archimedes referred specifically to Aristarchus's extremely large estimate for the size of the Universe (a necessary consequence of the heliocentric view). Archimedes himself did not accept or deny Aristarchus's heliocentric system in his writings. Very few thinkers in antiquity adopted the heliocentric position – although several prominent thinkers considered the geocentric-heliocentric debate to remain an open question. It is worth noting that geocentrists like Ptolemy felt the need to refute the possibility of a moving earth in their works.

The Pythagorean view of the cosmos is less clearly understood, having been obscured by its early origins and by the incomplete accounts of it that survive. What is clear is that the Pythagorean view included an earth that moved around a central fire (not the sun) and that there was also a "counter earth." In Copernicus's day, it was common to refer to the heliocentric system as the "Pythagorean," even though the two systems had only a moving earth in common.

[38] Rheticus and Giese were outraged by the addition of the anonymous preface and unsuccessfully appealed to the authorities in Nüremberg to have the edition corrected. Much has been said about Osiander's actions over the years; he is vilified more often than not. For a more charitable assessment of Osiander's contributions to the reception of Copernican thought, see Wrightsman (1975).

[39] A letter from Bishop Giese to Rheticus describes that Copernicus was unaware he was being presented with his text because he had suffered a severe stroke and saw it only in the last moments of his life.

[40] Kepler's important work on the orbit of Mars around the sun, the *Astronomia nova*, was published in 1609 and Galileo's early telescopic work, the *Starry Messenger,* was published in 1610. Both of these works provided stronger arguments for the Copernican view. From that point on, the number of thinkers who began to entertain and defend the Copernican view began to increase significantly (even if they may have remained in the minority).

[41] Westman (1975a).

[42] Ptolemy's description of the moon was reasonably accurate at describing *where* the moon would appear in the sky. However, the mechanism that Ptolemy employed would have caused the moon to approach the earth and recede from it to such a degree that its apparent size should have changed greatly. Ptolemy's lunar model could not have been true and Copernicus provided an alternative description of the moon's motion that didn't suffer from this problem.

[43] Reinhold's *Prutenic Tables* were published in 1551. The most widely used astronomical tables before Reinhold's were the *Alfonsine Tables*, which were based on Ptolemaic theory (and which Copernicus had repeatedly referred to during the development of his own theory).

[44] Pope Paul III, to whom Copernicus had dedicated his work, was given a copy of *On Revolutions* and gave it to Bartolomeo Spina who was Master of the Sacred and Apostolic Palace. According to Rosen (1984), "Spina 'planned to condemn' it. But he fell ill and died. His plan was carried out by his lifelong friend, Giovanni Maria Tolosani." Tolosani wrote a very negative appraisal of Copernicus's work – criticism that Copernicus avoided in death.

[45] The list of pre-1600 Copernicans is: Thomas Digges, Giordano Bruno, Galileo Galilei, Diego de Zúñiga, Simon Stevin, Rheticus, Michael Mästlin, Christoph Rothmann, Johannes Kepler, Bishop Tiedemann Giese, Cardinal Nicholas Schönberg, Achilles Gasser. Likely Copernicans (but not confirmed): William IV Landgrave, Robert Recorde, Christian Wursteisen. Possible: George Vögeli, Andreas Aurifaber, Thomas Harriot, Gemma Frisius, Johannes Stadius, Jost Bürgi.

[46] A lesser-known feature of Copernicus's theory was that the earth retained its special standing in his latitude theory of the planets. Historical discussions of planetary theories almost always refer to longitude theories of planetary motion – that is, those aspects of planetary theory that offer predictions about how far east or west a planet will appear in the zodiac. However, it was always well known that the positions of the planets vary in their height as well (relative to the ecliptic). Ptolemy and Copernicus each had elaborate latitude theories that are seldom described in historical accounts. Because the orbits of the planets and of the earth were not

exactly centered on the sun in Copernicus's theory, Copernicus needed to vary the inclination of the planets' orbital planes to improve his latitude model. But for a reason Copernicus never attempted to explain, *the rates at which these planetary inclinations changed were tied to the motion of the earth round the sun.* This was an unexplained coincidence, and it was very similar to the coincidental relationship that existed between the motion of the earth/sun line and the motions of the planets in Ptolemaic theory. Copernicus's latitude and longitude theories were applied independently and resulted in discrepancies (Neugebauer and Swerdlow, 1984). The problem in latitude theory was later solved by Kepler when he substantially modified Copernican theory and fixed the elliptical orbits of all of the planets (the earth included) directly on the sun.

[47] Galileo's contribution to putting the earth on an equal footing with the other planets resulted from his discovery of the moons of Jupiter. This discovery showed that the earth was *not* unique in its possession of a satellite. Kepler's contribution was his conclusion that the paths of *all* the planets, including the earth, were the same – ellipses that were centered on the sun.

Chapter Five – Tycho Brahe, His Science, and His Response to the Copernican System

Tycho Brahe (1546-1601) was a Danish scientist who is best known for his extensive record of highly accurate naked-eye astronomical observations. Less widely-appreciated today are his important and lasting contributions to theoretical astronomy and cosmology. Even so, he did not consider himself to be just an astronomer. Tycho had a wide-range of interests in the natural world; he explored the possibility of using astronomy to develop accurate weather prognostications, to produce astrological forecasts, and to inform his alchemy and medicinal practices.

Tycho Brahe's life was fascinating – he was born into Danish high nobility, which meant that his family helped co-manage the Danish realm along with other noble families and the king. He was kidnapped at the age of two by his childless uncle and aunt – an arrangement that his birth parents soon accepted.[1] As a member of either Brahe family branch, Tycho was assured of a high social status and a sizable inheritance.

Tycho attended the University of Copenhagen at the age of twelve (unremarkable in his day) so that he could acquire some of the knowledge and skills that he would find valuable as a warrior-lord in the service of the king. The role of highly-placed nobles, like the Brahes, included administrating fiefs, advising and serving the king, entertaining foreign dignitaries and delegations, and leading military forces in times of war. Furthermore, for a noble family to remain influential and successful, they needed to be constantly interacting with other nobles and the king. Royal court politics was a demanding task, but it was a necessary one for protecting and promoting one's interests.

Tycho was sent to the university to increase his knowledge of classical languages and European intellectual traditions. It was, in a sense, a finishing school that rounded out his early education prior to beginning his on-the-job training as a nobleman. Tycho did not stay at the University long enough to earn a degree. As Tycho's biographer, Victor Thoren described, "...boys of [Tycho's] rank were born with all the credentials they would need..." Tycho's brothers, like his father and grandfathers, followed a standard career path, which included apprenticeships that introduced them to the realities of politics, court etiquette, and, of course, war. Tycho would be different. By the age of fourteen he had developed a keen interest in the subjects of astronomy, trigonometry, and astrology. Later, he would become very active in the practice of medical alchemy as well. None of these subjects were essential

[Figure 5.1. Portrait of Tycho Brahe. Image Courtesy History of Science Collections, University of Oklahoma Libraries.]

to the life of a nobleman, but were instead activities normally pursued by university men, physicians, theologians, and other middle class intellectuals. In spite of his high-born status, these subjects greatly appealed to Tycho and he took great advantage of his time in Copenhagen to learn about them from knowledgeable practitioners.

Philip Melanchthon and the German Universities

Denmark was a Lutheran land, and the intellectual environment in Copenhagen was heavily influenced by the important co-founder of the Lutheran religion, Philip Melanchthon (1497-1560). As partners in early Protestantism, Philip Melanchthon and Martin Luther had very different instincts and concerns, but they also deeply trusted and relied upon each other as they transformed Luther's rebellion against the Catholic Church into a viable alternative to it. Together, they co-created the religious and cultural traditions that would serve as the basis for the Lutheran religion, which quickly replaced Catholicism as the dominant form of Christianity in Northern Europe.

Melanchthon was young humanist scholar when he began his association with Luther. He worked hard to systematize emerging Lutheran theological positions and to mediate disputes between opposing parties in his attempt to bring as many people into the Lutheran fold as possible. As a committed humanist, Melanchthon strongly believed that the success of the Lutheran faith and society depended on a firm understanding of God's creation. So, in addition to his religious work, Melanchthon undertook an enterprise to increase the quality of learning at Germany universities, beginning with the University of Wittenberg.

Melanchthon promoted the importance of mathematics and astronomy instruction at Wittenberg and hired talented instructors. He also had a deep interest in astrology and supported and encouraged its practice. As university graduates from Wittenberg took on teaching posts at universities across Northern Europe, Melanchthon's influence widened – he came to be called "The Teacher of Germany."[2] And Denmark, although not German, was well within his sphere of influence. Many of Tycho's teachers in Copenhagen had personally known Melanchthon as students in Wittenberg, and a few of them had even been lodgers in Melanchthon's house. Melanchthon's interests in mathematics, astronomy, and astrology would have a very important impact on what Tycho would learn at the University of Copenhagen.

Tycho's Career Path

As family tradition dictated, the young Tycho was under a great deal of pressure to take on the responsibilities of a young nobleman. But in spite of these well-established expectations, Tycho repeatedly withdrew to his bookish interests and managed, time and time again, to avoid the path that had been carefully laid out for him. Fortunately for Tycho, the times were beginning to change – at least to some extent. The allure of Renaissance Humanism had reached Denmark through the influence of Melanchthon and others, and higher learning had become more widely-appreciated. So while on the one hand there was tremendous pressure from the Brahe side of the family for Tycho to toe the line as a nobleman, on the other, Tycho's adoptive mother's family was well-steeped in humanism and seemed to be more accepting of Tycho's unusual interests. Still, even if nobility increasingly appreciated the products of humanism and learning, it did not mean they saw it as their business. After all, they had the much more important and pressing responsibility of co-governing the Danish realm than bothering with matters that concerned middle-class scholars. The Brahes had the ear of the king on a regular basis – there would be little to be gained and much to be lost by keeping one's nose in a book or one's eyes on the heavens. Tycho was torn between these two realms.

Tycho's Travels

Tycho left the University of Copenhagen at the age of fifteen and in 1562 traveled with his guardian-tutor into German lands, where he continued his studies at the University of Leipzig. As a responsible young noble, he was expected to study the classics and learn languages, fencing, horsemanship, and dancing. But while he was there, Tycho also encountered men who were as passionate about astronomy as he was, giving him many opportunities to learn from more knowledgeable astronomers and scholars. During this time, he began to study the heavens and made astronomical observations using instruments that he had purchased. By intensely pursuing his passion for astronomy, astrology, and alchemy, Tycho continued to stray from the path of nobility.

Tycho returned home after three years in Leipzig and found Denmark at war with neighboring Sweden. His extended family was actively involved in the war, but by now Tycho was already out of his element – he had neither the inclination nor the skills to contribute to the war effort like his brothers did. After a year in Denmark, Tycho returned to Germany –

first to the University of Wittenberg and then to the University of Rostock. While at Rostock, Tycho publicly tried his hand at astrology and, based on a recent lunar eclipse, predicted the death of the Turkish sultan Suleiman the Great. Unfortunately for Tycho, news soon arrived that the sultan had died six weeks *before* the eclipse occurred. In the weeks and months following this embarrassment, Tycho got into repeated quarrels with another young Danish nobleman (a distant cousin). Their arguments continued and the episode came to a head at an evening dinner when the young men took their disagreement outdoors to be settled with broadswords. During the duel, Tycho received a blow that glanced off his forehead and hacked open the bridge of his nose. Permanently disfigured, Tycho would wear a "flesh colored" prosthetic nosepiece made out of metal for the rest of his life. He considered the injury to be the result of a fair fight, and he and his cousin remained friends into adulthood. Tycho returned to Denmark for a year, but again found himself restless, uncomfortable, and unwilling to take on the roles expected of him. He headed south once again – this time to find a suitable intellectual environment that he might someday call home.

During all of his trips abroad, Tycho continued to exhibit an intense interest in astronomy, astrology, medicine, and weather forecasting.[3] He bought books, made observations, experimented with instruments, and attended universities. Eventually, Tycho returned to Denmark once again and took up residence as a twenty-five year-old nobleman in one of his family's estates, where his pursuit of astronomy and alchemy continued to cause tension between him and his family. To add to the discord, shortly after returning he created a scandal by marrying a local commoner – Kirsten Jorgensdatter. This arrangement could not be recognized as a legitimate marriage for a nobleman. Following Danish custom, Tycho and Kirsten's children would not be considered noble and would not be able to inherit the family name, let alone the castles and fiefs that went with it. It is not known why Tycho did this – whether it was a simple act of love, a public statement that he would refuse the traditional role of a nobleman, or both.

His marriage was quickly followed by another important event in his life – the spectacular supernova of 1572. Already an avid astronomer by this time, Tycho noticed a bright star in the sky one evening where no star had ever been observed. He was so surprised by its presence that he had his servants go outside to confirm that what he had seen with his eyes was real. Over the months that followed, he carefully observed the new star and attempted to measure its parallax (the apparent change in its position against the background of stars). He found none. The lack of parallax led him to conclude that the new star was extremely distant – either among or very near to the sphere of stars.[4] This conclusion, that the supernova was located far beyond the lunar sphere, was quite significant because it challenged the classical Aristotelian view that the heavens were perfect and immutable. Tycho published his observations, calculations, and conclusions in a text called *De stella nova* in 1573.

Tycho was quickly recognized as an expert astronomer by his intellectual peers in Denmark. He was invited to give a lecture series on astronomy at the University of Copenhagen even though university work had been traditionally reserved for the educated middle class. His lectures were well received, but he continued to be under intense social pressure to conform to the manner of a nobleman. Tycho cancelled the second half of his popular lecture series and sought out a new social environment – one that would be more supportive of his work. His options were severely limited since he wanted to avoid the responsibilities of nobility, but yet maintain the material advantages that went along with it.

Tycho decided that the only solution to his problem was to emigrate out of Denmark. With this possibility in mind, he undertook a fourth trip abroad to identify a permanent home, this time traveling as far south as Basle and Venice. When he returned to Denmark, he began to plan for the move of his family and wealth out of the country and made his intention apparent to the people around him. While his plan appears to have been serious, it may also have been a well-considered gambit to gain the king's patronage. If so, it was effective – King Frederick caught wind of Tycho's intentions and sent a messenger to Tycho, asking him to change his mind. To Tycho's pleasure, the king had invited him to pursue astronomy in Denmark and with the full support of the crown. Frederick offered Tycho the island of Hven for his observatory, a stipend, and an income from additional lands to support his effort. After some initial hesitation and negotiation, Tycho accepted and soon began construction of his new home and observatory on his new island fief. The king's act effectively legitimized Tycho's earlier actions and raised his standing among his Danish peers. In return, Tycho would become Frederick's court astrologer.[5]

The Lord of Uraniborg

With Frederick's support, the resources that Tycho was able to direct toward his astronomical studies were tremendous. Hven was an island with forty farms and a small village, but it represented only a fraction of the total income that Tycho had been granted. The isolation of the island fief helped to free Brahe from the many of the obligations that normally would have been part of his duties as a member of the King's court. On Hven, Tycho could pursue his scientific interests relatively undisturbed.

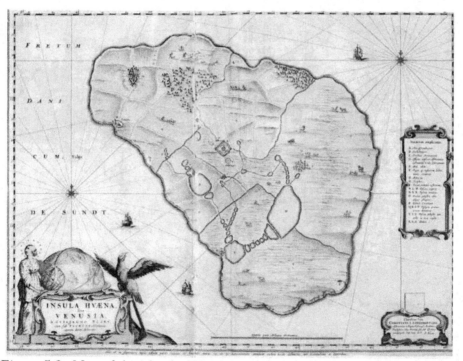

[Figure 5.2. Map of the island of Hven from a copper etching of Willem Janszoon Blaeu's Blaeu Atlas 1663. Public domain, Wikimedia Commons.]

Tycho expended a significant fraction of the crown's resources transforming his island home into a research institute. He dubbed his creation "Uraniborg" after Urania – the muse of astronomy in Greek mythology. The main house, or castle, included living quarters for his family, assistants, and guests; alchemical furnaces in the basement; a library on the first floor; and platforms on the second level for astronomical instruments. The grounds included gardens, aviaries, and fishponds and was surrounded by a square earthen rampart with outbuildings and gatehouses on its corners and sides. Uraniborg even had a jail for problem peasants.

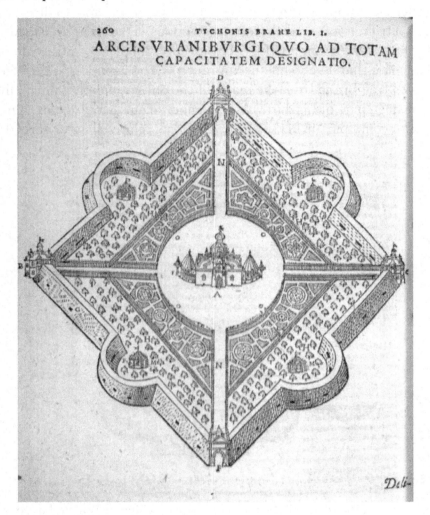

[Figure 5.3. Drawings of the house and grounds of Uraniborg. Photo of an image in Tycho Brahe's *Astronomical Letters*, 1596. Image courtesy History of Science Collections, University of Oklahoma Libraries.]

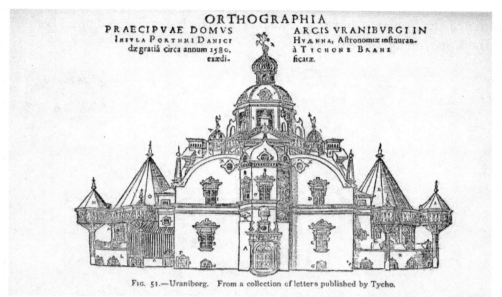

FIG. 51.—Uraniborg. From a collection of letters published by Tycho.

[Figure 5.4. Drawing of Uraniborg. From *A Short History of Astronomy* (Arthur Berry, 1899). archive.org]

Tycho periodically entertained visiting dignitaries, scholars, and noblemen who made the trek to Uraniborg to satisfy their curiosity. Though Tycho preferred to be left to his work, he enjoyed impressing occasional visitors with his scientific instruments and alchemical laboratory.[6] Tycho had created a self-sufficient operation at Uraniborg. It included a workshop for the production of new astronomical instruments, a printing press, and eventually a paper mill. Some historical accounts portray Tycho as a near-tyrant who treated his peasants and assistants harshly. This may well have been true – especially if one applies modern standards to his behavior.[7] On the other hand, many of Tycho's assistants stayed at Uraniborg for several years and left with great respect and admiration for him.

Tycho's Astronomy

Though he is most appreciated for his careful measurements of stellar and planetary positions, Tycho was no mere cataloger of astronomical data. Like many other astronomers in his day, he greatly admired Copernicus's accomplishment. And even more than most of his contemporaries, Tycho found the mathematical harmony of the Copernican system to be appealing. Still, he rejected the motion of the earth. Tycho aspired to develop a new astronomical system that would keep the earth at the center of the universe, but would also retain the harmony and "numbers" of the Copernican system.

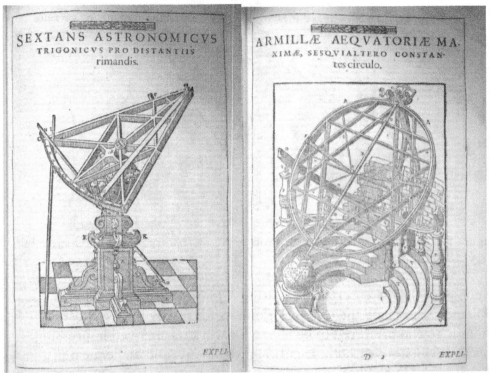

[Figure 5.5a (left). Tycho's large "mature" sextant (ca. 1582). The radius is over one and a half meters long. Figure 5.5b (right) Tycho's Large Armillary (ca. 1585). The large scale of the instrument can be appreciated by noting the arched entranceway to the observing area. Images courtesy History of Science Collections, University of Oklahoma Libraries.]

At the root of Tycho's cosmological thinking was his belief that there was a profound connection between the structure of the macrocosm (the universe with its stars and planets) and the microcosm (the earth and its inhabitants). In this view, the celestial influences acted directly on the earth and its inhabitants because they were at the center of the cosmos. In this way, it was natural for Tycho to consider the subjects of astrology, alchemy, meteorology, and medicine as astronomically-related disciplines. For example, he believed the influences of the heavens were manifested in the transformation of chemicals and elixirs that he worked with in his basement laboratory.[8] So strongly did Tycho feel this connection between the microcosm and the macrocosm that he referred to alchemy as "terrestrial astronomy."

Tycho had set his astronomical sights high: he wanted to create a credible astronomical theory that was mathematically precise. He understood early in his career that the astronomical tables and observations from the preceding millennia contained many inaccuracies and some outright errors. Tycho knew that to make further progress in astronomy using the existing data was impossible. Thus, he began to devote himself to recording high-quality naked-eye astronomical observations over many years. To do that, Tycho expended a tremendous amount of effort and money designing and manufacturing precision astronomical instruments. Many of his instruments were of new designs and had never been made before. After his craftsman completed the instruments that were built to his specifications, Tycho tested them critically. As often as not, the instruments failed to meet his high expectations and were never used again. The instruments in the figures are representative of the ones that Tycho used to map the heavens.

One of the most famous of the instruments at Uraniborg was the "Mural Quadrant," which was built into the central north-south wall of the main house. The Mural Quadrant was both an instrument *and* a work of art. The image of it (figure 5.6) can be somewhat confusing unless it is understood to be a drawing of an instrument, its operators, and a painting on the wall above the instrument. The actual instrument that Tycho used is the graduated brass arc attached to the wall. The "mural" was painted on the wall above the arc and depicted the various activities that occurred at Uraniborg; this is the "painting in the drawing." The three figures represented in the foreground are taking measurements at the quadrant. The assistant farthest to the right is measuring the position of a planet or a star by lining up the moveable sight attached to the brass quadrant with the sight in the opening of the wall (located in the upper left-hand corner of the drawing). The assistant at the table is recording the measurements as they are called out. This large fixed quadrant was capable of accurately measuring the altitude of astronomical objects as they crossed the southern meridian. The drawing also shows a third assistant with a candle, recording times taken from a set of three clocks.[9]

In addition to finding increasingly accurate ways of making astronomical observations, Tycho analyzed the data in new ways as well. He sometimes took multiple measurements of the same object in order to increase his

[Figure 5.6. Tycho's famous "Mural Quadrant." Image courtesy History of Science Collections, University of Oklahoma Libraries.]

confidence in the measurements; Tycho was one of the first scientists to engage in what is now called "error analysis." He also developed an early mathematical model to compensate for the effects of atmospheric refraction – a phenomenon that caused astronomical objects to appear in positions slightly different from where they really were (especially for those located near the horizon).[10]

The Comet of 1577

Shortly after Tycho began construction of Uraniborg, the second major astronomical event in his life occurred – the spectacular comet of 1577. Tycho had hoped for a chance to observe a comet so that he could measure its position and motion in the sky. When he did, he could detect only a small amount of parallax.[11] This analysis allowed him to conclude that the comet was located well beyond the sphere of the moon and was not an atmospheric phenomenon as many commentators had assumed.

Several astronomers carefully studied the comet of 1577 and the comets that followed in the years 1580, 1582, and 1585. These astronomers included Christoph Rothmann and Michael Mästlin.[12] Both of these men recognized that the celestial motion of comets was very different than the motion of the planets. For example, comets did not always travel within the zodiac like the planets did, and they often exhibited very large periods of retrograde motion. Mästlin calculated the path for the comet of 1577 and determined that it had passed right through the sphere of Venus. Tycho repeated the calculations and agreed. For this and other reasons, the three astronomers concluded that the motion of comets served as evidence that the celestial spheres were not real.[13] This episode also underscores the fact that in spite of his relative physical isolation, Tycho was not working in intellectual isolation – he frequently communicated with Rothmann, Mästlin, and others. Occasionally, a few of his peers even made the long trek to Hven for an extended visit with Tycho.

The comets made it apparent to many astronomers and natural philosophers that transient events could occur in the heavens as they do on earth. These findings posed a strong challenge to the traditional Aristotelian belief in an immutable and perfect celestial realm. So although Tycho would maintain the traditional view of a central and stationary earth, he helped contribute to the erosion of some long-standing Aristotelian assumptions about the cosmos.

[Figure 5.7. The Comet of 1577. Woodcut by Jiri Daschitzsky, 1577. Public domain image courtesy Ragesoss, Wikimedia Commons.]

Stjerneborg—"Star town"

Tycho quickly ran out of space to house the new instruments he had produced, so he built a separate observatory just beyond the walls of Uraniborg. He named this observatory "Stjerneborg" (Star Town).

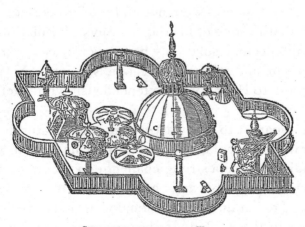

STJERNEBORG, SEEN FROM THE WEST.

[Figure 5.8. Diagram of Stellaborg. From *Tycho Brahe*, Dreyer, 1890. Public domain.]

In this new observatory, the instruments could be mounted directly on the ground, which provided them with a more stable foundation. Furthermore, because they were mounted slightly below ground level, both the observers and the instruments were protected from the wind. The rooms containing the instruments were covered by retractable roofs and were connected by tunnels to a central warming house.[14] This was the facility where Tycho and his assistants made most of their observations.

The measurements that they took were, on the average, within one and two minutes of accuracy (within 0.01% of their true values). In cases where Tycho was particularly interested in the position of an object, the measurements were accurate to considerably better than one minute and approached the physiological limit of naked-eye observation. Prior to this time, most planetary data was known only to about ten minutes of accuracy. Furthermore, the preexisting astronomical record had been marred by some gross errors that created serious problems for theoretical astronomers. Tycho corrected these errors and greatly improved upon that situation as well. Confident in the quality of the new data he was collecting, he began to apply them to a new theory for the motions of the sun, the moon, and the planets.

Tycho's Planetary Theory
While Tycho had an immense amount of respect for Copernicus, he ultimately rejected Copernicus's sun-centered cosmos. As with many astronomers, the Copernican system conflicted with Tycho's cosmological beliefs – including his conceptions of physics, alchemy, medicine and scripture. Tycho also strenuously objected to the fantastic size that Copernicans had conferred on the Universe. Tycho's careful measurements of stellar positions and his subsequent failure to detect any stellar parallax meant that the Copernican Universe would need to be far larger than the Copernicans had initially suggested.

Even though Tycho believed that the earth was in the center of the Universe, he found the order and coherence of the Copernican planetary arrangement to be very attractive.[15] Eventually he found a way to keep the Copernican "numbers" but still dispense with a moving earth.[16] He imagined that all of the planets except the earth revolved around the sun.

In the Tychonic model, instead of the earth revolving around the sun, *the sun revolved around the earth.* Consider Tycho's diagram (Figure 5.9).

In this planetary model, the earth is motionless at the center of the Universe with two bodies revolving directly around it: the moon and the sun. The sun is the second center of motion in the Tychonic model, with the planets Mercury, Venus, Mars, and Saturn revolving around it. Thus, the sun "carries" the planets with it as it travels on its annual passage on the ecliptic. Finally, superimposed on top of all of this relatively slow planetary motion is the rapid daily motion of the entire celestial sphere – stars, planets and all, around the earth every 23 hours and 56 minutes in an east-to-west direction.

When viewing the diagram of his planetary system, many of his contemporaries objected to the intersection of the sphere of the sun with the sphere of Mars. Some even thought that this meant Mars and the sun might collide! This last concern especially frustrated Tycho since he thought it was obvious from the diagram that Mars circled the sun at a fixed distance from it so that any collision between them was impossible. Tycho requested that mechanical models of his system be manufactured so that skeptics who were less-skilled at geometry could see this for themselves. For Tycho, the intersection of the sphere of Mars with the sphere of the sun was not a problem, because he, Mästlin, and Rothmann had already convinced themselves that the celestial spheres were not physically real.

Tycho's theory can be seen as a compromise between the Ptolemaic and Copernican theories. It is worth noting that, in spite of the huge cosmological differences between the Tychonic and Copernican systems, they both accounted for the astronomical observations of the planets in equivalent ways.[17] While the motions in the geoheliocentric Tychonic model may seem unrealistically complicated to us now, they appeared reasonable enough to people in Tycho's day – so much so that several people also claimed credit for the idea (including a former assistant of Tycho's who Tycho accused of plagiarizing his work.)[18]

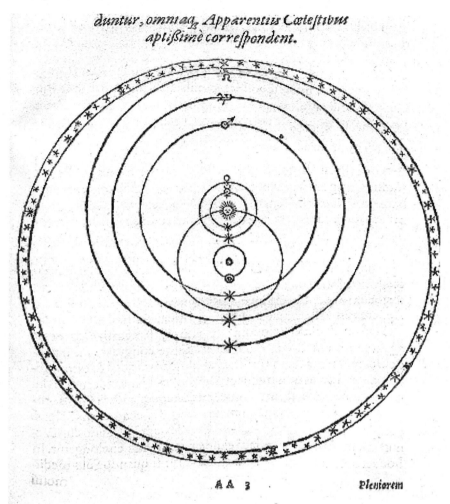

duntur, omniaq, Apparentiis Cœleſtibus
aptiſſimè correſpondent.

[Figure 5.9. The Tychonic system as presented in Tycho's *De mundi* of 1588.
Image courtesy Deutsche Fotothek, Wikimedia Commons.]

What distinguished Tycho's theory from the geoheliocentric theories of
his competitors was his decision to allow the "spheres" of the sun and
Mars to intersect – indeed, it was necessary for Tycho to have done this in
order to truly preserve the "Copernican numbers."[19] Because Tycho no
longer accepted the reality of the celestial spheres, he had no difficulty
including this important feature.

Tycho's astronomical objections to the Copernican system
In a purely astronomical sense, one could not logically distinguish
between Tycho's and Copernicus's system – with the important exception

of stellar parallax. The failure to detect stellar parallax in Copernicus's day meant that the stars had to be at least *40 times* farther away than had been previously believed. After Tycho's careful measurements of stellar positions and the continued absence of detectable stellar parallax, the stars in a Copernican Universe would now have to be at least *700 times* farther away (and the Universe 300 million times larger in volume) than what geocentric astronomers believed. This Copernican requirement for a Universe so vast in size struck Tycho as more unbelievable than any other feature of the Copernican system.

Absurdly Large Stars

Tycho recognized another problem the absence of observable stellar parallax presented to Copernicans: that their system obligated them to accept the existence of absurdly large stars. This conclusion was a consequence of two things: 1) the apparent visual diameters of stars, and 2) the vast distance away from the earth that the stars had to be in a Copernican Universe (given the absence of detectable stellar parallax). Tycho pointed out that for stars to have discernable size at such fantastic Copernican distances, they would need to be gigantic. Tycho calculated that some of the "Copernican stars" required diameters as large as the orbit of Saturn around the sun to appear in the sky as they do.[20] Tycho's new geoheliocentric system suffered from no such absurdities.

Loss of Uraniborg

Tycho's tenure on Hven came to an end with the death of King Frederick and the rise to the throne of Frederick's son Christian in 1596. Tycho was accustomed to the extremely generous treatment he had been receiving from Frederick and did not adjust very well to the decrease in support that came with Christian's rule. Because of this, and for reasons of his own doing, the situation soured – first in Hven, and then in Denmark itself. Tycho soon found it necessary to go into exile. During his preparation to leave Denmark, he managed to extract enough wealth from his estates and receive enough help from friendly nobles in Germany that he was able to live and travel fairly comfortably in exile – though the money ran through his hands quickly. Thus, with a sense of urgency, Tycho negotiated for employment with the Holy Roman Emperor Rudolph in Prague. Because of the uncertainty surrounding his future, the loss of some of his best instruments, the worry of providing for his family, and the anticipation of his own death, Tycho ceased making significant astronomical observations.

Tycho and the Copernican Revolution

Tycho was one of many astronomers who greatly admired Copernicus but chose not to believe in the reality of his system. He found it unlikely that the gross motions of the earth would go unnoticed to our senses. He couldn't believe in the absurd distances between Saturn and the stars that the Copernicans had proposed and all of the wasted space that would have existed. He also objected to the absurdly large stellar diameters that the Copernican viewpoint seemed to demand. Finally, Tycho believed that the passages in the Bible describing the stability of the earth were to be taken literally. He freely referred to scripture when he attempted to convert some of his Copernican contemporaries back to a geocentric view. Tycho believed in the reality of his astronomical system and considered it to be his greatest gift to science.

With the benefit of hindsight, we can see that a great deal of what Tycho had accomplished ended up benefiting the Copernican cause as well as his own. His careful astronomical measurements were used later by Kepler to create a highly accurate version of the Copernican system. And Tycho's contributions to the erosion of the traditional Aristotelian view of the cosmos helped lower some of the barriers to the acceptance of the Copernican system.

From Tycho to Kepler

At this late stage of his life, Tycho worked to create an enduring legacy by completing his planetary theory. Once this was done, he intended to apply his theory to the completion of astronomical tables that would supersede all others. But there was a problem. If the Tychonic system were to succeed as a model capable of accurately predicting planetary motion, it would, like the Copernican system, also need to include minor epicycles.[21] Tycho's excellent astronomical data made his effort to fashion an astronomical theory far more difficult to accomplish than it had for anyone before him. Because the data were so much better, any successful model would have to be correspondingly better as well. Tycho had set the bar quite high for anyone who would try to account for his data – this included himself...

To work out the details, large numbers of calculations needed to be carried out – a task too great for him to do on his own. He needed the assistance of talented and experienced mathematicians rather than the novices that he employed to make astronomical observations on Hven. Mathematicians of this caliber were not easy to come by, and Tycho's need was urgent. Though he wasn't terribly old, he sensed that his death was approaching. Tycho wanted enduring fame for himself and money for his family. As he became increasingly desperate to complete his life's work, the fate of another astronomer, Johannes Kepler, also hung in the balance. Having already made a name for himself as an astrologer, astronomer, and mathematician, Kepler was on the verge of going into exile himself; he was a Protestant who was caught up in the turmoil of the Catholic Counter-Reformation, and he needed to leave his home. A broad and brutal religious war threatened and Kepler would repeatedly find himself on its front lines. So at the same time Tycho needed Kepler, Kepler needed Tycho.

In the most famous scientific collaboration that fate has ever arranged, the two exiles came together in Prague. Their short relationship was awkward and acrimonious at first, but the deep mutual respect they had for each other as scientists prevented them from parting ways. While Tycho would have preferred not to have placed all of his eggs into one basket by relying entirely on Kepler, he could find no other person to help with the task. As we'll see, it is hard to imagine that Tycho could have found anyone more talented. Tycho set Kepler on the problem of the motion of Mars – a problem for which Tycho had excellent data but which he and his able assistant, Longomontanus, had been unable to solve.

Within a year after their partnership began, Tycho was dead. His death, due to a blocked bladder, was drawn out over five days – a consequence, according to some accounts, of his overly-polite withholding of "water" at a dinner party.[22] His deathbed plea to Kepler was, "Let me not seem to have lived in vain." Kepler acquired Brahe's data with the understanding that he would complete Tycho's project and co-publish his results with the Brahe family. The goal was to produce astronomical tables of very high predictive power – something far better than had ever existed before.

These tables would be called the *Rudolphine Tables,* after their patron, the Emperor Rudolph II.

We will see in the next chapter why it took Kepler many more years to produce the *Rudolphine Tables.* It was a delay that frustrated the Brahe family immeasurably. But in spite of this complication, and their exile from Denmark, the Brahe family story ended happily. As prominent foreigners associated with the Holy Roman Emperor, the Brahe children married into nobility. It would have been unlikely for them to have done so in Denmark.

[1]Tycho's noble uncle needed a son in order to pass on his legacy and inheritance, whereas Tycho's birth parents had other sons – so, in a sense, they could afford to lose Tycho. See Thoren, 1990.

[2] Melanchthon was responsible for having hired both Rheticus and Reinhold as professors of mathematics (astronomy) at the University of Wittenberg. Before this time, university professors in mathematics were uncommon. For a fascinating and detailed account of Melanchthon's role in the intellectual tradition in Northern Europe see Kusukawa, Sachiko, *The Transformation of Natural Philosophy: The case of Philip Melanchthon*, 1995.

[3] Tycho diligently recorded weather phenomena in the hopes that he would be able detect meteorological and astronomical patterns that would allow him to make accurate predictions of the weather.

[4] The astronomer Michael Mästlin reached a similar conclusion at about the same time. Tycho would come to regard Mästlin's opinions on astronomy highly.

[5] Many rulers employed court astrologers. Tycho would be called on repeatedly to cast horoscopes for his patron, Frederick. One impressive example of Tycho's astrological work was described by Thoren, 1990: "Tycho had a small volume 'bound in pale green velvet with gilded edges, containing about three hundred pages all written in [Tycho's] own hand' ready to deliver to the king."

[6] Tycho liked to impress his visitors in other ways as well. He had bells placed in his assistants' rooms tied with cords that ran down to the first floor so he could call them when he wanted. He would use this system to astonish visiting guests, surreptitiously pulling a cord and then quietly mentioning an assistant's name to have the assistant appear downstairs "magically." He also employed a dwarf named Jeppe whom Tycho believed could predict the future.

[7]As a boss, Tycho received mixed reviews from his student/assistants. Some of the young men spent only a short time on the island before leaving – others stayed several years. Brahe often complained about the poor quality and laziness of his assistants. It appears that competent assistants who accepted Brahe's position of authority and shared his obsession with accuracy faired quite well and left the island with fond memories. Others who stood out in the coldest, darkest winter nights when their hearts weren't in it may have felt differently. The peasants seemed to have had a relatively idyllic arrangement on Hven prior to Tycho's arrival and their lives had changed abruptly when Tycho took up residence on the island and demanded serious physical labor from them.

[8] Tycho's views on medicine and alchemy were strongly influenced by the famous German-Swiss alchemist physician Paracelsus (Philippus Aureolus Theophrastus Bombastus Von Hohenheim, 1493-1541).

[9] In an attempt to increase the efficiency of the inherently slow but highly accurate fixed quadrant, Tycho tried incorporating mechanical clocks into the data collection process. He understood that if he could record times within a specified range of accuracy, he could make more observations. After a great deal of expense and experimentation, Tycho concluded that the best clocks of his day were simply not up to the task.

[10] The phenomenon of refraction in water was well-known and frequently discussed in ancient times. Atmospheric refraction had been proposed as well in order to account for why it was possible that a lunar eclipse observed in antiquity occurred in a way that "the sun and the partially eclipsed moon could be seen simultaneously on opposite horizons." (Thoren, 1990, pp. 227). Thus, it was understood that atmospheric refraction caused a setting sun to appear above the horizon for a slightly longer time than it otherwise would have, while the moon appeared above the eastern horizon sooner. Tycho would be only partially successful at addressing atmospheric refraction.

[11] Determining parallax for an object in motion is not at all straightforward, because the observed motion of such an object is due to two components: 1) The object's actual motion and, 2) the apparent motion that is due to the parallactic effect. Thus, one needs to know how an object is moving before its parallax can be teased out. It is not surprising that Tycho was only partially successful when he attempted to determine parallax for moving objects – whether it was a comet, the sun, the moon, or the planets.

[12] It is worth noting that both of these astronomers were early Copernicans. Christoph Rothmann was a highly skilled astronomer who was employed by Wilhem IV, Landgrave of Hesse-Kassel, who was an astronomer himself. Michael Mästlin was a professor at the University of Tübingen and is most famous for being known as the teacher who later introduced a young Johannes Kepler to Copernicanism.

Tycho tried hard to convince Rothmann, who he thought highly of, to abandon Copernicanism, but the evidence that he succeeded is very weak (for an alternative opinion, see Barker, 2004).

[13] See Mosley, 2007, pp. 74, for more detail.

[14] The latitude of Hven is 56° N, which means astronomical observing in the summer would be very poor due to extremely long summer days and extended twilight. For

the same reason, the nights would be very long at Hven in the winter. Winter weather also provided for very low humidity and very clear winter skies, which made for optimum astronomical observing (but for a very uncomfortable observer). For these reasons, Tycho and his assistants spent many Scandinavian winter nights measuring the heavens. The design of Stellaborg was a reflection of that practice.

[15] Tycho sought a planetary theory that would show "how the appearances of the other planets could be adapted to the stability of the earth, while the Copernican numbers stayed the same." For an excellent description of Tycho's thoughts on the relative merits of the Copernican and Tychonic Systems, see Ann Blair's *Tycho's Brahe's Critique of Copernicus and the Copernican System*, Journal of the History of Ideas, Vol. 51, No. 3, 1990, pp. 355-377.

[16] Tycho was certain of the central position of the earth in the cosmos. However, he was less certain of whether or not the earth remained stationary in its central position – he thought it possible, but unlikely that the earth might spin in place. This particular kind of geocentrism no longer required the rapid diurnal motion of the entire stellar sphere to explain daily risings and settings of the celestial realm; rather, the daily motion of the heavens was explained by an earth rotating on its axis. When the notion of a spinning earth is added as a modification to Tycho's planetary theory, it is often known as "semi-Tychonic" theory. Semi-Tychonic theory had its occasional proponents – including Tycho's most important assistant and disciple, Longomontanus.

[17] As was pointed out by Kuhn (1957), "The Tychonic system is, in fact, precisely equivalent mathematically to Copernicus's system. Distance determination, the apparent anomalies in the behavior of the inferior planets, these and the other new harmonies that convinced Copernicus of the earth's motion are all preserved." For a view that underscores the differences between the Copernican and the Tychonic systems see Goldstein, 2002.

[18] It is clear from the historical record that Tycho freely borrowed ideas from others as well. Because there were many astronomical systems similar to Tycho's circulating about the same time, it is difficult for historians to establish priority for geoheliocentric systems in general. No doubt all of the men who considered geoheliocentric systems were familiar with and influenced by the ancient "Capellan system," which was a variation of the traditional geocentric system that had Mercury and Venus both revolving around the sun, while the sun revolves around the earth. In the Capellan system, the superior planets continue to revolve around the central earth as they do in the Ptolemaic system.

Priority claims aside, there is no doubt that Tycho fashioned the best version of a geoheliocentric system – one where the sphere of Mars and the sphere of the sun intersect each other; no other astronomers were willing or able to propose that particular innovation (Rothmann and Mästlin weren't inclined to bother with it, since they were Copernicans). See Thoren, 1990, and Gingerich and Westman, 1988 for more on the priority disputes and with Tycho's rocky relationship with Paul Wittich.

[19] The need for the intersection of the spheres of the sun and Mars can perhaps be more easily seen from the perspective of the mathematically equivalent Copernican System. In the Copernican System, the earth is sometimes closer to Mars than it is to the sun. This occurs when Mars is at opposition – that is, when it is directly opposite the sun in the sky and in the midst of its retrograde motion. Thus, for the Tychonic system to be mathematically analogous to the Copernican System, Mars must also be sometimes closer to the earth than the sun is – thus, the need for the intersecting spheres. With one's initial glance at a Tychonic diagram, it appears as though the sun and Mars might collide – however, since Mars revolves around the sun and maintains its distance from it, such a collision is impossible.

[20] It is now known that the apparent diameters of stars do not correspond to their actual dimensions, but are instead artifacts that result from the wave nature of light and the optics of the eye or that of a telescope. At the distances that stars are from the earth (light-years away), they are effectively point sources of light. See Graney 2010b for further discussion of the stellar size argument and apparent stellar diameters.

[21] Tycho was so staunchly opposed to the equant that, as Ann Blair describes it, "[He] would continue to perceive Copernicus's motion of the earth as a lesser evil than Ptolemy's use of the equant point..." This is the reason that Tycho would come to use many of the same modeling techniques that Copernicus had.

The total number of motions for a planet in Tycho's epicycle-on-epicycle-on-deferent was astonishing. The planet itself revolves around the center, K, of the smallest epicycle (sometimes called an *epicycle* or *epicyclet*), while the center of the epicyclus revolves around the center, F, of the larger epicycle (which is still a minor epicycle). The center of this epicycle travels around the sun, while the sun makes its annual revolution around the earth. Finally, we should not forget that the rapid daily motion by the celestial sphere is superimposed on all of these planetary motions. Therefore, the full version of the Tychonic system features five different circular motions for a single planet (see following diagram).

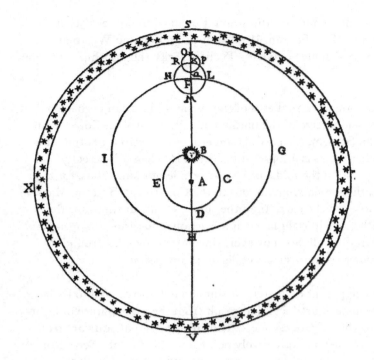

[Figure 5.10. Public Domain]

[22] A recent sensationalistic account (Gilder and Gilder, 2004) concluded that Kepler had poisoned Tycho with mercury, but that conclusion has been definitively shown to be false. Tycho's body was exhumed and shown to possess mercury concentrations well below lethal levels. There seems to be no good reason to doubt that Tycho died of a blocked bladder and that Kepler and Tycho remained on good terms until the end.

Chapter Six – Johannes Kepler and His New Astronomy

Johannes Kepler is one of the greatest scientists who ever lived – even if he isn't as well-known as Copernicus or Galileo. The likely reason that Kepler suffers from poor name recognition is that his primary scientific contributions are of a highly mathematical nature and are not easy to understand.[1] In contrast to Kepler, Galileo had little trouble communicating his discoveries and ideas – the non-mathematical nature of Galileo's astronomical discoveries made them easily accessible to ordinary people. However, by giving Kepler the consideration he deserves, it will become apparent that his contribution to the Copernican Revolution was every bit as important as Galileo's. Indeed, many people find Kepler's story to be the most compelling of them all.

In the previous chapter we witnessed how Kepler gained possession of Tycho's valuable astronomical data. In return for this treasure, he was expected to complete Tycho's work and produce a highly accurate set of astronomical tables that would be dedicated to Emperor Rudolph II – an effort for which both he and the Brahe family were to be compensated. After a long series of personal and scientific struggles, Kepler was able to satisfy most of this agreement. He made good on his promise to finish the *Rudolphine Tables*, but as a committed Copernican, he could not complete Tycho's planetary theory. Instead, Kepler radically modified the Copernican system by having the planets speed up and slow down as they moved on elliptical paths around the sun. This "new astronomy" violated the principle of uniform circular motion that his predecessors had held for two-thousand years.[2] But with Kepler's great transgression came an equally great reward: the accuracy of his *Rudophine Tables* vastly exceeded anything that had ever existed before.

Kepler's Life

Johannes Kepler was born in 1571 in the small city of Weil der Stadt in Württemberg, a southern duchy of the Holy Roman Empire (in modern day Germany).[3] Kepler's family ancestry was of Lutheran tradesmen and local politicians of modest, but comfortable means. Unfortunately for Kepler, his immediate family did not manage so well, and it suffered from some significant pathologies. His parents had an unhappy marriage. His restless father was frequently absent as a soldier of fortune and after one trip abroad simply failed to return home. One of his brothers was constantly troubled, and later in life, Kepler's mother was nearly burned as a witch.

His dysfunctional family managed to avoid poverty and Kepler was able to receive an education. The duchy of Württemberg supported schools and seminaries, and it offered financial support for promising young boys in order to produce well-educated bureaucrats and clergymen. Kepler

[Figure 6.1. Johannes Kepler, 1610. Painter unknown. Public domain.]

received one of these scholarships and attended a Latin school where he soon distinguished himself academically. By doing so, he won further support to continue his studies at the University at Tübingen in 1589.

At Tübingen, Kepler had the opportunity to learn mathematics and astronomy from one of the very few Copernicans of the time – Michael Mästlin.[4] Mästlin taught standard Ptolemaic astronomy in his lectures, but he also mentioned the advantages of the Copernican system to his students when he felt it was appropriate.[5] Kepler became very interested in astronomy and exhibited an aptitude and interest in mathematics that went well beyond what was normally expected of a student. In the meantime, Kepler continued to work on his general studies requirements and received the Master of Arts degree, which made him eligible to begin his training to become a Lutheran pastor. Kepler was well along in these theological studies when he was called to teach astronomy and mathematics at a Lutheran school in Graz.[6] Kepler was at first greatly disappointed that he would not become a pastor, but then soon came to accept the change in plan as an unexpected opportunity to reveal and praise God's works.[7]

Kepler was called to Graz to teach, but he also began to conduct original work in astronomy shortly after arriving there. Kepler had two principal motivations for doing astronomy, one of which was his conviction that he had been ordained to uncover the grandeur of God's design. His other aim was to apply astronomy to the creation of calendars, almanacs, and astrological forecasting – activities that were considered legitimate, practical and lucrative in his day.[8] One of Kepler's first publications was an almanac for the year 1595. In addition to weather predictions, almanacs featured warnings about pestilence, war, and religious or political turmoil. Kepler would publish several almanacs in his lifetime; they were quite popular and would serve as an important source of income.

Kepler and Astrology
Kepler was highly respected for his astrological forecasting – likely for two reasons: First, he *was* a good astrologer.[9] Second, the practice of astrology required knowledge of past, present, and future positions of the planets and stars – as a skilled astronomer, Kepler had a great advantage in being able to determine planetary positions himself. Astrologers who did not have a good working knowledge of astronomy either performed their tasks ineptly or else needed to rely on the astronomical work of others.

Kepler was both skeptical and hopeful about the possibilities for astrology. In this sense, his views weren't much different from Tycho's.

Kepler believed that the pursuit of astrology was worthwhile but that it was a difficult subject to master because of its complexity. In the early part of his career he pursued astrology avidly but still believed that there were practical limits to the accuracy of astrological prognostications. He frequently criticized the outlandish claims that other astrologers made. Like Tycho, he believed that the heavens influenced people and events, but that they didn't completely determine one's future. As Kepler grew older, he became less interested in practicing astrology and more interested in completing his new astronomy.

Mysterium Cosmographicum

Kepler's first major publication was the *Mysterium cosmographicum* (1597),[10] which was the first pro-Copernican work to be published since Copernicus's *De revolutionibus*. In his *Mysterium*, Kepler accepted all of the major premises of Copernican cosmology but ignored many of the details of Copernican mathematical astronomy.[11] In a sense, we can view Kepler as the antithesis of the Wittenberg astronomers, who had taken the opposite stance and denied Copernicus's cosmology but greatly admired his mathematical astronomy.

To understand Kepler's contributions to science, it is important to appreciate that he was a committed Copernican *before* he became a skilled astronomer. Under the influence of Michael Mästlin, Kepler had learned of the cosmological advantages of the Copernican system as a student. So for Kepler, the question was not *whether* the Copernican system was true, but *how and why* it was true. In the *Mysterium cosmographicum* he set out to explain why the Copernican cosmos had the features that it did. For example, he sought to address questions like the following: Why are there six planets orbiting the sun and no more or no less?[12] Why were the planets separated from each other by the distances they were? And why did planets farther from the sun move more slowly than those that were closer to it? Since both Mästlin and Tycho Brahe had recently concluded that the celestial spheres were not physically real, these questions took on new meaning.[13]

Kepler found his inspiration for the *Mysterium* while teaching. According to his own account, he was lecturing on the periodic conjunctions of Jupiter and Saturn when a thought occurred to him: might regular geometric shapes serve as a template for God's creation? After exploring the idea, Kepler determined that two-dimensional polygons such as triangles or squares would not suffice. Instead, he considered three-dimensional figures. Since antiquity, it had been well-known that there were five regular solid shapes enclosable by regular polygons: the tetrahedron, the cube, the octahedron, the dodecahedron, and the icosahedron. These figures are known as the "Platonic solids" after Plato, who had used them in his theory of matter.

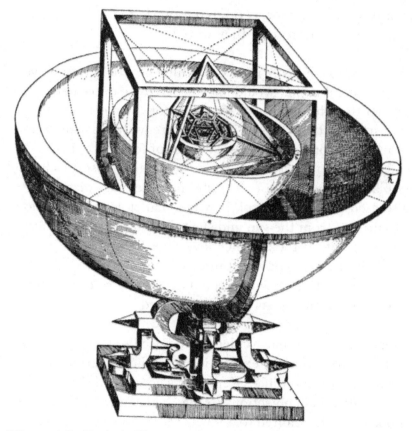

[Figure 6.2. Kepler's Platonic solid model of the Solar system from *Mysterium Cosmographicum* (1596).]

By invoking the five Platonic solids, Kepler was able to account for why six and only six planets existed *and* why they orbited the sun at the specific distances that they did. According to Kepler, the paths of the planets and the Platonic solids were nested one inside another so that the size of the gap between the paths of two adjacent planets was determined by the Platonic solid that separated them (see figure 6.2). For example, the outer boundary for the path of the earth was defined by the inner faces of a dodecahedron, while the vertices of that same dodecahedron served as the inner boundary for the path of Mars; Mars and Jupiter were separated by a tetrahedron, and so on... The spaces that were created by nesting the six planetary spheres and the five Platonic solids matched remarkably well to the known planetary dimensions of the Copernican model.[14] To get his scheme to work, Kepler had to determine where each Platonic solid should be positioned. In his mind, the order of the Platonic solids was not at all arbitrary, and he soberly offered esoteric reasons for why they were located in the positions that they were.[15]

Kepler included other ideas in his *Mysterium*, which he would refine over the years to follow. One idea that would later prove to be extremely fruitful was his belief that the sun was responsible for the motion of the planets. Kepler postulated that the sun spun in place with quasi-magnetic lines of force emanating from it. These solar lines of force swept the planets along and, by acting most strongly on the planets closest to it, caused the inner planets to move more quickly than the more distant planets.[16] He also used this idea to explain why a planet appeared to slow down when it was distant from the sun and sped up as it got closer – as occurs in Ptolemy's equant. It took Kepler several years before he was able to refine these ideas, but his basic intuitions first appeared in the *Mysterium*. In his later writings, Kepler would frequently refer back to his "little book" and the myriad ideas that it contained.

There was one important topic that Kepler was advised to leave out of his *Mysterium*: an introductory chapter explaining why the Copernican system was compatible with the Bible. Kepler was concerned that his readers would raise theological objections to the Copernican view that he promoted in his book, and he wanted to address those concerns at the very beginning. However, during the preparation for the publication and printing of the *Mysterium*, he was strongly counseled by local Lutheran theologians to drop the discussion. Their advice came with this explanation: *" There already reigns more dispute in the church of Christ than the weak can endure."*[17] The "dispute" referred to the increasing tensions between the forces of the Protestant Reformation and the

Catholic Counter-Reformation, as well as differences between the various Protestant sects themselves.

The *Mysterium* makes it clear that Kepler was completely confident that the Copernican system was true. Even so, he remained concerned that stellar parallax had not yet been observed, and he made repeated inquiries of other astronomers about how it might be measured. As a Copernican, Kepler had accepted that the Universe must be very large, but he also remained certain that it was finite and that stellar parallax would eventually be measured. Kepler did not believe that God would have created an infinite universe, which would have been without any unique center.[18]

Religious Troubles

By 1599 the political and social situation for Protestants in Graz had become dire as the Catholic Counter-Reformation gained ground.[19] At first, Lutheran preachers were expelled, forcing Lutherans to travel outside of the city to receive the sacrament. Soon, Lutheran parents were required to have their children baptized as Catholics. Kepler himself ran into trouble when his daughter died, and he arranged to have a Protestant funeral for her rather than a Catholic one. He was penalized for the transgression by the authorities who forced him to pay a fine before he was allowed to bury her. Other parts of the region suffered under forced conversions to Catholicism, which were frequently followed by riots. It became clear to Kepler that he should get out of Graz while he could. The decision to move away was not an easy one; the Keplers had property and would risk losing many of their assets. Other Graz Lutherans took a more pragmatic approach and converted to Catholicism in order to solve their problems, but Kepler would not compromise in matters of religion, so he felt that he had no choice but to move.

Kepler's employment options outside of Graz were limited. He had hoped he might be able to return to the University of Tübingen and find a position there, but his inquiries turned up no opportunities for employment and his old teacher Mästlin offered him no encouragement. An earlier invitation from Tycho Brahe began to look more and more attractive as Kepler's need to flee Graz intensified. Soon, he traveled to Bohemia to discuss the matter of employment with Tycho directly.

During negotiations over the terms of Kepler's appointment, a great deal of acrimonious posturing took place between the two men. Tycho was looking for an assistant who would help him complete his work, while Kepler viewed himself as much more than that. Both men also had ulterior motives: Kepler very much wanted access to Tycho's excellent astronomical data for his own purposes, and Tycho wanted Kepler to serve as an ally in an extremely bitter clash with another scientist.[20] Their first attempt at arriving at a mutually satisfying arrangement failed. At one point, Kepler exploded in rage, leaving the Brahe household. But after a short time, Kepler cooled off, apologized to Tycho, and rejoined him. Kepler then brought his family to Bohemia, and the famous association between Tycho and Kepler began.

In the beginning, Tycho only shared a small amount of his valuable astronomical data with Kepler, providing Kepler only with what was needed for the problem he had been assigned: He challenged Kepler to work out a theory for the motion of Mars within the framework of Tycho's planetary model – a solution to it had eluded Tycho and his other assistants. But after only a year, Tycho was dead. Kepler then gained access to all of Tycho's astronomical data and was free to use it as he saw fit.[21]

Kepler's War on Mars and His New Astronomy
At the beginning, Kepler was frustrated by Tycho's refusal to share all of his astronomical measurements – he had hoped to gain access to Tycho's planetary records so that he could confirm that his Platonic model for planetary distances was correct. But once Kepler had started his work on Mars, he continued until it was solved – even after the rest of Tycho's planetary data had been made available to him.

Kepler's approach to mathematical astronomy was unusual. Prior to Kepler, mathematical astronomers explained the motion of the planets by focusing their attention on the mathematical details of the geometric descriptions they were using, such as the epicycle-on-deferent, eccentric, and equant models. They didn't exhibit much concern over what caused the motions, since it wouldn't have any impact on how they went about their work. Furthermore, such an approach would have been seen as speculative and not the business of an astronomer.[22]

In contrast to this long-standing approach, Kepler began his astronomical work with a strong notion about what caused the planets to move in the way that they did: he believed that the sun, an obvious source of great power, caused the planets to travel around it.[23] Kepler posited that the sun extended quasi-magnetic lines of force into space while it spun on its axis. These moving lines of force pushed on the planets – sweeping them along.[24] This physical model of the cosmos accounted for why the inner planets took so much less time to revolve around the sun than the outer planets did: the sun's lines of force acted more strongly on planets closer to it.

When Kepler first began his work on Mars, he embraced Ptolemy's equant model for planetary motion – a model which both Copernicus and Tycho had deplored. For Kepler, the heliocentric equant was compatible with his physical ideas about planetary motion, since the equant has planets moving slower the farther they are from the sun and more quickly the closer they are to it. In Kepler's mind, one of the reasons planets *appeared* to speed up and slow down was because they actually *did* speed up and slow down!

But as hard as Kepler tried to make the equant work, he could not get it to match up to Tycho's excellent planetary observations, which were within two minutes of accuracy. Kepler understood that any planetary model that could not accommodate Tycho's data was simply not true – and Kepler wanted the truth. He did not solve this problem easily – he described his lengthy and difficult effort as his "war on Mars."[25] In this text, we can only provide a condensed description of the path that he took.[26]

Equal Areas in Equal Times

Kepler's first major innovation in mathematical astronomy was his "equal areas in equal times" description of planetary motion. In this model, Kepler placed Mars on a circular eccentric path around the sun, similar to the equant, but instead of using the equant point as a reference for the motion of the planet, Kepler had the speed of Mars vary according to a new mathematical relationship: the line drawn between the sun and the planet always swept out the same area over the same period of time.[27] This early Keplerian innovation is now known as "Kepler's Second Law."

Another extremely important innovation that is usually overlooked in introductory accounts of Kepler's work is that he treated the motion of the earth the same way that he treated Mars and the other planets: he placed the earth on an eccentric and subjected it to the equal area rule. Furthermore, the eccentrics for both Mars and the earth were referenced precisely to the "true" sun, unlike Copernicus who had instead referred the planets to the "mean sun."[28] Treating the earth's motion in the same manner as he treated Mars and the other planets was essential to Kepler's ultimate success. Because planetary positions are measured from a moving earth, it was important for Kepler to know where the earth was in order for him to know where Mars was in its orbit.

Thus, in order to solve the problem, Kepler needed to create a model for the earth's motion and, at the very same time, a model for the motion of Mars. However, since Kepler began with only the raw observational data of Mars, there was no straightforward way to determine the paths of Mars and the earth independently. It was simply not a problem that could be solved by the direct application of a fixed formula. Instead, it was a process that had to be solved using an intelligent mathematical game of "warmer-colder." Kepler first made an initial guess at the planetary paths for the earth and Mars separately. Then he assessed the results, made changes, and tried again.[29] As he did this, he considered the position of the earth as it would appear from Mars and then the position of Mars as viewed from the earth. Kepler reported that he carried out the entire series of calculations seventy times until they matched the accuracy of Tycho's data to within 2 minutes of arc accuracy. Other astronomers may have let out a great sigh of relief and admired their accomplishment, but Kepler critically appraised his work by selecting additional observations from Tycho's Mars data in order to confirm that they also properly "fit" his model. They did not. Kepler uncovered a discrepancy of eight minutes of arc in his theory – still better than anyone before him had accomplished, but a completely unacceptable error in Kepler's mind.[30]

Thus, Kepler failed in spite of his great effort. In a desperate attempt to "fix" the problem, Kepler began distorting the path of Mars from a circle into a variety of oval shapes. After experimenting with a number of figures, he discovered that the solution to his problem was the ellipse – a well-defined mathematical form, which, along with the circle, parabola, and hyperbola, is one of the conic sections.[31] Kepler concluded that every planet possessed an elliptical orbit with one of its two foci centered on the sun. This is now referred to as Kepler's "First Law of Planetary Motion" (even though he arrived at it *after* his so-called "second" law). The elliptical orbits of the planets differed in their size, the orientation of their major axes, and their degree of eccentricity.[32]

Consider the diagrams of planetary motion, which show 1) the structure of an ellipse with its two foci (figure 6.3) and, 2) the equal area in equal time rule superimposed onto an ellipse (figure 6.4). Keep in mind that the diagrams greatly exaggerate the elliptical shape of planetary paths – the actual paths would appear very nearly circular – if drawn to scale.[33]

KEPLER'S "FIRST" LAW:

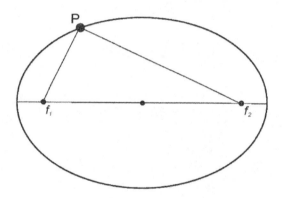

[Figure 6.3. Kepler's first law—the elliptical path of the planets. Figure courtesy Danica Oudeans.]

Note the different positions of a planet in the second diagram (figure 6.4). At "aphelion," when the planet is farthest from the sun, it moves most slowly; at perihelion, it moves most quickly. Though the speed that a planet moves on its elliptical path can change, the total area that it sweeps out in a given period is constant. These two innovations made it possible for Kepler to account for Tycho's accurate planetary data.

KEPLER'S "SECOND" LAW:

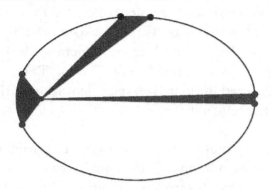

[Figure 6.4. Kepler's second law of planetary motion. Figure courtesy Danica Oudeans.]

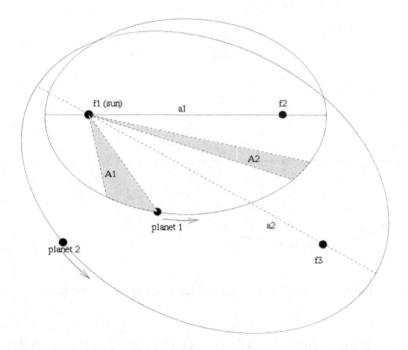

[Figure 6.5. A depiction of the orbit of two planets in Keplerian theory. Although planets have their own orbit on ellipses of different sizes, eccentricities, and orientations, the ellipses of all of the planets have one of their foci centered on the sun (f1 in the diagram). Planet 1 has its empty focus as f2, and planet 2 has its empty focus at f3. Although the ellipses appear to be coplanar in this diagram, they are in different planes (though typically not more than 5 degrees from each other). The eccentricity of the orbits is greatly exaggerated for clarity. Image courtesy Han-Kwang Nienhuy, Wikimedia Commons.]

A Bad Year in Prague

In 1611 Kepler's year began with the loss of his son to smallpox and a religious war that loomed around Prague. To add to his misery, later that year his wife died and his patron, the Emperor Rudolph, was forced to abdicate the throne in favor of his brother, Matthias, who was a more enthusiastic supporter of the Catholic Counter Reformation than Rudolf had been. So, once again for religious reasons, Kepler was forced to flee his home. After searching for a new place to live and work, he accepted a position as District Mathematician in Linz.

The religious turmoil affected everyone in central Europe at this time, but for Kepler it was particularly troubling since he had been warning others about its dangers for years. Kepler strongly advocated tolerance in religious matters and felt that religious belief wasn't something that should be forcibly imposed on people. Unfortunately for Kepler, and for the rest of Europe, many of his fellow countrymen didn't see things in the same way. What made matters worse for Kepler was that even though he considered himself a Lutheran, he was denied the sacrament by the Lutheran clergy in Linz for his heterodox opinions on the meaning of Holy Communion.

In Linz, Kepler remarried and had six children with his second wife – though three would die in childhood. To add still more distraction and anxiety to Kepler's life, as he worked to complete the *Rudolphine Tables*, his mother was charged with witchcraft. It was a charge that he had to take seriously since six women had been sentenced in her town for witchcraft in the preceding months. In the neighboring city of Weil der Stadt, thirty-eight women had been tortured to death for practicing witchcraft over the preceding fifteen years. An interesting story in its own right, it suffices to mention here that had Kepler not taken the time and care to personally defend his mother, she would almost certainly have suffered the same fate.

During this tumultuous period, Kepler continued to work on several projects simultaneously. One of his accomplishments is now referred to as Kepler's third law[35] – a mathematical relationship that tied the period of each planet's orbit to its distance from the sun.[36] This correspondence of mathematics with physical reality appealed greatly to Kepler's Pythagorean sensibilities. He compared the order of the planetary configurations to the ratios of vibrating strings and other "harmonies" of the universe and the mind. The discovery of his third law moved Kepler to great rapture.[37] This fundamental mathematical relationship could serve as the basis of an argument against *any* geocentric system – including the Tychonic system, which would become an increasingly popular geocentric alternative to the Ptolemaic system.[38]

Kepler published his third law in his *Harmonices Mundi (the World Harmony)* in 1619; at the same time he continued work to complete and publish additional sections of the *Epitome of Copernican Astronomy* (1617-1621). The *Epitome* was a comprehensive statement of Kepler's new astronomy and included a broad range of arguments for the heliocentric viewpoint – many of which later appeared in Galileo's *Dialogue*. Kepler also directly addressed theological objections to the heliocentric system in his *Epitome*. Not surprisingly, the book was soon listed in the Roman Catholic Church's Index of Prohibited Books, along with other Copernican works. All of these actions were a part of the Catholic Church's 1616 response to Galileo's aggressive campaign for Copernicanism, which followed his telescopic discoveries. Living north of the Alps, Kepler was beyond the reach of the Catholic Inquisition, although he did encounter some criticism to the *Epitome* from Lutheran clergy and theologians. But in spite of Kepler's strong advocacy for the heliocentric view, he never had trouble with religious authorities – probably because Lutheran Church orthodoxy wasn't as well established, and there existed no Lutheran organization comparable to the Catholic Holy Office of the Inquisition. Furthermore, Kepler was very well-liked and made very few enemies – characteristics that likely prevented many bad situations from getting any worse for him.

Kepler also published calendars that were based on his new planetary theory. One of the prognostications included in his 1618 calendar was particularly prophetic: he appears to have foreseen the watershed event that would begin the devastating "Thirty Years' War" – the Prague Defenestration of May of 1618. In the following year's calendar, Kepler suggested that comets might create something more for astrologers to consider, and in that year, *three* comets appeared. Of course, there are many reasons that Kepler may have appeared to be such a good astrologer: his good luck, a large number of prognostications, political astuteness, and an equivocation in the wording of his predictions that made failure less apparent. Kepler's calendars were quite popular.

Rudolphine Tables

After years of personal struggles and after performing extensive calculations using his planetary theory, Kepler was ready to publish the *Rudolphine Tables.* The *Tables* would publicize the success of his new conceptual scheme, and it would give others the resources to make highly accurate planetary predictions that only Kepler had had access to.[39] Unfortunately, at the time that Kepler was preparing the work for the printer, the Counter Reformation arrived in Linz. In 1626, a peasant uprising in the neighboring countryside broke out in response to forced conversions to Catholicism. The city was besieged for two months during which time the printing house where Kepler had planned to have his book printed went up in flames (the manuscript survived in Kepler's possession). Kepler's house in Linz stood at the city wall, and a company of soldiers occupied it. He was required to leave all of the doors of his house open so that the soldiers could come and go as they needed. In the turmoil, Kepler worked through the distraction of guns, fumes, and fires.

There were substantial barriers to getting the *Tables* printed: The negotiations with the Brahe family over the terms of their agreement, the difficulty in finding a printer who could carry out the highly specialized printing, the requirement of Kepler's presence during the printing to view the galley proofs, the need for money, and the distraction of an ever-worsening war. Eventually, life in Linz became intolerable. There was no longer a printing press to use, so he packed up his family and moved to Ulm, where the book was finally printed in 1627.[40] The *Rudolphine Tables* sold well due to the great demand from fellow astronomers, astrologers, calendar makers, mapmakers, and navigators.

The Reception of Kepler's Work

The value of Kepler's astronomical work was not widely appreciated until he published the *Rudolphine Tables.* When astronomers had the opportunity to compare Kepler's new tables with existing tables, it slowly became obvious that his were vastly superior to anything else that had existed before (we now know they were approximately 50 times more accurate). The tables also successfully predicted a rare event: the transit of Mercury across the face of the sun in 1631. These great accomplishments drew attention to Kepler's earlier theoretical works: his *Astronomia nova* and *Epitome of Copernican Astronomy*, the latter of which was reprinted in 1635.

[Figure 6.6. Frontispiece to Kepler's *Rudolphine Tables*—note the homage he pays to his astronomical predecessors. Frontispiece and title page of: *Tabulae Rudolphinae: quibus astronomicae ...* by Johannes Kepler, 1571-1630. Public domain.]

In spite of Kepler's great predictive success, his planetary theory was accepted in its entirety by very few astronomers. The least appealing aspect of Kepler's theory was his speculative physical explanation for planetary motion, which almost no one accepted.[41] The reception of his mathematical astronomy also posed challenges because it featured new mathematical techniques. This included the early use of logarithms and the muddling through of problems that really called for the use of calculus – a field of mathematics that hadn't yet been developed.

Kepler's equal area rule was particularly troublesome for his contemporaries because it didn't allow for the planet's position to be directly calculated, as had been possible for all previous astronomical theories. Instead, the planetary positions had to be determined indirectly through a cumbersome process. So while the end results were highly accurate and well-defined, the procedure was difficult and unfamiliar. Even astronomers who in principle accepted the equal area rule often resorted to alternative mathematical pathways to do their calculations. Others ignored it entirely and reverted back to equant-like mechanisms to vary the speed of the planets. Kepler himself acknowledged the awkwardness of applying his equal area rule.[42]

So, while not everyone accepted Kepler's equal area law, he *did* seem to convince many of his contemporaries that planets moved on elliptical paths and with varying speeds. With this change, the era of the epicycle was over and the Copernican system took on the simple form that we are now familiar with – the planets traveling on unadorned, roughly circular figures centered on the sun.[43] This was a considerable transition from the standard view of the previous generation for whom equant motion was considered abhorrent and circles or spheres seen as the only legitimate figures for describing the celestial realm. Furthermore, in Kepler's astronomical system the earth had acquired full status as a planet because its motion was finally described using all of the same principles that were applied to the other planets.[44] And while very few of his contemporaries accepted the details of his celestial physics, in a way Kepler was at the vanguard by having taken celestial physics so seriously. He was soon followed in this activity by scientists like Descartes and Newton. So although few were impressed by the details of Kepler's physics, others recognized that offering a physical explanation for the motion of the planets was an important objective necessary to complete the Copernican view. As we will see, eight decades after the *Astronomia nova* was published, Isaac Newton would create a new physics that was successful at "making sense" of Kepler's version of the Copernican system – including all three of Kepler's planetary laws.

Geocentrism and Keplerian Planetary Theory

Kepler's accomplishment convinced some astronomers to change their minds and adopt the heliocentric view. But others, in the tradition of the Wittenberg interpretation, accepted Kepler's ellipses only to then turn around and put them into a Tychonic framework. The most vocal proponent of this view was Jean-Baptiste Morin, a French astronomer who placed the earth at the center of the cosmos with the sun on an elliptical orbit around the earth and the planets on elliptical orbits around the sun.[45] With the "Keplerian" modification of the Tychonic system, the Tychonic system was once again mathematically equivalent to the heliocentric system and, as far as the planets were concerned, observationally indistinguishable from it. After the edict of 1616, the Catholic Church would not allow Copernicanism to be considered as anything more than an unprovable mathematical hypothesis (an outcome of the first phase of the "Galileo Affair," which we will consider in the next chapter). As we will see, Catholic Copernicans would have a variety of reasons to embrace a geoheliocentric model for the motion of the planets and Kepler's ellipses could be made compatible with that view.

Kepler's Other Works

Kepler was an extremely productive scientist. In addition to the astronomical works that we've already considered, he published a path-breaking work on optics, the *Dioptrice*, in 1611 (from which the modern ophthalmology term "diopter" is derived). He also made important contributions to mathematics in his early use of logarithms and in framing practical problems that led to advances in functional analysis and calculus. Some of his proto-calculus ideas appear in his study on the measurement and volume of wine in casks, *Nova stereometria doliorum vinariorum* (1615), which he later modified and published in German in order to make it more widely accessible.[46]

Kepler also publicly evaluated Galileo's telescopic discoveries, having first learned of them indirectly and then by reading Galileo's *Sidereus Nuncius (Starry Messenger)* of 1611. Kepler was so impressed that even without access to a telescope, he accepted the veracity of Galileo's reports. Kepler's response, as the Imperial Mathematician for the Holy Roman Emperor, was very important to Galileo, who was a relatively minor figure at that time. Kepler publicly supported Galileo's work by publishing an open letter: *Dissertatio cum Nuncio Sidereo (Conversation with the Starry Messenger)* at a time when Galileo's astronomical claims were under attack from many of Galileo's own countrymen. Kepler could not be accused of being overly polite: years earlier Kepler had attempted to correspond with Galileo, but, except for a short reply, Galileo ignored his overtures. Kepler simply stated what he believed about the telescopic observations and felt that Galileo, a fellow Copernican, deserved his support. Once again Kepler initiated a dialogue with Galileo, and once again Galileo broke it off.

Kepler's Final Days and His Final Work

Following the publication of the *Rudolphine Tables*, Kepler sought another employer and a place for his family to live. He also struggled to make ends meet since much of the money that he was promised by the Emperor was never paid out. He returned to Prague one more time where, to his surprise, he was well received. But soon, he was asked once again to convert to Catholicism. Firm in his religious convictions, he left Prague for Sagen, where Protestants were still tolerated, but the situation soon deteriorated there as well. Finally, he headed for Regensburg with the goal of collecting some money owed to him and where, on November 2nd, 1630, "he rode, tired, on a skinny nag, over The Stone Bridge into Regensburg."[47] He soon became ill and died several days later.

Kepler's final work was a curious little book, published posthumously through the efforts of his family: *Somnium seu Astronomia Lunari (Dream or Astronomy of the Moon)*, 1634. Appearing to be a fantastic science fiction account of a trip to the moon, it was at the same time a psychologically astute pro-Copernican work. In the *Somnium,* Kepler described how the inhabitants of the moon believed that their world was the unmoving center of the Universe – just as Kepler's earth-bound geocentric contemporaries believed their world to be.

Kepler went on and described, with great detail and accuracy, how the heavens appear when observed from the lunar surface. He pointed out that there are two distinct lunar hemispheres: one of which always had a large stationary "moon" (the earth, or what his imagined lunar beings called "Volva"), always visible and unmoving, "as though it were attached to the heavens with a nail",[48] and the other hemisphere – in which "Volva" was not present in the sky. A lunar day and a lunar night would take more than 29 earth days to pass – and Volva, which appeared 15 times larger than our moon, would cycle through all of its possible phases during the lengthy lunar day and night. Although Volva would always remain fixed in the same position above the lunar horizon, it would spin in place – the shapes of its continents clearly visible from the lunar surface.

Kepler went on to describe the kinds of observations that a lunar astronomer would make – how the sun, planets, and stars appear to whirl around over the course of a day and over the period related to Volva's position in the sky. Indeed, the motions of the planets viewed from the lunar surface are exceedingly complex.

The *Somnium* is a short 17 pages in translation, whereas the supporting notes for it are about four times as long. Thus, most of the book is comprised of highly detailed notes that elaborate on the ideas presented in the main story. Kepler's central message in the *Somnium* was that lunar astronomers would be physically unaware of lunar motion and would, therefore, be inclined to adopt a lunar-centric astronomical model that was untrue. The *Somnium* was a gentle admonition to his earth-bound geocentric colleagues who were making the same mistake.

[1]Kepler used mathematical techniques that even skilled astronomers in his day struggled to comprehend. It took his peers several decades to incorporate key features of his work into their own astronomical practices (Applebaum, 1996). Jeremiah Horrocks was an exception to this pattern and was an enthusiastic supporter of Kepler's work early on, but Horrocks died quite young and his work was not published until much later. Magini also made early use of some of Kepler's mathematical astronomy in constructing his tables, though he continued to be a geocentrist in his cosmology (Voelkel and Gingerich, 2001).

[2] Kepler's modifications to the Copernican system might seem minor to us today, but recall that the fundamental expectation of all his predecessors – from Plato, Aristotle, the medieval Ptolemaic astronomers in Islam and Europe through to Copernicus and Tycho Brahe – was that heavenly motion was caused by some underlying combination of uniform *circular* motion. Only Ptolemy had deviated in any way from uniform circular motion through his use of the equant, and he had been relentlessly criticized for it for centuries to follow. Even so, at least Ptolemy had kept the planets on perfectly circular paths – Kepler would discard the circle as well.

[3] Weil der Stadt was a small free imperial city, which meant that it was directly under the control of the Holy Roman Emperor and was, therefore, officially Catholic. The city was completely surrounded by the duchy of Württemberg, which was, like its duke, Lutheran. The Kepler family moved to a neighboring town in the duchy when Kepler was young.

[4] Mästlin was the only Copernican teaching in a university at the time. For more detail see Voelkel, 2001.

[5] Kepler found Mästlin's descriptions of the Copernican system appealing and noted that Mästlin mentioned that system in his lectures. See Caspar, 1948/1993. For a discussion of Mästlin's beliefs and teaching practices see: Methuen, 1996.

[6] Some commentators have suggested that the reason Kepler was chosen for the teaching position at Graz was because he held religious beliefs that were not in line with Lutheran orthodoxy. However, Kepler has indicated that he kept these thoughts to himself during his younger years. It seems more likely that Kepler was chosen for the position at Graz because he was skilled at mathematics and the unexpected death of the previous teacher created a vacancy that needed to be filled quickly. It is also sometimes said that Kepler was about to receive a master's degree in theology just before he was called to Graz, but Methuen (1998) has shown that there was no such degree at Tübingen and that Kepler was simply preparing to be a pastor and waiting to be appointed to a position when one became available.

[7] Kepler wrote Mästlin about his plans for the *Mysterium* and declared, "I wished to be a theologian; for a long time I was troubled, but now see how God is also praised through my work in astronomy." (In E.J. Aiton's introduction to A.M. Duncan's translation of Kepler's *Mysterium*)

[8] There were some vocal opponents to astrology in Kepler's day, but for the most part, it was considered to be a normal activity of astronomers and physicians.

[9] For more detail see Caspar (trans. Hellman), 1948/1993. Court astrologers, by the nature of their work, interacted with nobility, or even royalty, on a frequent basis and would have had access to the most current news of the day. They also tended to be very bright and politically astute (or they would not have held the positions that they did). For these reasons, people like Kepler would have been as likely as anyone else to see what was on the road ahead. And importantly, successful astrologers were skillful at *appearing* to be good astrologers. They carefully crafted their predictions so that more were perceived as successes than as failures.

[10] Mästlin took full responsibility for the publication and printing of his former student's work. It was Mästlin who decided to append a copy of Rheticus's *Narratio Prima* to the *Mysterium Cosmographicum*, for the benefit of readers who lacked familiarity with the Copernican system. *Mysterium cosmographicum* is the frequently used short Latin title for the book. In the English translation, A.M. Duncan rendered the title as *The Secret of the Universe*. The full title in English is: *The Secret of the Universe on the marvelous Proportion of the Celestial Spheres, and on the true and particular causes of the number, size, and periodic motions of the heavens, Established by means of the five regular geometric solids*. Such a lengthy title is not uncommon for books from this period.

[11] Indeed, it isn't clear how much mathematical astronomy Kepler was capable of at this early point in his career. Mästlin performed many astronomical calculations for Kepler's *Mysterium* – in particular, the distances of the planets from the sun.

[12] There were only six known planets until William Herschel discovered Uranus in 1781.

[13] Not only did the celestial spheres no longer exist in the minds of many astronomers, but for Copernicans, the cause of motion could no longer be the outmost "Primum mobile," which had accounted for the motion of the stars and the planets in ancient and medieval times.

[14] The scheme would work less successfully for Mercury, where Kepler found it necessary to make an ad hoc alteration to his scheme. Kepler lamented that "[Mercury] tormented me...with many twistings and toilings, in trying to explore its motion." (*Mysterium*). Kepler was not alone: the motion of Mercury would remain

problematic for astronomers and physicists until the twentieth century, when it would finally be addressed by applying Einstein's theory of general relativity.

[15] The justification that Kepler offers in the *Mysterium* for placing the Platonic solids seems strange to modern ears (and to most of his contemporaries as well). His rationalizations were related to the practice of "numerology" but as applied to geometry. For example, Kepler distinguished the five Platonic solids into two classes: The "primary solids" – the tetrahedron, the cube, and the dodecahedron, which have three faces that meet at their vertices; and the "secondary solids," the octahedron and the icosahedron, which have four and five faces that meet at their vertices. All the primary solids were positioned outside the sphere of the earth and the secondary solids beneath the sphere of the earth.

[16] An outer planet takes longer to complete its orbit than an inner planet for two reasons: (1) it has a longer path to complete and, (2) it moves more slowly on its path.

[17] Trans. Caspar/Hellman, 1948/1993.

[18] Kepler had a highly idiosyncratic religious cosmology: he believed that the universe was a spherical manifestation of God and of the Trinity. The sun represented the Father, the stationary outer sphere represented the Son, and the region in between represented the Holy Ghost.

[19] Graz is located in modern-day Austria and was, in Kepler's day, part of the Holy Roman Empire – a large confederation of hundreds of independent principalities, estates, and free cities that encompassed central Europe (lands that comprise modern-day Austria, Germany, the Czech Republic and parts of neighboring countries). By 1500, the Emperor of the Holy Roman Empire possessed only limited power to rule over the Empire. Instead, the independent states were effectively ruled by the local princes, landgraves, and bishops. The Emperor himself was elected by a select group of princes in the Empire called "Electors."

Luther's successful challenge to the Catholic Church was made possible by the internal power politics of the Holy Roman Empire. Many of the princes in the Empire had grown tired of the way the Catholic Church had been operating and were ready for a Reformation to occur – if not for religious reasons, then for political and economic ones. The princes endured the domination of the Catholic Church in both religious and secular affairs and believed that the Church was draining potential income by imposing costly tithes and indulgences on their subjects and by taking rents earned from Church ownership of valuable lands. Thus, resources that could have remained in their principalities were being syphoned off to Rome in order to underwrite the Italian Renaissance and increase the splendor of the Vatican. It was for reasons like these that Luther found himself protected by a powerful prince, and it is in large measure why his uprising was successful. Many other princes followed suit, and Luther's reformation spread to their principalities as well.

The religious fragmentation caused by the Lutheran Reformation created a great deal of tension within the Empire, because the Emperor and a large number of princes remained committed to defending the Catholic faith. The Emperor went to war with the Protestant princes over this issue, but over the long term failed to bring them and their territories back into the fold of the Catholic Church. In order to address the continuing instability that this caused within the Holy Roman Empire, an important compromise was reached: The Peace of Augsburg, 1555. This agreement gave each prince the authority to establish the religion of his realm as either Lutheran or Catholic – the religion of the principality was the religion of the prince. If his subjects didn't like it they would have to pack up and move to another principality.

Over the years, the Catholic Church reformed itself and launched its "Counter-Reformation," which was a concerted and sustained effort to educate and proselytize for the Catholic religion. In time, it won several Lutheran principalities back over to the Catholic faith through the conversion of its princes. Perhaps a prince was influenced by the arguments of a Catholic theologian, or perhaps a prince died and his son, the new prince, adopted the Catholic faith. In any case, the religion of the principality would change with the religion of the prince. This was the world that Kepler lived in, and he repeatedly found himself living in a former Lutheran principality that had suddenly became Catholic.

[20] Kepler was uniquely qualified to serve in this capacity. Years earlier, Kepler had corresponded with Tycho's opponent, a man named Ursus, who was the Emperor's astronomer. Kepler had sent a letter to Ursus in an effort to begin a correspondence with the socially well-placed astronomer and, in doing so, Kepler praised Ursus and his abilities profusely. Without Kepler's knowledge or permission, Ursus put Kepler's praises into print for all to read.

Before this time, Ursus had been a young guest of Tycho's on Hven, but he was expelled from the island when he was caught snooping around in Tycho's library and otherwise behaving strangely. Ursus later proposed a planetary theory similar to Tycho's, which Tycho accused him of plagiarizing. Ursus responded to Tycho's accusation in print with a vicious and slanderous personal attack on Tycho and his family. In Tycho's mind, Kepler was uniquely qualified to join the fray as a particularly well-positioned ally. When Kepler became Tycho's assistant, much of Kepler's time and energy was taken up with the composition of an essay designed to set the record straight. Tycho wished to be properly credited with the development of the geoheliocentric system and wanted Kepler to reveal Ursus's less than civilized behavior. Instead, Kepler produced a well-balanced piece of writing that was far less aggressive than what Tycho had hoped for. It was never published because both

Ursus and Tycho died soon after Kepler had written it. However, it is an extremely important document for historians of science, because it reveals a great deal about Kepler's philosophy of science, which does not appear prominently in his other works (Jardine, 1984).

[21] The other two potential heirs to Tycho's data had been distracted by their own careers. Longomontanus, Tycho's skilled right hand man, had recently left Tycho to take a position in Denmark. Tengnagel, Tycho's noble son-in law, was too busy engaged in politics and business to be able to use Tycho's data – even if he had the ability to do so. So, while neither Longomontanus nor Tengnagel saw eye-to-eye with Kepler, particularly with regard to his Copernicanism, they recognized his talent. Any money that would be earned from the use of Brahe's data to publish the *Rudolphine Tables* would be shared with the Brahe family, so their feeling towards Kepler was mixed – they wished him success at completing the *Tables*, but disliked his astronomical theory. During the many years that Kepler worked through Tycho's data, the Brahe family, particularly Tengnagel, interfered and delayed Kepler from publishing his works more than once. Both the Brahes and Kepler had control over any publication that was based on Tycho's data – at least until the *Tables* were published. In spite of the frustration this caused Kepler, he was aware of the great treasure he had in Tycho's data and believed that his possession of it was the result of divine fortune.

[22] Of course, most astronomers had *some* kind of physical ideas about why planets moved, whether it was Aristotelian, Ptolemaic or otherwise. Indeed, the handful of homocentric (concentric) shell astronomers that existed in the Renaissance adopted that view because they thought it was more physically plausible than the Ptolemaic mechanisms. And most (though not all) astronomers believed the spheres were real and that there were mechanisms that would allow spheres to turn in the ways that they did. It was, for example, an underlying assumption about the motion of the spheres that caused Copernicus to abandon the equant and to consider only uniform circular motion in his astronomical system. But these early and ancient physical ideas had only served as guides in a general sense; they didn't tell astronomers how many epicycles to use or whether an eccentric was better than an epicycle if they both did the job equally well.

Kepler proceeded very differently – perhaps because he was practicing Copernican astronomy right after the celestial spheres had been demolished by Mästlin and Brahe. If there were no spheres, then what would cause the regular motions of planets? Most astronomers didn't consider physical questions like this to even be part of their job. Kepler did. He began with an assumption about a spinning sun and solar lines of force and let that idea inform his new astronomy. So, what was "new" about his "New Astronomy" was that he allowed his celestial physics to guide his thinking about highly detailed aspects of planetary motion. It was this thinking that eventually led him to adopt the ellipse and his equal area law. It is unlikely he would have developed these ideas in the absence of the physical conceptual framework he was relying on.

[23] Keep in mind that Kepler did not have the modern Newtonian view that objects in motion stay in motion, so for Kepler and many of his contemporaries, something had to keep the planets moving. On one hand, this aspect of Kepler's physics was in line with traditional Aristotelian thinking; on the other, he did something very un-Aristotelian: he treated the planets like terrestrial objects by invoking a kind of magnetism as the cause of their motion, which was a terrestrial phenomenon.

[24] Galileo and Scheiner later confirmed (from their observation of sunspots) that the sun *did* spin on its axis. Both Kepler and Galileo were strongly influenced by William Gilbert, the English scientist who, in 1600, published a remarkable description and analysis of the magnetic lodestone, the compass, and the magnetic properties of the earth. The idea that there were magnetic lines of force had existed before Kepler applied them (or something analogous to them) to his physics of planetary motion.

[25] This would have been recognized by Kepler's readers as a pun – since antiquity Mars was known as the God of War.

[26] For detailed accounts of Kepler's "War on Mars," see Stephenson, 1987 and Voelkel, 2001.

[27] Kepler had also explored other rate laws, including an inverse distance relationship where the speed of the planet varied inversely to the distance from the sun. He eventually settled on this equal area equal time law, which, though difficult to calculate, gave excellent results.

[28] The planets in Copernicus's "sun-centered" system weren't centered exactly on the sun, but to the "mean sun" (the *average* solar position). Thus, in Copernicus's planetary theory, the planets effectively revolved around the empty center of the *earth's orbit*, which was very close to, but not directly located on the sun. Kepler thought this was absurd, in large part because he believed that the sun *caused* the motion of the planets. Kepler positioned one of the foci of each planet's ellipse directly on the sun, which then served as the planet's "true center" (the other focus of a planet's ellipse remained empty). This was a very important innovation that is often overlooked in introductory accounts of Kepler's work and it allowed Kepler to treat the longitudes and latitudes of the planets with a single theory, which was something that had never been done before.

[29] Iterative techniques continue to be used in physics today. For example, *ab initio* quantum mechanical calculations for the structure of molecules cannot be solved in a

single step but are done in a series of calculations that are repeated until the successive answers converge on an optimum value.

[30] Kepler (Caspar, 1948): "I would already have concluded my researches about world harmony, had not Tycho's astronomy so shackled me that I nearly went out of my mind...." And, "These eight minutes showed the way to a renovation of the whole of astronomy."

[31] The "conic sections" had been studied extensively by Apollonius of Perga (262-190 BCE), who was a gifted Hellenistic mathematician. His works were very well known in Renaissance Europe.

[32] The elliptical paths of Mars and the earth were in different planes and had their major axes pointed in different directions. Thus, Kepler's solution naturally provided both longitude and latitude positions for Mars and the other the planets. Earlier theories of planetary latitudes were not a natural consequence of the models that accounted for longitude.

[33] The orbits of Mercury and Mars were elliptical enough that it was essential for Kepler to use an ellipse for his calculations on those planets. In contrast, the orbit of the earth more closely approximates a circle.

[34] The *Epitome* (*Epitome astronomomiae Copernicanae*) was published in three parts, 1618-1621.

[35] Like Kepler's first two laws, the third law was not named as such until long after Kepler's death.

[36] The ratio of the period of two planets' orbits squared equals the ratio of their distances from the sun cubed. Or, as Kepler put it, " *The squares of the periodic times are to each other as the cubes of the mean distances.*" In modern notation: $P_1^2/P_2^2 = R_1^3/R_2^3$, where P is the period of a planet and R is its semi-major axis. Kepler also showed that the third law could be used to describe the orbits of the four moons of Jupiter around that planet. When astronomers later discovered moons of Saturn, they showed that the third law extended to those as well.

Put into words, the third law describes in a mathematically precise way how the planets, as they become increasingly distant from the sun, take a longer period of time to make a complete circuit. There are two reasons for this: 1) More distant planets have a greater distance to travel to make it around the sun, 2) the more distant planets are actually moving more slowly as well.

[37] Kepler in Lodge, 1905:

> What I prophesied two-and-twenty years ago, as soon as I discovered the
> five solids among the heavenly orbits – what I firmly believed long before
> I had seen Ptolemy's Harmonies – what I had promised my friends in the
> title of this book, which I named before I was sure of my discovery – what
> sixteen years ago, I urged as a thing to be sought – that for which I joined
> Tycho Brahe, for which I settled in Prague, for which I have devoted the
> best part of my life to astronomical contemplations, at length I have
> brought to light, and recognized its truth beyond my most sanguine
> expectations. It is not eighteen months since I got the first glimpse of
> light, three months since the dawn, very few days since the unveiled sun,
> most admirable to gaze upon, burst upon me. Nothing holds me; I will
> indulge my sacred fury; I will triumph over mankind by the honest
> confession that I have stolen the golden vases of the Egyptians to build up
> a tabernacle for my God far away from the confines of Egypt. If you
> forgive me, I rejoice; if you are angry, I can bear it; the die is cast, the
> book is written, to be read either now or by posterity, I care not which; it
> may well wait a century for a reader, as God has waited six thousand
> years for an observer.

[38] Kepler's third law cannot be mapped onto the Tychonic system, where the
correspondence between the mathematical relationship and the physical relationship
of the planets' distances and periods is seriously disrupted. As Kepler challenged his
Tychonic readers:

> What shall I say of the motion's periodic time of 365 days, intermediate
> in quantity between the periodic time of Mars of 687 days and that of
> Venus of 225 days? Does not the nature of things cry out with a great
> voice that the circuit in which these 365 days are used up also occupies a
> place intermediate between those of Mars and Venus about the sun and
> not of the sun about the earth? (*Astronomia nova*, trans. Donahue, 1992,
> pp. 53)

[39] Kepler had published some ephemerides, charts that reported daily planetary
positions, prior to the publication of his tables.

[40] Kepler responded to pressure to publish his tables with the statement, "I am as
eager for the publication as Germany is for peace." Caspar, 1948.

[41] Athanasius Kircher, 1641, said of Kepler, "concerning the mathematical, no one is
better and subtler than he; concerning the physical, no one is worse." (Applebaum,
1996.)

[42] Kepler, "It is artless, but the outcome is wholly determined and unique." (Voelkel, 2001.)

[43] This abrupt end to the hegemony of the circle in astronomy was likely due to a combination of factors – the weakening of the standard Aristotelian view of the "perfection of the cosmos," the striking success of Kepler's *Rudolphine Tables*, and the fact that the ellipse was one of the four conic sections (as was the circle). In this last sense, all Kepler had done was to exchange one idealized conic section for another.

[44] Recall that in Copernicus's original model, the earth was put into motion like the other planets, but it remained unique because it didn't possess a minor epicycle like the other planets did. Moreover, the earth's motion wasn't even centered on the sun in Copernicus's model, but on the "mean sun" which was slightly displaced from it. The motions of all of the planets were referenced to this empty center of the earth's motion (rather than directly on the sun). In these ways, the earth retained a special status in the Copernican system. This special status was removed in Kepler's astronomical system because all of the planets were placed on elliptical paths with one of their foci centered on the sun. They also followed the equal area rule – the earth was no exception.

On the other hand, from a cosmological perspective, Kepler continued to view the earth as a special part of Creation. In his view, God had placed the earth in a central location so that there were three astronomical bodies below us (the sun, Mercury, and Venus) and three astronomical bodies above us (Mars, Jupiter, and Saturn); thus, putting the earth and its inhabitants in the ideal location to appreciate Creation. Furthermore, in his nesting hypothesis, the earth retained a special place between these two classes of Platonic solids (see note 15).

[45] Giambattista Riccioli (1598 – 1671) was another astronomer who incorporated ellipses into a geocentric system.

[46] It is frequently noted that Galileo wrote many of his works in Italian in order to make his arguments evident to intelligent laypeople, who he believed could think as critically as academic philosophers. It is less well-appreciated that Kepler did the same thing by publishing some of his works in German.

[47] Caspar, 1948.

[48] Kepler, Johannes, *Somnium*, (translated by Rosen, Edward), 1634/1967.

Chapter Seven – Galileo Galilei: His Science and His Telescopic Discoveries

Galileo is one of the few scientists whose name is widely recognized by the general public. Many people are familiar with Galileo's famous telescopic discoveries and with his strong advocacy for the Copernican system – an activity which eventually led him into considerable trouble with the hierarchy of the Catholic Church. Of course, we will take an in-depth look at that episode, which is now known as the "Galileo Affair," but we will also consider the other important elements of his work. Indeed, most people are surprised to learn that until Galileo picked up the telescope at the age of 45 he wasn't an astronomer at all, but was instead a mathematician and physicist.

[Figure 7.1. Galileo at the age of forty. Painting by <u>Domenico Tintoretto</u>, 1605-1607). Public domain.]

Galileo's Early Life

Galileo Galilei (1564-1642) was born into a family of lesser nobility and of modest means in the Tuscan city of Pisa. His father, Vincenzo Galilei (ca.1525-1591), was a highly accomplished lute player and musicologist who made major contributions to music theory,[1] but who also struggled to make ends meet for his family and sold cloth on the side.

The Galilei family moved to nearby Florence when Galileo was ten. Like Pisa, Florence was part of the state of Tuscany, which was ruled by the powerful and wealthy de' Medici family. Florence was one of the centers of the Italian Renaissance and Galileo was able to receive an excellent education there – both formally and informally. In his teens, Galileo was enrolled in a monastery school and considered becoming a monk. However, before Galileo was able to take the vows, his father withdrew him. Vincenzo had no intention of letting his highly talented and oldest son live out his life as a monk. Instead, he groomed Galileo to be a physician, which was a reliably lucrative vocation that could provide the necessary income to support an extended family. So, in 1581 Galileo enrolled at the University at Pisa where he studied medicine. The standard medical school curriculum at this time was centered on the traditional theories of the authoritative Greek doctor Galen (129-199 CE), but it also included the subjects of philosophy, astronomy, and astrology. Medical students studied basic astronomy so that they would be able to cast horoscopes for their patients. In Galileo's day, astrology was an essential component of diagnostic medicine.

Galileo's first significant encounter with the study of higher mathematics began when he was home in Florence on break from his university studies. By his own account, he overheard a lecture on mathematics given by Ostilio Ricci to some pages at the Tuscan court, after which he began to study the subject on his own. Ricci soon recognized that Galileo had a special aptitude for mathematics and, before long, both petitioned Galileo's father to allow him to study it. An active intellectual himself, Vincenzo Galilei understood his son's wishes, but he was also a practical man who knew that it would be difficult for a mathematician to support an extended family. For that reason, the father pressured his son to continue the pursuit of a medical degree, although he did permit Galileo to study mathematics on the side. In the end, it was the mathematics that won out and Galileo left the University of Pisa without a degree. Galileo then began working hard to establish himself as a professional mathematician and to secure a teaching position at a university. Before we consider Galileo's intellectual and professional trajectory, we will first consider some of the influences on his thought.

Intellectual and Cultural Influences on Galileo's Thinking

Although Galileo was no longer at the university and was focusing his attention primarily on mathematics, he continued to read and study the works of Plato, Aristotle, and other philosophers. Nearly all of Galileo's contemporaries adhered to the natural philosophy of Aristotle in one form or another. Recall from Chapter Three that in the Middle Ages Aristotelian thought had been modified for Catholic use by St. Thomas Aquinas. By the late Renaissance this Aristotelian-Thomistic synthesis had been long since established as the officially sanctioned philosophy and was taught by Catholic Jesuit teachers in hundreds of Jesuit schools and universities across Europe.

In spite of this, "Thomism" was not the only version of Aristotelian thought that circulated in Galileo's day. Renaissance scholars had gained access to a large number of Greek texts that had been brought to Italy from the declining Byzantine Empire. These included authors like Plato, Leucippus, Zeno, Epicurus, Pyrro, and Plotinus – to name just a few. This expansion of the Greek tradition fostered a broader range of philosophical and scientific thought. And while Aristotelianism continued to be the dominant philosophical viewpoint, there was no longer a single version of it. Indeed, many Renaissance Aristotelians had strayed far enough from Thomism that it troubled the Church and caught the attention of the Inquisition (indeed, one of Galileo's professors at Pisa spent time in prison for his transgressions). However, even with this greater diversity of opinion, the main features of Aristotelian thought remained intact and continued to be shared by university philosophers. Some of the central and universally shared tenets of Aristotelian natural philosophy were: 1) the universe is spherical with the Earth at its center, 2) the physical nature of the celestial and terrestrial realms are different, and 3) the motion of all objects required some kind of cause – whether natural or violent.

For our purposes, any natural philosophers who did not hold the central tenets listed above, particularly the first two, will not be considered an Aristotelian – even though they continued to hold some Aristotelian ideas (as we will see, even Galileo retained vestiges of Aristotelian thought). So, when we use the term "Aristotelian," we refer to people who adhered to the fundamental features of Aristotelianism – even if they may have differed about the details. From our perspective, the two most important internal disagreements between Aristotelian natural philosophers involved questions about the reality of the crystalline spheres and the cause of projectile motion.

Galileo turned his back on Aristotelian natural philosophy at a very early stage in his career and followed a path that was considerably different from those of his academic contemporaries. This seems to have begun at home where he was exposed to an uncommon collection of experiences and ideas.

Galileo's Father
Vincenzo Galilei was a professional musician, expert lute player, composer, and music theoretician. Galileo was frequently enlisted to accompany his father in lute playing and was known to be a highly accomplished amateur. Vincenzo's second oldest son, Michelangelo Galilei (1575-1631), became a professional lutenist and composer and had a successful professional career in Poland and in the Holy Roman Empire.

Vincenzo Galilei is recognized as an important figure in the development of late Renaissance music and as a contributor to the development of what later became Baroque music. However, it is Vincenzo's work in music theory that interests us here. Vincenzo became interested in music theory because he knew that professional musicians and singers did not allow their work to be limited by theoretical constraints. The existing musical theory of harmony and tuning had been based on the ancient theories of the Pythagoreans and Ptolemy. Vincenzo's teacher, Zarlino, attempted to expand music theory by elaborating on that ancient system. Vincenzo, in contrast, approached the problem by considering the actual practices of contemporary musicians and used that to inform his new theory of music. His attention was drawn to musical relationships that sounded pleasing, but which weren't explainable within existing theory. He also investigated problems that arose in tuning instruments – particularly those that occurred when different types of instruments were played together. In Galilei's way of thinking, it was better to accommodate music theory to the ear than it was to accommodate the ear to a flawed theory of music.

To address the problems of tuning, Vincenzo conducted some basic investigations into the relationship between the physical conformation of an instrument and the sounds that it made. In an experimental study of stringed instruments, he determined the relationship between string tension and pitch in a mathematically precise way for the first time. To do this, he placed a known amount of tension on a string by hanging a standardized weight from it and then identified the resulting pitch by plucking it. By varying the amount of weight on a string, Vincenzo was able to relate its pitch to the string tension. He discovered that the pitch was not proportional to the string tension, as had been previously believed, but it was instead proportional to the *square root* of the string tension.

Learning about the precise mathematical association between pitch and string tension is not as important to us as appreciating the novelty and nature of Vincenzo's accomplishment: He carefully designed his experiments to uncover the precise mathematical relationships that existed between different physical magnitudes. In doing so, he was able to effectively challenge a well-accepted and long-standing theoretical viewpoint. None of what Vincenzo had accomplished was commonplace. He announced his new results and theories in his *Dialogo della musica antica e moderna* and in other manuscripts,[2] and he often adopted an aggressive and argumentative posture toward those who held a different opinion (particularly towards his former teacher, Zarlino). Vincenzo's famous son, Galileo, would later be known for conducting himself in a similar manner, although the nature of Galileo's discoveries would be much farther-reaching than those of his father.

It is very well worth noting that Vincenzo was conducting his acoustics experiments at about the same time that Galileo had returned home from the University of Pisa. Undoubtedly, Galileo knew about the experiments, probably witnessed them, and may have even helped conduct some of them.[3] In any case, his father's experimental and mathematically descriptive approach for addressing a theoretical controversy, along with his willingness to publicly challenge a well-entrenched view, was an important lesson for the young Galileo.

Other Philosophers and Mathematicians

The Renaissance fascination with ancient literature, philosophy, science, and mathematics resulted in the rediscovery and translation of many literary and scientific works from antiquity. At the same time, newer and better translations superseded older ones in order to satisfy a continuing appetite for ancient authors. One important consequence of this activity was that lesser-known works and authors came increasingly into view for Renaissance thinkers – as did the richness and diversity of other elements of ancient thought.

Instead of limiting himself to the work of philosophers, Galileo was drawn to the works of two outstanding Hellenistic mathematicians: Euclid of Alexandria (fl. 300 BCE) and Archimedes of Syracuse (287-212 BCE). Euclid was a mathematician who unified geometry as a coherent logical system. Archimedes lived and worked in the generation that followed Euclid's, and he benefited from the mathematical advances made by Euclid and others. Archimedes was a remarkable mathematician who extended the subject into a number of new fields, including an early attempt at the development of calculus. He is still considered to be one of the greatest mathematicians of all time, but because his work was highly technical and appreciated only by other skilled mathematicians, it eventually fell out of circulation and was nearly lost.[4] While Archimedes' passion was for pure mathematics, he was also renowned for his military inventions and routinely mixed the theoretical with the practical. In sixteenth-century Italy, a group of men had recovered Archimedes' mathematics by translating and publishing some of his works into Latin. One of these men was the famous Renaissance mathematician Tartaglia – reportedly a teacher of Ostillio Ricci.[5]

Getting a Job

In order to land a university position, Galileo needed to produce new mathematical works impressive enough to gain the attention of well-established mathematicians. He rose to the challenge by tackling a number of problems in applied mathematics – including one that dealt with the center of gravity in solid bodies.

Desperate to gain influential patrons, Galileo traveled to Rome to share the results of his work with the renowned Jesuit scholar Christopher Clavius. Clavius (1538-1612) was the chief mathematician for the Collegio Romano, which was the flagship campus for Jesuit colleges around the world.[6] Clavius considered Galileo's work carefully and was supportive – however, the logic of Galileo's proof eluded him, and he advised Galileo to get another opinion. Galileo then approached the highly regarded mathematician Guidobaldo del Monte, who, only after a careful second look, enthusiastically endorsed his work.[7] Del Monte was so moved by the brilliant reasoning in Galileo's proof that he immediately recognized Galileo as his equal and worked hard to help him secure an academic position. Del Monte proved to be one of Galileo's most reliable and persistent supporters and helped Galileo land his first position at the University of Pisa in 1589.

The pay at the University of Pisa was meager, but Galileo had gotten his foot in the door. During the three years that followed, Galileo began some of his early work on the physics of motion – including, if the story is true, the dropping of objects of unequal weights from the leaning tower of Pisa.[8] Traditional philosophers had held the opinion that heavy objects fall faster than lighter ones. Galileo arrived at a very different conclusion – one that put him greatly at odds with Aristotelians.[9]

We have only fragments of Galileo's work during this Pisan period, but we do know from these early writings there that he already held strongly anti-Aristotelian ideas about motion. He was also clearly influenced by Archimedes and by some of his contemporaries who also admired Archimedes.[10] It is also apparent that Galileo had already managed to aggravate university philosophers by criticizing Aristotle – the central subject of their discipline. From their point of view, the *mathematician* Galileo was not qualified to discuss philosophy let alone to find fault in the greatest philosopher who ever lived. In essence, Galileo had encroached upon their turf. Since the philosophy professors were among the most powerful in the university (along with the medical professors), it soon became clear that Galileo would not be invited to continue on at the university after his contract expired.[11] With nothing to lose, Galileo wrote a very humorous and extremely irreverent poem that poked fun at the wearing of the traditional academic toga. The toga was the traditional uniform of university professors and Galileo had been fined for not wearing it. Clearly, his unconventional views extended well beyond physics...

Galileo's father died while he was at Pisa, leaving Galileo as the head of the household. From this point on, Galileo was responsible for supporting the needs of an extended family – including the obligation to provide large dowries for his sisters' weddings and to offer periodic support to his musically talented but forever broke younger brother Michelangelo. Fortunately, after only three years working at Pisa, and with no prospect of being asked to continue, Galileo won a better position at the University of Padua in the Venetian Republic. Even so, with his burdensome family obligations, Galileo remained on the lookout for opportunities to increase his income. He augmented his salary in Padua by tutoring, taking on student boarders, and by designing and selling new instruments that he had manufactured in his shop.

It was in nearby Venice that Galileo met the young Marina Gamba. Galileo had a long-term relationship with Marina that resulted in three children born out of wedlock: two daughters and a son. Marina's low social standing precluded the upwardly mobile Galileo from marrying her. In any case, it was not uncommon for university professors to remain bachelors. Galileo supported his illegitimate family: he arranged for the security of convent life for his daughters[12] and had his son formally legitimized. Such informal family arrangements, especially those that crossed class lines, were not uncommon in the seventeenth century, and caused little scandal.

Galileo at Padua
At Padua, Galileo continued work on new ideas in physics while he taught and attended to his projects. He spent a great deal of his time teaching private students the "practical arts" of basic spherical astronomy, mathematics, mechanics, and military engineering. He designed and produced a popular new calculating sector (compass) and printed an instruction manual for its use. He even invented a horse-powered water

pump, which he had patented. All of these activities demonstrated Galileo's ambition, energy, and breadth of interest and skill.[13] They were also a reflection of his need for additional income.

It is clear that Galileo adopted the Copernican viewpoint early on – perhaps prior to arriving in Padua. The earliest written evidence for his Copernicanism is found in 1595 in the private writings of a friend who described Galileo's theory of tides in his notebook.[14] According to Galileo, the movement of water in large seas resulted from the combined motion of the earth spinning on its axis as it revolved around the sun. The two motions, taken together, caused the water in the earth's seas to slosh back and forth in an east-west direction as it moved around the sun. It would be many years before Galileo would present his theory of tides publicly – but when he did, it would serve as one of his central arguments in support of Copernicanism.

In 1597, Galileo admitted his preference for the Copernican system in letters to two correspondents. One of these letters was written to thank Johannes Kepler for sending him a copy of the *Mysterium cosmographicum*. When Galileo read the first few pages of the book he learned that Kepler was a deeply committed Copernican. In a hastily written letter to Kepler (the courier was returning to Germany), Galileo promised to read the rest of the *Mysterium*.[15] He confided to Kepler that he too held the Copernican opinion but hadn't announced it publicly because of its unpopularity:

> I have been for many years an adherent of the Copernican system, and it explains to me the causes of many of the appearances of nature which are quite unintelligible on the commonly accepted hypothesis. I have collected many arguments for the purpose of refuting the latter; but I do not venture to bring them to the light of publicity, for fear of sharing the fate of our master, Copernicus, who, although he has earned immortal fame with some, yet with very many (so great is the number of fools) has become an object of ridicule and scorn. (trans. Sturge in Gebler, 1879).

Galilean Physics and the Nova of 1604

On October 9, 1604, a new star shone brightly in the constellation of Sagittarius. It appeared near the conjunction of Saturn and Jupiter, which marked the beginning of an astrologically important period. These planets were also joined by Mars at the very same time, which made for a rare event that rendered the nova's appearance all the more conspicuous. Galileo and Kepler had each seen "Tycho's nova" of 1572 as children. Since that time, many astronomers had concluded that the nova of 1572 had been located far into the celestial realm,[16] although many dedicated Aristotelian philosophers continued to argue for the contrary view.[17]

Galileo enthusiastically welcomed the appearance of the nova of 1604 and it is worth taking the time here to understand why. If we consider his activity up to 1604, it is notable that Galileo had done little to publicly promote his work in physics – even though he was already forty years old and had devoted his entire career to the discipline. There are likely two reasons he had hesitated to publish his views at this time: The main reason was that his work was not yet complete. While he had managed to make a substantial amount of progress, he was not yet satisfied with what he had accomplished – there were simply too many loose ends remaining. The second reason for avoiding publication was the overwhelming authority of the Aristotelian view, which would have seriously prejudiced people against anything that Galileo had to say about physics. In this sense, Galileo was cautious and conservative as a scientist. If he had taken a stand early on, his ideas, which were those of a mere mathematician, would not have gotten a warm reception. The Aristotelian tradition was still too strong and Galileo's work too weak for him to weather a public dispute about physics. He chose to wait for another day before exposing his efforts to scrutiny.

It is worth taking some time to contrast the Aristotelian system with the new approach to physics that Galileo was taking. At this time, "physics" as an independent subject did not exist; rather, it was a part of Aristotelian philosophy. The appeal of the Aristotelian view was that it provided a single comprehensive theory of everything and it would be difficult for Galileo or anyone else to seriously challenge it. On the other hand, it is important to appreciate that Galileo never intended to replace the Aristotelian system with another *system*. Instead, he pursued a very different goal – the development of a descriptive mathematical physics that would exist independent of philosophy. What Galileo had hoped to achieve was much narrower in scope than the comprehensive system he was challenging.

Galileo's strategy for the investigation of nature was to study a particular phenomenon closely and attempt to describe it using geometry or mathematics. In this way, he could know more precisely what it was that he was observing. The disadvantage to Galileo's approach was that he didn't always offer explanations for the phenomena he observed. In short, he might know very well what was happening but not know *why* it happened. For Aristotelians, philosophizing about nature meant offering explanations – it was the whole point of philosophizing! To them, Galileo's effort would have seemed pointless; applying mathematics to nature held no promise of telling them anything they didn't already know. Besides, mathematics was the sort of thing that tradespeople did – engineers, architects, assayers, bookkeepers, and others. It was an activity that was beneath the dignity and station of an academic philosopher, but was instead for people who were accustomed to getting their hands dirty. In order for Galileo to make progress within this intellectual environment, he needed to convince his audience that physics without philosophy was a worthwhile venture.

Let's consider an important example of the difference between the Galilean and Aristotelian approaches to physics by considering the case of falling objects. Because objects fall too quickly to accurately measure their progress, Galileo retarded the phenomenon artificially by rolling balls down inclined planes and measuring their position as time passed. He altered the steepness of the incline planes and used his results to extrapolate the process to freely falling objects. In doing this, he was able to uncover a mathematical regularity in the relationship between the length of time an object traveled and the distance it traveled, which described falling objects in general.[18]

What Galileo did not attempt to do, however, was to explain *why* objects fell. In contrast, the Aristotelians offered an explanation for why they fell (the element earth was seeking its natural place at the center of the universe), but they did not offer a mathematical description of *how* they fell. In their mind, they already knew what caused motion so there was no pressing reason to measure it. From Galileo's point of view, the

Aristotelians were premature in offering an explanation since they didn't understand, in a precise way, how things actually fell.

The Nova of 1604

Astronomers determined that the nova of 1604, like the nova of 1572, showed no measurable parallax. That meant that the novae had to be very far away – certainly beyond the moon and perhaps even among the stars. This conclusion was a serious challenge to Aristotelian belief because Aristotle had maintained that no change ever occurred in the celestial realm. Could Aristotle be wrong? Some Aristotelian philosophers defended his view by explaining that the novae had always been there, but for one reason or another just hadn't been visible before.[19] Other philosophers ignored the conclusions of the astronomers and refused to acknowledge that the novae were located in the celestial realm at all.[20] With the Aristotelian view presenting a significant barrier to the acceptance of Copernicanism and to his work in physics, Galileo could not let the opportunity pass – he gave well-attended public lectures that supported the conclusion of the astronomers: The novae were new celestial objects, and Aristotle had been wrong.

Galileo's message inspired the publication of an interesting literary-scientific work entitled, *Dialogue Concerning the New Star*, published in 1605 under the pseudonym Cecco di Ronchitti. It is possible that Galileo was involved in the publication of the work since one of his associates had edited it.[21] It was written in a rough rural Paduan dialect, which suggested that uneducated farmers could reason better and more freely than the close-minded and bookish university philosophers. It was a sarcastic but effective literary device used to attack the Aristotelian philosophers from a distance.

After the nova declined in brilliance and the debate over its physical nature declined with it, Galileo continued to teach students, refine his theory of motion, and work on new inventions – including an early thermometer and the modification of a naturally occurring magnetic lodestone. Through trial-and-error, Galileo had managed to increase the lodestone's strength significantly by surrounding it with different shaped pieces of metal. Like Kepler, Galileo was greatly inspired by William

Gilbert's scientific work on the magnet, which had been published in 1600.

The Dutch Spyglass

In 1608 reports of a "spyglass" reached Italy from the Netherlands.[22] The device was a by-product of European spectacle-making where convex lenses were used for correcting farsightedness and concave lenses for nearsightedness. The "Dutch spyglass" was a combination of one convex lens and one concave lens that were placed at opposite ends of a tube.[23] Early spyglasses of this kind were limited to magnifications of two or three times that of normal sight and were sometimes described as toy-like. Upon hearing of the invention, Galileo thought he could do better and began fashioning one for himself. With the skill and perseverance of an experienced inventor, he went into his shop and began to grind lenses.

After fashioning dozens of lenses and selecting the best, Galileo managed to produce a significantly improved version of the device. His improved "telescope" (as it would later be called)[24] was capable of magnifying the images of objects by eight or nine times their actual size. Not surprisingly, Galileo found a way to cash in on his invention: He demonstrated its military value to Venetian authorities by showing them that ships traveling toward Venice could be seen long before they were visible to the naked eye. He also donated a high quality instrument to the Venetian Republic. His effort paid a large dividend: he was granted a permanent position at the University of Padua at twice his previous salary. Galileo described his successes to his brother-in law, Benedetto Landucci:

> I made a spy-glass which far surpasses the report of the Flanders one. As the news had reached Venice that I had made such an instrument, six days ago I was summoned before their highnesses the signoria, and exhibited it to them, to the astonishment of the whole senate. Many noblemen and senators, although of a great age, mounted the steps of the highest church towers at Venice, in order to see sails and shipping that were so far off that it was two hours before they were seen steering full sail into the harbor without my spy-glass. (trans. Sturge in Gebler, 1879).

Galileo continued to improve upon the early telescope by learning to grind lenses with better curvatures. He eventually succeeded at creating devices that were capable of magnifying objects up to thirty times their normal size, though it appears that some of his most useful telescopes had a magnification of about twenty.[25] There has been some debate over who invented the telescope. Many people have accused Galileo of stealing the invention from someone else, though Galileo never claimed to be its original discoverer. He did, however, take full credit for skillfully transforming the device into a useful scientific instrument. After reaping the financial rewards of his telescope, Galileo turned it toward the sky and made an astonishing series of new discoveries. In order to establish priority for his observations, he quickly published descriptions of them in a little book called *Sidereus Nuncius* or, *The Starry Messenger*.[26] These are some of the things that he saw:

The Moon

To the naked eye, the full moon appears mottled with light and dark patches so that some people might detect a figure resembling a "man in the moon" or others, the outline of a rabbit. The moon also exhibits partial phases over the course of a month – the cause having been understood since antiquity: The moon is a spherical body having no light of its own, but instead receives its light from the sun. Thus, only half of the moon is illuminated – the side facing the sun. Since the moon revolves around the earth, its illuminated side sometimes faces towards us, sometimes faces away, and most often shows us some fraction of its illuminated side.[27] Along with the geometric explanation for the lunar phases, the Aristotelians had an additional belief: They presumed that the moon was, like all celestial objects, perfectly spherical and flawless. The celestial-terrestrial distinction was one of the most fundamental Aristotelian expectations of the natural world.

When Galileo observed the moon telescopically it was, more often than not, in one of its partial phases. To the naked eye, the light-dark boundary line in a lunar partial phase is smooth and well-defined. However, when viewed through a telescope, Galileo found that the boundary instead had a ragged appearance. See one of Galileo's lunar drawings in figure 7.2.[28]

Galileo also noted that there were small spots close to the light-dark boundary. On the dark side of the boundary there were small illuminated spots and on the bright side of the boundary there were small dark spots. Since the light-dark boundary existed where lunar sunrises or sunsets were occurring, Galileo believed that the boundary's irregular shape and the associated spots were caused by the tops of tall lunar mountains and deep lunar valleys. During the lunar sunrise and sunset, the mountain tops would remain lit longer and the valleys would remain dark longer than the surrounding landscape – just as occurs in mountainous areas on the earth during dawn and dusk. Galileo had pointed his telescope into the celestial realm and discovered a terrestrial landscape! It was anything but the perfectly smooth sphere that the Aristotelians expected.

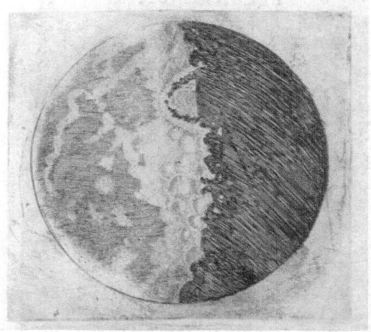

[Figure 7.2. A drawing of the moon in Galileo's hand from his booklet, *Sidereus Nuncius* (The Starry Messenger), 1610. Image courtesy of History of Science Collections, University of Oklahoma Libraries.]

"Earthshine"

Galileo also more closely investigated a phenomenon that was well-known prior to the invention of the telescope: During the thin crescent lunar phases that occur just before and just after new moon, the unlit portion of the moon is clearly visible – even if it appears only faintly (see a modern photo of the phenomenon in figure 7.3).

Natural philosophers had offered a variety of explanations for why the crescent moon had this appearance. One common explanation was that the moon was partially translucent and that some of the sun's rays passed through it. Another was that the planet Venus provided the light that faintly illuminated the dark half of the moon. But both of these explanations suffered from serious objections (particularly the last one). For this reason, Michael Mästlin had offered another explanation for this effect: he believed that the phenomenon was caused by light reflecting off of the surface of the earth, which then faintly illuminated the lunar surface.

[Figure 7.3. A picture of earthshine during a conjunction of Venus (in upper left hand corner) with the moon. Image courtesy Claude Schneider, Wikimedia Commons.]

Galileo investigated the phenomenon with his telescope. By partially obstructing his view of the moon to avoid the visual distraction of the bright crescent, he was able to observe only the dark region of the moon through his telescope (in the same way that you can use your hand to cover up the lit, lower right-hand portion of the moon in the picture above). When his eyes adjusted to the darkness, an illuminated lunar surface appeared to him. Where was the light coming from? Galileo adopted Mästlin's earlier explanation: The moon is illuminated by light reflected off the surface of the earth![29] This analysis also accounted for why the effect was most pronounced during a thin crescent phase: When the moon was in that position, the earth would appear to be nearly full and very bright in the lunar sky (see figure 7.4 and note 27 for a discussion of lunar phases).

[Figure 7.4, Earthshine showing the reflected light from the earth illuminating the surface of the "dark" side of the moon in one of its crescent phases. Figure courtesy Gringer, Wikimedia Commons.]

In his *Starry Messenger*, Galileo described how the moon and the earth share each other's reflected light and how this sharing of light changes as the moon moves around the earth over the course of a month:

> What must we assert? Shall we assert that the body of the moon, or some other dark and sunless orb, receives light from the earth? Why should it not be the moon? And most certainly it is. The earth, with fair and grateful exchange, pays back to the moon an illumination like that which it receives from the moon nearly the whole time during the darkest gloom of night. Let me explain the matter more clearly. At conjunction, when the moon occupies a position between the sun and the earth, the moon is illuminated by the sun's rays on her half towards the sun which is turned away from the earth, and the other half, with which she regards the earth, is covered with darkness, and so in no degree illumines the earth's surface. When the moon has slightly separated from the sun, straightway she is partly illumined on the half directed towards us; she turns towards us a slender silvery crescent, and slightly illumines the earth; the sun's illumination increases upon the moon as she approaches her first quarter, and the reflexion of that light increases on the earth; the brightness in the moon next extends beyond the semicircle, and our nights grow brighter; at length the entire face

of the moon looking towards the earth is irradiated with the most intense brightness by the sun, which happens when the sun and moon are on opposite sides of the earth; then far and wide the surface of the earth shines with the flood of moonlight; after this the moon, now waning, sends out less powerful beams, and the earth is illumined less powerfully; at length the moon draws near her first position of conjunction with the sun, and forthwith black night invades the earth. In such a cycle the moonlight gives us each month alternations of brighter and fainter illumination. But the benefit of her fight to the earth is balanced and repaid by the benefit of the light of the earth to her; for while the moon is found near the sun about the time of conjunction, she has in front of her the entire surface of that hemisphere of the earth which is exposed to the sun, and vividly illumined with his beams, and so receives light reflected from the earth. Owing to such reflexion, the hemisphere of the moon nearer to us, though deprived of sunlight, appears of considerable brightness. Again, when removed from the sun through a quadrant, the moon sees only one-half of the earth's hemisphere illuminated, namely the western half, for the other, the eastern, is covered with the shades of night; the moon is, therefore, less brightly enlightened by the earth, and accordingly that secondary light appears fainter to us. (trans. Carlos, 1880).

The significance of Mästlin's "earthshine" explanation, and Galileo's confirmation of it, isn't readily obvious to us today. Galileo's support for the Copernican system was multifaceted, and it addressed a wide range of beliefs in order to win over potential converts to the Copernican side. The earthshine analysis challenged a fundamental Aristotelian expectation – and it did so both philosophically and psychologically. On a *philosophical* level, the earthshine analysis presumed that the earth reflects light in the same way as the moon and planets do. The resulting implication was that the physical properties of the earth and the physical properties of celestial objects were very similar. But there was also a subtle *psychological* element to the analysis: Anyone who followed the earthshine argument was forced to change their reference point and visualize the phases of the earth from the surface of the moon. This change of reference point could also have caused a person to view the moon as a place on which they might stand and view the earth as a kind of celestial object – even if for only very briefly. So while the earthshine analysis didn't serve as proof for the Copernican system, at the very least it helped to further undermine the celestial/terrestrial distinction of the Aristotelian view. And there was more...

Beyond the Moon

Before the advent of the telescope, planets and stars were often distinguishable by their visual appearances – stars tended to "twinkle" while planets shone steadily.[30] When Galileo looked at them through his telescope, stars and planets still appeared to be different from each other, but in a new way – he saw that planets revealed themselves as small but distinct moon-like disks, whereas stars appeared to be smaller and "blazed" – shooting out beams and sparkling. But other telescopic observers soon began reporting disk sizes for stars and eventually Galileo detected them too. Through their telescopes the brighter stars appeared to be larger, and dimmer stars appeared to be smaller.[31] The apparent size of a star was very important to the geocentric-heliocentric debate.

One of the arguments leveled against the Copernican system, and a favorite of Tycho Brahe's, was that the Copernican system required stars to be unbelievably large. The reasoning was as follows: If stars were as far away as the Copernicans said they were (a necessity due to the absence of stellar parallax) and in order for them to have the apparent visual diameter that they did, then the stars in a Copernican Universe had to be physically gigantic. Tycho estimated, using Copernican distances, that the brightest stars had diameters larger than the orbit of Saturn around the sun! Galileo claimed that stellar disk sizes were much smaller than his opponents claimed, and he performed an ingenious non-telescopic experiment that supported his view. His conclusion was that stellar diameters were similar to that of our sun.[32] However, the arguments he used to support that view were not entirely conclusive, and the issue of stellar sizes remained an unsettled matter.

Galileo also reported seeing a tremendous number of new stars through his telescope that had never been observed before. To demonstrate how many new stars there were, he carefully examined small portions of the sky and then recorded the positions of the newly visible stars alongside of the positions of stars that had been known since antiquity.[33]

As one example, Galileo examined an asterism known as the Pleiades, in which most people are able to identify either six, seven or nine stars without the aid of a telescope (the number of stars seen depends on the quality of one's eyesight). By using his telescope, Galileo identified an additional forty stars in the Pleiades that were too faint to be seen with the naked eye.

[Figure 7.5. Galileo's diagram of the Pleiades from the Starry Messenger, 1610. Public domain.]

Galileo also noted that the Milky Way, which to the naked-eye has a cloud-like appearance, was largely made up of innumerable stars (though portions of it retained its cloudy appearance and could not be resolved into individual stars).

Jupiter

Galileo then turned his telescope toward the planet Jupiter, which was in opposition when he viewed it in January 1610 (recall that opposition is when a superior planet is closest to the earth, at its brightest, and in retrograde motion against the background of the stars). Galileo described what he saw in his *Starry Messenger*.

On the 7th day of January in the present year, 1610, in the first hour of the following night, when I was viewing the constellations of the heavens through a telescope, the planet Jupiter presented itself to my view, and as

I had prepared for myself a very excellent instrument, I noticed a circumstance which I had never been able to notice before, owing to want of power in my other telescope, namely, that three little stars, small but very bright, were near the planet; and although I believed them to belong to the number of the fixed stars, yet they made me somewhat wonder, because they seemed to be arranged exactly in a straight line, parallel to the ecliptic, and to be brighter than the rest of the stars, equal to them in magnitude. The position of them with reference to one another and to Jupiter was as follows. (trans. Carlos, 1880).

[Figure 7.6a. *Starry Messenger*. Public domain.]

At first, Galileo believed that these faint stars were "fixed stars" that just happened to be located near Jupiter. However, on the next night, they remained close to Jupiter even though Jupiter had moved through the zodiac. On this night, they were all located on Jupiter's western side.

[Figure 7.6b. *Starry Messenger*. Public domain.]

Since Jupiter was in the midst of its retrograde motion (moving in an east-to-west direction through the zodiac), Galileo had expected the newly observed fixed stars to appear *east* of Jupiter on this second evening – not to the west as he found them. Galileo was intrigued by this and continued to observe Jupiter and the "stars" intently through the course of many nights. He found that there were always two, three, or four "stars" and that they were all lined up with each other and with Jupiter. Most importantly, the "stars" followed Jupiter on its retrograde motion through the zodiac and appeared to be tethered to it. Galileo soon recognized them for what they were: moons of Jupiter.[34]

The discovery of Jupiter's moons had important implications for the reception of Copernican theory. Before this time, geocentric astronomers had a critical question for Copernicans: If the earth is indeed a planet, then why is it the only one that possesses a satellite of its own? Wouldn't it be easier to believe that that there is only one center of motion in the cosmos and that the moon and everything else went around the earth? This was an exceptional feature of the Copernican system: The earth had a satellite while the other planets did not, which reinforced geocentrists' doubts that the earth had anything in common with planets. However, when Galileo discovered that Jupiter also had moons, he showed that planets in motion could indeed carry lesser planets (moons) along with them as they traveled. By demonstrating this he demonstrated that the earth was not an exception in the Copernican system; rather, it had something in common with the other planets. Galileo put it thus:

> We have a notable and splendid argument to remove the scruples of those who can tolerate the revolution of the planets round the sun in the Copernican system, yet are so disturbed by the motion of one moon about the earth, while both accomplish an orbit of a year's length about the sun, that they consider that this theory of the constitution of the universe must be upset as impossible; for now we have not one planet only revolving about another, while both traverse a vast orbit about the sun, but our sense of sight presents to us four satellites circling about Jupiter, like the moon about the earth, while the whole system travels over a mighty orbit about the sun in the space of twelve years. (trans. Carlos, 1880).

Although Galileo wrote *Starry Messenger* with the main motivation of claiming the telescopic discoveries as his own, he did not shy away from pointing out how his discoveries put the Copernican system into a more favorable light.

Critics and Supporters of Galileo's Starry Messenger
Starry Messenger sold out within a week of being printed. It created quite a stir and people quickly realized that it had major implications for the debate over cosmological systems. The British ambassador to Venice, Henry Wotton, sent a report about Galileo's discoveries to the Earl of Salisbury in England,[35] as well as a copy of *Starry Messenger* to King James I.

Now touching the occurrents of the present, I send herewith unto his Majesty the strangest piece of news (as I may justly call it) that he hath ever yet received from any part of the world; which is the annexed book (come abroad this very day) of the Mathematical Professor at Padua, who by the help of an optical instrument (which both enlargeth and approximateth the object) invented first in Flanders, and bettered by himself, hath discovered four new planets rolling about the sphere of Jupiter, besides many other unknown fixed stars; likewise, the true cause of the Via Lactea [Milky Way], so long searched; and lastly, that the moon is not spherical, but endued with many prominences, and, which is of all the strangest, illuminated with the solar light by reflection from the body of the earth, as he seemeth to say. So as upon the whole subject he hath first overthrown all former astronomy — for we must have a new sphere to save the appearances — and next all astrology. For the virtue of these new planets must needs vary the judicial part, and why may there not yet be more? These things I have been bold thus to discourse unto your Lordship, whereof here all corners are full. And the author runneth a fortune to be either exceeding famous or exceeding ridiculous. By the next ship your Lordship shall receive from me one of the above-named instruments, as it is bettered by this man.

In his letter, Wotton portrayed Galileo's reports as true, but then near the end, prudently left open the possibility that Galileo might make a fool of himself. Other people were far more doubtful of Galileo's fantastic descriptions, and they refused to believe that his reports could be true at all. This skepticism was not something that Galileo could quickly or easily remedy, since he was one of the few people who had access to a telescope. He worked diligently to solve this problem by manufacturing and distributing telescopes to key figures in Europe, but it was a slow and laborious task. The chief hang-up was that only a small percentage of the lenses he produced were of a sufficient quality to be included in his telescopes.

Furthermore, Galileo did not share his telescope production techniques with others because it would have undercut the value of those that he produced. There were other investigators across Europe who produced good telescopes and used them, but few who could replicate the quality of Galileo's – especially at the beginning. Galileo wanted it both ways: an effective monopoly over high quality telescopes but enough of them circulating so that people could see what he had described in his *Starry Messenger.* This was especially an issue for the moons of Jupiter, which required a high quality telescope in order to be seen. When he had telescopes available, Galileo usually gave them to powerful princes. By doing this, he won potential patrons' favor and simultaneously made the telescopes available to large numbers of people, since their recipients would naturally show them off to visitors at their courts.

However, even with a good telescope in hand, the confirmation of Galileo's discoveries was not straightforward: the "Dutch" or "Galilean" telescope design had an extremely narrow field of view, so to find and keep an object in sight was difficult.[36] Determined skeptics who preferred not to believe that the moons of Jupiter existed could fail to see them easily enough. Moreover, many philosophers declined the invitation to look through a telescope, justifying their refusal by claiming that whatever Galileo had seen through the telescope had been created by it.[37] They didn't believe that an imperfect terrestrial device could be trusted to reveal what truly existed in the celestial realm. In any case, they didn't expect that anything new was to be found there.[38]

For these reasons, Galileo had great difficulty establishing the truth of his discoveries at the beginning, and this put his reputation at risk – at least temporarily. As one example of the difficulty that Galileo encountered in winning over new converts, he demonstrated a telescope for the highly regarded Italian astronomer Magini and some of Magini's associates in Bologna. Galileo was very disappointed when he was the only one present who was able to see the moons of Jupiter, and this was with him on hand to provide instruction to the other astronomers! Magini's negative opinion was devastating. Other commentators similarly criticized Galileo.

Yet, Galileo managed to win the confidence of his potential patron, Cosimo II de Medici. He accomplished this in two ways. First, Galileo sent Cosimo one of his best telescopes so that Cosimo could view the moons of Jupiter with his own eyes, which he did.[39] Secondly, Cosimo's ambassador to the Emperor asked the Imperial Mathematician, Johannes Kepler, to give his frank assessment of Galileo's claims – at Galileo's

request. It is important to appreciate that at this time Galileo was not
well-known in Europe, whereas Kepler was the highly-regarded
astronomer and mathematician to the Emperor of the Holy Roman
Empire. Kepler responded with a long published letter, *Conversation
With the Starry Messenger* (April, 1610), in which he publicly approved
of Galileo's *Starry Messenger*. In the letter, Kepler reasoned that Galileo
would not publish untrue reports if they could be easily verified or refuted
by someone else. In other words, Kepler simply would not believe that
Galileo would be so foolish as to destroy his own career by spreading false
reports. As the best known astronomer in Europe at the time, Kepler's
words carried a great deal of weight.[40]

In spite of Kepler's support, there remained some strongly negative
reviews of Galileo's telescopic discoveries – particularly in Italy. With
this, Kepler was put in the awkward position of supporting Galileo even
though he wasn't able to confirm the telescopic observations himself.
Soon, Kepler was petitioning Galileo for a telescope so that he could
respond to the skeptics more knowledgeably. Although Galileo never did
send him one, Kepler finally did get the opportunity to look through one
that he had borrowed.[41]

Galileo's fortunes slowly turned in his favor as other astronomers,
including those at the Jesuit Collegio Romano, began to confirm his
telescopic discoveries. Before long, he was triumphant and made a trip to
Rome where Jesuit scientists arranged a special reception on his behalf in
order to discuss his new discoveries and their significance.[42] While in
Rome, Galileo attended a banquet and was invited to join the Academy of
the Lynxes (Lynceans), an early scientific society composed of a small
group of men who were free-thinkers in many matters. Galileo's
membership in the Lyncean Academy provided him with an important
social network to replace the one he had lost when he left the University
of Padua. The Lynceans also offered great moral and financial support to
Galileo through the patronage and leadership of Prince Cesi – its
founding member. Eventually, Galileo's former critics, Magini included,
changed their minds and accepted the validity of his telescopic
discoveries. This even included Horky, one of his most virulent
detractors, whose less than civil conduct towards Galileo eventually
caused him to lose his reputation and flee the country. Indeed, it wasn't

long before others began to step forward and claim that they had made the telescopic discoveries before Galileo had.[43]

A New Employer and the Starry Messenger

The fantastic telescopic discoveries provided Galileo with yet another opportunity to improve the terms of his employment. With his recent raise at Padua, money was no longer a pressing issue. Instead, he sought a new work environment – one where he could be relieved of teaching responsibilities. Teaching at Padua took up valuable time and it obligated him to teach Aristotelian ideas to his students, since Galileo was expected to follow a traditional university curriculum in his instruction. His employment at the university also meant that he was engaged in constant turf battles with the Aristotelian professors. He found both activities distasteful. Yet as long as he was a public employee of the Republic of Venice, there was no possibility that Galileo could focus solely on his research.[44] To get what he wanted, he would need to win the support of a powerful and independent patron – similar to the relationship that Kepler had with the Holy Roman Emperor.

Galileo had had his eye on such a position for some time: Chief Mathematician to the Grand Duke Cosimo II de Medici in Florence. The role was attractive to Galileo for a number of reasons – first and foremost because the Grand Duke was a wealthy absolute ruler who could grant Galileo what he desired. Another reason Galileo was drawn to the position was that it would enable him to return to his native Tuscany. It is not difficult to detect homesickness in some of Galileo's letters, and he often returned to Tuscany in the summer – frequently serving as a personal tutor to the young Cosimo II while he was there. Galileo and Cosimo had a good relationship and a long standing mutual fondness between the two men existed into adulthood. Even prior to his telescopic discoveries, Galileo had petitioned the Tuscan court for the role of court mathematician. And although it had been an entirely realistic goal, nothing had yet come of his inquiries.

With the spectacular telescopic discoveries to his credit, Galileo had an excellent opportunity to approach the court with a request once again. With this in mind, he dedicated his hastily written book, *Starry Messenger,* to the Grand Duke Cosimo II de Medici in March of 1610. In the dedication, he named the moons of Jupiter "The Medicean Stars" after the Grand Duke and his three brothers (his discovery of *four* moons was more fortuitous than he could have first imagined).[45] The following passage from the dedication to *Starry Messenger* illustrates how one went about gaining favor from an absolute ruler in sixteenth-century Europe:

> I was the first to investigate them, who can rightly blame me if I give them a name, and call them the Medicean Stars, hoping that as much consideration may accrue to these stars from this title, as other stars have brought to other heroes? For not to speak of your most serene ancestors, to whose everlasting glory the monuments of all history bear witness, your virtue alone, most mighty sire, can confer on those stars an immortal name; for who can doubt that you will not only maintain and preserve the expectations, high though they be, about yourself, which you have aroused by the very happy beginning of your government, but that you will also far surpass them, so that when you have conquered others like yourself, you may still vie with yourself, and become day by day greater than yourself and your greatness?
>
> Accept, then, most clement Prince, this addition to the glory of your family, reserved by the stars for you; and may you enjoy for many years those good blessings, which are sent to you not so much from the stars as from God, the Maker and Governor of the stars.
>
> Your Highness's most devoted servant,
>
> Galileo Galilei
> (trans. Carlos, 1880).

Galileo's accomplishments and dedication were rewarded. He won dual appointments as the Mathematician and Philosopher to the Grand Duke and to the University of Pisa as the Chief Mathematician, where he drew a salary but had no teaching obligations.

It is worth noting here that Galileo made a special request of Cosimo to be granted the title "philosopher" in addition to that of "mathematician."[46] He did this because philosophers were able to make a broader range of statements about the natural world than mathematicians could, and philosophers could draw conclusions about what "caused" things to happen. In contrast, mathematicians were expected to limit themselves to the study and instruction of mathematics, mathematical astronomy, astrology, and engineering. Mathematicians were not considered properly qualified to provide opinions about the fundamental nature of the world; although in the sixteenth century, the disciplinary barrier between "philosophy" and "mathematics" had begun to break down. With increasing frequency, mathematicians and astronomers arrived at conclusions that intruded on the philosophers' territory. The work of Galileo, Kepler, and others marked the beginning of the end for this long-standing separation of disciplines – one that Aristotle himself had originally helped to establish. In this light, we can consider Galileo's appointment as "philosopher" to the Grand Duke as an end-run around the exclusive guild of academic philosophers. No doubt his new title and position greatly annoyed his Aristotelian opponents.

Galileo gained a considerable amount of new freedom by moving to Florence to work for Cosimo II. But as we will see, he also lost some freedom by leaving the Serene Republic of Venice. Even though Venice had always remained firmly committed to the Catholic faith, it had a long standing reputation of fierce independence from the secular authority of the Roman Catholic Church.[47] Venice was rich and cosmopolitan, the result of its lucrative shipping trade and powerful navy. The Republic had ignored edicts from the Pope and the Inquisition in the past and had a particularly strong tradition of protecting the intellectual freedom of faculty members at the University of Padua.[48] As Galileo finalized his plans to leave Venice, some of his friends warned him that he was taking a risk by leaving the protection of the Republic.[49] In Florence, Galileo would be more subject to the authority of the Church – a fact that he undoubtedly took into consideration. Still, he was supremely confident that his anti-Aristotelian arguments and new telescopic discoveries would result in success for the Copernican cause and his new physics. He considered the Jesuits at the Collegio Romano among his potential converts. Some historians of science have even speculated that Galileo found Florence to be an attraction *because* it was closer to Rome, where he could more effectively conduct his campaign among the important intellectual and cultural leaders of the Italian peninsula. As we will see, Galileo greatly overestimated his powers of persuasion and underestimated the resistance to the Copernican system and his anti-Aristotelian ideas.

More Telescopic Discoveries

Several of the planets had not yet made their appearance in the night sky until after the publication of *Starry Messenger.* Among the most important of the new planetary observations was the discovery that Venus exhibited phases. Galileo privately claimed his discovery by sending an anagram to Johannes Kepler. Decoded, the poetic message read: "The Mother of Love emulates the figures of Cynthia." What Galileo and others found when they observed Venus through the telescope over several months was that Venus exhibits phases that are similar to the phases of the moon – except that the size of its disk varied greatly during its cycle.[50]

[Figure 7.7. The phases of Venus by Galileo's hand. Public domain.]

The Discovery of Sunspots

The discovery and study of sunspots was a collective effort in which Galileo was a principal contributor.[51] Another important investigator of sunspots was Father Scheiner, a Jesuit professor at the University of Ingolstadt in Bavaria. Galileo and Scheiner effectively collaborated in their study of sunspots – though far more in the spirit of competition than in cooperation. Over the course of many years each of them made important discoveries that would influence the other. Galileo first became aware of Scheiner's work through a mutual correspondent, Mark Welser, a wealthy science enthusiast from Augsburg in Bavaria. Scheiner made the initial contact by asking Welser to forward his letter on sunspots to Galileo. As a Jesuit, Scheiner found it prudent to remain anonymous and presented his work under the pseudonym "Apelles."[52]

In the beginning, the correspondence between Galileo and Scheiner was very cordial, although Galileo disagreed with many of the conclusions that Scheiner had reached. For example, Scheiner originally believed that the appearance of the spots was caused by numerous little "stars" orbiting the sun, which took on the appearance of a spot when they happened to be grouped near one another. It was an interpretation of sunspots consistent with the view that the cosmos is immutable.

Galileo, on the other hand, believed that the sunspots were similar in form to clouds on the earth. In doing so, he proposed that the sun was not perfect, but was instead an active place that underwent a series of changes on its surface. He even speculated that the spots might be exhalations or excrement resulting from intense solar activity.

Thanks to a new drawing technique invented by his protégé Castelli, Galileo had an early advantage in sunspot research: the capability to render highly accurate drawings of the solar disk.[53] This allowed him to carefully study how the spots appeared, grew, changed shape, and dissipated as they slowly moved across the face of the sun. Galileo was then able to conduct a geometric analysis that allowed him to draw a number of conclusions – most importantly, he was able to show that the spots were either on or very close to the surface of the sun.[54] Galileo also provided strong arguments that the spots were similar in appearance to the clouds on the earth – even if they were made out of a very different material. He noted, too, that some of the spots were sufficiently long-lived that they reappeared from the backside of the sun in the same period of time that it took them to travel across the face of the sun. By following the progression of the spots over an extended period of time, he concluded that the sun rotated on its axis with a period nearly equal to that of the lunar month.

Scheiner eventually changed his mind about the "solar stars" and conceded many points to Galileo. As the correspondence between the two men continued, Galileo grew increasingly impatient with Scheiner. He probably viewed him as a competitor and became patronizing toward him. The two men eventually became bitter enemies. In the end, Galileo underestimated Scheiner, who, with great devotion and persistence, studied sunspots carefully and over many years. Scheiner eventually published his complete sunspot work in his magnum opus, the *Rosa ursina,* in 1630.

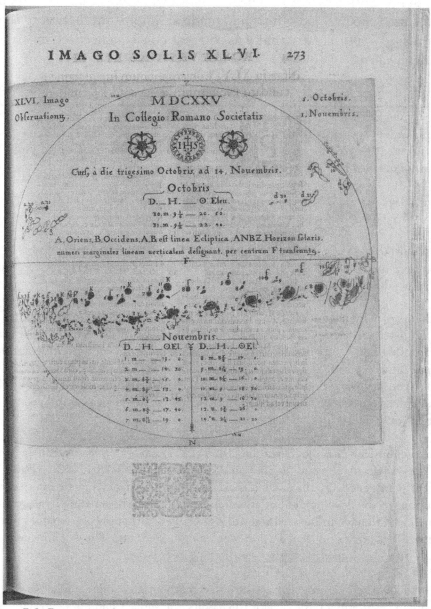

[Figure 7.8. Drawing of sunspots and their movement across the face of the sun by Christoph Scheiner in his *Rosa Ursina*, 1630. Image courtesy Avron, Wikimedia Commons.]

But however low Galileo's opinion of Scheiner may have been, it is clear that Scheiner inspired Galileo to spend more time considering sunspot motion than he otherwise would have. As we will see, Galileo eventually realized that Scheiner and others had made an important discovery that he had missed – a discovery that was of great consequence to the Copernican cause.

---

[1] Vincenzo Galilei's work is still performed, as is that of his less famous son, Michelangelo. (See youtube.com for performances of their work.) Galileo himself was an accomplished lute player and frequently accompanied his father.

[2] Johannes Kepler was considerably influenced by Vincenzo Galilei's *Dialogo della musica antica e moderna,* which he read with great enthusiasm.

[3] Some historians of science have speculated that Galileo's familiarity with his father's experiments with hanging weights led to Galileo's well-known interest in the physics of pendulums.

[4] Indeed, one of Archimedes' works has only recently been recovered through a careful, high-tech x-ray analysis of the *Archimedes Palimpsest.* A palimpsest is a manuscript that had been scraped clean and then used to copy a different work on top of the (partially) removed old text. In the case of the Archimedes Palimpsest, a thirteenth-century prayer book was eventually found to contain erased texts by the Hellenistic mathematician. A modern spectroscopic technique was employed to uncover the original script that remained.

[5] The mathematician Niccolo Tartaglia (1499-1557) made important translations of Archimedes works and he and his student, Giambattista Benedetti (1530-1590), were greatly influenced by the ancient mathematician. Benedetti made many early contributions to the development of a non-Aristotelian mathematical physics and is widely believed to have influenced the work of Galileo, although Galileo does not credit him. (See entries on Benedetti in Applebaum, 2000 and The Archimedes Project at http://archimedes2.mpiwg-berlin.mpg.de/ .)

[6] Clavius had worked vigorously to ensure that mathematics found a place in the curriculum of Jesuit universities. Prior to Clavius, the subject had not been regarded highly in the Jesuit curriculum. Philip Melanchthon served a similar role for Lutheran universities.

[7] Del Monte claimed that the conciseness of Galileo's proof had led him astray in his first reading of it. Only after Galileo responded to Del Monte's concerns did Del

Monte understand the nature of Galileo's proof and offered his full endorsement of its reasoning.

[8] Viviani, Galileo's young personal secretary and scientist, tells us that at the end of Galileo's life, Galileo told the story of his Leaning Tower of Pisa experiments. According to Viviani's account, Galileo had dropped objects of the same material and different weights from the tower "to the dismay of the philosophers" and that the experiments were conducted repeatedly and in the presence of teachers, philosophers, and students (Heilbron, 2010, pp. 59). The story is plausible, but because it hasn't been confirmed by other sources, some historians have unnecessarily assumed that it didn't happen and is merely a myth.

[9] Galileo could show, through repeated experiments, that heavy objects arrived at the ground only slightly ahead of the light ones – a very different result from what Aristotelian theory claimed. But Galileo also showed that Aristotle's theory could not be true on purely logical grounds. To do this, he described a "thought experiment":

Consider two weights: A is heavy and B is light. Following Aristotelian theory, A would fall faster than B. However, consider what would happen to the rate that A fell if it were *connected* to B: the fall of A would be *retarded* by the more slowly falling B to which it was attached. On the other hand, if A and B were connected, their total weight would be greater, so they should both fall faster! Galileo illustrated that Aristotelian theory predicted both outcomes – a logical impossibility.

[10] Some of Galileo's early ideas about falling objects were derived from ideas that had been expressed by an older contemporary of his, Giovanni Benedetti (1530-1590).

[11] At the time, Galileo also had a disagreement with a Medici related to the ruling family who had invented a pump. Galileo criticized the design and ended up being proved right when the device failed to work as advertised. Galileo's contribution to the embarrassment of a Medici also did not make staying in Pisa any more likely or comfortable. Allan-Olney, Mary, *The Private Life of Galileo*, 1870.

[12] Galileo's placement of his daughters in a convent would have been seen as a responsible act by his peers, since it was a common alternative to marriage at this time. Galileo did not consider his illegitimate daughters "marriageable" except to someone of a lower class, and such a marriage would have been socially awkward and an embarrassment to Galileo. His two daughters responded quite differently to convent life, as did many young women. Some accepted their lot with devotion, but others were very unhappy about having being taken out of the world to live behind the grate of a convent. See *Galileo's Daughter* by Dava Sobel, 1999 for an excellent and readable account of his daughters' experiences.

[13] Galileo had remarkable hand-head intelligence. He was extremely skilled at doing things with his hands and was an inventor, a musician, and an artist. He was also very interested in the interactions between the practical and the theoretical. In Venice, he spent time in the Arsenal, where the ships of the huge Venetian navy were produced. He admired the skill of artisans and engineers to an extent that might have seemed strange to his university colleagues. Like Archimedes, whom he emulated, Galileo had his feet in two worlds.

[14] This evidence exists in a theory of tides that was described in one of Fra Paolo Sarpi's notebook entries of 1595. Sarpi was a good friend of Galileo's and, although Sarpi does not describe the tidal theory as Galileo's, he doesn't describe it as his or anyone else's either. For a convincing explanation of why this tidal theory is probably Galileo's, see Drake, 1978.

[15] It appears unlikely that Kepler knew of Galileo before receiving his letter of thanks. Galileo had received the book (actually two copies of it) from Paul Hamberger. Kepler had given Hamberger copies of the *Mysterium* to distribute to mathematicians while he was in Italy. It appears that he discharged his duties just before leaving the Venetian Republic. For that reason, Galileo had little time to read the *Mysterium* before he gave Hamberger a note of thanks to carry back to Kepler.

[16] Astronomers attempted to measure the parallax of the novae against the background of stars. They found the parallax of the novae to be very small (which placed them well beyond the sphere of the moon) or measured no parallax at all (which meant that the novae were near or among the stars). The novae of 1572 and 1604 (sometimes called "Kepler's" nova) are now referred to as supernovae. Remarkably, these were the last two supernovae in our galaxy to have made an appearance. Kepler and Galileo were fortunate to have witnessed not one but two of these rare events.

[17] Many Aristotelians were remarkably persistent in their opposition to the idea that novae were located far beyond the sphere of the moon – in spite of the strong geometric arguments that highly-regarded astronomers had offered. Indeed, nearly thirty years after the nova of 1604, Galileo was still obligated to devote over 40 pages to the subject in his famous *Dialogue* in order to refute the position of Lorenzini, who had published a treatise in 1605 that maintained the nova was *below* the sphere of the moon. In the *Dialogue*, Galileo carefully considered the accounts of twelve astronomers who had already tackled the problem and presented the relevant geometric arguments patiently (and in Italian) so that anyone could understand them. The need for an extended passage on basic principles illustrates the contempt with which Aristotelian philosophers viewed mathematical arguments, and it highlights the effort Galileo was willing to make in order to appeal to people who didn't have formal training in astronomy or geometry.

[18] Galileo addressed the free fall problem by identifying a system that exhibited a similar kind of motion and invented a variety of apparatuses that would allow him to make the measurements he needed. In one experiment, Galileo and a friend rolled an inked ball up and across an inclined flat surface at an angle; then they released the ball and carefully analyzed its motion by measuring the ink path that it left behind (a parabola). In a particularly thorough series of experiments, Galileo fashioned some extremely smooth grooved inclined planes and released a ball at the top of them. He carefully measured how far balls moved over a fixed period of time in order to understand the way in which they accelerated. Galileo was extremely handy and designed the equipment himself. He even found new and ingenious ways to measure time. As just one example, he allowed water to flow from a very narrow opening and then stopped it like a stop watch. He could determine the time between the beginning and the end of the experiment by weighing the water.

Galileo's work on bodies that rolled down planes mimicked the phenomenon of free fall well enough for him to identify the mathematical law of falling bodies (that is, the distance a freely accelerating object travels is proportional to the square of the time it has traveled). Galileo had actually overlooked another factor that influenced the rate at which rolling bodies accelerate – the changing angular momentum of the balls, which tends to retard the forward motion of the balls down the plane. He also worked hard in the design of his apparatuses to reduce friction and wind resistance – effects which he understood to be secondary phenomena. Neither friction nor his ignorance of angular momentum was so great as to cause Galileo trouble reaching his conclusions.

[19] A few Aristotelians accepted the findings of the astronomers but then adopted an explanation that continued to maintain that there had been no change in the celestial realm. They proposed that the crystalline spheres that carried the planets could act as giant lenses. In this way, stars that had been too dim to see could become visible for short periods of time as the spheres moved past each other and manifested their effect. Thus, they argued that the novae resulted in no real change in the heavens – only the appearance of one. See Drake, 1978, pp. 118.

[20] Some commentators either didn't understand or they didn't care about the geometric arguments used to establish the nova's position. Many didn't believe that terrestrial geometry, as was used in land surveying, could be confidently applied to the celestial realm (see also note 17).

[21] See Fantoli, 2012.

[22] From the historical record, it is not at all clear who the inventor of the earliest version of the spyglass was. We do know that there were three or four Dutchmen in 1608 with early spyglasses in hand – all hoping to benefit from sales of the

instrument. As Van Helden, 1977, stated, "It now appears that we may never know the identity of the inventor(s) of the telescope..."

[23] The first spectacles were manufactured in Europe near the end of the 13th century and were used for correcting the far-sightedness (difficulty seeing objects close up) that plagued older readers. The glass lenses for correcting far-sightedness were convex. Later, in the middle of the fifteenth century, concave lenses were ground in order to correct for near-sightedness (myopia). On or before 1608 someone, most likely in the Netherlands, looked through both a convex and a concave lens at the same time. The trick was that for the "spyglass" effect to be noticed, the lenses needed to be of a proper curvature and held at the correct distance from each other. Van Helden (1977) describes a plausible discovery scenario. See also Van Helden's introduction to his translation of Galileo's *Sidereus Nuncius*. Galileo's telescopes had lenses that were planar on one side and convex or concave on the other.

[24] Galileo originally referred to the devices as "perspicilli" in *Starry Messenger.*

[25] Galileo had the good fortune of having access to high quality optical glass from both Venice and Florence, which each had a long tradition of spectacle manufacturing. Many other investigators and inventors had set out to improve upon the telescope at the same time Galileo did, but they didn't experience the same degree of success.

[26] The *Sidereus Nuncius,* is somewhat ambiguous in its original Latin. Galileo originally intended it to be read "Starry Message," but Kepler and others read it instead as "Starry Messenger" as though Galileo himself were the messenger. Galileo made no effort to correct this interpretation, so the name stands today (see Van Helden's 1989 introduction to his translation of *Sidereus Nuncius*).

[27] For example, during a full moon, when the earth is positioned between the sun and the moon, we can see the entire side of the moon that is lit by the sun. In the lunar quarter phases, when the sun, the earth, and the moon are at right angles to each other, we can see only half of the illuminated side of the moon. In the thin lunar crescent phases, the moon is almost between the earth and the sun so that we can see only a small fraction of the illuminated side of the moon. Finally, in the "new moon" phase, which is not visible, the moon is between the earth and the sun so that the unlit half of the moon is facing the earth, and the lit side is facing away from us.

The cause and rarity of eclipses was also understood in antiquity. A lunar eclipse occurs during a full moon – but only when the moon happens to be crossing the ecliptic (in the plane of the earth/sun system) and the earth's shadow is cast on the moon. Recall that the moon's orbit around the earth is in a different plane than the orbit of the earth around the sun (or, in the geocentric view, the sun around the earth). In other words, during a full moon, it isn't very likely that the earth will lie *exactly* between the sun and the moon, but it will normally be somewhat above or below the line between them. On those rare occasions when the full moon occurs just as it is crossing over from one side of the ecliptic to the other, and the moon finds itself directly on the earth-sun plane, a lunar eclipse occurs. Likewise, when the new moon crosses the ecliptic, a solar eclipse occurs.

[28] Thomas Harriot (1560-1621) in England also produced an improved version of the telescope and applied it in a similar manner to observing the moon. Indeed, Harriot's drawings of the moon preceded Galileo's by four months. However, since Harriot did not promote or publish his work in the way Galileo did, his work wasn't widely known.

[29] Kepler later took Galileo to task for not acknowledging that the earthshine explanation was originally proposed by Mästlin. Heilbron, 2010, pp. 156, reports that, "Several astronomers had already traced moonglow to earthshine, notably Kepler and his teacher Mästlin. And Sarpi had puzzled it out before either of them."

[30] Some Aristotelians had explained the twinkling as "an effect that happens only in very distant bodies and because our vision is weakened by traveling so far." Drake, Stillman, *Galileo Against the Philosophers* (English translations with introduction and notes), 1976.

[31] The size of stellar disks was in dispute for over two hundred years. Some astronomers claimed to observe the disks, whereas others claimed that stellar light was essentially point-like. It wasn't until the early 1800s that George Airy, the Royal Astronomer of England, offered an explanation for the conflicting reports: the diffraction of light due to its wave-nature causes an essentially point source of light (like the light from a distant star) to appear as a pattern of concentric rings, which appear disk-like to the eye through a telescope – even in an optically perfect telescope. Thus, in retrospect, the apparent magnification of stellar disks was an artifact and not real. See Graney and Grayson, 2010a for a more detailed discussion.

[32] Tycho estimated that the apparent diameter of a first magnitude star was 3 minutes of arc. Galileo designed and performed a non-telescopic experiment that showed that Tycho's estimates of stellar diameters were far too large. Galileo's experiment involved sighting a star with one eye and then covering the star from view with a thin cord stretched taut. Keeping the star hidden from view with the cord, he then moved his eye farther from the cord so that the cord's apparent width became thinner and thinner. Eventually, Galileo reached a distance where the apparent (angular) width of the cord was too small to continue to hide the star. Considering the width of the cord, the distance his eye was from the cord when the star reappeared, and the size of his pupil, Galileo applied geometry to determine that the stellar diameter of a first magnitude star was, at most, 5 seconds (which, however, did not entirely eliminate the problem of stellar sizes for Copernicans).

This is in great contrast to Tycho's estimate of 3 minutes. See Frankel, 1978, for more experimental details, as well as Galileo's "Third Day" in his *Dialogue*.

[33] A telescope as powerful as Galileo's was not necessary for seeing some of the previously unseen stars. There were reports from the Netherlands in 1608 that some new stars could be seen using the relatively weak Dutch spyglass. See Van Helden, 1977.

[34] There are a number of reasons that Galileo did not immediately recognize there were four moons of Jupiter. One reason was that his telescope had such a narrow field of view that he was not able to see the outermost moon, which was some distance from Jupiter. Another reason that it took time for Galileo to recognize there were four moons was that his early telescope was incapable of resolving the moons if they were too close together (that is, two moons sometimes appeared to be one). Furthermore, the moons of Jupiter also "disappeared" as they passed in front of or behind the planet. See Stillman Drake, 1978, pp. 152-3. Dozens of other satellites of Jupiter have since been discovered, but the four original Galilean moons are far larger than any of the others.

[35] Smith. L.P. (ed.). (1907). *The Life and Letters of Sir Henry Wotton*. Oxford: Clarendon Press, Accessed Internet Archive Cornell University Library.

[36] Because of their narrow field of view, the most powerful of Galileo's telescopes showed only one quarter of the moon's image at a time. Thus, small objects were difficult to find and difficult to keep sighted. Furthermore, there was a significant challenge to getting a clear image. Minor hand movements and even breathing tended to disturb the telescope enough to cause the image to bounce around. The telescope needed to be kept stable. However, the problem could not be solved by simply clamping it down and holding it in place because any heavenly body would quickly disappear from view as it traveled from east-to-west on its daily journey across the sky. In order to appreciate just how fast this east-to-west diurnal motion would appear through a telescope, consider the example of the moon: it travels across the sky at the rate of one lunar diameter every two minutes! Therefore, a telescope needed to be panned slowly, but somehow steadily in order to follow an object. Galileo was skilled at doing this and offered advice to others about how to do it. Later, as telescopes became increasingly powerful, astronomers would eventually devise clockwork-like mechanisms that would automatically and smoothly move a telescope at a constant rate to keep an astronomical object sighted.

[37] The telescope represents a watershed moment in the history of science because, for the first time, one of the human senses was augmented artificially. Some people in Galileo's day did not believe that looking into a man-made device was the same as seeing. They feared that the instrument might do unexpected things. Galileo's position on the issue was that, since a telescope could magnify terrestrial objects

accurately and did not seem to create false images when pointed at earth-bound objects, then it ought to behave just as accurately when pointed to the heavens. But then Galileo assumed that the rules of geometry and light would apply the same way in both the celestial and terrestrial realms. In contrast, many Aristotelians believed that the heavens and the earth were completely different realms, so they objected to Galileo's basic assumption. For these Aristotelians, there were no solid conclusions that could be made about the images that appeared in a telescope.

[38] Galileo remarked that the recently deceased Aristotelian professor at Pisa, Guilio Libri, who had refused to look through the telescope might finally have the chance to see the new astronomical discoveries on his way to heaven, since he hadn't bothered to take a look at them while he was on the earth (This is just one example of the biting sense of humor that won Galileo so many admirers and detractors). Drake, 1978, pp. 165.

[39] When the tide of public opinion was turning against Galileo, he sent a letter to a member of the Medici court who had the ear of the Grand Duke, "...I pray you therefore to take a fitting opportunity to entreat his Highness not to retard the flight of fame by showing himself doubtful of a thing which he has seen so many times with his own eyes." Galileo to Vincenzo Giugni, June 25, 1610 (trans., Mary Allan Olney, 1870).

[40] Although Kepler's letter indicated support for Galileo's discoveries, it didn't uniformly praise everything that Galileo had said or done. For this reason, some of Galileo's critics had wishfully misread Kepler's letter as being in opposition to Galileo's reports; in doing so, they missed Kepler's main point. It would have been clear to most people at the time that Kepler had done Galileo a great favor, and not without risking his own reputation. Yet in spite of the support and acknowledgement from the Imperial Mathematician, Galileo would never be as interested in maintaining a correspondence with Kepler as Kepler would be with Galileo.

[41] Kepler was able to use the telescope that Galileo had given to the Elector Archbishop of Cologne in August, 1610. By the end of that year, Galileo's discoveries were no longer disputed in the imperial city of Prague.

[42] Even though they accepted the telescopic observations as real and as posing a challenge to the existing understanding of the heavens, this isn't to say that the astronomers at the Collegio Romano were won over to the Copernican side by Galileo's discoveries. Still, the Jesuits astronomers were far more open-minded than what they have usually been given credit for. Even the conservative Christopher Clavius, who was staunchly opposed to the Copernican view, stated that the telescopic discoveries created a demand for a new understanding of the heavens – even if he couldn't provide that new understanding himself.

[43] There was at least one person who claimed he observed the moons of Jupiter before Galileo had – Simon Marius. And while Marius's claim is questionable, it seems likely that he did observe them independently shortly after Galileo had. On the other hand, it is clear that the singular and talented Englishman Thomas Harriot had already been observing the moon with his six-power telescope (and made drawings of it) when Galileo was still impressing the Venetian Senate with his nine-power telescope. In any case, Harriot's habit of moving quickly from one activity to another without publishing resulted in his observations not being shared until much later. Harriot was one of several European astronomers who confirmed Galileo's discovery of the moons of Jupiter the following year (Van Helden, 1977).

[44] Galileo described to a friend that it would be impossible to get the kind of position he wanted in the Venetian Republic, because he was serving the public rather than an absolute ruler. Drake, in *Discoveries and Opinions of Galileo*, 1957, pp. 65.

[45] Galileo named the moons collectively for the Medici brothers and had not given them individual names. The names now used for the moons of Jupiter were suggested by Simon Marius, who named them after the lovers of Jupiter (Zeus): Io, Europa, Ganymede, and Callisto.

[46] We should also note that when Galileo originally asked to be granted the title "philosopher," the Medici court accepted his request, but then dropped the original title "mathematician" in order to change his title to "philosopher." They likely assumed that since Galileo had already been granted the position of "mathematician" at the University of Pisa, it would have been redundant for him to retain the title of mathematician to the Grand Duke. Galileo responded to this change with a clarification: he wanted to be known as the "Philosopher *and* Mathematician" to the grand duke. While mathematics was not held in as high esteem as philosophy by most of his contemporaries, it appears that Galileo had plans to change that state of affairs. He may also have desired to use the two titles as a description of what he was trying to accomplish – the mathematization of physics. In the words of Stillman Drake, "...it is not too far-fetched to say that what Galileo was seeking...was the world's first post as a mathematical physicist."

[47] Indeed, just a few years before Galileo left Padua for Tuscany, Pope Paul V excommunicated the Venetian leaders and placed the entire Venetian Republic under Interdict, which forbade the Venetians from receiving the normal sacraments. The heavy handed act was a response to the Venetian Republic's arrest of two Catholic clergy and the recent restriction of the amount of land that could be donated to the Church. The Venetian authorities responded to the excommunication and the Interdict aggressively: They ordered the churches to remain open and for priests to ignore the orders from Rome. They also removed the threat of the strongest pro-Roman faction by expelling all of the Jesuits from the Republic. The standoff was witnessed with great interest by Protestants who hoped that the Venetians might

even break from the Catholic Church. The long and bitter standoff ended at last with a compromise peace agreement and the lesson was quite clear to all observers: Venice would not be pushed around by the Church.

[48] Crimonini, Galileo's Aristotelian colleague and friend at the University of Padua, was continually under investigation for his heretical Aristotelianism. Recall from Chapter 4 that many of Aristotle's original ideas were incompatible with Christianity and that not all elements of Aristotelian thought were included in the Thomistic synthesis. There were also medieval contributions to Aristotelian philosophy made by Islamic commentators that some free-thinking Aristotelians found appealing. The Church strongly discouraged the latter and forbade the former. But in spite of the opinion of the Church, Crimonini was free to speak his mind in the Republic of Venice, where he was actively protected from the authority of the Church under the principle of academic freedom.

The fascinating case of Fr. Paolo Sarpi (a good friend of Galileo) is another example. Hated by Roman authorities and beyond their reach as a citizen of the Venetian Republic, he was the target of numerous assassination attempts orchestrated by Church leaders.

[49] Galileo's good friend Sagredo was particularly concerned. He wrote to Galileo, "Where will you find freedom and self-determination as you did in Venice?" And, "...I am much disturbed by your being in a place where the authority of the friends of the Jesuits counts heavily." (trans. Drake, 1957).

[50] Prior to Galileo's sending the anagram to Kepler, Galileo's former student and friend Benedetto Castelli sent a letter to Galileo, in which he proposed that Venus might have phases similar to that of the moon. For this reason, some historians have claimed that Galileo stole Castelli's idea. Instead, it seems most likely that Galileo, as well as the astronomers at the Collegio Romano, had turned their telescope on Venus as soon as it appeared from behind the sun. That they would have done this is not at all surprising – Galileo's *Starry Messenger* made it quite obvious that there were fantastic discoveries to be made by looking at planets through a telescope. We don't know if Galileo or the astronomers at the Collegio Romano had anticipated the Venusian phases or if they were simply checking to see whether Venus had moon(s) like the earth and Jupiter.

[51] The observation of sunspots was actually something of a "rediscovery" since there are records of sunspots being sighted in ancient times in China and in the Greek World – as well as the in early European Middle Ages. However, these earlier sightings were rare and, in order for them to be noticeable to the naked eye, were dependent on extremely intense solar activity. Furthermore, they were usually observed through clouds or on the horizon when the intensity of the sun was diminished. With the discovery of the telescope, several researchers began to

independently study them on a regular basis (though taking care to use techniques that would prevent immediate blindness). It appears that Thomas Harriot and Galileo were the first to notice them, with Fabricus and Scheiner following shortly thereafter. Fabricus would be the first to publish on sunspots in 1611 and Scheiner would conduct the most thorough studies (See the Galileo Project website: http://galileo.rice.edu/sci/observations/sunspots.html).

[52] As a Jesuit professor, Scheiner was under pressure to keep his published works within the increasingly narrow bounds of accepted Jesuit teachings. Using a pseudonym gave him the freedom to publish. His choice, "Apelles," is a reference to the legendary painter of Alexander the Great, who was known to stand hidden behind his paintings so that no one could see him when they shared their criticisms. In this way, "Apelles" could learn what people really thought about his paintings (and Scheiner could learn what Galileo thought about his work on sunspots).

[53] Benedetto Castelli (1578-1643), a Benedictine monk, was one of Galileo's best pupils and most committed supporters over the years. Among other things, Castelli pioneered an ingenious technique for producing sunspot drawings that allowed unprecedented accuracy and reproducibility. There were a number of challenges associated with accurately recording the location, shapes, and sizes of the sunspots. To begin with, it was downright dangerous to one's eyesight to look through a telescope into the sun – to do it, a filter of some sort was necessary, but even that was often insufficient. Another problem was the inherent inaccuracy of rendering on paper by hand what one saw with the eye.

Castelli avoided both these problems by allowing the full light of the sun to pass through the telescope and land on a piece of paper that was placed perpendicular to it. Held at the appropriate distance, a large and clear image of the sun and its spots appeared on the paper (albeit inverted). To record the sunspots, all one needed to do was to make a tracing directly over the image (the procedure had its own challenge – the entire apparatus needed to be moved in order to follow the sun through the sky and to keep the image centered).

[54] The part of the geometric analysis that allowed Galileo to reach this conclusion was dependent on the apparent "foreshortening" of the spots as they approached the edge of the solar disk. All of the spots retained the same north-south dimensions as they approached the edge, but their width became greatly diminished because they presented themselves at an acute angle on the surface of a sphere. Furthermore, when the spots were located right at the edge of the solar disk, they never appeared to be floating above it. In this way, Galileo could conclude that the spots were either on the surface of the sun or, if not, very close to it.

Chapter Eight – Galileo's Copernican Campaign

We will now examine what Galileo's is most famous for: his enthusiastic advocacy for the Copernican system. Many histories on Galileo focus on this aspect of his work to the near exclusion of his other activities. This emphasis is understandable since Galileo took a great deal of time and energy battling to establish the Copernican system – an effort that ultimately resulted in his being sentenced to house arrest for the last years of his life. The primary reason the "Galileo Affair" continues to be analyzed and discussed four hundred years later is largely because of the questions it raised about the relationship between religion and science.

A few historians of science have portrayed Galileo's Copernican campaign as a distraction of little substance when compared to his important work in physics. While this informed challenge to the standard storyline is worth considering, in the end it fails to account for why Galileo proselytized for Copernicanism for more than ten years. In this text, we will assume that Galileo had good reasons to do what he did. In his own words:

> To investigate the true constitution of the universe – [is] the most important and most admirable problem that there is. For such a constitution exists; it is unique, true, real and could not possibly be otherwise; and the greatness and nobility of this problem entitle it to be placed foremost among all questions capable of theoretical solution. (Galileo's *Letters on Sunspots* 1613. Trans. Stillman Drake, 1957).

On the other hand, while we must try to understand Galileo on his terms, it *is* important to have an appreciation for Galileo's work in physics, since most historians of science agree that his work in physics was his most original and longest lasting contribution to science. Indeed, even before Galileo had run into trouble with the Church, some of his own friends were expressing their wishes that he spend more time completing his work in physics rather than getting wrapped up in the acrimonious geocentric-heliocentric debate. But regardless of what others thought – modern historians of science *or* his friends, it seems that Galileo himself considered his advocacy for the Copernican system and his project in physics as inextricably linked. It is worth noting that both physical and astronomical arguments were important to the case that he presented in his famous *Dialogue Concerning the Two Chief World Systems*.

Earlier, we considered the barriers that Galileo faced in promoting his work. He had been limited to making occasional attacks on the Aristotelian system as he continued to work on physics. With his spectacular telescopic discoveries, his situation changed dramatically– he now had a new found fame and had identified fresh critiques of the Aristotelian system. Before we consider the ways in which Galileo used his telescopic discoveries to support the Copernican view, it is worth taking stock of the first three scientific works that he published:

Starry Messenger, 1610 (in Latin). Galileo's main motivation for publishing this short and remarkable book was to claim ownership for his telescopic discoveries. While the book is mostly descriptive, in a few places he discussed the possible theoretical implications of his discoveries and in doing so, revealed his Copernican sympathies. However, Galileo did not provide direct or sustained arguments for the Copernican view in this work. Of all the things Galileo had described in the *Starry Messenger* it might be surprising to learn that it was his report of a rough lunar surface that drew the greatest number of objections from his critics. And while it might be difficult for us to appreciate why the appearance of the lunar surface was such a big deal, we shouldn't be tempted to ignore it. The lunar controversy offers us an opportunity to gain an appreciation for just how deep-seated the Aristotelian celestial-terrestrial distinction was at that time: When people looked up into the heavens, they saw something that was wholly different from what was immediately around them on earth – they had had little reason to believe that the stuff "up there" was anything like the stuff "down here."

Bodies that Stay atop Water or Move in It, 1612 (in Italian). This was Galileo's first published work on physics. It was inspired by a debate that began over dinner at the de' Medici palace. Those in attendance included Galileo, some Aristotelian professors, Cosimo II, and other dignitaries – including two cardinals. One of these cardinals, Maffeo Barberini, who would later become Pope Urban VIII, argued alongside Galileo. The debate arose over the question of why ice floats. The Aristotelians maintained that it was the shape of ice that kept it from sinking in water, whereas Galileo argued that ice floated because it was less dense than water. Galileo reasoned that if the shape of an object was important in determining how ice moved in water, then a piece of ice held under the water ought not to move upward in it when it was released. Following the dinner, the debate continued for weeks with many arguments and counter-arguments offered and the threat of many more to follow. Eventually, the plans for a public debate led the Grand Duke to end the bickering. He believed that it was inappropriate for his Chief Mathematician and Philosopher to be caught up in the circus-like atmosphere and asked Galileo to put his thoughts to paper instead.[1]

In the book, Galileo provided a remarkable modern mathematical analysis and explanation of buoyancy and displacement of bodies in water. He pointed out the faulty reasoning of his Aristotelian opponents and addressed a key criticism that Aristotelians had leveled at him: that he had no adequate explanation for why bodies denser than water can sometimes be induced to float on its surface. His critics had referred specifically to items such as thin chips of ebony or fine metal needles. Galileo, in turn, responded to this criticism carefully and brilliantly. In doing so, he was able to illustrate the full strength of his original explanation.

Galileo offered much more than a discussion of floating bodies in his book: The nature of the arguments and analyses he offered revealed that he was proposing a new approach for addressing physical questions. The form his reasoning took was as novel as the conclusions he reached. The book was extremely popular, sold out immediately, and was soon offered in a second edition. There was no doubt that it got the attention of Aristotelians: four books were published in opposition to it. Galileo and his friends determined that none of the Aristotelian responses had enough merit or influence to warrant a reply.

The printing of *Bodies that Stay atop Water* also afforded Galileo a convenient opportunity to lay claim to some of his latest telescopic discoveries. These new discoveries included the phases of Venus, the "three-bodied" nature of Saturn, sunspots, evidence that the sun spins, and finally, the individual periods of the Medicean stars.[2]

<u>Letters on Sunspots</u>, 1613 (in Italian). Galileo published the letters of correspondence that circulated between himself, Scheiner, and Welser on the subject of sunspots. The publication marked his first unambiguous display of support for the Copernican system. The *Letters* also publicly revealed that Galileo had little regard for the Jesuit Scheiner and his work; this created some friction between Galileo and other Jesuits, because they were not inclined to tolerate an attack on one of their own. Importantly, Galileo wrote both *Bodies that Stay atop Water* and *Letters on Sunspots* in Italian, which is evidence that he was appealing to an intelligent lay audience beyond the universities.[3]

The Theoretical Implications of Galileo's Telescopic Discoveries

In this section, we will more carefully consider the implications of the new astronomical observations on the cosmological debate and the ways in which Galileo used them to support the Copernican cause. Here, we find Galileo engaged in astronomy – not the traditional mathematical astronomy of Ptolemy or Copernicus but a new "physical astronomy." Galileo was interested in determining the basic physical arrangement of the cosmos – not in making accurate predictions of planetary positions. He had little concern for astronomical "hypotheses," which were mathematical devices that may or may not be true. He rarely mentioned epicycles, equants, or deferents and chose to ignore Kepler's ellipses. For Galileo, the circular paths of the Copernican system were "close enough" and he left the astronomical details to be worked out by others.[4] So without delving into the complexities of mathematical astronomy, Galileo set out to establish that the basic Copernican system was the true system of the world. In doing this, he was painfully aware that until stellar parallax was observed, purely astronomical arguments would be insufficient for settling the debate over world systems.

Venus and its Phases

Venus is the third brightest object in the sky (after the sun and the moon). It can appear as the "morning star" near the eastern horizon just before sunrise, or it can appear as the "evening star" near the western horizon just after sunset. Like the planet Mercury, Venus never appears very far from the sun, and it is never seen high in the nighttime sky. In the geocentric Ptolemaic system, this well-known fact was explained by postulating that the epicycle centers for both Mercury and Venus remained fixed to the line between the earth and the sun. Ptolemaic astronomers never provided an explanation for *why* the epicycle centers for Mercury and Venus tracked the sun as the sun revolved around the earth; they just accepted that it was so. It worked well enough.

Once Galileo discovered that Venus, like the moon, goes through a full range of phases, he realized that he had proof that the Ptolemaic arrangement was not true. To understand Galileo's reasoning, let's consider how the phases of Venus would appear if the Ptolemaic system *were* true and then consider what the phases of Venus would look like if the Copernican system were true. In both cases, it is assumed that the light that is coming from Venus is sunlight reflected from its surface.[5]

Phases of Venus in the Ptolemaic System
We will first consider how the phases of Venus would appear if the Ptolemaic system were true. Figure 8.1 shows the earth on the left, the center of Venus's epicycle in the middle, and the sun on the right. This basic arrangement never changes as the sun revolves around the earth, since the epicycle center for Venus always remains on the line between the earth and sun. The planet Venus is shown in four different positions on its epicycle.

In this arrangement we would occasionally see a small portion of the Venusian disk being illuminated by the sun. A quick glance at the diagram should convince the reader that the illuminated side of Venus always, for the most part, faces away from the earth in the Ptolemaic system. Thus, we would expect to find that Venus displays a series of very thin crescents and nothing more. This conclusion may be more evident if we carefully consider how Venus would appear in each of the four positions shown in the diagram (figure 8.1).

When Venus is at the top position in its epicycle circuit (at the 12 o'clock position), only a small fraction of its illuminated side would be visible from the earth. It would appear as a thin crescent and as the evening star.

As Venus moved on its epicycle so that it was closest to earth and directly on the earth-sun line (at the 9 o'clock position), Venus would not be visible from the earth for two reasons: 1) It would be too close to the sun in the sky and thus hidden by its glare, and 2) Only the dark, unlit side of Venus would be facing the earth, so that no reflected light would reach us.

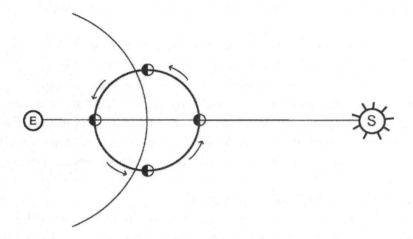

[Figure 8.1. Figure courtesy Danica Oudeans.]

After Venus moved to the bottom of its epicycle (at the six o'clock position), a small fraction of its illuminated side would again be visible from the earth except that the crescent would appear on the opposite side of its disk, and it would appear as the morning star.

After Venus moved on its epicycle so that it was closest to the sun and directly on the earth-sun line (at the 3 o'clock position), it would again be lost in the glare of the sun with its unlit side facing the earth.

The Phases of Venus in the Copernican Model
We will now consider how the phases of Venus would appear if the Copernican system were true. In figure 8.2 Venus is shown orbiting the central sun in a counterclockwise direction. Several positions of Venus on its circuit around the sun are illustrated. The earth is located to the right in the diagram and farther away from the sun than Venus is. Recall that Venus orbits the sun more frequently than the earth; so, for simplicity, we can use the following diagram without considering the motion of the earth.

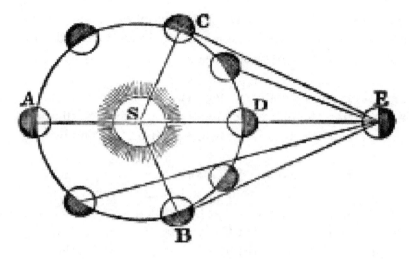

[Figure 8.2. Copernican explanation for the observed phases of Venus. From *Letters on Astronomy*, Olmsted, 1841. Public domain. archive.org]

When Venus is located in position "A" all of its illuminated side would be facing toward us, but it would be lost from our view by the glare of the sun.

When Venus arrives at the intermediate position between "A" and "B" (about 7 o'clock in the diagram), it would become visible because it is no longer directly behind the sun. Here, most of its illuminated face would be seen from the earth, and it would appear to be nearly full. However, because it is still a great distance from the earth, its disk would appear small.

When Venus arrives in position "B," less of its illuminated side would be visible from the earth, and it would appear about half full. However, because it is closer to the earth in this position, the size of its disk would be larger than it was in the previous position on its path.

When Venus arrives at a position intermediate between "B" and "D" (at about 4 o'clock), only a very small fraction of its illuminated side would be visible from the earth, and it would appear to be a very thin crescent. However, because it is so close to the earth in this position, its disk would appear to be very large.

When Venus arrives at position "D," it would not be visible for two reasons: none of its illuminated side would be directed toward the earth, and it would be lost in the glare of the sun.

As Venus continues on its counter-clockwise path, it would appear first as a large thin crescent, the phases becoming progressively fuller and the disk becoming smaller as it moves toward position "C" and beyond.

This is exactly what Galileo and others observed through the telescope, and it confirmed the prediction that Castelli had shared with Galileo. But while the Venusian phases proved that the Ptolemaic system could not be true, the phases did not prove that Copernican system *was* true. The phases only proved that Venus orbited the sun, which was the case in both the Copernican and Tychonic systems. Thus, figure 8.2 can also be used to explain the Venusian phases in the Tychonic system; the only difference is that in the Tychonic analysis, the earth remains stationary as the sun moves around the earth (as Venus moves around the sun).

The Moons of Jupiter

Galileo's discovery of the moons of Jupiter could be used to defend the Copernican system – but, once again, wasn't proof for it. Prior to the discovery of the moons of Jupiter, the earth was an anomaly in the Copernican system: it was the only planet that possessed a satellite – the moon. Because of this, there were really *two* physical centers of motion in the Copernican system: one centered on the earth and one centered on the sun. This would have seemed needlessly complicated to Ptolemaic astronomers, since their system possessed only one physical center of motion – the earth. In this sense, having two centers of motion in the Copernican system violated the principle of simplicity.[6] With the discovery of the moons of Jupiter, the earth was no longer unusual – moreover, it required the Ptolemaic system to adopt a second center of motion, because Jupiter clearly had satellites. Galileo also suspected that Saturn was more than a lone planet – he reported it as "three-bodied."[7]

The moons of Jupiter could be accommodated by the Ptolemaic and Tychonic systems, but they added a level of complexity to those systems that hadn't existed before. For example, recall that in the Tychonic system all of the planets revolved around the sun as the sun revolved around the earth. With the addition of the moons of Jupiter, the dynamics in the Tychonic system became more cumbersome: the moons revolved around Jupiter, while Jupiter revolved around the sun, while the sun revolved around the earth, while the celestial sphere carried all of these bodies around the earth with a rapid diurnal motion. In this way, the moons of Jupiter had four different motions associated with them in the Tychonic system, whereas they had only two motions in the Copernican system. On the other hand, those who were inclined to the Tychonic view in the first place would not necessarily have seen this as a problem.

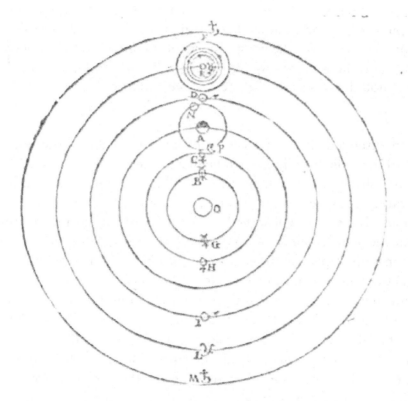

[Figure 8.3. Galileo's diagram of the Copernican System including the moons of Jupiter. From Day Three of Galileo's *Dialogue*. Public domain.]

Sunspots

The discovery and study of sunspots increased the plausibility of the Copernican system in three ways:

1) Their mutability further eroded the celestial-terrestrial distinction of the Aristotelian view: they appeared, changed shape, and disappeared on the surface of the sun as clouds do on the earth.

2) The sunspots provided evidence that the sun spun on its axis. This also rescued the earth from being an exceptional planet in the Copernican system. Prior to this, the only celestial object that spun, as near as the Copernicans could tell, was the earth (which was obviously a major problem, since the earth didn't *feel* like it was in motion...).

3) The paths the sunspots take across the solar surface change predictably over the course of a year. Galileo had originally missed making this observation and even after hearing reports of it continued to overlook its significance until he was writing his *Dialogue*.[8] The importance of the discovery is not obvious at first glance, so we will discuss it at some length below.

Careful and extended observations of sunspots revealed that the sun does not spin with its axis directly perpendicular to the earth-sun plane but rather with it slightly inclined, or "tilted." This became evident because the spots rarely appeared to move across the solar disk in perfectly straight lines. Instead, the observed pattern of sunspot motion changed throughout the year in the following way: 1) For only a few days each year, the sunspots appear to move in straight lines that are inclined upwards as they move from the left side of the solar disk to the right. This occurs when the sun's axis is tipped to the left and is perpendicular to a line between the earth and the sun. 2) For nearly half the year, the spots appear on the left side of the solar disk, rise up slightly, and then sink down again before disappearing from the right side of the disk, following curved, concave down paths as they move across the sun's surface. This occurs when the sun's axis is pointed away from the earth. 3) Once again, for only a few days each year, the sunspots appear to move in straight lines, but this time inclined downward as they move from the left side of the solar disk to the right. This occurs when the sun's axis is perpendicular to the earth-sun line and tipped to the right. 4) Finally, for nearly half the year, the spots appear on the left side of the sun, dip down, and then rise again before disappearing from the right side of the solar disk, tracing out concave up shaped arcs. This occurs when the sun's axis is pointed toward the earth.[9]

While Galileo did not discover this phenomenon, he did recognize its theoretical significance. He noted that the changing annual appearance of sunspot motion was most easily explained within the framework of the Copernican system as the result of the changing perspective from which we view the spinning sun as we travel around it during the year. As he put it in his *Dialogue* (trans. Drake), "The sun itself bears witness that the annual motion belongs to the earth."

Galileo's sunspot argument was heavily dependent on physical assumptions about how objects move, and once again, Galileo applied his understanding of terrestrial physics to celestial objects. In this case, he compared the motions and apparent motions of the earth and the sun to the behavior of a wooden ball floating in a bowl of water.[10]

Galileo argued that this changing orientation of the sun's axis is difficult to explain in a geocentric system. In contrast to the Copernican sunspot explanation, sunspot motion in a geocentric system can be explained only if one accepts an unusual and coincidental motion. The problem that sunspot motion created for the geocentric view boiled down to this: Why would it take precisely a year for the sun's axis to change its orientation relative to the central and stationary earth when the sun was spinning around the earth daily? That is, why would the motion of the sun need to include an additional and independent precessional motion of its axis that took precisely a year and no more and no less to complete?[11] It was an unexplained coincidence in any geocentric system.

Galileo's sunspot argument demanded that he compare his proto-inertial Copernican cosmology with the standard Aristotelian physical geocentric cosmology – underscoring the astronomical and physical differences of both. Because the argument required him to compare all of the elements of the two cosmologies, including the very different physical assumptions behind the two systems, Galileo's argument is frequently underappreciated today.[12]

The Moon

It is difficult for us today to imagine how critical the telescopic discovery of the moon's surface features was to the debate over the world systems. Galileo spent a great deal of time describing the surface of the moon and included several careful sketches of it in his *Starry Messenger*. Through his observations and the application of geometry, he estimated that the tallest lunar mountains were about four miles high.[13] His lunar discoveries were at odds with the traditional Aristotelian notion that everything in the cosmos was perfect. The subsequent commentary and intense criticism of Galileo's conclusions provides us with important insight into the way Aristotelians had conceived of the cosmos.

Indeed, so greatly did Galileo's lunar discovery conflict with prevailing expectations that several Aristotelians independently suggested that the apparently rough lunar surface was actually covered with a transparent and perfectly spherical crystalline material. This proposed invisible shell rescued the moon from imperfection. Advocates of this position included the elderly Jesuit mathematician Christopher Clavius as well as Ludovico delle Colombe, an early and tenacious Florentine opponent of Galileo's. Galileo responded to this desperate but imaginative proposal playfully: he expressed his willingness to entertain the possibility that an invisible crystalline material covered the moon, as long as his opponents would consider the possibility that the invisible material might not be smooth, but was instead so uneven that it made the mountains thirty times *taller* than they appeared to be through the telescope! It was this sort of clever and biting response that won Galileo both admirers and detractors. The discovery of mountains and valleys on the moon and the previously discussed earthshine analysis worked to erode the celestial-terrestrial distinction. The discovery of sunspots eroded it even further.

Galileo's Successes and the Rising Opposition

By the end of 1613, Galileo's broad and persistent strategy in support of Copernicanism and against Aristotelianism had been working well. He won some converts to his side, but his successes frustrated and worried many of his detractors. A few of his opponents attacked him angrily and with little provocation, while other intellectual rivals remained on cordial terms but earnestly disagreed with his conclusions. However, over time, some of the friendly disagreements became more pointed as Galileo's impatience and frustration with other thinkers led him to respond to their correspondence and written works with a patronizing and condescending tone. His forceful personality was not the only personal characteristic that won him enemies – he was also disinclined to share credit for scientific discoveries when it may have been appropriate or advantageous for him to have done so. Both of these tendencies were at play during Galileo's sunspot studies and in his interactions with Scheiner. Whether Galileo's constant need for recognition was inspired by a need to fulfill his obligations to a powerful patron or whether it was a personal idiosyncrasy is unclear. In any case, many of Galileo's contemporaries felt professionally stymied and personally slighted by him. Over the years, the good feelings toward Galileo that once existed at the Collegio Romano had cooled considerably. In a few cases, former admirers chose to watch with indifference and inaction as Galileo ran into trouble.

The public debate over the world systems took a more serious turn when a handful of Aristotelians inside and outside the universities became increasingly frustrated with Galileo's successes. Discouraged by their inability to effectively dismiss his arguments using philosophical or mathematical reasoning, some turned to the Bible as a final defense of the Aristotelian tradition. In order for us to gain a full understanding of what happened next, it is critical for us to appreciate how easy and natural it was for Galileo's opponents to bring theology into the debate.

Recall that in the Middle Ages the Aristotelian system was "Christianized" in a fusion of theology, logic, and cosmology that had been forged by St. Thomas Aquinas. By Galileo's day, the Thomistic-Aristotelian synthesis had become so thoroughly embedded in Catholic thought that many of Galileo's contemporaries had simply forgotten that Catholicism had once flourished in its absence. Thus, some of Galileo's most dangerous opponents viewed his attacks on the Aristotelian Universe as an attack on St. Thomas and Christianity. Before the year was out in 1611, there were treatises by two authors who suggested that the Copernicanism they detected in *Starry Messenger* was heretical.[14] The writers were relatively minor figures who had no official positions in the Church, and Galileo felt it best to remain silent in order to avoid drawing further attention to the matter. Galileo hoped that if he held his tongue, the matter might simply be dropped – for a time, it was.

In his *Sunspot Letters* of 1613, Galileo unambiguously proclaimed his support for the Copernican view in print. This act accelerated the debate between the world systems and the controversy began to take on more serious proportions. The first worrisome challenge came from the pious Grand Duchess Dowager Christina de' Medici, the matriarch of the Medici family that employed Galileo. She raised the theological question over a palace lunch in 1613 in the presence of the rest of the family, members of the court, and Benedetto Castelli, Galileo's chief disciple and good friend. As a member of the clergy and a trained theologian, Castelli was particularly well-positioned to defend the Copernican opinion from charges that it went against scripture. By all accounts, the debate at the palace was friendly but intense. Castelli reported the episode to Galileo and shared his assessment that by the end of his visit Christina had been satisfied by his responses to her. However, Galileo remained concerned and sent Castelli a short theological treatise in the form of a letter that is now known as Galileo's *Letter to Castelli*. It was an early effort by Galileo to demonstrate that scripture and Copernicanism did not need to be taken as incompatible with one another. The letter was copied and circulated so that the theological arguments he offered in it were more widely known.

In late 1614, the year following the famous Medici family lunch, a second and more public challenge was issued against Galileo. This time a Dominican Father, Tommaso Caccini, angrily denounced Galileo and other Copernicans from the pulpit during a sermon he delivered in a Florentine church. Caccini accused Copernicans of holding heretical beliefs. Caccini was not officially authorized to offer such an opinion and his superior, the Dominican general Fra Luigi Maraffi, personally apologized to Galileo.[15] However, the damage had been done, and Galileo could see clouds looming on the horizon. He began to prepare for the kind of struggle he had hoped he could avoid. In the meantime, his daughters had moved from Venice to Tuscany. Because of all the disturbance, and because his daughters were illegitimate, Galileo thought it best to have them placed in the convent of San Matteo – even though they were barely in their teens.[16]

The issue over scripture came to a head in 1615 when authorities in Rome became increasing aware of the noisy theological objections to Copernicanism and to Galileo's active support of it. We will briefly consider the issues, events, and actions that shaped the outcome in this important episode, which has come to be known as the "Galileo Affair." There are several excellent historical accounts that examine the events in much greater depth than what follows here.[17] Before describing the nature of the debate, we will first consider a chronology of how the controversy escalated.

In January 1615, a remarkable work was published in Naples by Carmelite friar and theologian Antonio Foscarini, entitled *Letter on the Opinion, Held by Pythagoreans and by Copernicus, of the Earth's Motion.* In his letter, Foscarini argued that Copernicanism is compatible with the Bible and is probably true. Galileo was gratified to see a trained theologian support his views in a published work. He was also very hopeful that Foscarini's letter would be influential in Rome. However, some of Galileo's friends feared the letter could have the opposite effect and make matters worse by inciting Galileo's adversaries to respond in even stronger terms.

In February 1615, another Dominican, Niccolo Lorini, sent a letter denouncing Galileo to the Congregation of the Index (the bureau of the Church responsible for approving and censoring books). Lorini complained to the Index:

> [They] explain the Holy Scriptures after their own fashion, and differently from the usual interpretation of the fathers, and should defend an opinion which the Holy Scriptures appear to be entirely opposed to...They tread the entire philosophy of Aristotle, of which scholastic philosophy has made so much use, under foot...in short, to show how clever they are, they (the Galileists) say a thousand shameless things and scatter them abroad in our city, which holds fast to the Catholic faith... (trans. Sturge in Gebler, 1879).

Along with his letter, Lorini included a copy of Galileo's *Letter to Castelli* that he had acquired. When Galileo was later informed of Lorini's actions, he expressed concern that the copy of the *Letter to Castelli*

Lorini had given to the Index was different from the one he had written.[18] In the end, it turned out not to be a problem because the members of the Index found little to be concerned about in what they read. Their only complaint was over Galileo's choice of words, which it considered inappropriate, but not heretical. As we will see, Galileo had adopted well accepted and long standing theological principles in his *Letter to Castelli* – even if he had applied them to a very new situation.

In March 1615, Caccini traveled to Rome and volunteered his testimony to the Holy Office of the Inquisition. He also shared his concern about Galileo's pro-Copernican activities.

In April 1615, the chief theologian to the pope and leader of the Catholic Counter Reformation, Lord Cardinal Robert Bellarmine, responded to Antonio Foscarini, who had specifically asked for the cardinal's opinion on his *Letter*. The cardinal did so respectfully, but with a firm and implicit warning to both Galileo and Foscarini: they were free to consider the Copernican system *hypothetically* but should not maintain that it was true in an absolute sense.

There were two ways of advocating for an astronomical system – one as a mere hypothesis (i.e. for calculating planetary positions), the other as a bona fide description of reality. This was an important distinction to everyone involved in the controversy. Bellarmine, and others like him, believed that it was impossible to prove that a particular astronomical system was true. In their way of thinking, the Copernican system was no different from other astronomical systems, because it was both unproven and *unprovable*.[19] In contrast, some thinkers were realists, in that they believed astronomical systems could provide an accurate description of a reality that was ultimately knowable. These were very different views about the kind of knowledge that one is able to have of the natural world, and they had very different implications for making sense of scripture. Copernicans who wished only to discuss their astronomical view hypothetically and who stopped short of maintaining that it was true in an absolute, physical sense encountered no trouble – at the end of the day, they could always yield to a literal account of scripture. On the other hand, when Copernicans insisted that their astronomical system was more than a mere idea, but actually described reality, their view was no longer compatible with a strictly literal account scripture. This latter perspective would require the intervention of professional theologians to assess the true meaning of the Bible.

Bellarmine's position was simple: Why should Galileo insist on creating problems with scripture when he had not *proven* that the Copernican view was true and that he would be unlikely to do so in the future? In Bellarmine's way of thinking, Galileo and Foscarini's insistence that the Copernican system was true was simply philosophically unwarranted and divisive to the Christian faith.

In Spring 1615, Galileo had begun to expand on his *Letter to Castelli* – probably with Castelli's help as a theologian. This longer work was addressed to the Grand Duchess Dowager Christina Medici and is now known as the *Letter to the Grand Duchess Christina*. It was not published at the time and had a limited circulation in manuscript.[20] Galileo's *Letter to Christina* is one of his finest pieces of prose and is a remarkable work of theology – especially for a person unqualified to express an opinion on the subject. It continues to be relevant to discussions concerning the relationship between science and religion today.

Catholic Theology in the Reformation and Counter-Reformation

Before describing Galileo's *Letter to Christina*, it is worth noting the circumstances that led Galileo to write an extended theological treatise. Prior to his *Letter to Christina*, Galileo had limited his theological arguments to the relatively short and informal *Letter to Castelli*. However, by 1615, Galileo's most dangerous opponents had given up on making physical and philosophical arguments against him and had instead invoked the authority of the Bible. The nature of their attacks carried the unavoidable implication that Copernicans were heretics. At that point, Galileo felt he needed to provide reasoned arguments to support a theology that was compatible with Copernicanism – he could only hope that his suggestions might be taken up by someone who had the influence to have an impact on the outcome.

The Vatican theologians were not necessarily obligated to conclude that Copernicanism was incompatible with Christianity. Catholic theologians had never presumed that a purely literal reading of scripture was always the proper one even if they tended toward that view for most Biblical passages. Early on, they understood that authors of the Bible used metaphor and allegory in order to effectively convey important messages about salvation and morality. In their view, an overly strict literal reading of the Bible could even cause an important religious message to become lost on its readers. For these reasons, the Church took on the responsibility for interpreting the meaning of the Bible for the laity. It had assumed this important role because individual worshipers didn't have the apostolic inspiration or training to make these decisions on their own. Only the Fathers of the Church, in councils, had the Holy authority to uncover the intended meaning of the Bible.

The Church assumed this interpretive authority because it had been the central organ of Christianity for centuries. It traced its origin to the earliest Roman churches and considered its popes to represent an unbroken line of succession beginning with the chief apostle of Christ, Peter. In this view, the Catholic Church inherited Holy traditions and knowledge that predated the Bible by centuries.[21] Indeed, it had been the early Catholic Church that had determined which gospels and books appeared in the Bible in the first place, so it would have seemed natural for the Church to take on an interpretive responsibility as well.

Martin Luther challenged this view. His objection to Catholic custodianship of the Bible was one of the central criticisms that led to the Protestant Reformation. He believed that the Bible could be read by anyone and that it did not require a middleman to explain its message of salvation.[22] A consequence of this view was that Luther and other Protestants tended toward literal readings of the Bible over more high-minded ones. As Luther's message of reform and anti-Catholic sentiment spread across Northern Europe, other Protestant leaders emerged. Much to Luther's dismay, when these leaders read the Bible in a literal sense they often uncovered different messages than Luther had. A diversity of theological viewpoints arose, which led to a further fragmentation of Christian sects in Europe. In this way, the "Lutheran Reformation" became the "Protestant Reformation," with several new denominations arising including the Calvinists, Zwinglians, Anabaptists, and a diversity of smaller sects. Many of these Protestants detested each other as much or more than they did the Catholic Church, but they all believed that the path to salvation was to be found in the Bible – even if their readings of it led them to different conclusions.

So in principle at least, the Catholic Church was freer to interpret the Bible than the Protestants were. Catholic theologians had understood that messages in the Bible were inspired by the Holy Spirit, but were written by and for men. One of the roles of the Church was to explain messages that were potentially confusing. Given the outcome of the Galileo Affair, it might seem ironic that Catholicism had the greatest potential, at least in theory, for reconciling scripture and Copernicanism.

Obviously, what appeared to be possible in principle did not turn out to be possible in practice. There existed an important complicating factor that trumped such a simple view: Catholic leaders were very anxious about the ongoing conflict between Reformation and Counter-Reformation forces north of the Alps. Catholics had made great territorial gains and had won important new converts during this period (as we witnessed in the great personal struggles of Johannes Kepler). The continuing success of the Counter-Reformation was heavily dependent on Catholic unity, so any threat to unity was seen as a threat to the Counter-Reformation.

It is worth taking time here to briefly consider the Catholic response to the Protestant Reformation. Luther's first challenge to the Church in 1517 was answered by Rome with his excommunication. In the beginning, Church authorities simply viewed Luther as the problem. However, once the rebellion had extended beyond the leadership of a few dissident preachers, the Catholic Church appeared to be paralyzed and was unable to formulate a meaningful response. Only after it had long been obvious that the Protestant problem was not going to go away did the Catholic Church begin to answer the challenge. It did this in two important ways.

The Council of Trent
The pope called for a Church council of bishops and other leaders to help address some of the problems posed by Protestantism. The Council of Trent (1545-1563) accomplished two main goals: 1) it answered the Protestant heresies by clarifying proper Catholic theological positions,

and, 2) it set in motion reforms that resulted in the Church becoming more professional and less corrupt than it had been before.

The Jesuits

Following the Protestant Reformation a number of Catholic preachers began new religious orders that worked to teach and proselytize for the Catholic faith. The most successful of these was the Jesuit order, or "Society of Jesus," which was founded by a former soldier, St. Ignatius of Loyola, and recognized by the pope in 1540. The Jesuits were committed to education and to responding to the confessional needs of Catholics and potential Catholic converts everywhere. By 1615, there were over 15,000 Jesuit priests, and the order operated over two hundred schools and colleges in Europe, the Far East, and the New World. They were the major force of the Catholic Counter-Reformation.

An important element of Jesuit influence and success was its uniformity of doctrine, which exhibited itself in military-like discipline. Both religious and secular instruction was highly standardized and codified in a document called the *Ratio Studiorum*, which was completed in its final form in 1598.[23] It is particularly important for our story to note that the *Ratio Studiorum* had designated Aristotelian-Thomistic philosophy as the only philosophy to be taught. Therefore, when it came to discussions of physics and astronomy, the official Jesuit position was Aristotelian.

The Jesuit professors at the Collegio Romano, which was the flagship campus for all Jesuit schools, were afforded a significant amount of intellectual freedom by virtue of their positions. In practice, they did not strictly adhere to the *Ratio Studiorum* in their own thinking since they were the academic leaders that helped to determine what appeared in the document in the first place. Indeed, Christopher Clavius had raised the status of mathematics in the Catholic world by carving out a sizable place for it in the *Ratio Studiorum*.[24] However, with the Counter-Reformation in full swing, the need for discipline in the Jesuit ranks became crucial. By 1611, the Jesuit General Acquaviva was seriously concerned that Jesuits had strayed too far from orthodoxy and needed to more closely follow the *Ratio Studiorum*. He ordered that at the beginning of each academic year, Jesuit teachers take an oath to uphold proper teachings and follow prescribed doctrine in their teaching or be threatened with dismissal.

This meant that the Jesuits had effectively redoubled their commitment to teaching a conservative Aristotelian view of the cosmos at the very same time new discoveries about it were being made. It was a limitation that many Jesuit scientists were unhappy about, but which they accepted as members of the Order.[25] This move, towards a more conservative position, even extended to the Jesuit scientists at the Collegio Romano, who now had far less freedom of expression than Galileo expected of them.[26] To a very significant degree, the scientists at the Collegio Romano were constrained in the ways they could respond to the new reports that Galileo had been challenging them with.

Toward a Unified Catholic View

As complaints against Galileo became more frequent and more vociferous, the leaders of the Church found themselves under increasing pressure to settle the matter. The increasing tension between the Protestant and Catholic Counter Reformation forces in Germany called for solidarity among Catholics – not the sort of divisiveness that Galileo and his opponents were inciting. Discord had threatened Catholic unity several years earlier when a theological argument between the Dominican and Jesuit orders threatened to spin out of control. On that occasion, Pope Paul V successfully promulgated a decree that demanded the cessation of the debate between the two orders.[27] The quarrel between Galileo and his opponents presented a new kind of threat – and by mid-1615, it was clear to most people that Pope Paul V would soon need to end this disagreement as well. Galileo held hope that the Church authorities would determine that Copernicanism was compatible with scripture and that he and his opponents would be able to continue to debate it as an open question.

Galileo and his adversaries maneuvered quickly to make their points before the Church offered a final ruling on the matter – each hoping to influence the outcome in their favor. In this, Galileo had a considerably more difficult task than his opponents. While his scientific arguments were strong and persuaded many people to the Copernican side, they were far from logically decisive. He was also limited in being able to offer theological opinions since he didn't have the proper qualifications to engage in theology.[28] His opponents, most of whom were also not trained as theologians, had considerably more freedom to express their views because of the position they adopted – they simply quoted scripture and let it speak for itself. Reading scripture in the literal sense had always been the preferred or "default" approach unless Catholic theologians found a need to determine it otherwise. Since a literal reading of scripture on an open question was a safe position to take, and since it also reflected public opinion and common sense concerning the earth's stability,[29] Galileo's opponents were free to attack with little risk to themselves. They only needed to point out what was so obvious to nearly everyone: The earth didn't move. They were confident that the earth was stationary and knew it to be so in many different ways: through common sense, by the authority of Aristotle and, finally, because the Bible said it didn't move. This was the well-entrenched position that Galileo was challenging, and it was an uphill battle.

The Biblical passages that geocentrists most frequently cited as being in conflict with the heliocentric view are provided here:

- "Who founded the earth on its foundations, it will not be shaken forever" (Psalm 104:5)

- "God made the orb immobile" (1 Chronicles 16:30)

- "Heaven is up; the earth is down" (Proverbs 30:3)

- "The sun rises, and sets, and returns to its place..." (Ecclesiastes 1:5)

- "And the sun and the moon stood still, till the people revenged themselves of their enemies. Is not this written in the book of the just? So the sun stood still in the midst of the heaven, and hasted not to go down the space of one day" (Joshua 10:13)

The last biblical passage listed above was the one the Grand Duchess Christina had challenged Castelli with during the famous lunchtime encounter of 1613. In this Old Testament story (Joshua 10:12-13), Joshua had petitioned God to grant him more daylight so that he had time to vanquish his enemies. The passage describes how God satisfied Joshua's request by stopping the sun in the "midst of the heaven." It was an act that strongly implied that the sun had previously been in motion – a motion that was incompatible with the Copernican system.

Galileo responded brilliantly to the challenge of the Joshua passage in his *Letter to Castelli* – once again turning an important criticism into an advantage. He was able to clearly show that his critics were being hypocritical in demanding that Copernicans yield to a purely literal reading of scripture. Because his critics adopted the Thomistic-Aristotelian view, a literal reading of Joshua would have meant that God had stopped the sun's slow west-to-east motion against the background of the celestial sphere. But the Joshua passage makes no mention of stopping the entire celestial sphere, which rotates around the earth in a rapid east-to-west direction every 23 hours and 56 minutes. Thus, if God had stopped the sun, but not the celestial sphere, the sun would have set four minutes *earlier* than normal!

By remarking on this, Galileo was clearly inviting his opponents to explain how the Aristotelian view was compatible with the Joshua passage. But to do this, the Aristotelians needed to argue that it was actually the celestial sphere that had stopped – not the sun. By forcing his opponents to embellish the passage with such a science-minded explanation, Galileo forced them to concede that the Joshua passage was written in the "normal manner of speaking." Thus, Galileo showed his readers that the Aristotelians needed to adopt the same kind of non-literal reading of the Bible that they had intended to deny Galileo.[30] Galileo then went on to argue that the Copernican system could be seen as being *more* compatible with a literal reading of Joshua than the Aristotelian system was.[31]

Galilean Theology

Galileo responded to the theological challenge against Copernicanism more thoroughly in his *Letter to Christina*. It was also a more aggressively pro-Copernican work than his *Letter to Castelli* had been – in some places daringly so.[32] Moreover, although the work is ostensibly addressed to the Grand Duchess Christina, the document reads as though he is speaking to theologians directly and is giving them advice. He did this with some risk to himself because he had no training or authority to make theological pronouncements. Even so, Galileo managed to stay out of trouble for a number of reasons – with the most important one listed first: 1) The *Letter to Christina* was not published but was copied and its distribution limited to those whom Galileo trusted. 2) The theological position Galileo adopted was a conservative view that had been established much earlier by St. Augustine (354-420 CE). 3) His theological positions avoided issues of "faith and morals." The Council of Trent had specifically forbade individuals from offering new theological opinions on "matters of faith" – that was a responsibility that belonged to the Church alone. Galileo understood Trent to mean that he was free to offer other theological opinions – as long as they were not matters of faith. 4) Earlier Catholic theologians appear not to have rendered an opinion on the motion of the earth, so it wasn't clear that Galileo was even disputing a belief that had been previously established by the Church.[33] As we will see, not everyone agreed with him on these last two points.

St. Augustine

Galileo's *Letter to Christina* relied heavily on the theology of St. Augustine. St. Augustine had been the most highly regarded of the early church Fathers, and his wisdom on theological matters was unquestioned by later theologians. For this reason, Galileo was on safe ground. St. Augustine was from the Roman city of Hippo in North Africa where he served as its bishop shortly after his conversion to Christianity. Earlier in his life, he had been a professor of rhetoric, so he was well acquainted with the Greek intellectual tradition. In his role as Bishop of Hippo, St. Augustine worked diligently to win more converts to Christianity. At that time in the declining Roman Empire, there were many religious traditions and cults in competition with each other.

St. Augustine sought to convert the most influential pagans. These pagans were educated in Greek science and cosmology as Augustine himself had been. The educated classes in the Mediterranean world believed in a round earth and in the Greek two-sphere model of the heavens. St. Augustine understood that it would be problematic and counter-productive for Christians to demand a purely literal reading of scripture, because that would have required potential converts to accept a more primitive cosmology than what they already had available. In Augustine's way of thinking, Christians could ruin their credibility and lose potential converts by exhibiting their ignorance of natural philosophy.

Old Testament Cosmology

The Jewish or Hebrew cosmology that appears in the Old Testament has very little in common with the cosmology of the Greeks. Furthermore, we should appreciate that the "Old Testament" was not at all old for most Christians, but was an entirely new document, since most converts to Christianity were Gentiles who had never practiced Judaism.[34]

The Hebrew or Old Testament Bible describes an earth that is flat and that rests on pillars. Some passages appear to describe a flat earth that is square or rectangular, in others it is portrayed as a round disk. There is nothing in the Bible that corresponds to the spherical earth of the Greeks:

> "...in his anger; who shakes the earth out of its place, and its pillars tremble; who commands the sun and it does not rise" (Job 9:5-6)

> "...from one end of the earth to the other" (Deut. 13:7 and 28:64)

> "He will raise a signal for a nation far away, and whistle for a people at the ends of the earth" (Isaiah 5:26)

> "...and gather the dispersed of Judah from the four corners (kanefot) of the earth" (Isaiah 11.12)

> "The end has come upon the four corners of the land" (Ezekiel 7:5)

The Hebrew Bible also describes the sky as resting on pillars, which is very different from the Greek two-sphere model of the heavens.

> "The pillars of heaven tremble, and are astounded at his rebuke" (Job 26:11)

In some places, the sky is described as stretched like a tent or fabric and in others, as though it is a dome that has been hammered out of metal. Celestial waters exist beyond the sky (the "firmament" or "dome").

> "And God said, 'Let there be a dome in the midst of the waters, and let it separate the waters from the waters.' So god made the dome and separated the waters that were under the dome from the waters that were

above the Dome. And it was so. God called the dome Sky" (Genesis 1:6-8)

A few early Christians read these biblical passages in a strictly literal sense and concluded that the earth was flat. An early church father named Lactantius (240- ca.320 CE) was known for this view. St. Augustine was concerned that ill-informed Christians might squander their influence over potential converts by seeming foolish – an appearance that would likely result in the tragic loss of souls. Furthermore, Augustine was thinking beyond his own time. He was concerned that new and untested ideas about the natural world that might first appear to be in conflict with scripture could later be shown to be true. For this reason, he counseled Christians against too hastily proclaiming against new ideas, because they ran the risk of being proved wrong somewhere down the road. If that happened, it would show potential converts that Christians weren't just wrong about science, but that they were wrong about properly understanding their own religion as well. In Augustine's view, the Bible was not written to be a guide to the natural world for the use of scientists and philosophers – rather, it was written as a religious guide for the benefit of all believers in pursuing eternal salvation.

Galileo modeled his *Letter to Christina* on the opinions of St. Augustine and quoted him and other Church Fathers extensively. Since St. Augustine was arguably the most influential and important Father of the Catholic Church, Galileo had adopted a centuries' old conservative theological viewpoint in his *Letter* that was tried and true. He echoed St. Augustine's belief that the Holy Ghost had inspired the authors of the Bible to write about salvation – not about the natural world. Galileo quoted one of his contemporaries, Cardinal Baronio, who had cleverly summed up the idea: "The intention of the Holy Spirit is to teach us how one goes to Heaven, not how Heaven goes."

In order to explain why descriptions in the Bible sometimes seemed to conflict with what natural philosophers knew to be true, St. Augustine had postulated that Biblical authors simplified their language for the common person. By using language and imagery "in the normal manner of speech," they were able to deliver important religious or moral messages to everyone. St. Augustine explicitly stated that the Lord had not intended to teach science or mathematics and did not include the subjects in the Bible to avoid confusing the readers. This interpretive idea has come to be known as the "principle of accommodation" – sometimes also known as "benevolent condescension."

Galileo borrowed all of these ideas from St. Augustine. Galileo also argued that the Holy Ghost's message in the Bible is to help us to understand things that we could know in no other way. In contrast, when it comes to knowing something about nature, which is not a matter of faith, man must rely on his senses and on reason – not on scripture because scripture was not written with that purpose in mind. As he stated in his Letter to Castelli:

> I am inclined to think that the authority of Holy Scripture is intended to convince men of those truths which are necessary for their salvation, and which being far above man's understanding cannot be made credible by any learning, or any other means than revelation by the Holy Spirit. But that the same God who has endowed us with senses, reason, and understanding, does not permit us to use them, and desires to acquaint us in any other way with such knowledge as we are in a position to acquire for ourselves by means of those faculties, that it seems to me I am not bound to believe, especially concerning those sciences about which the Holy Scriptures contain only small fragments and varying conclusions; and this is precisely the case with astronomy, of which there is so little that the planets are not even all enumerated. (trans. Sturge in Gebler, 1879).

Galileo then made the explicit claim that in order to understand what scripture has to say about the natural world, one should first understand the natural world through experience and reason. So when we find cases in which science *appears* to be in conflict with scripture, we can conclude that scripture had not been correctly understood in the first place.

God's Two Books

Galileo's line of reasoning was supported by another important theme that he emphasized in his letters to Castelli and Christina – that God had written two books: the Bible and the "Book of Nature." The centuries-old metaphor that God had authored two books found some support in scripture: "Ever since the creation of the world his eternal power and divine nature, invisible though they are, have been understood and seen through the things he has made" (Romans 1:20). And, "The heavens are telling the glory of God; and the firmament proclaims his handiwork" (Psalm 19:1).[35]

The Bible was written because it contained essential messages of salvation and morality, whereas the Book of Nature was written in order to create a temporal home for us to live in. Both Galileo and Augustine maintained that scripture was not written to instruct man about the workings of nature. Galileo repeated this view in his *Letter to Christina* and supported it further by pointing out that the Bible made no references to astronomy except for the sun and the moon and "...only once or twice Venus, under the name of the Morning Star."[36] Galileo used an analogy to explain why theologians should not become overly concerned about the work of natural philosophers:

> If then theology occupies herself solely with the highest problems, maintains her throne by reason of the supreme authority conferred on her, and does not condescend to the lower sciences as not affecting salvation, the professors of theology should not assume authority on subjects which they have not studied. For this is just as if an absolute ruler should demand, without being a physician or an architect, that people should treat themselves, or erect buildings, according to his directions, to the great peril of poor sick people and obvious ruin of the edifices. (trans. Sturge in Gebler, 1879).

Instead, it was left to the philosopher-scientists to "read" the book of nature. In his *Letter to Christina*, Galileo quoted the following passage as an indication of the difficulty of the task: "God hath delivered the world to their consideration, so that man cannot find out the work which God hath made from the beginning to the end" (Ecclesiastes 3). Galileo's point here was that the structure of God's creation was hidden from view and was not to be understood through ordinary common sense.

In the High Middle Ages, when the scientific works of Aristotle were being studied by Christian scholars in Europe for the first time, there was an increasing awareness that the "Book of Nature" and the Bible sometimes seemed to disagree. A few imaginative interpreters proposed to solve the dilemma by claiming that what was true in nature might not be true in scripture and vice versa. However, most thinkers found the notion of such a "double truth" to be absurd, and the idea was dismissed as a logical impossibility from that time on: If God was the author of both books, then the books must be compatible with each other. Christians had established that their God would not contradict himself. This principle was a fundamental assumption that held together philosophical, theological, and scientific ideas in European thought. It was left to theologians to determine how the Bible and the "Book of Nature" should be reconciled when there were *apparent* incompatibilities.

In the fall of 1615, Galileo became increasingly concerned that the Congregation of the Index was about to ban Copernicanism. Desperate to avoid having a large part of his scientific effort prohibited or circumscribed, Galileo traveled to Rome to make a series of personal appeals to influential churchmen and intellectuals. He arrived in December, against the Tuscan ambassador's recommendation and began an intense campaign of persuasion. Accounts of Galileo's activity at this time show him to be a master of argument. In public debates he restated his opponents' views and amplified their ideas in order to make them as strong as possible before he proceeded to demolish them in front of their supporters. He impressed his admirers and angered his opponents. The Tuscan ambassador grew uneasy witnessing the Medici's court philosopher going against popular sentiment and engaging in theological debates in the holy city of Rome. During this period, the ambassador referred to Galileo in his reports to the Medici court as " *The Galileo*"– as though Galileo were some sort of phenomenon unto himself. One is left with the image of a bull in a china shop. The ambassador predicted an unhappy outcome, while Galileo's hope was that his pro-Copernican project might not be thwarted. It is important to note that not all theologians were opposed to Copernicanism – indeed, there appears to have been a greater diversity of viewpoints among Catholic theologians on the Copernican controversy than there were among university philosophers.

Pope Paul V, Cardinal Bellarmine, the Index, and the Holy Office

Pope Paul V (1552-1621) was the leader of the Roman Catholic Church as well as the secular prince of the Papal States – a sizeable territory that extended across the midsection of the Italian peninsula. Thus, Pope Paul

V had concerns both as a secular leader who ruled over a significant physical realm and as the religious leader of the Catholic Church. Another key figure at the Vatican was the Lord Cardinal Robert Bellarmine (1542-1621). St. Bellarmine, as he is now known by Catholics, was a highly-regarded cardinal who served in the Papal Curia as an advisor to Pope Paul V in theological and other matters. As a powerful and successful leader in the fight against the Protestant movement and heresies in general, Bellarmine's foreboding nickname was "the hammer of the heretics." Early in his career as a cardinal, Bellarmine had been appointed a member of the Holy Office of the Inquisition and served as a judge in the famous trial of Giordano Bruno.

Bruno (1548-1600) was a Dominican monk who held a variety of heretical religious beliefs. The most important of these had to do with his heterodox views about the nature of Christ and the Trinity. He was also an early Copernican who believed that the Universe was infinite in its extent and that it harbored numerous worlds like our own – a belief to which he applied his own religious interpretations. In the face of his transgressions, even the normally protective Venetian Republic turned Bruno over to the Inquisition where he was found guilty of heresy. He refused to recant his beliefs and was burned at the stake in 1600. While Bruno mixed his religious heresies with his unique version of the Copernican system, it was his religious beliefs that got him into trouble with the Inquisition – he was not burned at the stake simply because he was a Copernican, as some early commentators and historians have suggested.

The key point here is that Bellarmine had experience dealing with heretics – both Catholic and Protestant. Bellarmine hated the Protestant religions, which were all heresies by definition. He energetically led the fight against them with considerable success and while it is important to appreciate that maintaining Catholic orthodoxy was Bellarmine's main concern, there was a great deal more to the man than this. It is worth noting that at the same time Bellarmine was dealing with Galileo, Bellarmine himself had views about the heavens that went against the orthodox Jesuit position.[37] Thus, Bellarmine was able to see in shades of grey and was generally empathetic, but he also believed that Christianity was at great risk. He took his role as defender of the Catholic faith very seriously.

It is useful to distinguish between the two Catholic Church bureaus or "congregations" that worked to maintain Catholic orthodoxy: 1) The "Congregation of the Index" or, more commonly, "The Index," was the body of the Church that was specifically charged with censoring books and offering guidelines on what type of books were publishable. 2) The "Congregation of the Holy Office" or, more commonly, "The Holy Office," or "The Inquisition," was the body responsible for maintaining the faith and identifying individuals who held false doctrines. The Holy Office operated as an investigating body and as a court. It collected information and rendered judgments against individuals according to an established legal procedure.

Banning Copernicanism – the Decree of 1616

The publication of Foscarini's pro-Copernican theology and Galileo's boisterous advocacy of heliocentrism in Rome brought the issue to a head. The theological battle between conservative philosophers and the "Galileists" was creating discord among Catholics. Pope Paul V ordered consultants to the Holy Office to address the theological correctness of the following Copernican propositions:

> I. The sun is the center of the world and immovable from its place.

> II. The earth is not the center of the world and is not immovable, but moves, and also with a diurnal motion.

The consultants responded with their conclusions in only four days. They determined that the first proposition, that the sun was central and stationary, was philosophically absurd and formally heretical. Similarly, they determined that the second proposition, that the earth moves, was philosophically absurd and was "at least erroneous in faith." It is quite significant that the consultants' theological conclusions depended on arriving at philosophical (scientific) conclusions first.

This judgment is sometimes mistakenly referred to as "Galileo's First Trial." In fact, it had been physical Copernicanism that was on trial. And although the decision of the Holy Office was made with Galileo in mind, there was no public mention of Galileo or his works. Even so, Pope Paul V and Bellarmine decided that it was necessary to have a special meeting with the determined and forceful Galileo in order to ensure that he got the message. According to a Vatican manuscript of February, 1616:

> His Holiness [Pope Paul V] has directed the Lord Cardinal Bellarmine to summon before him the said Galileo, and admonish him to abandon the said opinion; and in case of his refusal to obey, that the Commissary is to intimate to him, before a notary and witnesses, a command to abstain altogether from teaching or defending this opinion and doctrine, and even from discussing it; and if he does not acquiesce therein, that he is to be imprisoned. (trans. Sturge in Gebler, 1879).

Bellarmine's strategy was to deal with Galileo as diplomatically as possible, but to also ensure that the gregarious Philosopher and Mathematician to the Grand Duke of Tuscany would fully comply with the decree. Galileo was to be told to stop advocating for the reality of the Copernican system and, if he exhibited any reluctance to do so, would be formally served a binding legal injunction that was more strongly worded. The meeting took place between Bellarmine and Galileo with some Dominican witnesses and the Commissary of the Holy Office, Father Segizzi, present. Segizzi was prepared to formally present the injunction if it became necessary. We don't know precisely the manner in which Galileo was told to cease his advocacy of the Copernican cause, but it appears certain that he was made aware of the formal injunction at some point during this meeting. Whether or not it was properly served on him remains a matter of debate. As we will see, this will all have important implications for Galileo's trial in 1633. What is clear is that Galileo complied with Bellarmine's orders after the meeting:

> The Lord Cardinal Bellarmine having reported that Galileo Galilei, mathematician, had in terms of the order of the Holy Congregation been admonished to abandon the opinion he has hitherto held, that the sun is the center of the spheres and immovable, and that the earth moves, and had acquiesced therein; (trans. Sturge in Gebler, 1879).

Thus, Galileo's Copernican activities were seriously circumscribed by the decree of 1616. The works of Copernicus, Foscarini, and Diego Zuñiga had been restricted or banned entirely. On 5 March, 1616 the Congregation of the Index publicly issued its formal decree, which was based in part by the recommendation of the consultants:

> The Holy congregation has decreed that the said Nicholas Copernicus,
> De revolutionibus orbium, and Diego di Zuñiga, on Job, be suspended
> until they be corrected; but that the book of the Carmelite Father,
> Paolo Antonio Foscarini, be altogether prohibited and condemned,
> and that all other works likewise, in which the same is taught, be
> prohibited... (trans. Sturge in Gebler, 1879).

Thus, the works of Copernicus and Zuñiga were prohibited until certain passages were corrected. Copernicus's *De revolutionibus* remained largely intact, but passages that described or advocated the physical reality of the Copernican system were censored. Foscarini did not fare so well – his entire work was banned, and he died while standing trial for having published his work without securing the proper permissions. Galileo, in his position as the Chief Mathematician and Philosopher to the powerful Duke of Tuscany, fared much better. The obviously pro-Copernican works like his *Sunspot Letters*, and his unpublished *Letter to Castelli* and *Letter to Christina* were not mentioned at all.

Although Galileo was not specifically mentioned in the decree, rumors spread that he had been forced to recant and had been punished at the hands of the Inquisition. To respond to the rumors, Galileo remained in Rome for a time in order to project a sense of normalcy. He also described the damaging rumors to Bellarmine and asked him for a public letter that would certify that they were untrue. Bellarmine, in the interest of clearing Galileo's name and maintaining amiable relations with the Medicis, provided Galileo with such a document:

> We, Robert Cardinal Bellarmine, have heard that it is calumniously
> reported that Signor Galileo Galilei has in our hand abjured, and has
> also been punished with salutary penance, and being requested to state
> the truth as to this, declare, that the said Signor Galileo has not
> abjured, either in our hand, or the hand of any other person here in
> Rome, or anywhere else, so far as we know, any opinion or doctrine

held by him, neither has any salutary penance been imposed upon him; but only the declaration made by the Holy Father and published by the sacred Congregation of the Index, has been intimated to him... (trans. Sturge in Gebler, 1879).

At the ambassador's recommendation, "The Galileo" was finally called back to Florence before he could cause any more trouble. He returned to Tuscany in June, which marked the beginning of a long period during which he no longer publicly promoted the Copernican system.

Work and Publications post-1616
During this time, Galileo was forced to watch in silence as anti-Copernican authors attacked Copernicanism without fear of being answered. Galileo was no doubt frustrated by this. He also felt betrayed by the Jesuits for not having supporting him more actively during the time that led up to the decree. But as was described earlier, Jesuit scientists, especially those who shared Galileo's Copernican sentiments, did not have the same freedom that Galileo did. Galileo had a powerful and independent patron who enthusiastically supported his project. In contrast, the patron of Jesuit scientists was the Jesuit Order itself and its general, who had repeatedly admonished individual Jesuits for straying from orthodoxy. A Copernican Jesuit had a clear choice – conceal his Copernicanism or lose his position. Indeed, even prior to the decree, a few Jesuits were removed from their posts for too enthusiastically discussing the Copernican view. Galileo's Jesuit friends could not help him in 1616, and Galileo never forgave them for that. While Galileo may have been justifiably disappointed by the Jesuits' silence, his feeling of betrayal seems to have been out of place.

Work on the Problem of Longitude in Navigation
Anxious to continue reaping the benefits of his telescopic discoveries, Galileo began to work on solving the problem of determining longitude at sea. Large monetary rewards had been offered by seafaring nations to anyone who could provide a method for navigators to determine their longitude while at sail. It had always been easy to determine one's latitude (north-south position) by simply noting the angular distance between the North Star and the northern horizon or by measuring the height of the sun in the sky. But there were no astronomically fixed east-

west reference points from which to measure longitudes. Longitude positions were only referenced relative to another location on the earth's surface; there were not absolute reference positions like those in latitude determinations (such as the poles or the equator). For example, today by agreement, everyone references longitude to a line marked at the British Royal Observatory in Greenwich, England, which is conventionally defined as 0°. In Galileo's day, one could determine the relative longitude between two points in one of two ways: 1) By taking direct distance measurements over the earth's surface – a task that was difficult enough to accomplish with any accuracy over land and nearly impossible to do so by sea. 2) By recording an astronomical event at two places simultaneously and then comparing the local time difference between the two points.[38] Such a method provided the angular distance between two points on the globe. The disadvantage in the second method was that the determinations could only be made on rare occasions and with questionable accuracy. The inability to easily and accurately determine longitude made both long-range navigation around the globe and map-making problematic.

Galileo carefully observed the four moons of Jupiter and was able to determine the individual orbits and periods for each of them – by doing so, he was able to predict their future positions. Because their locations changed noticeably over a few hours' time, and their disappearance and reappearance from behind the Jovian disk were well-defined and frequent, they held great promise for determining longitude. Galileo spent a large amount of time recording his predictions onto tables and inventing apparatuses that would allow a navigator to telescopically observe the moons from a tossing and turning ship. His basic observational design included a telescope attached to a helmet that a navigator would wear. He worked with the Spanish government on his project, but was ultimately unsuccessful and won no reward. The unfortunate navigators who attempted to use the device had difficulty sighting the moons and were often overcome by intense seasickness. In any case, Galileo's tables for the Jovian moons were not accurate enough to satisfactorily determine longitude, although the same principle was later applied to the eclipses of the Jovian moons by Cassini. Cassini's method proved to be very accurate for the determinations of longitude by surveyors who worked on solid ground.[39]

Controversy of the Comets 1618

As Kepler had so famously predicted, the year 1618 brought with it multiple comets and along with them, multiple commentaries on their nature and location. Galileo was extremely ill at this time and was confined to his bed, so he had little opportunity to observe them himself. But he did read the reports of others. The author of one of the commentaries was the Jesuit Orazio Grassi of the Collegio Romano, who published his work under the pseudonym "Sarsi." Galileo, in a foul mood from his illness and looking for an opportunity to pay the Jesuits back for their failure to support him in 1616, responded nastily to Grassi's work. Galileo's publication was entitled *Discourse on Comets* (1619) and although Galileo's student Guiducci was listed as its author, interested readers understood who was really behind its writing and publication.

In *Discourse on Comets,* Galileo-Guiducci took Grassi to task about the methods, assumptions, and conclusions he used in his work and decided to publicly teach Grassi a thing or two about proper reasoning. The *Discourse* had little to do with Copernicanism, beyond creating uncertainties about the nature and motion of comets that could be used to make attacks against it.[40] Mostly, the *Discourse* appeared to be written with the goal of establishing Grassi's incompetence. In any case, Galileo criticized much but proposed little in this book. With the decree of 1616 in force, Galileo was constrained from speaking freely – perhaps if he had been able to do so, he may not have been so disagreeable toward Grassi. As with so many of Galileo's writings, the *Discourse* was skillfully written and full of biting sarcasm and wit – all at Grassi's expense. The Jesuits at the Collegio Romano were not at all pleased with Galileo's insulting one of their own. Any warm feelings toward Galileo that existed at the Collegio Romano had run cold by this point.

Galileo – Still a Copernican...

Galileo was extremely frustrated that he was never able to bring his "theory of tides" to print. In his mind, the theory all but proved that the earth was in motion. The tidal variations that Galileo had observed first-hand in the lagoons of Venice begged for an explanation that he believed only a moving earth could provide. He had various manuscript versions of his tidal theory on hand, but he had published nothing yet – and with the decree of 1616 in force he would not be able to. Although the decree allowed a *hypothetical* discussion and treatment of Copernican astronomical theory, it forbade Copernicanism to be entertained as physical reality. Since the theory of the tides was a physical proposition, it would be a big stretch for Galileo to claim that it was a mere hypothesis similar to the epicycles and eccentrics of mathematical astronomy. In any case, Galileo didn't want to portray his theory of tides as anything less than solid evidence in support of the earth's motion. Thus, Galileo was in no position to follow through with his desire to publish on the subject – at least in Italy. It seems that Galileo may have made a veiled attempt to have his theory of tides published in Germany. At one point, he approached a powerful admirer and acquaintance of his, Duke Leopold of Austria, the brother of Grand Duchess Christina. In a letter of May 1618, Galileo sent Leopold some telescopes, a copy of his treatise on tides, and an interesting letter – a portion of which appears below:

> I consider this treatise which I send you merely to be a poetical conceit, or a dream, and desire that your Highness may take it as such, inasmuch as it is based on the double motion of the earth, and indeed contains one of the arguments which I have adduced in confirmation of it. But even poets sometimes attach a value to one or other of their fantasies, and I likewise attach some value to the fancy of mine. Now, having written the treatise, and having shown it to the Cardinal above-mentioned [Orsini], and a few others, I have also let a few exalted personages have copies, in order that in case anyone not belonging to our church should try to appropriate my curious fancy, as has happened to me with many of my discoveries, these personages, being above all suspicion, may be able to bear witness that it was I who first dreamed of this chimera. (trans. Sturge in Gebler, 1879).

There is plenty that could be read between the lines in the preceding passage. Leopold was well aware that Galileo believed in the reality of the Copernican system and that Galileo thought that his theory of tides served as a proof for it. Given the decree of 1616, Leopold would have understood that Galileo used the words "conceit" or "dream" or "fancy" for safety's sake – in case someone unfavorable to Galileo or Copernicanism were to read it. It also appears that Galileo was suggesting to Leopold that he was unconcerned about the possibility of someone "stealing" his treatise and having it published outside of Italy. If that happened without Galileo's knowledge or consent, Galileo would be able to deny his responsibility for its publication, but still claim ownership for an idea that pre-dated the decree of 1616. If this was indeed Galileo's suggestion, Leopold did not take him up on it.[41]

Grassi (Sarsi) soon published a response to Galileo-Guiducci's *Discourse on Comets*. The Jesuit's work was entitled *The Astronomical and Philosophical Balance* (1619), after a device that was used for weighing one object relative to the weight of another. In his *Balance*, Grassi advocated for Aristotelian physics and positioned himself against Copernicanism – full well knowing that Galileo could not freely respond. Galileo took the advice of Cesi and his other friends in Rome by not taking the bait – at least not at the time.

Deaths and a New Era

The deaths of 1621 included those of Cardinal Bellarmine, Pope Paul V, and Galileo's patron, Cosimo II. The College of Cardinals then elected a pope who took the title Gregory XV. Old and infirm, Gregory XV reigned for only two years before dying. After numerous ballots were cast by a long sequestered College of Cardinals, a new pope was elected in 1623 – the fifty-five year old Cardinal Maffeo Barberini, who took the title Urban VIII. This was great news for Galileo because Maffeo Barberini had been a great admirer of Galileo and his work – so much so that Barberini had once penned a poem in admiration of Galileo and sent it to him. Pope Urban VIII was an intellectual who appreciated Renaissance literature, art, and science. He was not as conservative as his predecessors had been. Galileo wasted no time in taking advantage of the situation. He sent a letter of congratulations to the brother of Urban VIII (a direct letter to the new pope would have been inappropriate).

In this new political climate, Galileo was at last able to gain approval to publish his rejoinder to Grassi's *Balance*. Published in 1623, this work was cleverly titled the *Assayer*, after a weighing instrument that was far more accurate than the crude *Balance* of Grassi's. Galileo avoided any direct references to Copernicanism, but he did take on the Aristotelian view in a masterful and eloquent way. In his *Assayer*, Galileo not only presented his physical conclusions and reasoning, but presented the kind of strategy one should take when engaged in the study of nature. It was nothing less than a manifesto for a new kind of philosophizing about nature. The writing was so impressive that it is still considered a classic in Italian literature. It won rave reviews from admirers and complaints from opponents, including an anonymous letter to the Holy Office that claimed Galileo's atomistic views on the nature of substances were incompatible with proper Catholic belief about the real presence of the body and blood of Christ during the Holy Sacrament (Communion). There were also objections that the *Assayer* discreetly defended the Copernican position. None of the complaints inspired the Holy Office to action.

Another treatise that may well have caused Galileo some trouble if he had allowed it to circulate widely, was his *Letter to Ingoli* (ca. 1624). The letter was a belated response to a work written immediately after the decree of 1616 by Francesco Ingoli – a work to which Galileo was unable to respond. Galileo's friend and the pope's personal secretary, Ciampoli, had read carefully selected portions of Galileo's *Letter to Ingoli* to Pope Urban VIII, who found what he heard to be clever and amusing. Still, Galileo and his friends decided that circulating the entire *Letter* might bring trouble, so they never gave a copy of it to Ingoli. Galileo remained cautious about bringing up the subject of Copernicanism.

With his hopes for the publication of a new Copernican work on his mind, Galileo traveled to Rome in the spring of 1624. He had several audiences with Urban VIII, which included lengthy discussions about Galileo's hope to once again raise the Copernican issue. Galileo and Urban VIII both wanted to see Galileo's work in print, but each had a very different goal in mind. Urban VIII believed that the decree of 1616 was a bad decision, and he wanted Galileo to show to the world that Catholics had understood all of the mathematical and philosophical reasons in favor of the Copernican view. Urban VIII wanted to make it clear that Catholics had not denied the physical reality of Copernicanism because they were poor scientists, but because they were devout and pious Christians. Galileo, on the other hand, simply wanted a second shot at selling the Copernican view. As we will see, although their goals were superficially related, they were not at all compatible.

It was clear to both men that Galileo would need to treat Copernicanism hypothetically and not absolutely. Their extensive discussions appear to have revolved around just what each of them meant by "hypothetically." After six audiences with Urban VIII, and believing that he understood the pope's instructions and had his blessing, Galileo returned to Tuscany to begin the writing. Urban VIII was very impressed and pleased with Galileo at this time and was enthusiastic about their mutual plan. The Pope's sentiment was positive enough that he wrote a strongly favorable letter on Galileo's behalf to Galileo's patron, the young Grand Duke of Tuscany, Ferdinando II:[42]

> We have observed in him not only the literary distinction, but also the love of religion and all the good qualities worthy of the papal favor. When he came to congratulate us on our accession, we embraced him affectionately, and listened with pleasure to his learned demonstrations which add fresh renown to Florentine eloquence. We desire that he should not return to his native country without having received by our generosity manifold proofs of our papal favor. (trans. Sturge in Gebler, 1879).

It was undoubtedly advantageous for Galileo to be held in high regard by both the new Duke and Pope Urban VIII. In a sense, Galileo had two great patrons.

---

[1]In addition to the scientific relevance of the dispute, there is also a backstory concerning Galileo's motives for so enthusiastically engaging in the controversy: When Galileo originally petitioned the Medici court to be granted the title "philosopher," he had no formal credentials to justify the request. In a sense, by showing Cosimo II that he was capable of successfully debating with academic philosophers, he had proved his worth as his employee.

[2] Galileo's telescopes were not of sufficient quality to resolve the rings of Saturn. Because of this, Galileo described Saturn as being "three-bodied" and remained unsure of what he was looking at. Even more perplexing to Galileo was the fact that these "bodies" disappeared two years later when he looked at Saturn again (*Sunspot Letters*). It wasn't until 1655 when Christiaan Huygens, employing a considerably more powerful telescope, explained the planet's changing appearance as the result of a ring encircling it, which was inclined to the ecliptic.

Galileo was also successful at identifying the individual periods for the four moons of Jupiter – an impressive accomplishment that Kepler had considered impossible. Finally, in the second edition of *Bodies that Stay atop Water*, Galileo reported that the sun was spinning.

[3] One disadvantage of writing in Italian was that it limited Galileo's audience to Italians. Indeed, he often made requests that his books be translated into Latin so that intellectuals across Europe would have access to them as well.

[4] Galileo seems not to have been aware that Kepler had, in large measure, solved the problem of the planets, which Kepler had reported in his *Astronomia Nova* and *Epitome of Copernican Astronomy*. Knowledge of Kepler's success grew slowly among astronomers following the publication of his *Rudophine Tables*. We have firm evidence that Galileo knew about Kepler's ellipses through letters from Cesi, but we don't know what he thought of them. It may have been that Galileo could simply not be bothered with that level of astronomical detail when he was caught up in his own work. However, one could also speculate that Galileo may have found the ellipse troublesome given his emerging concept of inertial circular motion (akin to the modern concept of angular momentum) and his continuing commitment to the special standing of the circle (in this regard, Galileo was conservative). In any case, Galileo remained silent on the issue of Kepler's ellipses.

[5] Not everyone in Galileo's day agreed that the planets shone with reflected sunlight – some believed that planets generated their own light or that they were illuminated by stars. Kepler was one of those who believed that planets had light of their own and he was quite surprised when Galileo reported his discovery of the phases of Venus. In fact, it was this discovery that caused Kepler to change his opinion and adopt the view that planets were illuminated by light from the sun.

[6] This idea is often referred to as "Ockham's Razor," after the medieval philosopher William of Ockham (1287-1347), even though the sentiment precedes him. It is also referred to as the principle of parsimony, which is based on the expectation that nature is simple and well-organized. Therefore, if one is comparing two theories that are otherwise equally successful in explaining the facts, one should choose the simpler theory as the one more likely to be true.

[7] This appearance of Saturn through early telescopes was later understood to be due to its rings. Christiaan Huygens (1629-1695), a Dutch scientist, discovered the rings of Saturn in 1655 using a more powerful telescope of his own design. In the same year, he also discovered a moon of Saturn, which later came to be known as Titan. Titan was the fifth moon of another planet that was discovered. There are now many dozens of moons known to exist in our solar system.

[8] Francesco Sizzi and his colleagues in France had noted before Scheiner that there were seasonal changes in the paths of the sunspots; he described the phenomenon in a 1613 letter to Galileo. At the time, Galileo had his hands full and failed to note the significance of the discovery with regard to the debate over cosmological systems. Only when Scheiner had announced the impending publication of his magnum opus,

Rosa Ursina (1630), did Galileo reassess everything he knew about sunspots and finally recognized the significance of the seasonal pattern.

[9] For an excellent discussion and helpful diagrams, see Mueller, Paul R., S.J., 2000.

[10] Galileo held a concept of motion that had features in common with those that were later developed and clearly articulated by Isaac Newton. However, Galileo's "proto-inertial" concepts were considerably different than Newton's – especially concerning straight line motion, which Galileo did not consider to be a "natural motion." Galileo's proto-inertial ideas appear to be the most modern when applied to objects possessing circular motion – as occurs in the motion of a planet around the sun or the spinning motion of a spherical object about its own axis.

[11] Most Aristotelian-Ptolemaic astronomers would have expected the orientation of a spinning sun to remain fixed within the crystalline sphere that carried the sun around the earth. Thus, they would have expected that the orientation of the sun's axis relative to the earth would remain unchanged over time – not dissimilar to the way that one side of the moon always faces the earth. For the spin axis of the sun to change its orientation in the Aristotelian-Ptolemaic system, it would have to have had an additional motion that slowly caused its axis to precess 1/365th of the way around every day.

[12] The presentation of Galileo's sunspot analysis that I've provided here is consistent with that provided by Paul Mueller, S.J. in "An Unblemished Success: Galileo's Sunspot Argument in the Dialogue," *Journal for the History of Astronomy*, 31, no. 4, 2000. For dissenting views, see Smith (1985), Topper (1999) and (2003), and Gingerich (2003). Regardless of what modern historians think of Galileo's sunspot argument, a report on the *Dialogue* given to the Inquisition in 1633 listed Galileo's sunspot argument as a substantial physical argument in support of Copernicanism.

[13] Using the length of the lunar shadows and the dimensions of the moon (as it was known then), he calculated the height of the lunar mountains. Today we know that the tallest lunar mountains visible from earth are closer to three miles in height, so Galileo's estimate was quite respectable.

[14] One treatise was by Ludovico delle Colombe, who would become a determined enemy of Galileo. Another work was by the young Francesco Sizzi, for whom Galileo had a surprising amount of patience and who, over the years, eventually came around to seeing things from Galileo's point of view. See Blackwell, 1991, pp. 57-60.

[15] Mary Allan-Olney, 1870.

[16] See *Galileo's Daughter* by Dava Sobel, 1999, for an excellent introductory account of Galileo's life and his relationship with his daughter Maria Celeste.

[17] For a good brief account of the Galileo Affair see Sharratt, 1994. For the most thorough account and one which details the interactions between Galileo and the Catholic Church see Fantoli, 1994. For an examination of the relationship between theology in science with regard to the Affair and its actors, see Blackwell, 1991. More recently, Heilbron, 2010, has offered a highly regarded and readable account.

[18] It seems as likely as not that Galileo was concerned that Lorini *did* have an accurate copy of the *Letter*, and he simply did not want to take responsibility for it. Repeated attempts by the authorities to get their hands on the original from Castelli failed.

[19] This kind of epistemology, where it is believed that the correspondence between facts and a theory can never be shown to be true or real is called "instrumentalism" or "fictionalism" by philosophers and historians today. There are many reasons that thinkers have for claiming that a theory cannot be proven – so there are many versions of "instrumentalism" or "fictionalism." As Barker and Goldstein (1998) have pointed out, it is not appropriate to describe Bellarmine, and others who shared his view, with modern terminology, since they adopted a somewhat different view. Bellarmine was, in fact, a realist. He believed that there was a real and absolute constitution for the universe and that, in principle, there was a theory to explain it. But Bellarmine believed that it stood outside the realm of possibility for human intelligence to ever uncover that true description of cosmos.

[20] For an English translation of *The Letter to Christina* and other selected works by Galileo, see *The Essential Galileo*, edited and translated by Maurice Finnochiaro, 2008. The *Letter to Christina* was eventually published in Galileo's lifetime but outside of Italy and in Latin.

[21] In the Catholic tradition, there are extra-Biblical sources that are no less important than the Bible itself. One example of a tradition that predates the Bible is *The Divine Office*, a collection of prayers and hymns that are recited at regular times. These were first developed in the earliest period of Christianity and reflect a tradition that has its origins in Judaism. The prayers and hymns continue to be a particularly important element in Orthodox and Western Roman Catholicism as well as in the Anglican and Lutheran faiths.

[22] Luther also refused to recognize the special Catholic claims of authority, which resided in the pope. He didn't believe that the Catholic Church, in the form it had taken, reflected the holiness and wisdom of the early Catholic Church – a tradition to which he wished to return. Furthermore, he and most other Protestant leaders

believed that it was the Bible and only the Bible that existed as the source of authority for a proper Christian faith. This doctrine is called *Sola scriptura.*

[23] Contibutors to the *Ratio Studiorum* included both Acquaviva and Bellarmine. It was published in 1598. See Fantoli, 1996, and Blackwell, 1991, for further discussion.

[24] Clavius served a role similar to that which Phillip Melanchthon played in advancing mathematics in the Lutheran educational curriculum.

[25] It is important to appreciate that there was no uniformity of belief or motivation among the members of the Jesuit order. There were as many reasons for a man to become a Jesuit as there were Jesuits. Some were drawn to the order's deep commitment to the maintenance and propagation of the Catholic faith. Others found in it the opportunity to continue their studies and become men of letters or the sciences, ostensibly in the service of the church. There were a limited number of positions for intellectuals in the universities and in the courts of princes – so in this way, the Jesuit order frequently served as a "patron" to those who otherwise would have had to pursue a less intellectual trade. Given the diversity of motivations and interests, it was not at all uncommon for individual Jesuits to stray from orthodoxy. Indeed, this is what led General Acquaviva to issue such strict orders for Jesuits to toe the line. In the face of such demands, obedience and compromise was required; service as a Jesuit preacher was a coveted position, and it was rare for a Jesuit to leave the order. These were facts of Jesuit life that Galileo never acknowledged.

[26] Christoph Grienberger (1561-1636) who succeeded Clavius as professor of mathematics at the Collegio Romano, explained this in a letter of 5 February 1613 to Galileo, "Do not be surprised that I say nothing about your [writings]: I do not have the same freedom as you do" (trans., Sharratt, 1994, pp. 106).

[27] The Dominican-Jesuit rift was known as De Auxiliis, which concerned a theological question over the relative importance of free will and grace. Pope Paul V put an end to the debate with the understanding that he would later rule on it. He never did. The problem went away because the debaters stopped debating.

[28] The Council of Trent had been very explicit about forbidding anyone but Catholic Church hierarchy from expressing new theological opinions on "matters of faith and morals." Indeed, it had been such activity that had set the Protestant Reformation in motion in the first place.

[29] A friend of Galileo's, Paolo Gualdo, advised Galileo in May 1611 to maintain the Copernican system only as a possible hypothesis rather than as absolute reality. Gualdo underscored the danger of going against a deeply entrenched public opinion: "...for many things can be uttered by way of disputation which it is not wise to assert,

especially when the contrary opinion is held by everyone, imbibed, so to speak, since the foundation of the world..." (trans. Fantoli, 1996, pp. 122).

[30] Galileo in his *Letter to Christina*: "I shall demonstrate further below that, regardless of the world system one assumes, it is in fact necessary to gloss and interpret the words of the text in Joshua." (trans. Finocchiaro, 1989, pp. 110).

[31] Galileo speculated that the spinning sun was the cause of planetary motion, so that if God stopped the sun, the earth would cease to rotate and the day would be longer. It was a view that had a surprising commonality with Kepler's views of celestial motion and raises questions about Galileo's concept of circular inertia.

[32] Galileo in his *Letter to Christina*: "...the Supreme Pontiff always has the absolute power of permitting or condemning [propositions]; however, no creature has the power of making them be true or false..." (trans. Finocchiaro, 1989, pp. 114).

[33] Many of Galileo's opponents claimed that the Church Fathers had recognized the earth was stationary and that Galileo's opinion was contrary to Catholic belief. However, they were never able to show any documentation that this was the case. In fact, one of Galileo's pro-Copernican compatriots, Thomas Campanella, (an exceedingly interesting character in this drama), wrote a pro-Copernican treatise, *Apologia pro Galileo*. In this work, Campanella pointed out that many of the early Church Fathers, including John Chrysostom, expressed uncertainty about whether or not the earth was in motion and that this was evidence that they never made a claim one way or another.

[34] Jewish theologians had many centuries of experience addressing the differences between the well-known and highly regarded Greek cosmology and certain passages found in the Hebrew Bible (Old Testament). Philo the Jew of Alexandria wrote some interesting speculations on how to decode the Bible to learn more about the natural world, but most Jewish theologians appeared to take the view that the Hebrew Bible was not written with the intent to inform its readers about the natural world. For example, the advice of the early 2nd century BCE Talmud commentator Ben Sira was, "Do not pry into things too hard for you or examine what is beyond your reach. Meditate on the commandments you have been given; what the Lord keeps secret is no concern of yours."

[35] Galileo in his *Letter to Castelli*: "For the Holy Scripture and nature both equally derive from the divine Word, the former as the dictation of the Holy Spirit, the latter as the most obedient executrix of God's commands" (trans. Finocchiaro, 1989, pp. 50).

[36] Galileo in Fantoli, 1994, pp. 192, "...one does not find there even the names of the planets, except for the sun, the moon..."

[37] Bellarmine believed, like many thinkers in his day, that planets were not attached to crystalline spheres, but that they moved through fluid heavens. This went against the standard Aristotelian view. Indeed, in 1614 a Jesuit teacher ran into trouble for teaching this to his students. The Jesuit General, Acquaviva, personally counseled Christopher Scheiner not to advocate for it: "One ought not to publish against the universal teaching of the Fathers and the scholastic doctors a new hypothesis which, basing itself on yet uncertain observations, maintains that the heavens are fluid, and that stars propel themselves there like fish in the ocean and birds in air" (Feingold, 2003, pp. 20).

[38] The simultaneity could be established during special astronomical events that could be anticipated – such as a lunar eclipse or the occultation of a star by the moon. The difference in (local) times at which the event occurred would give an indication of the longitude difference between the two points of observation. For example, if a lunar eclipse was observed to begin right at sunset in one location, but observed at sunrise in another, then the two points would be approximately 180° apart from each other on the globe.

[39] The great Italian astronomer Giovanni Domenico Cassini (1625-1712), who later in his career lived and worked in France, developed highly accurate tables for the eclipses of Jupiter moons. This work made it possible to extend Galileo's original idea into a practical technique for accurate surveying and map making. Upon surveying France, astronomers discovered that the east-to-west extent of France was considerably less than had been originally believed – so much so that the King of France wittily complained that he had lost more territory to his astronomers than he had ever lost on the battlefield.

Another example of longitude determinations using this technique can be found in the exploration of the American West by Lewis and Clark (1804-6). They traveled with a telescope so that they could record the positions of the moons of Jupiter at different locations. In doing this, astronomers would later be able to accurately map where they had been when they returned home.

[40] Tycho and others had argued that the apparent motion of the comets made the Copernican system appear unlikely.

[41] Drake, 1978, pp. 262.

[42] Ferdinando was only eleven when, upon the death of his father, he had become Duke. Thus, the letter the pope sent was to a Duke who was barely in his teens. Tuscan rule at this time was held in regency, which included the hand of the Grand Duchess Christina.

Chapter Nine – Galileo's Dialogue Concerning the Two Chief World Systems

Galileo began working on his *Dialogue* in 1624. The subsequent delay in publishing was caused by a number of factors, including the difficulty of the task and the repeated illnesses from which he suffered. Galileo was also taken up with his work on physics, magnetism and the development of the compound microscope. Many of his friends became concerned with the amount of time he was taking to bring the *Dialogue* to completion. Some begged him to finish it, while others wished that he would drop his obsession with the Copernican cause and complete his more important work in physics. We know of at least one friend who warned against the publication of the *Dialogue* after seeing a manuscript version of it – a young protégé of Galileo's in Venice.[1] Finally, in 1630, his *Dialogue* was complete and Galileo traveled to Rome to secure its imprimatur (official permission to print).

In order to gain approval for the *Dialogue's* publication, Galileo needed to submit his work to the Master of the Sacred Palace, Father Riccardi, who was responsible for the licensing of books in Rome. Galileo detected some advantages to having Riccardi serve as the licenser, since Riccardi had been well-disposed to Galileo in the past and was also a cousin to the Tuscan ambassador's wife. Galileo, upon believing his work to be well on the way to approval and publication, left Rome in June, 1630. However, not long after his departure, serious complications arose. Riccardi turned out to be more cautious than Galileo had anticipated and was slow to approve the manuscript. And in August 1630, Prince Cesi, the founding patron of the Lynceans and Galileo's Roman agent for shepherding the licensing and publishing process, died. As a result, the Lynceans effectively ceased to exist.

Without someone in Rome to guide the manuscript through the approval process, the *Dialogue* would not be easy to publish. Galileo proposed to Riccardi that his book be published in Florence instead. However, Riccardi was not willing to relinquish a task that he had already begun, and he insisted that the book be licensed in Rome. Then yet another complication intervened: an outbreak of plague spread across Italy. The subsequent quarantines made travel and mail between Rome and Florence impractical. A manuscript might take months to travel between Florence and Rome – if it would arrive at its destination at all.

Riccardi had been justifiably cautious to approve a work that threatened to violate the decree of 1616, while Galileo, who had believed the approval for publication would come quickly, now began to fear that his great work would never be published. Having lost patience and desperate to see some progress, Galileo appealed to the young Grand Duke Ferdinand for help. With the combined pressure of the Medici court, the Tuscan ambassador in Rome, and Galileo himself, Riccardi finally budged and allowed the licensing process to move ahead. He agreed to have the Inquisitor of Florence approve most of the manuscript following his instructions. Riccardi would remain responsible for approving the first and last sections of the *Dialogue.*

Galileo believed that Urban VIII's papacy and the great favor that Urban VIII had shown him would allow him to push the limits of the decree of 1616. Early in the approval process, Galileo had even proposed that his work be titled *Discourse on the Ebb and Flow of the Tides.* However, Urban VIII, through Riccardi, ordered that the title be changed to a dialogue on the world systems. The book was difficult for Riccardi to approve because Galileo continued to adopt a strongly pro-Copernican position. Furthermore, Riccardi was not entirely clear about what Pope Urban VIII and Galileo had agreed upon in the first place.

It is important to appreciate that the decree of 1616 hadn't just limited Galileo's freedom; it limited everyone's – including the pope's, since he was responsible for maintaining Catholic orthodoxy. His actions and decisions were also constrained by the political, religious, and military challenges he was facing at the time. The Thirty Years' War had been raging for over a decade, and the warring factions had formed alliances that were based as much on the strategic interests of its leaders as they were on differences over religion that led to the war in the first place. Urban VIII had consistently favored the interests of the Catholic French king over those of the Catholic Habsburgs. The Habsburgs, who ruled over both Spain and the Holy Roman Empire, were furious at this –

especially because France had allied itself with the Lutheran King of Sweden, Gustavus Adolphus, on the battlefield. Thus, the pope appeared to condone a Catholic alliance with a powerful Protestant force – and one that had recently won major territories in Central Europe. The critics of Urban VIII objected strongly to the pope's policies and pointed out that this was no way for the leader of the Catholic Church to act. They accused him of not defending and upholding the Catholic faith. The Spanish cardinals at the Vatican complained and plotted against him – activities which made Urban VIII extremely nervous. To add further to his stress, in 1630 some astrologers offered predictions that he would soon die. So credible were the predictions that some cardinals traveled to Rome in anticipation of the election to be held for the next pope. Urban VIII responded angrily to the astrologers.[2] One of them, a former acquaintance of Galileo, was arrested and died in prison within a year. The most important point of all this is that Urban VIII was besieged in many different ways and from many sides as the *Dialogue* was being approved.

Gaining approval to publish the *Dialogue* had required a considerable amount of discussion and negotiation – first between Galileo and the pope, and then between Galileo and the Roman licensor, Riccardi. The strategy that Galileo used in writing the *Dialogue* was, in principle, a safe one: he would treat the Copernican system and his discussions of it in a purely hypothetical way.[3] This was the understanding that was reached between him and Urban VIII – and in light of the decree of 1616 it was probably the only approach that could have been taken. But given Galileo's belief in the physical reality of the Copernican system and his passion for sharing it, having him provide a purely hypothetical account of Copernicanism was probably an unrealistic expectation. It had never been Galileo's practice to treat astronomical systems as mere devices for calculating planetary positions because he was not a mathematical astronomer. As we have seen, his ideas in astronomy were tied to his ideas in physics.

Finally, in 1632, after great delay and great anticipation, Galileo's *Dialogue* was printed. The vast majority of the book addressed physical propositions – both celestial and terrestrial. As its full title indicated, the *Dialogue Concerning the Two Chief World Systems* was a comparison of the geocentric system with its associated Aristotelian conceptual scheme and the Copernican system as presented in the context of Galileo's new proto-inertial physics. The astronomical ideas presented in the *Dialogue* are very basic and never reach beyond an introductory level of understanding. A medical student or well-educated lay person could have easily understood all of the astronomical arguments presented in the book. This stands in great contrast to Kepler's work, which contained lines of reasoning so complex and convoluted that it took other professional astronomers decades to fully comprehend them. The *Dialogue* was written neither for experts in mathematical astronomy nor for academic philosophers. Instead, it was written in Italian and in a style that spoke to intelligent readers from many walks of life.

Galileo had been counseled repeatedly not to advocate for the Copernican system in an absolute sense when writing his *Dialogue*. In spite of this, he offered very strong astronomical and physical arguments in support of the Copernican system. He hoped to convince his readers that the Copernican system was true, but he tried do it in such a way that he could deny that was actually his intention. The primary strategy he employed to have it both ways was the dialog format. This allowed Galileo to present the pro-Copernican arguments through the mouths of fictitious characters and not his own. The characters he invented were: Salviati, who was essentially a Galileist; Sagredo, who was intelligent and open-minded yet unsure about the new ideas that Salviati was proposing; and Simplicio, whose role in the dialogue corresponds well to his name. Both Salviati and Sagredo were gentlemen who were once close personal friends of Galileo, but had since died. Galileo expressed his wish to resurrect them once more for vigorous conversation and debate like those they used to have in the old days. The name "Simplicio" had a connotation in Renaissance Italian similar to that which it has for us today in English – that of "simpleton." At that time, "Simplicio" would also have been recognized as a reference to Simplicius, the famous and highly regarded Aristotelian philosopher from late antiquity. In this sense, the name was a pun – it simultaneously referred to a simpleton and to an Aristotelian. When Galileo wished to reference himself in the *Dialogue*, he had his characters refer to him as the "academician." Galileo also occasionally included his own voice as a narrator in the form of marginal comments (postils).

Galileo divided the *Dialogue* into four days:

<u>The First Day:</u> Following a brief introduction of the characters, which also foreshadowed the purpose of the conversation, Galileo addressed the key physical principles behind the two world systems. The discussion was wide-ranging. In addition to considering the individual points of contention, he embarked upon a broader examination of the assumptions and methods that Aristotelians relied upon. In fact, Galileo spoke highly of Aristotle, saying that the philosopher properly founded his theories on the limited knowledge he had of the natural world during the time he lived. Galileo criticized contemporary Aristotelians for not following Aristotle's method, because they did the opposite of what Aristotle had done: they were trying to make new knowledge of the natural world fit an old theory. He also pointedly criticized Aristotelians for assuming the very thing that was in question: namely, the centrality of the earth. Galileo had his characters address several physical propositions and questions, including: whether there is a center of the universe, what might exist at such a center, the tendency of a large body to unite around its own center, the moon's appearance and why its surface must be rough, and the reason for earthshine.

Galileo also included an extended discussion designed to break down the Aristotelian distinction between the celestial and terrestrial realms. Here, he included a broad range of persuasive techniques and appealed directly to his readers' understanding and expectations of the physical world. He suggested that the Aristotelian portrayal of the earth as a bilge of corruptibility, generation, and decay said more about Aristotelians than it did about the earth. Interestingly, Galileo went on to speculate that the Aristotelian need for a perfect and unchanging cosmos was derived from their deep-seated fear of death. He warned the Aristotelians about the implications of getting what they wished for. He pointed out that if they saw perfection in the cosmos, then surely they desired perfection for the earth as well. If that was the case, Galileo concluded, Aristotelians seemed to wish that the earth were composed of a crystalline and unchanging material that would render it unfit for human habitation.

In this and other ways, Galileo attacked Aristotelian belief using language, imagery, and metaphor as often as he relied on geometry and logic. The *Dialogue* was a broad intellectual and emotional appeal for others to see the world in the way that Galileo did.

The Second Day: Here, Galileo addressed the earth's motion. He argued, like Copernicus, that heavy objects fall to the center of the body in which they are a part – not to some singular and abstract "center of the universe." The complexity of the debate over motion required Galileo to consider a diversity of issues that are too lengthy to describe here. However, it is worth considering the most important issue that he addressed in Day Two:

Galileo responded at length to an important criticism put forth by geocentrists regarding the earth's motion. It is one that had been first offered in antiquity by Aristotle, Ptolemy, and others, and it appealed greatly to common sense: If the earth were turning on itself at a rate of nearly one thousand miles an hour at the equator, then its motion should be easily detectable by its passengers. Objects dropped from a tower ought not to land near the base of the tower but to the west of it. Projectiles, like cannon balls, ought not to travel in one direction as far as in the other. This understandable belief about the nature of motion caused most people to dismiss the Copernican system out-of-hand. In his *Dialogue*, Galileo needed to address it in a convincing way if he was going to have any chance of success with the rest of his book.

Galileo postulated that objects in circular motion have a tendency to remain in motion unless they are otherwise disturbed.[4] This was a view that ran counter to what Aristotle had maintained. With regard to falling or moving objects on the earth, Galileo believed that all objects on the earth's surface possessed the circular motion that they shared with the earth – whether or not the objects happened to be in contact with it at all times. So, to Galileo's way of thinking, an object held at the top of a tower possesses the same west-to-east motion that the tower does, which in turn, possesses the same west-to-east motion that the earth does. When an object is released, it continues to possess its original west-to-east motion as it falls, which is why it lands at the foot of the tower.

Galileo sought to establish that it didn't matter whether the earth moved or not, an object dropped from a tower would land at the foot of it in either case. He provided similar arguments for projectile motion. In general terms, he proposed that the observed motion of an object is always detected relative only to the motion of other objects near it. He illustrated this point through the use of an analogy that is now well-known:

> Shut yourself up with a friend in the large Cabin between the decks of some large Ship, and there place gnats, flies, and such other small winged creatures. Get also a great tub (or other vessel) full of water, and within it put certain fishes; let also a certain bottle be hung up, which allows water to flow drop by drop forth into another bottle placed underneath, having a narrow neck. With the Ship lying still, observe diligently how those small winged animals fly with like speed towards all parts of the Cabin; how the fishes swim indifferently towards all sides; and how the distilling drops all fall into the bottle placed underneath. And casting anything towards your friend, you need not throw it with more force one way then another, provided the distances are equal. If you jump, as the saying is, with your feet closed, you will reach as far one way as another. Having observed all these things, though no man can doubt that so long as the vessel stands still... [Now] make the Ship to move with what speed you please – as the motion is uniform and not fluctuating this way or that, you shall not discern the smallest change in all the previously mention effects – nor can you determine by any of them whether the Ship is moving or standing still. In jumping you shall reach as far across the floor as before and would not make a greater leap towards the front of the ship than the back of it... and throwing anything to your friend you shall not need to cast it with more strength to reach him if he was standing towards the front of the ship or near the back. The drops would all land into the lower bottle and not so much as one shall fall towards the front, even though while the drop is in the Air, the Ship shall have run many feet. The fish in their water would not swim with more trouble towards the front than towards the back of the aquarium, but would with equal speed make it to food placed on any side of the aquarium. And lastly, the flies and gnats would continue their flight indifferently in any direction, nor shall they ever happen to be driven together towards the side of the Cabin next the prow, as if they were made tired following the swift course of the Ship, from which through their time in the Air they had been long separated. And if by burning

a few grains of incense you make a little smoke, you would see it ascend up and like a cloud suspend itself and move indifferently – not inclining more in one direction or another. And of this correspondence of effects the cause is for that the Ships motion is common to all the things contained in it... (original trans. Thomas Salusbury, 1661, rendered into modern English)

Those of us who have not had this experience might find Galileo's description unbelievable since sailboats and ships usually encounter waves that rock the vessels in perceptible ways. But those of us who have sailed on smooth water in steady winds know that in these conditions there is absolutely no perception of motion unless we look out the window. This was an experience that Galileo's contemporaries would have been quite familiar with.

The Third Day: In this section Galileo considered the relative merits of the Ptolemaic and Copernican systems. Notably, he did not explicitly discuss the Tychonic system, which is a significant and curious omission, since many geocentrists had adopted it by this time. Some of the arguments that Galileo leveled at geocentrists applied only to the Ptolemaic system – an important one of these was the analysis of the phases of Venus, which plainly disproved the Ptolemaic system (but yet was fully compatible with the Tychonic view). Still, while Galileo was explicitly attacking the Ptolemaic system, whenever possible he used arguments that could be used against the Tychonic system as well – even if he didn't mention that system by name.

In Day Three of the *Dialogue*, Galileo used pro-Copernican strategies that had been employed earlier by Copernicus, Rheticus, and Kepler. These ranged from carefully constructed geometric arguments to appealing analogies. The extent to which his more conservative Aristotelian opponents had maintained a non-mathematical conception of the universe is revealed in the exceptionally long passage that Galileo devoted to the nature and location of the novas of 1572 and 1604. Recall that professional astronomers had determined that the novas were located well beyond the sphere of the moon, with most concluding that they were among the stars. Yet there remained many Aristotelians who refused to believe the novas were located beyond the sphere of the moon – in spite of the careful parallax measurements and distance determinations by the astronomers. Galileo devoted over forty pages of his *Dialogue* to this issue alone. He carefully led his readers through the geometric reasoning that twelve independent astronomers used in order to conclude that the novas are located in the celestial realm. Upon reading this passage of the *Dialogue*, one is left with the sense that Galileo was not just showing his readers how to *use* geometry to draw physical conclusions, but that he was, to some extent, showing his readers how to *do* geometry. Finally, in true Renaissance fashion, Galileo invoked ancient authorities in order to add credibility to his Copernican view; he reminded his audience that the idea was held by the Pythagoreans and by Aristarchus of Samos.[5]

Most of the astronomical issues that Galileo dealt with on Day Three have to do with how far away things are, how big they are, and how they move. It was not a detailed mathematical astronomy like Kepler had so thoroughly and successfully created. Rather, Galileo was interested in addressing big picture questions about where things were and what was moving around what. In one section, Galileo attempted to address the problem of stellar parallax and provided an explanation for why it had not yet been observed – he even suggested a future experiment that could someday detect the very small effect. In Day Three, he also shared the results of an experiment he conducted whereby he was able to determine an upper limit to the very small visual diameter of stars in an attempt to answer Tycho's objection about absurdly large stellar sizes in the Copernican system. Finally, it is in this section that he presented his important and physical "sunspot argument" in support of the Copernican view.

The Fourth Day: In the last section, Galileo presented what he believed was his strongest argument in support of Copernicanism – his theory of tides. He believed that the double motion of the earth, with its simultaneous daily rotation on its axis coupled with its revolution around the sun, caused the water in ocean basins to slosh back and forth in an east-west direction. This was a strictly mechanical view of the tides, which differed from the more commonly-held view that the moon was somehow responsible for the cause of the tides. The lunar connection was undoubtedly an important one and could not be entirely ignored since both tidal frequency and intensity had been correlated with the position and motion of the moon. Kepler had maintained that any theory of the tides had to include the moon as its cause and had proposed that the moon and the earth's ocean had a mutual attraction that caused the oceans to rise and fall in concert with the moon's position. Galileo claimed that an invisible attraction between the moon and the ocean was absurd – though he didn't provide a fair representation of Kepler's views on the tides in his criticism of it.[6]

Galileo postulated that the earth's two motions were the primary cause of the tides, but that the moon contributed to a secondary effect, which accounted for the monthly changes in tidal intensity. Galileo was so confident that his theory of the tides was correct that he portrayed it as though it were a proof for the motion of the earth. Indeed, near the end of the fourth day he had Sagredo claim that it would be impossible for the tides to occur if the earth stood still. Of course, such a strong statement was in clear violation of the decree of 1616, so he quickly had Salviati point out that the theory of tides might be a mere dream or paradox. Galileo had awkwardly inserted such disclaimers in the *Dialogue* in numerous places – often after his pro-Copernican arguments threatened to be too conclusive. His disclaimers usually came across as disingenuous and rarely rang true.

Near the end of the fourth section, and as a final disclaimer, Galileo included the pope's favorite argument against the possibility of having certain knowledge of nature, which Urban VIII had specifically requested of Galileo. The argument went along these lines: No matter what man might choose to believe about nature, God could have constructed it differently – and in ways that no one could have imagined. Galileo placed this potentially powerful qualification in the mouth of Simplicio, who was portrayed throughout the entire *Dialogue* as an unimaginative and clichéd Aristotelian. Thus, Galileo allowed the pope's poetic and profound message to fall flat and minimized much of its intended effect.

Reception of the *Dialogue*

In the *Dialogue*, Galileo put forth his best effort to have his cake and eat it too: he provided strong reasons for adopting the Copernican view, but then inserted periodic disclaimers to assure readers that he held the opinion in only a hypothetical sense. Short of adopting a position of "double truth," which neither he nor his opponents would have accepted, it seems that Galileo was attempting to fool his readers, delude himself, or both.

The *Dialogue* was extremely popular and sold out quickly. Many of Galileo's contemporaries later cited its arguments as the reason for their conversion to Copernicanism. It was printed in Florence, and copies reached Rome many weeks later. When it did, the same licensor who had approved the *Dialogue* for publication ordered that sales of it be halted and that all available copies be returned. Father Riccardi had done this at the pope's directive, and it was the first indication that something was wrong. The official Vatican response was too late; the book had sold out and only a handful of copies would ever be returned. As was typical, official attempts to suppress a book guaranteed its popularity and drove up its price.

Francesco Niccolini, the Tuscan ambassador who had helped pressure Riccardi into licensing the book, had multiple audiences with Urban VIII in order to try to understand what the difficulties were. Initially, Niccolini was concerned only about the status of the book and whether it could be rescued from prohibition with minor corrections. However, the pope made it clear to Nicolini that it was Galileo who was in trouble – not just the book. The pope had been besieged by complaints and unfavorable reports about the *Dialogue*. He was also notified that his favorite doctrine had been placed into the mouth of the fool. The final straw was the discovery of the special injunction against Galileo in the files of the Holy Office. This was the document that had been prepared for Cardinal Bellarmine's private meeting with Galileo in 1616. The wording of the injunction was far stricter than the public decree of 1616 had been:

> Friday, the 26th [1616] –At the Palace, the usual residence of the Lord Cardinal Bellarmine, the said Galileo having been summoned and brought before the said Lord Cardinal...[was] warned of the error of the aforesaid opinion [Copernicanism], and admonished to abandon it; and immediately thereafter, before me and before witnesses...Galileo was by the said Commissary commanded and enjoined, in the name of His Holiness the Pope, and the whole Congregation of the Holy Office, to relinquish altogether the said opinion that the sun is the center of the world and immovable, and that the earth moves; nor henceforth to hold, teach, or defend it in any way whatsoever, verbally

or in writing; otherwise proceedings would be taken against him in the Holy Office; which injunction the said Galileo acquiesced in and promised to obey. Done at Rome, in the place aforesaid, in the presence of [several witnesses listed]. (trans. Sturge in Gebler, 1879).

Whether or not the injunction had ever been formally served on Galileo remains uncertain, but considering Galileo's subsequent trial testimony, it seems that he was familiar with it. Perhaps the injunction hadn't been officially served on him during his meeting with Bellarmine so that Galileo hadn't felt bound by it. Or perhaps with the deaths of Bellarmine and Pope Paul V, Galileo believed the injunction had been forgotten. In any case, Urban VIII was now informed that Galileo had been ordered in 1616 not to "...hold, teach, or defend [Copernicanism] in any way whatsoever..." The wording was perfectly clear. Urban VIII concluded that the *Dialogue* should never have been written and was enraged that Galileo had misled him by not informing him of it. The pope was livid. Ambassador Niccolini received the news from Riccardi privately:

> it had been discovered in the books of the Holy Office, that sixteen years ago, it having been heard that Galileo entertained that opinion, and disseminated it in Florence, he was summoned to Rome, and forbidden by Cardinal Bellarmine, in the name of the Pope and the Holy Office, to hold that opinion, and this alone is enough to ruin him entirely. (trans. Sturge in Gebler, 1879).

With this, it was clear that Galileo would need to stand trial at the Holy Office. And it wasn't just the injunction that Galileo would need to be concerned about. Galileo had strongly advocated for the Copernican system, and it had appeared to go well beyond the hypothetical treatment that he had promised the pope. Only a week earlier, Urban VIII explained to Niccolini,

> Your Galileo has ventured to meddle with things that he ought not, and with the most important and dangerous subjects which can be stirred up in these days. (trans. Sturge in Gebler, 1879).

The ambassador had attempted to defend Galileo on the grounds that the *Dialogue* had received prior licensing from the Church. But the pope didn't buy that argument. Urban VIII complained that Galileo had misled Riccardi and others while he secured the imprimatur. The pope forwarded the matter to the Holy Office.

The Trial of Galileo

The workings of the Holy Office were conducted in secret, so it was difficult for anyone outside the Inquisition to know what might happen next. Galileo had been called to Rome in October 1632, but the Medici and Galileo vigorously negotiated with Urban VIII to allow Galileo to stay in Tuscany. Galileo was 68 years of age and reportedly ill. Yet Urban became increasingly impatient with the excuses coming from Tuscany, and he explained to Niccolini in no uncertain terms that

> He can come very slowly in a litter, with every comfort, but he really must be tried here in person. May God forgive him for having been so deluded as to involve himself in these difficulties, from which we had relieved him when we were cardinal. (trans. Sturge in Gebler, 1879).

After even more attempts to delay the inevitable, the pope explained that either Galileo would come to Rome on his own, or he would come as a prisoner in irons. With this, the Medici and Galileo yielded: Galileo set out for Rome on what would be his sixth and final trip to the city. He arrived at the Tuscan embassy in Rome on 13 February, 1633, where he was received by the Niccolini as their guest. His house arrest at the Tuscan ambassador's residence was an extremely unusual arrangement for someone being tried by the Holy Office – normally the accused would have resided in the prison of the Holy Office as they awaited trial. The special accommodations made for Galileo were in deference to the Grand Duke of Tuscany. The secular politics of the Italian peninsula loomed in the background.

During this time, ambassador Niccolini continued to have audiences with Urban VIII and attempted to negotiate a way out of formal trial proceedings at the hands of the Inquisition. Urban responded:

> It would not do to act otherwise. May God forgive Galileo for having intruded into these matters concerning new doctrines and Holy Scripture, when it is best to keep to universally recognized opinions. May God help Ciampoli [the pope's former secretary and friend of Galileo's], also, about these new notions, as he seemed to have a

leaning towards them, and to be inclined to the modern philosophy. (trans. Sturge in Gebler, 1879).

Niccolini assured the pope that Galileo would be able to explain himself, but the pope was not moved by the ambassador's words:

> He would be heard when the time came; but there was one argument which had never been answered, namely, that God was omnipotent, and therefore everything was possible to Him; but if so, why should we impose any necessity upon Him. (trans. Sturge in Gebler, 1879).

This, of course, was the argument that Galileo had put into the mouth of Simplicio.

On 12 April, 1633, Galileo was finally called to stand trial. This was after a long delay during which the pope and members of the Holy Office collected information and deliberated over how to proceed against him. Because the trial would last for more than a day, Galileo was now incarcerated at the Holy Office. However, once again in deference to the Grand Duke, Galileo was given a large apartment and allowed to have a servant (the normal arrangements would have had Galileo locked up in an ordinary prison cell). After his extensive discussions with Urban VIII, Niccolini strongly advised Galileo to fully submit and to forego making any further attempts to defend his views. With that advice, Galileo became seriously depressed – to the point that Niccolini worried about his well-being.

At the trial, the first series of questions that Galileo was asked had to do with the 1616 injunction against him, which had been found in the Vatican files:

> Inquisitor: "Was this decision then communicated to you, and by whom?"

> Galileo: "This decision of the Holy Congregation of the Index was made known to me by Cardinal Bellarmine."

Inquisitor: "You must state what his Eminence Cardinal Bellarmine told you about the aforesaid decision, and whether he said anything else on the subject, and what?"

Galileo: "Signor Cardinal Bellarmine signified to me that the aforesaid opinion of Copernicus might be held as a conjecture, as it had been held by Copernicus, and his eminence was aware that, like Copernicus, I only held that opinion as a conjecture, which is evident from an answer of the same Signor Cardinal to a letter of the Father Paolo Antonio Foscarini, provincial of the Carmelites, of which I have a copy, and in which these words occur: 'It appears to me that your reverence and Signor Galileo act wisely in contenting yourselves with speaking ex supposition, and not with certainty.' This letter of the cardinal's is dated 12th April, 1615. It means, in other words, that that opinion, taken absolutely, must not be either held or defended."

Galileo was then told to describe what was communicated to him in his February 1616 meeting with Bellarmine:

Galileo: "In the month of February, 1616, Signor Cardinal Bellarmine told me that as the opinion of Copernicus, if adopted absolutely, was contrary to Holy Scripture, it must neither be held nor defended, but that it might be held hypothetically, and written about in this sense. In accordance with this I possess a certificate of the said Signor Cardinal Bellarmine, given on 26th May, 1616, in which he says that the Copernican opinion may neither be held nor defended, as it is opposed to Holy Scripture, of which certificate I herewith submit a copy."

Inquisitor: "When the above communication was made to you, were any other persons present, and who?"

Galileo: "When Signor Cardinal Bellarmine made known to me what I have reported about the Copernican views, some Dominican fathers were present, but I did not know them, and have never seen them since."

Inquisitor: "Was any other command communicated to you on this subject, in the presence of those fathers, by them or anyone else, and what?

Galileo: "I remember that the transaction took place as follows: Signor Cardinal Bellarmine sent for me one morning, and told me certain particulars which I was to bring to the ears of his Holiness before I communicated them to others. But the end of it was that he told me that the Copernican opinion, being contradictory to Holy Scripture, must not be held nor defended. It has escaped my memory whether those Dominican fathers were present before, or whether they came afterwards; neither do I remember whether they were present when the Signor Cardinal told me the said opinion was not to be held. It may be that a command was issued to me that I should not hold nor defend the opinion in question, but I do not remember it, for it is several years ago."

Inquisitor: "If what was then said and enjoined upon you as a command were read aloud to you, would you remember it?"

Galileo: I do not remember that anything else was said or enjoined upon me, nor do I know that I should remember what was said to me, even if it were read to me. I say freely what I do remember, because I do not think that I have in any way disobeyed the injunction, that is, have not by any means held nor defended the said opinion that the earth moves and the sun is stationary."

After being informed by the Inquisitor that the injunction commanded that Galileo "must neither hold, defend, nor teach that opinion in any way whatsoever," Galileo responded,

I do not remember that the command was intimated to me by anybody but by the cardinal verbally; and I remember that the command was, not to hold nor defend. It may be that, 'and not to teach' was also there. I do not remember it, neither the definition 'in any way whatsoever,' but it may be that it was; for I thought no more about it, nor took any pains to impress the words on my memory, as a few months later I received the certificate now produced, of the said Signor Cardinal Bellarmine, of 26 May, in which the injunction given me, not to hold nor defend that opinion, is expressly to be found. The two other definitions of the said injunction which have just been made known to me, namely, not to teach, and in any way, I have not retained in my memory, I suppose, because they are not mentioned in the said certificate, on which I rely, and which I have kept as a reminder. (trans. Sturge in Gebler, 1879).

In the next line of questioning the Inquisitor asked whether he had told the Master of the Palace (Riccardi) about the command that had been issued to him in 1616:

Galileo: "I did not say anything about that command to the Master of the Palace when I asked for the imprimatur for the book, for I did not think it necessary to say anything, because I had no scruples about it; for I have neither maintained nor defended the opinion that the earth moves and the sun is stationary in that book, but have rather demonstrated the opposite of the Copernican opinion, and shown that the arguments of Copernicus are weak and not conclusive."

With this, the first part of the trial came to a close. No doubt the members of the Holy Office were shocked to hear Galileo claim that his *Dialogue* presented the arguments of Copernicus as "weak and inconclusive"! A special panel was assigned to consider Galileo's statement, and they concluded that, not only did he provide strong pro-Copernican arguments in the *Dialogue,* but that he appeared to believe it was true in an absolute sense. The panel's opinion seems quite fair and reasonable in its conclusion since anyone who reads the *Dialogue* today is left with the same impression. The trial proceedings were going to be exceedingly difficult and troublesome if Galileo continued to adopt such an untenable position.

The Inquisitors needed to find Galileo guilty in order to silence him and in order to display their authority in uncertain times. But it also appears that at least several of the inquisitors wished to show the world that their treatment of Galileo was fair-minded – he was, after all, a highly respected and famous scientist as well as the client of a powerful prince. In order to address the conundrum, Commissary Maculano spoke with Galileo informally and pointed out the seriousness of the problem he had created by claiming his *Dialogue* was an argument *against*

Copernicanism. At last Galileo saw that he would need to admit his error. He was given some time to formulate a credible explanation for his behavior up to that point. At the second hearing his confession on 30 April, Galileo's volunteered testimony takes the following form,

> It occurred to me to re-peruse my printed dialogue, which for three years I had not seen, in order carefully to not whether, contrary to my most sincere intention, there had by inadvertence, fallen from my pen anything from which a reader or the authorities might infer not only some taint of disobedience on my part, but also other particulars which might induce the belief that I had contravened the orders of the Holy Church. And being, by the kind permission of the authorities, at liberty to send about my servant, I succeeded in procuring a copy of my book, and having procured it I applied myself with the utmost diligence to its perusal, and to a most minute consideration thereof. And as, owning to my not having seen it for so long, it presented itself to me, as it were, like a new writing and by another author, I freely confess that in several places it seemed to me set forth in such a form that a reader ignorant of my real purpose might have had reason to suppose that the arguments adduced on the false side, and which it was my intention to confute, were so expressed as to be calculate rather to compel conviction by their cogency that to be easy of solution...I resorted to that of the natural complacency which every man feels with regard to his own subtleties and in showing himself more skillful than the generality of men, in devising, even in favor of false propositions, ingenious and plausible arguments...my error, then, has been – and I confess it – one of vainglorious ambition, and of pure ignorance and inadvertence." (trans. Sturge in Gebler, 1879).

At the end of his testimony, Galileo left the room, but then returned again shortly afterwards. He suggested to the cardinals of the Holy Office that he could write additional days to his *Dialogue* in order to make it clear that he did not actually hold the Copernican opinion. As we know, the Holy Office did not choose to take Galileo up on this offer. At the end of this second hearing, Galileo was allowed to return to the Tuscan embassy – even though the trial had not ended. He was again recalled to the Holy Office on 10 May to provide a defense, which he submitted in the form of a written statement reiterating the explanation for his behavior as, "owing to a vainglorious ambition..." He also pled for mercy and asked that they consider his age and health.

After a long delay and total silence from the Holy Office, Galileo was called before the Inquisition on 21 June. He was interrogated, under threat of torture, as to whether he believed that the sun was the center of the world and that the earth is not at the center, but moves. Galileo's catholic response:

> A long time ago, i.e., before the decision of the Holy Congregation of the Index, and before the injunction was intimated to me, I was indifferent, and regarded both opinions, namely, that of Ptolemy and that of Copernicus, as open to discussion, inasmuch as either one of the other might be true in nature; but after the said decision, assured of the wisdom of the authorities, I ceased to have any doubt; and I held, as I still hold, as most true and indisputable, the opinion of Ptolemy, that is to say, the stability of the earth and the motion of the sun. (trans. Sturge in Gebler, 1879).

The examiner challenged Galileo's statement pointing out that it appeared that Galileo held the Copernican opinion and that unless he confessed the truth, "recourse will be had against him to the appropriate remedies of the law." To this serious challenge, Galileo was forced to submit convincingly and conclusively to the authority of the Church,

> I do not hold, and have not held this opinion of Copernicus since the command was intimated to me that I must abandon it; for the rest, I am here in your hands, – do with me what you please.

It is doubtful any inquisitors actually believed Galileo's words, but it was a necessary ritual that was required for the trial to be resolved. The threat of torture was a normal step in the interrogation process, and it served to confirm the truth of the testimony that witnesses provided. Torture itself was rarely applied. It was in this manner that Urban VIII and the members of the Holy Office effectively silenced Galileo. However, the seriousness of the interrogation and the punishment that followed were both unexpected. This revealed that the inquisitors and the pope had not all been of the same mind in how to deal with Galileo.[7] Galileo received his sentence the following day; the final portion of it read as follows:

We say, pronounce, sentence, declare, that you, the said Galileo, by reason of the matters adduced in process, and by you confessed as above, have rendered yourself in the judgment of this Holy Office vehemently suspected of heresy, namely, of having believed and held the doctrine – which is false and contrary to the sacred and divine Scriptures – that the sun is the center of the world and does not move from east to west, and that the earth moves and is not the center of the world; and that an opinion may be held and defended as probable after it has been declared and defined to be contrary to Holy Scripture; and that consequently you have incurred all the censures and penalties imposed and promulgated in the sacred canons and other constitutions, general and particular, against such delinquents. From which we are content that you be absolved, provided that first, with a sincere heart, and unfeigned faith, you abjure, curse, and detest the aforesaid errors and heresies, and every other error and heresy contrary to the Catholic and Apostolic Roman Church in the form to be prescribed by us.

And in order that this your grave and pernicious error and transgression may not remain altogether unpunished, and that you may be more cautious for the future, and an example to others, that they may abstain from similar delinquencies – we ordain that the book of the 'Dialogues of Galileo Galilei' be prohibited by public edict.

We condemn you to the formal prison of this Holy Office during our pleasure, and by way of salutary penance, we enjoin that for three years to come you repeat once a week the seven penitential Psalms.

Reserving to ourselves full liberty to moderate, commute, or take off, in whole or in part, the aforesaid penalties and penance. (trans. Sturge in Gebler, 1879).

The sentence was signed by seven of the ten cardinals of the Holy Office.[8] The conviction of "vehemently suspected of heresy" was serious. It was, in effect, a sort of "second degree" heresy, which was a grave offense. Galileo was then presented with the abjuration, which he read aloud. The last part of the abjuration is presented here:

Therefore, desiring to remove from the minds of your Eminences, and of all faithful Christians, this strong suspicion, reasonably conceived against me, with sincere heart and unfeigned faith I abjure, curse, and detest the aforesaid errors and heresies, and generally every other error and sect whatsoever contrary to the said Holy church; and I swear that in future I will never again say or assert, verbally or in writing, anything that might furnish occasion for a similar suspicion regarding me; but that should I know any heretic, or person suspected of heresy, I will denounce him to this Holy Office, or to the Inquisitor and ordinary of the place where I may be. Further, I swear and promise to fulfill and observe in their integrity all penances that have been, or that shall be, imposed upon me by this Holy Office. And, in the event of my contravening, (which God forbid!) any of these my promises, protestations, and oaths, I submit myself to all the pains and penalties imposed and promulgated in the sacred canons and other constitutions, general and particular, against such delinquents. So help me God, and these His holy Gospels, which I touch with my hands.

I, the said Galileo Galilei, have abjured, sworn, promised, and bound myself as above; and in witness of the truth thereof I have with my own hand subscribed the present document of my abjuration, and recited it word for word at Rome, in the Convent of Minerva, this twenty-second day of June, 1633.

Urban VIII allowed Galileo to exchange imprisonment at the Holy Office for house arrest at the Tuscan embassy. Niccolini then requested that Galileo be allowed to return to Florence, but Urban VIII responded that it was too soon for that. Instead, Galileo was allowed to stay with the Archbishop of Siena, Ascanio Piccolomini. Within two weeks of the trial, Galileo left for Siena. The archbishop was a great admirer of Galileo and provided the traumatized man with the emotional and intellectual support that he needed at the time. In fact, the environment at the archbishop's residence proved to be a bit too supportive and lively for the pope's taste so, after several months, he ordered Galileo to return to his home of Arcetri, near Florence. Galileo would be allowed to entertain very few visitors in his prison home where he would live under house arrest for the rest of his life.

In Arcetri, Galileo began collecting his papers and his thoughts. He still had enough life in him to finish the work on motion and statics that he had begun decades earlier. He also began taking occasional visitors and started corresponding with other intellectuals again – though in a very circumscribed way. Then he was struck by another tragedy – his favorite daughter and frequent correspondent, the Sister Maria Celeste, died at her convent. After taking some time to recover from his grief, Galileo began to work with remarkable vigor for someone of his age and health who had weathered so many difficulties. To complete and publish his final work, he would receive a great deal of help from disciples and admirers inside and outside of Italy.

In the meantime, the popular *Dialogue* had found its way to lands north of the Alps – well beyond the authority of Rome. In 1635, the *Dialogue* and Foscarini's *Letter* were translated into Latin and published by Bernegger, a friend of Kepler's. The Latin translation of Galileo's *Letter to Christina* was delayed, and thus could not be included along with the *Dialogue*, but it was eventually published in 1636. Remarkably, none of these activities brought trouble for Galileo – most likely because he could disclaim responsibility for all of them.

Galileo's final goal was to complete and publish his work on physics. After some delay in identifying a foreign publisher, he had his most important scientific work, *Discourses on Two New Sciences,* printed in the Netherlands in 1638. The book included nearly everything that Galileo had learned about motion and statics. It marked a new period in the scientific tradition because of its heavy reliance on mathematical analyses in describing physical phenomena. Galileo was aware that he had only managed to begin a project that others would need to complete.

Galileo was completely blind by the time the *Discourses on Two New Sciences* was published. Toward the end of his life, he was aided by close friends and by a young and talented personal secretary, Vincenzo Viviani, who not only read to him and took dictation, but intellectually challenged Galileo and inspired him to continue to improve upon his work. In 1639, a request to the Vatican to free the blind and frail Galileo from house arrest was again denied by his former friend and admirer, Pope Urban VIII. Galileo died early in 1642 at Arcetri – his personal prison. The

Medici proposed to build a mausoleum, but Urban VIII and his brother, Cardinal Barbarini, objected strongly. His body was instead buried in an unmarked grave under the bell tower in the church his family had attended. Viviani vowed to have his master's life and works properly recognized and raised money to build a mausoleum at a later date. It would eventually be built, but not in Viviani's lifetime.

The Aftermath

The actions the Catholic Church had taken against Galileo had a broad effect on scientists across the Catholic world – particularly for those living on the Italian peninsula. Jesuit scientists were limited in what they could do or say about physical astronomy. But, in the decades following the publication of the *Dialogue*, it slowly became obvious that the Copernican system was the true system of the world – by 1700 it was the predominant cosmological belief among the educated. Still, the Catholic Church responded very slowly to the new consensus, and it wasn't until 1758 that the Congregation of the Index no longer forbade "all books teaching the earth's motion." And even with that loosening of the prohibition against Copernicanism, Galileo and Foscarini's works remained on the list of banned books. It wasn't until 1835 that Galileo's *Dialogue* was finally removed from the Index – a full two hundred years after it was published.

Galileo's abjuration may have marked the end of *his* trial, but it also marked the beginning of another one. In the centuries to follow, social critics and historians would deliberate over the Church's actions in the Galileo Affair – and the Church would be repeatedly found to be guilty. Aside from a few Church apologists, the Church's action against Galileo and his science was generally considered to be unjust, and Galileo's stature as a martyr and hero continued to grow over the centuries.

The Galileo Affair reached closure only in 1992, when the Catholic Church finally admitted its error without qualification. Though appearing to rehabilitate Galileo by doing this, in a sense the Catholic Church was rehabilitating itself as well. What is remarkable about Pope John Paul II's apology is that he didn't just admit that Galileo was right about the Copernican system, which had long been obvious to everyone, but that Galileo had been right about the theology as well.[9]

[1]Paolo Aproino, a former student of Galileo's, was concerned about the danger of making the *Dialogue* available to those who were uniformed or ill-disposed toward Galileo. He suggested a different course: have numerous manuscript editions copied by hand and placed in major libraries around Europe for interested intellectuals to read, and if desired, copy. See Allan-Olney, 1870, pp. 208-9.

[2] The predictions likely made Urban VIII all the more nervous because he was a firm believer in astrology. While good Catholics were not to put stock in astrology, many of them still did – including Urban VIII. He was so concerned about the astrological predictions that were circulating and the omen of an upcoming lunar eclipse that he had a famous astrologer, Tomaso Campanella, released from a Naples prison in order that he could serve as Urban's personal astrologer. Campanella assured Urban VIII that he could avoid the effects of the eclipse if they conducted special astrological rites together in a darkened room. The effort was successful, but their strange activity was made public by some of Campanella's enemies. Both Urban and Campanella quickly denounced the practice of astrology in order to distance themselves from the accusations (See Heilbron, 2010, pp. 288-290).

[3] The word "hypothetical" had, and still has, different meanings to different people. In Urban VIII's view, which was shared by many in his day, stating that an explanation was "hypothetical" meant that it may or may not be true and has no chance of ever being shown to be true. Galileo, on the other hand, tended to consider an explanation as "hypothetical" if there wasn't clear proof for it – but that did not mean that it could never be shown to be true in the future.

[4] Galileo did not have a modern (Newtonian) take on inertial motion and is a transitional figure with regard to the physics of motion. He possessed an assumption that circular motion was natural and that objects should move indefinitely on the surface of the earth if they encountered no resistance (because they were traveling on the surface of a sphere). However, he did not at all view straight line motion in the same way.

[5] Aristarchus of Samos (310 – ca. 230 BCE) was a renowned astronomer who was known for his early measurements of the distance from the earth to the moon and the sun. He was also clearly "Copernican" given his belief that all of the planets revolved around the sun. Although his was a minority opinion, it was not entirely ignored or dismissed by other thinkers: a later Mesopotamian astronomer, Selucius, also adopted the heliocentric view, and the Roman writer Seneca treated it as an open question that hadn't yet been definitively addressed. Although Ptolemy and other geocentrists clearly represented a majority view, they still found it necessary to provide arguments to refute heliocentricity.

The beliefs of the earlier Pythagoreans were not as well-understood, since these are known to us only indirectly. Many sixteenth and seventeenth century thinkers speak of the Pythagoreans as though they were early Copernicans, but this is not the case. The Pythagoreans did believe in a moving earth, but one that moved around a "central fire" rather than the sun. They also postulated the existence of a "counter earth." Written accounts of their beliefs are ambiguous, however, and it is difficult to confidently draw a diagram that represents their system.

[6] Since we now know that Galileo was wrong about his theory of the tides, there has been considerable debate among historians of science concerning the value of his contribution and whether he should have known that his theory of the tides was incorrect from the beginning. For us, it is most important to appreciate what exactly Galileo was attempting to accomplish and why his theory of the tides appeared quite plausible to him.

Ultimately, however, Kepler was right – any theory of the tides has to include the moon as a cause. While Galileo was able to account for why tidal intensity was greater at full moon and new moons, he was unable to explain why the *timing* of the tides also followed the position of the moon. Instead, he ignored the details and stated that tidal periods were daily – which is almost true, but not true. In reality, the periods of high and low tides occur at different times from one day to the next, and in a way that corresponds to the position of the moon in the sky – a fact which was known in Galileo's day.

[7] See Fantoli's *The Case of Galileo*, 2012, for a detailed account of the trial.

[8] The significance of the missing signatures of the three cardinals has been debated. Some historians have suggested that they serve as evidence of a dissenting opinion that existed among the cardinals of the Holy Office. We do know that some cardinals serving on the Inquisition had been well-disposed toward Galileo in the past and continued to be somewhat sympathetic to him. However, it is difficult to draw a solid conclusion about this point, since it was not uncommon for signatures to be missing on such documents.

[9] Pope John Paul II: "The problem posed by theologians of that age was, therefore, that of the compatibility between heliocentrism and scripture. Thus, the new science, with its methods and the freedom of research which they implied, obligated theologians to examine their own criteria of scriptural interpretation. Most of them did not know how to do so." See Sharratt, 1994.

Chapter 10 – An Epilogue: Catholic Science, Newton, and Proof for the Copernican System

In this epilogue, we will consider the fate of the ideas and decisions that we encountered in the preceding chapters. First, we will survey the impact of the 1633 trial of Galileo on science in the Catholic world and examine how Catholic scientists were affected by the prohibition of the Copernican view. Next, we will consider how scientists all across Europe responded to the mathematical astronomy of Kepler and to the physical astronomy and physics of Galileo. Finally, we will see how the Copernican view eventually became accepted as the true system of the world.

Catholic Science after 1633

The prohibition of Copernicanism in the Catholic world began in 1616 when Cardinal Bellarmine, Pope Paul V and the Holy Office of the Inquisition determined that physical Copernicanism was incompatible with scripture and that the view could not be held. Their decision tied the hands of future Church leaders and helped create an environment that led to Galileo's later trial and condemnation. When Galileo's sentence was broadcast across Europe, the message was heeded immediately by scientists and philosophers who worked within the jurisdiction of the Catholic Church. This meant that Copernicans in Italy and, to a lesser extent, other Catholic countries and outposts tended to keep their Copernican opinions to themselves.

It is sometimes difficult to discern what individual Catholic scientists thought about the Copernican system following the decree of 1616 and the trial of 1633. However, we do know that many Catholic Copernicans publically adopted the astronomical hypothesis of Tycho Brahe in order to avoid controversy. Some carefully shared their doubts about the decision to ban Copernicanism by explicitly stating their only reason for rejecting Copernicanism: *because they wished to remain pious and obedient Catholics.* In many cases, one does not need to read too closely between the lines to sense the frustration of these authors. Remarkably, there were a few who continued to teach Copernicanism as an astronomical model while pointing out that there was nothing in the published decrees that had forbidden them from discussing it as a hypothesis.

In response to the continuing Copernican grumblings and in order to show the rest of the world that educated Catholics fully understood the science behind the decision, the Italian Jesuit Giambattista Riccioli (1598-1671) argued against Copernicanism and in support of the Tychonic view in his detailed treatise, *Almagestum novum*, 1651. In it, he described 49 reasons in support of the Copernican system and 77 reasons against it in a spirited and well-informed attempt to justify the Church's decision against Galileo and against Copernicanism. He dismissed most of the arguments on both sides as inconclusive but believed that the remaining arguments tipped the balance in Tycho's favor.

However, by the end of the 1600s it became increasingly obvious to intellectuals everywhere that Copernicanism was the true system of the world. In response to this slowly emerging consensus, Catholic scientists began to more openly teach and discuss Copernicanism and many Catholic administrators had lost their enthusiasm for enforcing what increasingly seemed to have been a bad decision. Like all good bureaucrats responsible for carrying out a problematic policy, they often ignored it. To make it easier for the Church hierarchy to look the other way, Catholic Copernicans publicly maintained the pretense that they held the Copernican system only as an astronomical hypothesis. As the historian John Heilbron so aptly put it, Catholics could advocate for the Copernican view "...using the convenient fiction that it was a convenient fiction."

The extent to which Italian and Catholic science had been damaged by the decisions of 1616 and 1633 is difficult to determine, but it probably was not as bad as has been commonly portrayed. Of course, any Italian scientist who publicly espoused physical Copernicanism would have been asking for trouble. One could fairly ask, "Would Catholic authorities have tolerated an 'Italian Isaac Newton' immediately following Galileo?" The answer to this question is almost certainly "no." Still, Italian scientists continued to do important work in physics and in mathematical and observational astronomy while avoiding controversy with the Church.

The prohibition against physical Copernicanism was very real, but it was also limited in scope and was enforced infrequently after a few decades. In the end, the prohibition probably harmed the Church more than it harmed Italian science.

As the Copernican view became the dominant cosmology in the early 1700s, the Church continued to loosen its enforcement of the decrees against it. Its first significant act was to approve the re-publication of some of Galileo's works in 1741, though with the stipulation that the Copernicanism of the *Dialogue* be presented as a hypothesis; that Galileo's postils be removed and that it be printed with the decrees against Copernicanism included. Much later, in 1818, Thomas Settele requested permission to publish a blatantly pro-Copernican work that minced no words about the truth of the system. The Master of the Sacred Palace, Filippo Anfossi, denied Settele's request, saying that it violated the prohibition. Settle appealed the decision and won over Anfossi's superiors – but still, Anfossi refused to give his consent. Finally the Commissary of the Holy Office of the Inquisition ordered the book approved and warned future censors to approve similar works or risk punishment and/or the loss of their position. Thus, two hundred years after the decree of 1616, the situation had been reversed with the Commissary of the Holy Office threatening to punish someone for *interfering* with the publication of a Copernican treatise. However, as we saw in the last chapter, the Catholic Church did not fully come to terms with its responsibility for the Galileo Affair until 1992.

Protestant Science

There was no Protestant institution comparable to the Roman Catholic Church. Instead, there were a large number of Protestant denominations and an even larger number of political jurisdictions spread across Northern Europe – from large parts of the Holy Roman Empire, to the Dutch Republics and the British Isles. There were no systematic Protestant efforts to prohibit Copernicanism, and we can conclude that Protestant scientists had a greater measure of freedom than did Catholic scientists. Still, there remained limits to how far one could express novel religious beliefs or engage in radical philosophizing. The most tolerant land for either of these was the United Netherlands, which often became a destination for free thinkers.

The Acceptance of the Copernican System

After considering Galileo's famous encounter with the Inquisition, it might be tempting to adopt a commonly-held view of the affair: 1) Galileo had decisively argued what was already obvious to any intelligent person and, 2) the Church was a medieval organization blindly opposed to change. Hopefully, after considering this episode in its entirety, it is evident to the reader that such a view is a gross caricature at best. It should be clear from Galileo's actions that the Church was not his greatest concern in the years leading up to the publication of his *Dialogue*. His greatest anxiety, and the one that likely kept him up at night, was how to deal with the knowledgeable, anti-Aristotelian Tychonists in his audience – and by 1632, these people had become increasingly numerous and vociferous.

Galileo's core problem was that the vast majority of his "pro-Copernican arguments" were really only anti-Ptolemaic and anti-Aristotelian rather than unambiguously pro-Copernican. These arguments fell flat with well-informed Tychonists who could honestly respond, "I agree with you Galileo, but so what? How is that proof that the earth moves?" These opponents didn't need to rely on scripture to attack the Copernican system and to support their Tychonic viewpoint. Galileo had a difficult task at hand and had many different kinds of opponents. The fact that there was a large and diverse geocentric majority in Galileo's day is made evident by his need to take several years to write a book that was over 500 pages in translation. If the motion of the earth had been obvious to Galileo's contemporaries, the book would have been a great deal shorter.

It is worth noting that after considering all of the new telescopic discoveries and arguments that Galileo employed, the central reason for a person to become a Copernican in the first place continued to depend on the appealing mathematical and physical harmony of that system. And the remarkable coherence of the heliocentric view had already been clearly laid out by Copernicus's protégé, Rheticus, a century earlier in his *Narratio prima*, a book that had been reprinted several times over. During the intervening years, what remained at the center of it all, both literally and figuratively, was the sun.

Since antiquity, the sun was understood to be a unique celestial body in two ways: 1) It is luminous and provides light for the earth and its life forms and 2) It is the largest body in the heavens and is far larger than the earth. Interestingly, this last fact was proven by the person who is also known to be the first "Copernican," Aristarchus of Samos (310-230 BCE).[1] Aristarchus determined the relative size of the sun geometrically by using 1) solar and lunar eclipse observations and, 2) angular measurements of the relative position of the moon and sun when the moon was exactly half full. By doing this, he determined that the sun's diameter was about six times greater than the diameter of the earth.[2]

Aristarchus's estimate for the size of the sun is much lower than the modern value (approximately 110 earth diameters), but his geometric reasoning was sound and his basic conclusion was accepted from his day up through Copernicus's time. Although we don't know much about Aristarchus, it seems likely that his determination of the sun's size and his belief in a sun-centered system are related. While Aristarchus was ultimately unsuccessful in advocating for his heliocentric view in antiquity, his conclusion about a large solar diameter was adopted by Greek, Islamic, and European astronomers from that point on. It was a fact that a handful of Europeans seventeen hundred years later would find to be exceedingly relevant – heliocentrists, from Copernicus through Rheticus, Kepler, and Galileo all made allusions to the unique nature of the sun. In pleading their cases, they insisted that the largest and most luminous object is best suited to be the center of planetary motion – smaller things ought to move around larger things not the other way around.

So, even if we choose to classify Aristarchus's failed heliocentrism as historically insignificant, his solar size determination *was* essential to European heliocentrism. In this sense, the story of the "Copernican Revolution" has its earliest chapter in Greek Antiquity – a fact which calls into question the appropriateness of the term "revolution" in describing this great transition in thought. Furthermore, as we will see shortly, the Copernican Revolution didn't even come to a close until the early 1700s with the work of Newtonians. The adoption of the Copernican viewpoint was groundbreaking, but it was hardly a revolution in the temporal sense of the word. Indeed, the very title of this book was chosen because it reflects a long-standing historical convention – not because it accurately summarizes a series of events that unfolded over many centuries.

Kepler and Galileo

Kepler and Galileo each made essential contributions in support of the Copernican cause. As we saw, Kepler's new astronomy was not immediately appreciated by many of his contemporaries because it contained ideas that were strange and technically difficult to understand. In contrast, Galileo's physical arguments in support of the Copernican system were far more accessible and required only that his audience possess a rudimentary understanding of astronomy and geometry.

As different as the two approaches were, Kepler and Galileo shared at least one common goal: to account for the Copernican universe using physical principles that had previously been applied to terrestrial phenomena. Kepler's physical Copernicanism relied on magnetic lines of force emanating from the sun – akin to the magnetic lines of force that William Gilbert had invoked in his study of terrestrial magnets. Similarly, Galileo began to extend some of his ideas about the physics of terrestrial motion to the heavens – though he hadn't yet worked out any details. Galileo's strategy is revealed in the analogies that he drew between his terrestrial physics and motion as it existed in the Copernican system – an approach is particularly evident in his sunspot argument (Day Three of his *Dialogue*).

Galileo was acutely aware that his work was incomplete and understood that someone else would need to complete what he had begun. As we will see, Galileo's unfinished mechanics turned out to be far more fruitful than Kepler's elaborate physical system. The key point here is that both men used ideas and analogies taken from terrestrial physics to guide their thinking about how the celestial realm worked. This underlying commonality between the two men is often overlooked – probably because of the otherwise striking differences in their intuitions and goals.

Kepler's Legacy

Only after the stunning success of the *Rudolphine Tables* revealed the extent of Kepler's genius did many mathematical astronomers decide to roll up their sleeves and begin to seriously study his theoretical works.

Upon doing so, many of them adopted Kepler's planetary ellipse, which brought the 2,000 year old tradition of using the circle to describe heavenly motion to an end.[3] Kepler's other ideas were not as well received. His "area law of motion," which later became known as his "second law" of planetary motion, was ignored or avoided by most astronomers in the beginning, because it required the application of an unusual mathematical approach that seemed peculiar. Kepler himself acknowledged the awkwardness of the calculations required for the area law and apologized for it, but he also pointed out that it was the best method for reconciling Tycho's data with theory and that it gave well-defined answers. He reasoned that if it worked so well, it must be true. Some astronomers accepted it in principle, but then continued to use the equant or other approximations in order to avoid struggling with the awkward calculations.

The physical ideas that served as the inspiration for Kepler's mathematical astronomy – the magnetic lines of solar flux mechanism for the movement of the planets, won him virtually no converts. So, the key concept that motivated Kepler and guided him in solving the problem of the planets was rejected by his contemporaries. Many historians of science doubt that anyone other than Kepler could have accomplished what he did when he did, because he had adopted a highly idiosyncratic physical theory and then employed his outstanding mathematical talents to create a new astronomy. It was an unlikely combination of intuitions and skills.

It is reasonable to expect that Kepler's stunningly accurate mathematical astronomy would have convinced his fellow astronomers of the truth of the Copernican view – and, in fact, it did help many of them make the transition. But once again, we find that the expectation of a stationary earth can trump other considerations. And so it proved possible for some thinkers to incorporate elements of Kepler's astronomy into a *geocentric* framework. Jean Morin and other Tychonic astronomers placed the sun on an elliptical orbit around the earth and the planets on elliptical orbits around the sun.[4] For them, Kepler had offered a way to strip the Tychonic system of its minor epicycles and make it more elegant. When they were done with their modifications, the geoheliocentric system of

Tycho was once again mathematically and observationally equivalent to the Copernican system (with the obvious exception of stellar parallax).

However, not all Kepler's laws could be successfully accommodated into the Tychonic system – particularly the distance-period relationship of the planets, which is now called Kepler's third law. Recall that his distance-period law precisely related the length of time that planets take to circle the sun with their distances from it (with more distant planets taking longer to traverse their circuit). This simple mathematical relationship could not be integrated into the Tychonic system because that system possessed two separate centers of planetary motion.[5]

Galileo's Legacy

Many thinkers cited Galileo's *Dialogue* as the work that won them over to the Copernican side. In addition to offering pro-Copernican arguments that had previously been made by Copernicus, Rheticus and Kepler, Galileo presented new and powerful arguments based on his own discoveries and physical ideas.

Ironically, Galileo's greatest legacy to science is less well-known – his *Discourse on Two New Sciences*, 1638, which included discussions on statics, dynamics, and the strength of materials. This work was a major influence on physicists who followed Galileo – both because of the physical ideas that Galileo presented in it and because of the approach or "method" that he promoted in it. We will see how this apparently cosmologically-neutral work helped Isaac Newton establish the Copernican system as the true system of the world.

Other Scientists

In order to keep this book to a manageable length, I've passed over the contributions of many outstanding men whose intellects and contributions were important to the story, even if they were not central to it. As an introduction to the Copernican Revolution, the account that I have provided here has been necessarily abbreviated and circumscribed. Still, it is important to acknowledge that other men interacted frequently with the main characters – often times inspiring them to take paths in their work that they may not otherwise have taken. Following the deaths of Kepler and Galileo, this dynamic network of European scientists remained active and its members continued to work on the unresolved problems of the day. Indeed, it was *because* these bright and talented people adopted many of Kepler and Galileo's ideas that we now regard Kepler and Galileo so highly. We will now consider the work of the two of most influential natural philosophers or "scientists" who followed some of Kepler and Galileo's thinking.

Rene Descartes and a New Philosophy

Aristotelian natural philosophy was losing its dominant position during the early 1600s. Even geocentric scientists who continued to oppose Copernicanism had jettisoned many of their Aristotelian beliefs. After the works of Brahe, Kepler, Galileo and others, European thinkers in the 1630s were increasingly able to ignore Aristotelian natural philosophy if they wished to. One of these men was Rene Descartes (1596–1650), a Jesuit-trained French nobleman of modest but independent means.

[Figure 10.1. Portrait of Rene Descartes. Artist, Frans Hals – 1648, Louvre Museum. Image courtesy André Hatala, Wikimedia Commons.]

He became convinced of the truth of Copernicanism early on and admired much of Galileo's work, but he was also extremely disappointed in Galileo for not creating a system with firm philosophical foundations.

As much as Descartes respected Galileo's discoveries and conclusions, he believed that Galileo's approach could only produce an ad hoc and jumbled mess of knowledge about the natural world. Descartes was first and foremost a philosopher, and he believed that any understanding of nature should be based on fundamental principles. Thus, he set out to create a new philosophical system that could be used to inform future investigations of nature in an orderly way.

Cartesian Cosmology

Descartes was also a mathematician, and he desired a philosophical system that had the same rigorous foundations as mathematics did. He began his effort by stating the only thing about the world that he knew with absolute certainty: "I think, therefore I am." With this as his starting point, he built up his philosophical structure. We don't have the time here to pursue the novelties and idiosyncrasies of Cartesian philosophy (the word "Cartesian" refers to the works of Descartes), but we will focus on the major feature of his thought that we are most concerned with – his unique account of the Copernican system. Descartes provided yet another physical explanation for the motion of the planets – and one that was considerably different from either Kepler's or Galileo's.

Descartes assumed that the natural motion of a celestial body was in a straight line. However, he also believed that a vacuum was impossible and that heavenly objects did not move freely through empty space. Instead, he posited a Universe filled with an extremely fine material – an "ether" – and that the circular motion of the planets was a consequence of the continual contact of the planets with the ether as they moved through it. Based on these physical ideas, he imagined a vast array of swirling planetary and stellar vortices that surrounded every heavenly body and that accounted for the basic features of the Copernican system. This physical model was appealing to many thinkers, but it was also problematic in that it was extremely complex. It suffered from several difficulties – one of which was that it was inherently non-mathematical and could not be used for calculating planetary positions.

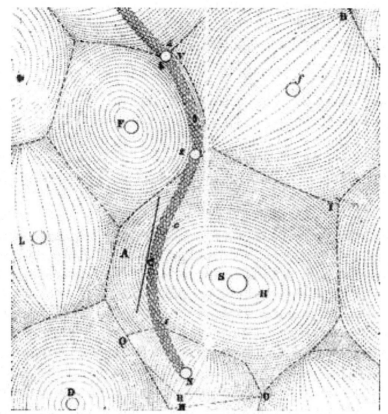

[Figure 10.2. Aether vortexes surrounding individual stars. René Descartes, *Principles of Philosophy*, 1644. Public domain.]

Descartes' influential works in philosophy, mathematics, and natural philosophy captured the imagination of many other thinkers of the time – including a young Isaac Newton. It is worth noting that Descartes abandoned an early effort to present his physical Copernicanism to the public in his manuscript titled *The World.* A Catholic, Descartes explained that he withdrew his work from publication after learning of Galileo's 1633 trial.

Later, Descartes published a somewhat amended version of his physical Copernicanism – one that included an imaginative solution for the problem of earth's motion: He proposed that each planet was stationary relative to its own vortex *and* stationary relative to the motion of the other planets and their vortices. This "Cartesian relativity" made every planet the center of celestial motion. Whether such a view of relative motion was believable or logically consistent was a matter of debate, but, by adopting it, Descartes was able to advocate for a version of the Copernican system while minimizing potential controversy.

On "Scientists" and "Philosophers"

I have conveniently used the term "scientist" throughout this book. It is important to note that my usage has been somewhat imprecise and anachronistic since the word was not coined in English until the early 1800s. Here, near the end of the book, we finally have a convenient place to discuss the terms that have been used to label people who investigated nature.

The "natural philosophers" of the past had many things in common with "scientists" of today – however, the two did possess significantly different goals and outlooks. These differences are perhaps best illustrated by the contrast in the methodologies of Descartes and Galileo. As we've just seen, Descartes believed that it was important to place all knowledge of the natural world on sound philosophical foundations before moving forward. In contrast, we saw that Galileo neglected to use philosophy to guide his work, and he didn't even attempt to fashion a new philosophy from his own discoveries. Instead, Galileo's study of nature was "a little of this and a little of that" with no strong sense of obligation to relate one thing that he learned about nature with other things that he knew about nature. This is one of the key features of Galileo's approach that he has in common with modern scientists. At the risk of oversimplification, but without exaggeration, we might describe Galileo as one of the first scientists and Descartes as one of the last natural philosophers.

Isaac Newton

Isaac Newton (1642-1727) was born in the same year that Galileo died – though this can be said only because the English had not yet accepted the Catholic Gregorian calendar.[6] Newton was born to a farm family of modest means and was raised by his grandmother after his father died and his mother remarried. Newton seems to have been difficult as a child and did not get along well with very many people. The young Newton was known to be good with his hands and comfortable around tools. He impressed local children and adults with his unusual knack for invention, which included a working model of a windmill and numerous sundials.

When he began grammar school, Newton's intellectual gifts were recognized, and his genius set him apart from the other children.

As an only son, Newton was expected to take over the thriving family farm. However, repeated attempts to groom him to accept his birthright failed. At farming, he proved to be inattentive at best and out-and-out irresponsible at worst. He even bribed hired hands to do his chores. His talent was instead for daydreaming, inventing, and thinking. After a time it became clear to the adults in Newton's life that he was not suited for farm work. Fortunately for young Isaac, and for English science, his schoolmaster and his maternal uncle persuaded his mother that he should be sent to the University. After some additional preparation at the local school, Isaac found himself at Cambridge. In his capacity there as a relatively poor scholarship student, he performed chores for well-to-do students, which included emptying their chamber pots.

[Figure 10.3. Portrait of Isaac Newton at forty-six. Sir Godfrey Kneller, 1689. Public domain.]

When Newton attended the university, Cambridge still adhered to Aristotelian and classical forms of education. By this time, neither staff nor students were particularly enthusiastic about the antiquated curriculum, so much of it was undertaken half-heartedly. Students had access to a tutor but were otherwise expected to study for the exams on their own. This environment proved to be a great advantage to Newton because it gave him the freedom to explore his own interests most of the time. He developed a strategy of ignoring the traditional curriculum until the occasional exam forced him to cram for it.

At this early phase in his life, Newton was drawn to two subjects in particular – the natural philosophy of René Descartes and mathematics. Newton had received very little formal instruction in mathematics since it did not have the place in the curriculum that it does now. With no one guiding him, Newton overlooked the basics and neglected to even study the geometry of Euclid. Without knowing any better, he managed to struggle through the advanced works of contemporary mathematicians on his own. That he was at all successful at understanding these authors is noteworthy – that he managed to master the material in a relatively short period of time and then began making original contributions to mathematics was remarkable. Not long after Newton had immersed himself in the subject, a plague epidemic hit Cambridge and the university closed for two years. He returned to his home village of Woolsthorpe in order to avoid the disease.

Newton had won a great deal of freedom and solitude at Cambridge by keeping his social interactions to the barest minimum. At Woolsthorpe, he had even more private time and used it to take full advantage of his remarkable concentration. During this period, Newton invented geometric versions of differential and integral calculus and explored and extended infinite series. By the end of his stay at Woolsthorpe and without anyone being aware of it, Newton became the leading mathematician in Europe. And, as if this were not enough, Newton also found time to conduct important experimental and theoretical work on optics and began to apply his powerful mathematical techniques to the development of a new inertial physics. These two remarkable years at Woolsthorpe are often referred to as Newton's *annus mirabilis*. When he returned to Cambridge, he shared the results of his mathematical work with Isaac Barrow, the Lucasian Professor of mathematics. Barrow quickly recognized Newton's gift for mathematics and, because he was in the process of abandoning his professorship for other pursuits, recommended that Newton replace him. It was in this way that a relatively young Isaac Newton won a permanent professorship at Cambridge.

Of all of Newton's works, we will focus our attention on his physics since he was able to use it to explain planetary motion in the Keplerian-Copernican system. It was also the work that had the greatest influence on later scientists. Newton's other accomplishments were also impressive, but they did not have the great impact that his physics did. For example, although Newton had invented calculus, he never published it. A younger mathematician, Gottfried Leibniz (1646-1716), later independently developed a more fruitful formulation of calculus, which was then extended by other mathematicians. And while Newton's work in optics was important and his invention of a new type of reflecting telescope notable, other men were working in these areas too. However, his creation of a new mathematical physics stood apart as a singular achievement, and it conferred onto Newton enduring fame.[7] Thus, we will consider Newton's physics, which he presented in his masterful *Philosophiae Naturalis Principia Mathematica* (*Mathematical Principles of Natural Philosophy*), 1687 – a book that is usually referred to simply as the *Principia*. Newton's new mathematical physics opened the door to the precision analysis of many phenomena. His success can be measured by the fact that his ideas are still taught in high schools and universities today and continue to be used by scientists and engineers. While we haven't the space here to describe how Newton managed to create his physics, a brief outline of its essential form is in order.

Newton's Laws of Motion

Newton developed four foundational ideas, or postulates, to establish his physics – three laws of motion and a theory of gravity. His first law of motion essentially stated the fundamental idea of his inertial physics: that an object at rest remains at rest or that an object in motion remains in motion until an interaction with another object causes it to change its speed and/or direction. Newton's second and third laws essentially described how such changes took place. According to this Newtonian view, moving objects continue moving at a constant speed and in a straight line unless they interact with another body.

Newton's Law of Gravity

Newton also proposed that there is an attractive force between all objects and that the strength of the force between any two objects is proportional to the product of their masses and inversely proportional to the square of the distance between them. Newton was not the first person to propose some version of gravity, but he was the first person who was able to mathematize it and rigorously show that it accounted for all of Kepler's planetary laws and Galileo's law of free fall.

Newton also illustrated that gravity was universal – that it existed between all objects in the Universe. In the first step toward demonstrating this, he analyzed the effect of gravity between the moon and the earth – then he analyzed the effect of gravity between a terrestrial object and the earth. He found that his theory worked in both cases. The mathematical calculations that Newton needed to perform in order to accomplish this were extremely challenging. For example, he showed that the path of the moon around the earth could be explained by two things: 1) the gravitational attraction between the earth and the moon and 2) the inertial motion of the moon. In his analysis, the moon was essentially "falling" towards the earth but, because of its tangential motion, was constantly missing it. His mastery of mathematics allowed him to illustrate this in a rigorous way.

In order for Newton to show that gravity also acted between a terrestrial object (like an apple falling from a tree) and the earth, he had to calculate the force of gravity between the entire earth and the object. The gravity calculation was difficult enough for the moon, but in the case of an object very close to the earth's surface, it was more troublesome. This is because earth's matter is distributed throughout its sphere in various distances, amounts, and directions from the object. All of the earth's matter contributed to the gravitational pull on the object – but how could one account for it all mathematically? Newton was able to solve the problem by first proving that the combined gravitational attraction of earth's matter acted as though it was concentrated at the earth's center. By simplifying the problem in this way, he was able to illustrate that gravity could account for Galileo's law of free fall.

Newton's Accomplishment

By invoking gravity to show that a falling object, an orbiting moon, and the planets' motion around the sun were all the result of the same cause, Newton established once and for all that physics in the terrestrial realm and physics in the celestial realm were the same. However, as great as Newton's accomplishment was, it is important to appreciate that he had not been working in complete isolation. Prior to his efforts, the Copernican system had been well-received in England, and Kepler's laws of planetary motion were widely appreciated there as well. Other scientists were struggling with the same problems that Newton was working on, and some of them had important insights – often times before Newton himself. However, none of these scientists were able to carry their speculations very far. Newton's mastery of mathematics and his ability to rigorously show that his physical system corresponded to reality is what set him apart from his peers.

Newton continued to illustrate the fruitfulness of his physics by explaining a number of subsidiary phenomena – these included the parabolic paths of comets, the solar and lunar gravitational influences on the tides, and the deviation of Jupiter and Saturn from perfect elliptical orbits (a result of their mutual attraction as they passed by each other). Finally, Newton made an additional prediction that would have important implications for the final reception of his theory outside of England: the earth was not a perfect sphere but was instead slightly flattened at the poles.

Newton's achievement was so compelling that it helped to finally establish the consensus that the Copernican system was the true system of the world. Newton did this not by offering direct proof for the Copernican system, but by providing a quantitatively accurate explanation for why the Copernican system behaved as it did. Given the outstanding success of his explanation, most thinkers found it unfathomable that Newton had somehow managed to account for something that did not exist. The Copernican system was, at last, a complete system. Interestingly,

Newton's work had at last validated the intuition and speculation of the early Copernicans – that smaller things ought to circle larger things...

Reception of Newton's Theory

Newton's *Principia* had a print run of only 300 copies. It was very well-received in England in spite of its very difficult geometric and mathematical passages. But only experts in mathematics were able to follow its key arguments. Even highly educated readers, like John Locke, had to rely on the opinion of expert mathematicians to confirm the veracity of Newton's conclusions. Newton won over many scientists with his *Principia*, and he quickly became famous in England.

Newton's work was not nearly as well-received in Continental Europe where Descartes' work was highly regarded. Furthermore, the prevailing "mechanical philosophy" in Europe presumed that all physical effects related to motion were to be explained by direct physical contact between objects – as occurred in Descartes' vortices. In this mechanical view, matter-on-matter interactions were necessary for one object to have an effect on another. From this perspective, the mysterious through-space attraction of Newton's gravity was viewed with great suspicion. Leading scientists like Huygens and Leibniz, while impressed by Newton's accomplishment, remained unconvinced of his gravitational force. They and others believed that Newton's gravity was an occult notion and represented a step backwards toward the magical thinking of the past rather than a step forward toward hard-nosed science. Indeed, even Newton had his doubts about his force of gravity and privately wondered about its underlying physical cause. But in remaining true to his method of science, which was to withhold speculation about things that could not be supported by evidence, Newton said nothing more. He described gravity but did not explain it.

For these reasons and others, the view of Descartes continued to dominate on the Continent, even though Newton had expertly criticized Cartesian vortex theory and revealed its failings. In particular, Newton pointed out that the vortex theory was incapable of explaining all of Kepler's laws. Still, Newton's criticisms seemed not to be enough to put the issue to rest. In the end, it was the debate over the shape of the earth that helped settle the matter once and for all. Both Newtonian and Cartesian physics had led to predictions that the earth was not a perfect sphere. Newtonian theory predicted that because the earth spun, it would bulge at the equator and be slightly compressed at the poles, while Cartesian theory predicted the opposite – because of its vortex, the earth would be narrower around the equator and elongated along its axis like an American football. Astronomers knew that careful distance measurements of the earth's surface between the lines of latitude near the North Pole and between the lines of latitude near the equator could help settle the debate between the two systems. Surveying expeditions were sent to Lapland and Peru. Upon their return, the matter was settled in favor of Newton – the earth, although nearly spherical, bulges slightly near the equator.

Newtonian Mechanics

While Newton's *Principia* was not immediately popular on the Continent, a handful of men and women there began to promote it nonetheless.[8] And once Newtonian physics finally caught on, it was extended rapidly through the contributions of highly skilled Continental mathematicians. An important example of their accomplishments was Alexis Claude Clairaut's (1713-1765) remarkably accurate prediction of the reappearance of Halley's Comet in 1759. It was a success that caused the Newtonian achievement to be more widely appreciated by the European public.

Continental mathematicians continued their work on refining and generalizing techniques in calculus, which allowed them to solve increasingly difficult puzzles in Newtonian dynamics. They improved upon Newton's solutions and tackled problems that he could not. In one case, the mathematician Pierre-Simon Laplace (1749-1827) was able to show that the Newtonian-Copernican universe was an inherently stable clock-like system that could run on its own forever. This was in great contrast to Newton's earlier conclusion: that a Universe following his laws of physics was unstable and required the continual intervention of God to keep it in working order. So whereas God's presence was an essential element of Newton's physical/cosmological scheme, he was not in Laplace's. Indeed, when asked by Napoleon Bonaparte where God was in his World System, Laplace famously responded, "I have no need for that hypothesis." This secular, God-optional Newtonian universe was not one that Newton would have been comfortable with. Over the years Newton's physics had been so greatly transformed that it has been said that Newton himself was not a "Newtonian" – at least as the term later came to be understood.

At Last: Proof for the Copernican System

Physical evidence that was accepted as proof for the Copernican system was a long time in coming. Observation of stellar parallax had been considered the gold standard, but for the three hundred years following Copernicus it eluded many spirited attempts to detect it. In the early 1700s, a number of investigators attempted to measure stellar parallax by directing their large telescopes to stars located directly overhead. Their efforts were rewarded, but instead of detecting it, they uncovered an unexpected kind of evidence for the motion of the earth – a phenomenon called *stellar aberration*. The effect was reported in 1725 and was explained by James Bradley two years later. Like stellar parallax, stellar aberration is manifested by changes in the apparent position of stars during the course of the year – though the annual changes of stellar aberration are very different from those of stellar parallax.

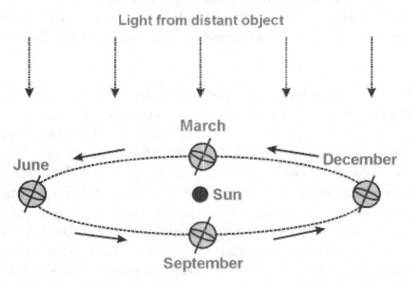

[Figure 10.4. The light from a distant star arrives from above (north) of the earth's orbit. Because of its great distance, a star's light arrives at the solar system in nearly parallel rays.[9] Figure courtesy Portnadler, Wikimedia Commons.]

Bradley's explanation for stellar aberration depended on an understanding that light travels at a finite speed.[10] He determined that the earth's motion around the sun, while much slower than the speed of light, still has a significant effect on the direction that a telescope must be pointed in order to capture the light emanating from a star. Consider figure 10.4, which illustrates the earth's motion around the sun and the direction that light arrives from a northern star.

This curious effect of the earth's motion is such that one cannot point a telescope straight upward to see a star that is directly overhead! This is very much like the way in which one uses an umbrella in the rain: While it is effective to hold an umbrella directly overhead when standing still, in order to capture the rain drops when walking or running, it needs to be tilted forward. The same holds for a telescope. If the earth were stationary, a telescope could simply be pointed upwards to sight a star directly overhead. But if one points a telescope directly overhead on a moving earth, the light that is falling down into it will hit the side of the telescope before it reaches the eye piece. To keep this from happening, the telescope must be tipped in the direction of the motion of the earth in order to see the star. Consider figure 10.5.

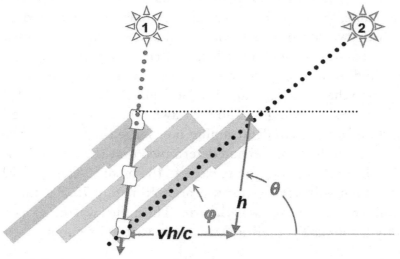

[Figure 10.5. Stellar aberration. Figure courtesy Brews ohare, Wikimedia Commons.]

The observed star is in position #1. The earth (and therefore the telescope) is moving from left to right in the diagram. The telescope needs to be pointed in the direction of its motion so that the light entering the telescope (when it is in the left hand position) can fall to the bottom of the telescope and hit the eye piece without hitting the inside of the telescope first. The actual path that the light takes is indicated by the line from #1. As the light falls downward the telescope continues to move forward (left-to-right) so that the light remains in the tube until it hits the bottom (the eye piece), which is portrayed by the telescope position shown on the right. However, unless observers know that this is what is happening, they might instead conclude that the star is located in the direction that the telescope is pointed. To such observers, it would appear as though star #1 is located where star #2 is shown in the diagram. Stellar aberration changes throughout the year, because the direction of the earth's motion around the sun changes throughout the year. So, while stellar aberration was not a phenomenon that anyone was looking for, it nonetheless served as the first direct evidence that the earth was in motion around the sun.

Stellar parallax

Reports of stellar parallax measurements were made from the mid-1600s onward. However, none of them stood up to scrutiny until Friedrich Bessel described his careful parallax measurements of the star *61 Cygni* in 1838. By this time, the Copernican system had long been accepted as the true system of the world, so that the observation of the long sought-after stellar parallax had no impact on the heliocentric-geocentric debate. Still, Bessel's finding was of great interest to astrophysicists because they had begun to map the stars and galaxies and address the question of the size of the Universe. Knowing just how far away the closest stars were was an important first step in determining how large the Universe was. By measuring its parallax, Bessel had determined that the star, *61 Cygni*, was over 10 light-years distant (quite close to the modern value). This meant that the relatively nearby star was approximately 75,000 times more distant from the sun than was Saturn. Thus, the "wasted space" that so greatly troubled Tycho Brahe was truly vast in its extent.

Proof for the Earth's Rotation

The wait was even longer for direct physical evidence that the earth rotated daily on its axis. The proof appeared in the motion of a large pendulum that had been designed and built in 1851 by a professor of

physics named Léon Foucault.[11] It was fashioned with a heavy metal bob
that was hung by a 200 foot long wire from the ceiling of the great dome
of the Pantheon in Paris.

[Figure 10.6. A Foucault's pendulum at the Pantheon in Paris. Public domain image
courtesy Arnaud, Wikimedia Commons.]

In order to make sure that the pendulum moved in a simple back-and-
forth planar motion (and did not possess any circular motion), he
designed a special release mechanism. He pulled the pendulum bob back
and tied it in place with a cord. After it steadied, he burned the cord to
free the bob and the pendulum began its motion. The pendulum remained
in motion for many hours and as the day progressed, the plane of its
oscillation did not remain fixed with respect to the floor of the Pantheon,
but instead rotated slowly.

It is easiest to understand the phenomenon by considering a Foucault's
pendulum constructed at one of the earth's poles. A pendulum set into
motion there will continue to oscillate back and forth with its plane of
oscillation fixed due to the inertial motion of the bob as the earth rotates
underneath it (see figure 10.7). However, since the observers of the

pendulum are standing on the rotating earth they will see things differently – they will note that the plane of the bob's motion rotates every twenty-four hours since they naturally perceive the earth to be stationary.

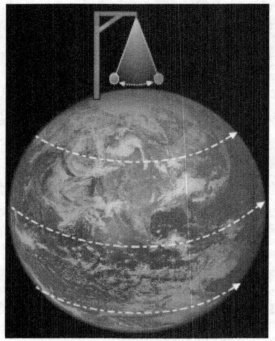

[Figure 10.7. A Foucault's pendulum at the North Pole. Figure courtesy Krallja, Wikimedia Commons.]

As a practical matter, the experiment was not first performed at the North or South Pole, but in Paris. At that latitude, the length of time that the plane of a pendulum's motion takes to complete its rotation is considerably longer than 24 hours – approximately 33-35 hours for the mid-latitudes of France and the northern United States. At the equator, the plane of a Foucault's pendulum would show no motion at all.

At first, many people reported difficulty reproducing Foucault's careful work. The experiment was not easy to perform unless the bob was heavy and the pendulum long. Furthermore, the peculiar length of time for the period of the pendulum did not sit well with non-scientists who expected the period to be exactly 24 hours.[12] Scientists, on the other hand, sorted out the experimental discrepancies and noted that the observed periods of rotation at the various latitudes matched theoretical expectations. Only much later was it practicable to actually carry out the experiment at one of the earth's poles. The expected period of rotation of 24 hours was reported for a pendulum that was hung in the unheated 6-floor stairwell of the South Pole Amundsen-Scott station in 2001.[13]

Loose Ends and Challenges for Newtonian Mechanics

There were two phenomena that continued to defy a Newtonian analysis: 1) a detailed account of the moon's motion and 2) a detailed account of Mercury's motion around the sun – in particular, the precession of its perihelion.

The Moon

Although Newton was able to explain the fundamental features of the moon's orbit around the earth, it took another two hundred years before scientists were able to fully account for the finer features of its motion. Newton had struggled mightily with the details, but was ultimately unsuccessful and admitted defeat only in the third edition of his *Principia*. He understood the nature of the problem but couldn't find a way through to a workable solution. The challenge was this: the moon is strongly attracted to two bodies simultaneously – the earth *and* the sun. This kind of physical interaction is referred to as a "three body problem," which has since been shown to have no exact mathematical solution – a fact which Newton himself had suspected.

In the case of the sun-earth-moon system, the gravitational attraction between the moon and the sun is twice as strong as the attraction between the moon and the earth. Indeed, if one traces out the path of the moon around the sun, it is always concave with respect to the sun. Viewing the matter in this way, we can consider the orbit of the moon to be centered on the sun with the presence of the nearby earth as perturbing its orbit. This "three body" system was analyzed through a series of successive mathematical approximations, and it consumed the efforts of several Newtonian physicists, with one even suggesting that Newton's simple inverse square law for gravity might need to be modified by the addition of a second term (although he soon retracted his own suggestion). Eventually, the moon's motion was accounted for using Newtonian physics after mathematicians developed increasingly sophisticated mathematical models. The problem was solved, for the most part, by G.W. Hill in the 1870s.[14]

Mercury

The path of Mercury around the sun is essentially elliptical. But as Newton realized early on, the orbit of a planet around the sun is also affected by the gravity of the other planets. One effect of these smaller gravitational forces is that the major axis of a planet's elliptical path tends to sweep slowly around the sun so that the closest point of a planet's orbit changes its location slightly from one orbit to the next. This, "precession of the perihelion" could be explained for all of the planets except Mercury, which didn't quite match expectations. The deviation of Mercury's orbit from Newtonian theory was very small, but because of the high degree of confidence in the astronomical observations and in Newtonian theory it posed a major puzzle to scientists.

Some astronomers postulated that there were undiscovered asteroids orbiting very close to Mercury that perturbed its orbit. The astronomer, Le Verrier (1811-1877), even proposed the existence of an undiscovered planet that orbited very close to the sun – a planet he dubbed "Vulcan." Le Verrier had been successful at making this sort of prediction before: he was one of the scientists who successfully anticipated the existence of the planet Neptune based on irregularities found in the expected orbit of Uranus. But while Le Verrier was correct about Neptune, the planet "Vulcan" was never found.

The solution to the problem of Mercury's orbit came from a completely unexpected quarter: Einstein's general theory of relativity (1916), which offered a very different account of gravity. Einstein's theory could be used to successfully predict the orbit of Mercury. So for this and many other reasons, Einstein's gravitational theory superseded Newton's. Interestingly, even though physicists now fully accept the superiority of Einstein's theory over Newton's, they continue to teach Newtonian theory to students. The reason for this is that in most terrestrial applications, the results of Newtonian theory so closely approximate the results of Einstein's that they are practically indistinguishable. Furthermore, Newtonian theory is much easier to apply and is more intellectually accessible to engineers and scientists who have no occasion to use the mathematically and conceptually challenging relativity theory.

The Impact of the Copernican Revolution

We have just considered a remarkable episode in the history of human understanding. The realization that the earth is a big spinning ball orbiting the sun raised as many questions as it answered. Not only did it forever alter mankind's relationship to the cosmos, but it also changed expectations regarding what could be learned about nature in the future. The great reverence for ancient thinkers had come to an end and was replaced with an unbridled self-confidence in all things European. No investigation about nature seemed too difficult. Hundreds of scientists pursued lines of inquiry on a wide variety of subjects – often times with considerable success. During the two hundred years following Newton, key discoveries in chemistry, biology, and physics occurred, and the subsequent growth in these disciplines accelerated. In the second half of the 1800s, the great progress in chemistry and advances in understanding electricity and magnetism were largely responsible for the subsequent growth of technology and industry. This impact of science on technology and society was unprecedented and was so wide-reaching that the period has often been described as a "second scientific revolution."

The Scientific Revolution and the Nature of Scientific Knowledge

After examining the history of the geocentric-heliocentric debate in some detail and getting a glimpse of the subsequent progress in physics and the other sciences, it may now seem appropriate to say something about the "nature of scientific knowledge" or the "scientific method." Indeed, it is difficult to resist the temptation to do so. I only have the space here to say that it is a much more difficult undertaking than one might first think – a fact that philosophers of science have proven over the years. In the meantime, it is probably more fruitful to glean lessons and rules-of-thumb directly from the history of science rather than to try to propose a philosophical system of rules and generalizations that hold true in all possible circumstances. By studying different historical episodes closely, we can develop a more realistic sense for the nature of scientific knowledge, and we can also more easily jettison naïve views about science that we have somehow picked up along the way. While fundamental questions about the philosophy of science are unavoidable and fascinating, those questions should be informed as much or more by what science *has been* than by what we might think it *ought* to be. Finally, it would be premature to begin a serious discussion on the philosophy of science without considering as many features of science as possible – these include episodes in the development of astronomy, geology, electricity, chemistry, biology, and modern physics. In spite of its limited scope, I hope this book has helped to provide meaningful insight into the scientific mindset – in spite of my never having articulated exactly what that mindset is.

---

[1] See endnote 37 in Chapter Four and endnote 5 in Chapter Nine for brief discussions of Aristarchus and early geokinetic theories.

[2] See Crowe, 2001, pp. 25 for a clear description of Aristarchus's solar diameter calculation. I thank Prof. Crowe for drawing my attention to the significance of the solar diameter determination.

[3] This rapid demise of the circle in mathematical astronomy was likely made possible by three factors: 1) The accuracy of Kepler's *Rudolphine Tables* – particularly for the case of Mars, which demanded that the orbit possessed an oval shape of some sort if the calculations were to account for Tycho's data. 2) The ellipse was a conic section along with the circle, parabola, and hyperbola. Thus, the ellipse had a respectable pedigree having been closely studied by the ancients, including the Hellenistic mathematician Apollonius, who was well-known by Renaissance mathematicians. In a sense, Kepler was simply replacing one conic section with another. 3) Finally, the perfection of the circle had been associated with the Aristotelian view of the cosmos. Since the fundamental Aristotelian premise of the immutability and perfection of the celestial realm was being dismissed on other grounds, there may have been an associated loss of confidence in the circle as the ideal shape to describe motion in the cosmos.

[4] Giambattista Riccioli also incorporated ellipses into his geocentric views.

[5] Kepler's third law mathematically describes an existing qualitative relationship that Copernicus was quite aware of: that the farther a planet is from the sun, the longer it takes to complete its circuit around it. In the Tychonic system, this simple qualitative relationship and Kepler's third law becomes fragmented, because the earth is taken from its Copernican orbit and placed stationary at the center of the system. Now, instead of the earth taking 365 days to circle the sun, a period

intermediate between those of Venus and Mars, it is stationary while the sun circles the earth.

[6] The Catholic Church had adopted the Gregorian calendar to solve a significant _____ eveloped after centuries of using the Julian Calendar, _____ days so that the spring equinox began occurring _____ ndar year. To solve the problem, in the 1500s the _____ Gregory, eliminated 10 days from the calendar and _____ ears (three leap years every four hundred years). This _____ diately adopted in the Catholic World under the _____ rotestants, always anxious to disagree with Catholics, _____ he disagreement created an awkward situation in _____ rs because, on a given day, the calendar read differently _____ lian calendar is sometimes called the "old style" and the _____ style." European historians customarily refer to the calendric system that was in use in the region that they study, unless otherwise noted. England used the old style calendar, so Newton's life span was reported using it: 25 December 1642 – 20 March 1727 OS, (which was actually 4 January 1643 – 31 March 1727 NS). Thus, only if the two different calendars are used is it possible to claim that Newton was born in the same year Galileo died.

[7] In addition to Newton's works in mathematics, optics, and physics, he was also extremely active in the practice of alchemy. He devoted a tremendous amount of time conducting alchemical experiments and in explaining the results of his experiments. An examination of Newton's alchemical writings have shown that Newton's concept of a "force" was wider-ranging and more general than the single force of gravity that he is now known for. Many historians have drawn attention to the relationship between Newton's alchemical ideas and his work in physics. Newton also indulged in Hermetic or "occult" beliefs about the origins of human knowledge. He believed that much of what he wished to learn about the natural world had been known much earlier – going all the way back to King Solomon. Privately, Newton was a devoted theologian who held heterodox views on the nature of Christ. He believed that the concept of the Trinity was a heresy that had been imposed on the Church very early on. Except for a few confidants, he kept his religious views to himself during his lifetime. In doing so, he managed to avoid certain personal troubles that would have included him being socially ostracized and losing his professorship at Cambridge. Only after his death and the examination of his voluminous writings on theology were discovered, did the world become aware that Newton was not a traditional Christian.

[8] One of these French Newtonians was the remarkable woman, Émilie du Châtelet (1706-1749), a mathematician and physicist who translated Newton's *Principia* into French and provided commentary on it – thus significantly increasing the accessibility of Newton's work in France.

[9] The fact that the rays of light from a distant star are very nearly parallel when they reach the solar system is the same reason that stellar parallax was so difficult to observe.

[10] The speed of light was determined in the 1670s by Cassini and Ole Rømer. Rømer determined the speed of light by carefully analyzing the way in which the timing of the eclipses of the moons of Jupiter changed depending on earth's distance from Jupiter.

[11] Foucault's pendulum provided the most convincing direct evidence for the earth's rotational motion on its axis, but it was preceded by the measurement of a slight eastward deflection of a falling body by Giambattista Guglielmini. Guglielmini repeatedly dropped objects from a high tower in Bologna in 1789-92 using a carefully determined plumb line. His work was confirmed by others in Europe using high towers or deep mine shafts. The effect was slight, but the measurements approximated the theoretical prediction from Newtonian physics for a spinning earth. An object on a high tower has a greater radius from the earth's center than an object below it – thus it is moving more quickly. As it falls, it "overtakes" the ground beneath it and lands slightly ahead of it in the direction it was traveling – to the east. Guglielmini measured an average deflection of 1.9 centimeters to the east (slightly less than an inch) for an object dropped 78.3 meters (over 250 feet). See Wallace, 1995.

[12] The period of rotation for a Foucault's pendulum is 24 hours at the poles (90° latitude). At the equator (0° latitude), the pendulum would not rotate at all since it would be positioned perpendicular to the earth's rotational axis. At intermediate latitudes, the period is longer than 24 hours and follows the equation:
$T = 24 \text{ hrs}/\sin \phi$, where ϕ is the latitude and T is the period. To be precise, the length of time that the earth takes to rotate once on its axis is closer to 23 hr and 56 min, though 24 hours is usually given as the approximate time.

[13] As reported by Mike Town, John Bird and R. Allen Baker, 2001.

[14] Hill showed that the path that the moon takes around the earth was highly sensitive to the initial conditions of motion and that the orbital path of the moon could have been much more complex and interesting than it is. One possibility was a double figure eight path. See the diagram in Neugebauer, 1969, pp. 153.

Bibliography

Aaboe, Asger, *Scientific Astronomy in Antiquity*, Phil Trans. R. Soc. Lond. A. **276**, pp. 21-42 (1974).

Aaboe, Asger, *Episodes from the Early History of Mathematics*, Mathematical Association of America, 1997.

Aaboe, Asger, *Episodes from the Early History of Astronomy*, Springer, 2001.

Achinstein, Peter (ed.), *Science Rules: A Historical Introduction to Scientific Methods*, The Johns Hopkins University Press, 2004.

Africa, Thomas W., *Copernicus' Relation to Aristarchus and Pythagoras*, Isis, Vol. 56, No. 1961), pp. 403-409.

Aiton, E. J., *On Galileo and the Earth-Moon System*, Isis, Vol. 54, No. 2 (Jun., 1963), pp. 265-266.

Aiton, E. J. and Burstyn, Harold L., *Galileo and the Theory of the Tides*, Isis, Vol. 56, No. 1 (Spring, 1965), pp. 56-63.

Aiton, E. J., *Celestial Spheres and Circles*, History of Science, Vol. 19, 1981, pp. 75-114.

Alexander, David, *Dante and the Form of the Land*, Annals of the Association of American Geographers, 76(1), 1986, pp. 38-49.

Allan-Olney, Mary, *The Private Life of Galileo: Compiled Principally from his Correspondence and that of his Eldest Daughter, Sister Maria Celeste.* London: Macmillan, 1870.

Applebaum, Wilbur, *Keplerian Astronomy After Kepler: Researches and Problems*, History of Science, (1996), pp. 451-504.

Applebaum, Wilber and Baldasso Renzo, *Galileo and Kepler on the Sun as Planetary Mover*, from *Largo Campo Di Filosofare – Eurosymposium Galileo 2001*, Jose Montresinos and Carlos Solis (eds).

Arciniegas, Germán, *Amerigo and the New World: The Life and Times of Amerigo Vespucci*, Alfred Knopf, 1955.

Baigrie, Brian S., *Kepler's Laws of Planetary Motion, Before and After Newton's Principia: An Essay on the Transformation of Scientific Problems*, Studies in the History and Philosophy of Science, 1987, pp. 177-208.

Baldasso, Renzo, *Galileo's Celestial Dynamics*, Master of Arts Thesis, University of Oklahoma, 1998.

Barker, Peter; Goldstein, Bernard R., *Is Seventeenth Century Physics Indebted to the Stoics?* Centaurus, 1984, pp. 148-164.

Barker, Peter; Goldstein, Bernard R., *Realism and Instrumentalism in sixteenth Century Astronomy: A Reappraisal*, Perspectives on Science, vol. 6, No. 3, 1998, pp. 232-258.

Barker, Peter, *Constructing Copernicus*, Perspectives on Science, Vol 10, No. 2, 2002, pp. 208-227.

Barker, Peter, *How Rothmann Changed His Mind*, Centaurus, Vol 46, 2004, pp. 41-57.

Barnes, Jonathan (ed), *Early Greek Philosophy*, Penguin Classics, 2001.

Beltran, Antonio, *Wine, Water, and Epistemological Sobriety: A Note on the Koyre-MacLachlan Debate*, Isis, Vol. 89, No. 1 (Mar., 1998), pp. 82-89.

Blair, Ann, *Tycho Brahe's Critique of Copernicus and the Copernican System*, Journal of the History of Ideas, Vol. 51, 1990, No. 3, pp. 355-377.

Blair, Ann and Grafton, Anthony, *Reassessing Humanism and Science*, Journal of the History of Ideas, 1992, pp. 535-540.

Blackwell, Richard J., *Galileo, Bellarmine, and the Bible*, University of Notre Dame Press, 1991.

Blackwell, Richard J., *Behind the Scenes at Galileo's Trial – Including the First English Translation of Melchior Inchofer's Tractatus syllepticus*, University of Notre Dame Press, 2006.

Blåsjö, Viktor, *A Critique of the Arguments for Maragha Influence on Copernicus*, Journal for the History of Astronomy, May, 2014, 45, pp. 183-195.

Bucciantini, Massimo and Camerota, Michele, *Once More about Galileo and Astrology: A Neglected Testimony*, Galilaena, II, pp. 229-232.

Burstyn, Harold L., *Galileo's Attempt to Prove That the Earth Moves*, Isis, Vol. 53, No. 2 (Jun., 1962), pp. 161-185.

Burstyn, Harold L., *Galileo and the Earth-Moon System: Reply to Dr. Aiton*, Isis, Vol. 54, No. 3 (Sep., 1963), pp. 400-401.

Carlos, Edward Stafford, *The Sidereal Messenger of Galileo Galilei and a Part of the Preface to Kepler's Dioptrics*, Rivingtons, London, 1880.

Carolino, Luis Miguel, *The Making of a Tychonic Cosmology: Cristoforo Borri and the Development of Tycho Brahe's Astronomical System*, 2008, pp. 313-344.

Cartwright, David Edgar, *Tides: A Scientific History*, Cambridge University Press, 1999.

Casanovas, Juan, *G. Settele and the Final Annulment of the Decree of 1616 Against Copernicanism*, Memorie della Società Astronomia Italiana, Vol. 60, 1989, pp. 791-805.

Casanovas, Juan, *The Problem of Annual Parallax in Galileo's Time*, in *The Galileo Affair: A Meeting of Faith and Science*, eds.: G.V. Coyne, S.J., M. Heller and J. Zycinski (Vatican City State: Vatican Observatory Publications, distributed by the Libreria Editrice Vaticana), pp. 67-74.

Caspar, Max, *Kepler*, Translated and Edited by C. Doris Helman, Dover, (1948/1993)

Christianidis, Jean; Dialetis, Dimitris; and Gavroglu, Kostas, *Having a Knack for the Non-intuitive: Aristarchus's Heliocentrism Through Archimedes's Geocentrism*, History of Science, 2002, pp. 147-168.

Christianson, J.R., *Copernicus and the Lutherans*, Sixteenth Century Journal, Vol. 4, No. 2, 1973, pp. 1-10.

Christianson, John, *Tycho Brahe's Cosmology from the Astrologia of 1591*, Isis, Vol. 59, No. 3, pp. 312- 318.

Christianson, J. R. *Tycho Brahe in Scandinavian Scholarship*, History of Science, 1998, pp. 467-484.

Christianson, John Robert, *On Tycho's Island: Tycho Brahe and His Assistants, 1570-1601*, Cambridge University Press, 2000.

Clagett, Marshall, *The Impact of Archimedes on Medieval Science*, Isis, Vol. 50, No. 4 (Dec., 1959), pp. 419-429.

Clutton-Brock, Martin, *Copernicus's Path to His Cosmology: An Attempted Reconstruction*, Journal for the History of Astronomy, 2005, pp. 197-216.

Clutton-Brock, Martin and Topper, David, *The Plausibility of Galileo's Tidal Theory*, Centaurus, 2011, pp. 1-15.

Cohen, H. Floris, *Quantifying Music: The Science of Music at the First Stage of the Scientific Revolution, 1580-1650*, D. Reidel Publishing Co., 1984, pp. 78-85.

Cohen, H. Floris, *The Scientific Revolution: A Historiographical Inquiry*, University of Chicago Press, 1994.

Cohen, H. Floris, *How Modern Science Came into the World: Four Civilizations, One 17th-Century Breakthrough*, Amsterdam University Press, 2010.

Conlin, Michael F., *The Popular and Scientific Reception of the Foucault Pendulum in the United States*, Isis, Vol. 90, No. 2 (Jun., 1999), pp. 181-204.

Copernicus, Nicolaus, *On the Revolutions of Heavenly Spheres*, Translated by Charles Glenn Wallis (St. John's Bookstore 1939), Prometheus Books, 1995.

Crombie, A.C., *The History of Science From Augustine to Galileo*, Dover (1970/1995).

Crowe, Michael J., *Theories of the World from Antiquity to the Copernican Revolution*, Dover, 2001.

Danielson, Dennis, *Achilles Gasser and the Birth of Copernicanism*, Journal for the History of Astronomy, 2004, pp. 457-474.

Danielson, Dennis, *The First Copernican: Georg Joachim Rheticus and the Rise of the Copernican Revolution*, Walker and Company, 2006.

Delong, H. *A Profile of Mathematical Logic*. Addison-Wesley, 1970.

Di Bono, Mario, *Copernicus, Amico, Fracastoro and Tusi's Device: Observations on the Use and Transmission of a Model*, Journal for the History of Astronomy, 1995, pp. 133-154.

Dicks, D. R., *Early Greek Astronomy to Aristotle*, Cornell University Press, 1970.

Donahue, William H., *The Solid Planetary Spheres in Post-Copernican Natural Philosophy*, In *The Copernican Achievement*, ed. Robert S. Westman, University of California Press, 1975, pp. 244-275.

Drake, Stillman, *Discoveries and Opinions of Galileo* (translations with notes), Anchor Books, 1957.

Drake, Stillman and O'Malley, C. D., *The Controversy on the Comets of 1618*, University of Pennsylvania Press, 1960.

Drake, Stillman, *Galileo Studies*, University of Michigan Press, 1970.

Drake, Stillman, *Galileo Against the Philosophers* (English translations with introduction and notes), Zeitlin and Ver Brugge, 1976.

Drake, Stillman, *Galileo at Work—His Scientific Biography*, University of Chicago Press, 1978.

Drake, Stillman, *Cause, Experiment, and Science: A Galiean dialogue incorporating a new English translation of Galileo's "Bodies That Stay atop Water, or Move in It,"* University of Chicago Press, 1981.

Dryer, J.L.E., *History of the Planetary Systems From Thales to Kepler*, Cambridge: at the University Press, 1906.

Eastwood, Bruce and Grassoff, Gerd, *Planetary Diagrams—Descriptions, Models, Theories: from Carolingian Deployments to Copernican Debates*, Max Plank Institute for the History of Science, Preprint 132, 2000.

Edson, E. and Savage-Smith, E., *Medieval Views of the Cosmos—Picturing the Universe in the Christian and Islamic Middle Ages*, Bodleian Library, 2004.

Evans, James, *The History and Practice of Ancient Astronomy,* Oxford University Press, 1998.

Fantoli, Annibale, *Galileo: For Copernicanism and for the Church*, (trans: Coyne, George V.), Vatican Observatory Publications, 1994.

Feingold, Mordechai ed., *Jesuit Science and the Republic of Letters*, MIT Press, 2003.

Feke, Jacqueline, *Ptolemy in Philosophical Context: A Study of the Relationships Between Physics, Mathematics, and Theology*, PhD Dissertation, University of Toronto, 2009.

Ferngren, Gary B. (ed.), *Science and Religion: A Historical Introduction*, Johns Hopkins University Press, 2002.

Finocchiaro, Maurice A. (ed.), *The Galileo Affair: A Documentary History*, University of California Press, 1989.

Finocchiaro, Maurice A., *Retrying Galileo, 1633-1992*, University of California Press, 2005.

Finocchiaro, Maurice A (ed. and trans.), *The Essential Galileo*, Hackett Publishing Company, Inc., 2008.

Finocchiaro, Maurice A, *Defending Copernicus and Galileo: Critical Reasoning in the Two Affairs*, Volume 280 Boston Studies in the Philosophy of Science, Springer, 2010.

Fletcher, John E., *Astronomy in the Life and Correspondence of Athanasius Kircher*, Isis, Vol. 61, No. 1, 1970, pp. 52-67.

Foglia, Serena; Mirti, Grazia; and Kollerstrom, Nick, *Galileo's Horoscopes for his Daughters*, Culture and Cosmos: A journal of the history of astrology and cultural astronomy, Vol. 7, No 1, 2003.

Frankel, Henry R., *The Importance of Galileo's Nontelescopic Observations Concerning the Size of the Fixed Stars*, Isis, 1978, pp. 77-82.

Galilei, Galileo. *Dialogue Concerning the Two Chief World Systems*, Translation by Stillman Drake, The Modern Library, 2001.

Galilei, Galileo, *Sidereus Nuncius, or The Sidereal Messenger*, Translated by Albert Van Helden, University of Chicago Press, 1610/1989.

Gebler von, Carl, *Galileo Galilei and the Roman Curia*, 1876, Stuttgart. Translated by Mrs. G. Sturge, C. Kegan Paul and Co., 1878.

Geymonat, Ludovico, *Galileo Galilei: a Biography and Inquiry into His Philosophy of Science*, Translated by Stillman Drake, McGraw-Hill, 1957/1965.

Gies, Frances and Joseph, *Cathedral, Forge, and Waterwheel: Technology and Invention in the Middle Ages*, HarperCollins, 1994.

Gilbert, William, *De Magnete*, 1600 (Translated by P. Fleury Mottelay, 1889) Dover, 1958.

Gilbert, William, *De Mundo*, (1608/1653) (trans: Sister Suzanne Kelly), Menno Hertzberger and Company, 1965.

Gilder, Joshua and Gilder, Anne-Lee, *Heavenly Intrigue: Johannes Kepler, Tycho Brahe, and the Murder Behind One of History's Greatest Scientific Discoveries*, Doubleday, 2004.

Gingerich, Owen, *From Copernicus to Kepler: Heliocentrism as Model and as Reality*, Proceedings of the American Philosophical Society, Vol 117, No. 6, December 1973.

Gingerich, Owen, *Did Copernicus Owe a Debt to Aristarchus?* Journal for the History of Astronomy, 1985, pp. 37-42.

Gingerich, Owen, *Islamic Astronomy*, Scientific American, April, 1986, pp. 1-7.

Gingerich, Owen, and Westman, Robert S., *The Wittich Connection: Conflict and Priority in Late Sixteenth Century Cosmology*, Transactions of the American Philosophical Society, Vol 78, Part 7, 1988.

Gingerich, Owen, *The Trouble with Ptolemy*, Isis, Vol. 93, No. 1 (Mar., 2002), pp. 70-74.

Gingerich, Owen, *Kepler Then and Now*, Perspectives on Science, 2002, Vol. 10, no. 2, pp. 228-240.

Gingerich, Owen, *The Galileo Sunspot Controversy: Proof and Persuasion*, The Journal for the History of Astronomy, February 2003, No. 114, Vol. 34(1), pp. 77-78.

Gingerich, Owen, *The Book Nobody Read: Chasing the Revolutions of Nicolaus Copernicus*, Walker Publishing Company, 2004.

Gingerich, Owen and van Helden, Albert, *How Galileo Constructed the Moons of Jupiter*, Journal for the History of Astronomy, 2011, pp. 259-264.

Gingerich, Owen, *How Galileo and Kepler Changed the Face of Science*, Euresis, Vol. 2, Winter 2012, pp. 9-19.

Goldstein, Bernard R., *Theory and Observation in Medieval Astronomy*, Isis, Vol. 63, no.1, 1972, pp. 39-47.

Goldstein, Bernard R., *Copernicus and the Origin of his Heliocentric System*, Journal for the History of Astronomy, August, 2002, pp. 219-235.

Goldstein, Bernard R. and Barker, Peter, *The Role of Rothmann in the Dissolution of the Celestial Spheres*, British Journal for the History of Science, 28, 1995, pp. 385-403.

Goddu, Andre, *Reflections on the Origin of Copernicus's Cosmology*, Journal for the History of Astronomy, 2006, pp. 37.

Goody, Jack. *The Power of the Written Tradition*, Smithsonian Institution Press, 2000.

Granada, Miguel, A., *The Discussion between Kepler and Roeslin on the Nova of 1604*, 1604-2004: Supernovae as Cosmological Lighthouses, ASP Conference Series, Vol. 342, Proceedings of the conference held 15-19 June, 2004 in Padua, Italy. Edited by M. Turatto, S. Benetti, L. Zampieri, and W. Shea. San Francisco: Astronomical Society of the Pacific, 2005, pp. 30.

Granada, Miguel, A., *Did Tycho Eliminate the Celestial Spheres Before 1586?* Journal for the History of Astronomy, 2006, pp. 125-145.

Granada, Miguel A., *Michael Maestlin and the New Star of 1572*, Journal for the History of Astronomy, 2007, pp. 99-124.

Graney, Christopher, M. and Grayson, Timothy, P., *On the telescopic disks of stars – a review and analysis of stellar observations from the early 17th through the middle 19th centuries*, preprint arXiv:1003.4918

Graney, Christopher, M., *The Telescope against Copernicus, Star Observations by Riccioli Supporting a Geocentric Universe*, Journal for the History of Astronomy, 2010, 453- 467.

Graney, Christopher, M., *Riccioli Measures the Stars: Observations of the telescopic disks of stars as evidence against Copernicus and Galileo in the middle of the 17th century.* arXiv preprint arXiv:1004.4034 (2010).

Graney, Christopher, M., *Teaching Galileo? Get to Know Riccioli! What a Forgotten Italian Astronomer Can Teach Students about How Science Works*, Physics Teacher, 50, 2012, pp.18.

Graney, Christopher, M., *Science Rather than God: Riccioli's Review of the Case For and Against the Copernicus Hypothesis*, Journal for the History of Astronomy, Vol. 43, No. 2, 2012, pp. 215-226.

Grant, Edward, *Were there Significant Differences between Medieval and Early Modern Scholastic Natural Philosophy? The Case for Cosmology*, Nous, 1984, pp. 5-14.

Grant, Edward, *Celestial Orbs in the Latin Middle Ages*, Isis, Vol. 78, No. 2 (Jun, 1987), pp. 153-173.

Grant, Edward, *The Foundations of Modern Science in the Middle Ages*, Cambridge University Press, 1996.

Grant, Edward. *God and Reason in the Middle Ages*, Cambridge University Press, 2001.

Green, Jonathan, *The First Copernican Astrologer: Andreas Aurifaber's Practica for 1541*, Journal for the History of Astronomy, 2010, pp. 157-165.

Guerrini, Luigi, *Echoes from the Pulpit: A Preacher against Galileo's Astronomy (1610-1615)*, Journal for the History of Astronomy, 2012, 377-389.

Hall, A. Rupert, *The Revolution in Science: 1500-1750*, Longman, 1954/1995.

Hall, Marie Boas, *The Scientific Renaissance, 1450-1630*, Dover, 1962/1994.

Hannaway, Owen, *Laboratory Design and the Aim of Science: Andreas Libavius versus Tycho Brahe*, Isis, Vol. 77, No. 4, 1986, pp. 584-610.

Harrison, Edward, *Whigs, prigs and historians of science*, Nature, 329 (1987), pp. 213–14.

Henry, John, *The Scientific Revolution and the Origins of Modern Science, 3rd ed.*, Palgrave/Macmillan, 2008.

Heilbron, J. L., The Sun in the Church: Cathedrals as Solar Observatories, Harvard University Press, 1999.

Heilbron, J. L., *Galileo*, Oxford University Press, 2010.

Heilbron, J. L., *Robert Westman on Galileo and Related Matters*, Perspectives on Science, 2012, vol. 20, no.3, pp. 379-388.

Hill, G.W., *Researches in Lunar Theory*, American Journal of Mathematics, Vol.1, No.1, 1878, pp. 5-26.

Hooykaas, R., G.J., *Rheticus' Treatise on Holy Scripture and the Motion of the Earth*, North-Holland Publishing Company, 1984.

Hooykaas, R., *The Aristotelian Background to Copernicus's Cosmology*, Journal for the History of Astronomy, 1987, pp. 111-116.

Hoskin, Michael, ed., *The Cambridge Concise History of Astronomy*, Cambridge University Press, 1999.

Howell, Kenneth J., *God's Two Books: Copernican Cosmology and Biblical Interpretation in Early Modern Science*, University of Notre Dame Press, 2002.

Hunt, L., Martin, T.R., Rosenwein, B.H., Po-chia Hsia, Smith, B.G., *The Making of the West Peoples and Cultures—A Concise History, Volume I: To 1740, 2nd Ed.*, Bedford St. Martin's, 2007.

Hutchison, Keith, *Sunspots, Galileo, and the Orbit of the Earth*, Isis, Vol. 81, No. 1, (Mar., 1990), pp. 68-74.

Jacobs, Rabbi Louis, *Jewish Cosmology*, in *Ancient Cosmologies*, Blacker, Carmen and Loewe, Michael, Allen and Unwin, 1975.

Jardine, Nicholas, *The Significance of the Copernican Orbs*, Journal for the History of Astronomy, Vol. 13, 1982, pp. 168-194.

Jardine, Nicholas, *The Birth of History and Philosophy of Science: Kepler's "A Defence of Tycho against Ursus" with Essays on its Provenance and Significance*, Cambridge University Press, 1984.

Jardine, Nick, *Whigs and Stories: Herbert Butterfield and the Historiography of Science*, History of Science, 41(2003): pp. 125–140.

Jarrell, Richard A., in *Encyclopedia of the Scientific Revolution*, Wilbur Applebaum ed., 2000, Garland Publishing.

Jarrell, Richard A., *Maestlin's Place in Astronomy*, Physis, 1975, pp. 5-20.

Jones, Alexander. *The Adaptation of Babylonian Methods in Greek Numerical Astronomy*, Isis, 1991, 82: pp. 441-453.

Kagan, Donald; Ozment, Steven; Turner, Frank M., *The Western Heritage, 4th Ed.*, Macmillan, 1991.

Keller, A. G., *A Byzantine Admirer of 'Western' Progress: Cardinal Bessarion*, Cambridge Historical Journal, Vol. 11, No. 3 (1955), pp. 343-348.

Kepler, Johannes, *Conversation with the Sidereal Messenger*, (1610) (trans. Edward Rosen), Johnson Reprint Corporation, 1965.

Kepler, Johannes, *Somnium*, (translated by Rosen, Edward), University of Wisconsin Press, 1634/1967.

Kepler, Johannes, *Astronomia nova*, (translated by William Donahue), Cambridge University Press, 1609/1992.

Kepler, Johannes, *The Epitome of Copernican Astronomy, Books Four and Five and Harmonies of the World, Book Five, (trans. Charles Glenn Wallis)*, Annapolis: The St. John's Bookstore/ Prometheus Books, 1618-1621/1939/1995.

Kepler, Johannes, *Mysterium Cosmographicum: The Secret of the Universe*, 2nd edition, (trans. A. M. Duncan), 1621/1981.

Klein, Richard G, *The Human Career: Human Biological and Cultural Origins, 2nd ed.* The University of Chicago Press, 1999.

Koyre, Alexandre, *From the Closed World to the Infinite Universe*, Johns Hopkins University Press, 1957.

Kraai, Jesse, *Rheticus' Heliocentric Providence: A Study Concerning the Astrology, Astronomy of the Sixteenth Century*, PhD dissertation, Ruprecht-Karls-University Heidelberg, 2003.

Kremer, Richard L., *Calculating with Andreas Aurifaber: A New Source for Copernican Astronomy in 1540*, Journal for the History of Astronomy, 2010, 483-502.

Krupp, E. C. *Echoes of the Ancient Skies: The Astronomy of Lost Civilizations*, Oxford University Press, 1983.

Kuhn, Thomas S. *The Copernican Revolution*, Harvard University Press, 1957.

Kuhn, Thomas S. *Structures of Scientific Revolutions*, University of Chicago Press, 1962.

Kusukawa, Sachiko, *The Transformation of Natural Philosophy: The case of Philip Melanchthon*, Cambridge University Press, 1995.

Laird, W. R., *Archimedes among the Humanists*, Isis, vol. 82, No. 4 (Dec., 1991), pp. 628-638.

Lattis, James, M., *Between Copernicus and Galileo: Christoph Clavius and the Collapse of Ptolemaic Cosmology*, University of Chicago Press, 1994.

Laudan, Larry, *The Demise of the Demarcation Problem*, in *Physics, Philosophy and Psychoanalysis*, Cohen, R. S. and Laudan, L. (eds), pp. 111-127, Reidel Publishing Company, 1983.

Laudan, Larry, *Science and Relativism: Some Key Controversies in the Philosophy of Science*, University of Chicago Press, 1990.

Laven, Mary, *Encountering the Counter-Reformation*, Renaissance Quarterly, Vol. 59, No. 3, pp. 706-720, 2006.

Lindberg, David C. *The Transmission of Greek and Arabic Learning to the West*, pp. 52-90 in *Science in the Middle Ages.* Edited by David C. Lindberg, University of Chicago Press, 1978.

Lindberg, David C. and Numbers, Ronald L. (eds.), *God and Nature: Historical Essays on the Encounter Between Christianity and Science,* University of California Press, 1986.

Lindberg, David C. *The Beginnings of Western Science*, Chicago University Press, 1992.

Lloyd, G.E.R., *Early Greek Science: Thales to Aristotle*, Norton, 1970.

Lloyd, G.E.R., *Greek Science after Aristotle*, Norton, 1973.

Lloyd, G.E.R., *Magic, Reason and Experience: Studies in the Origins and Development of Greek Science*, Oxford University Press, 1979.

Lodge, Sir Oliver, *Pioneers of Science*, Macmillan, 1905.

Machamer, Peter (editor), *The Cambridge Companion to Galileo*, Cambridge University Press, 1998.

Magee, Brian. *The Story of Philosophy*, Dorling Kindersley, 1998.

Mandrou, Robert, *From Humanism to Science: 1480-1700*, (translated by Brian Pearce), Humanities Press, 1979/1973.

Margolis, Howard, *Patterns, Thinking, and Cognition: A Theory of Judgment*, University of Chicago Press, 1987.

Magruder, Kerry V., *Jesuit Science After Galileo: The Cosmology of Gabriele Beati*, Centaurus, 2009, Vol. 51, pp. 189-212.

Marr, Alexander, *Between Raphael and Galileo: Mutio Oddi and the mathematical culture of late Renaissance Italy*, University of Chicago Press, 2011.

Martin, Jean-Pierre and McConnell Anita, *Joining the Observatories of Paris and Greenwich*, Notes and Records of the Royal Society of London, Vol. 62, No. 4, 2008, pp. 355-372.

Martin, Thomas R., *Ancient Greece*, Yale University Press, 2000.

Martins, Roberto de Andrade, *Natural or Violent Motion? Galileo's Conjectures on the Fall of Heavy Bodies*, Dialoghi – Rivista di Studi Italici, 2, 1998, 45-67.

McClellan, James, E. and Dorn, Harold. *Science and Technology in World History—An Introduction*, Johns Hopkins University Press, 1999.

McIver, Robert K., *"Cosmology" as a Key to the Thought-world of Philo of Alexandria*, Theology Papers and Journal Articles, Paper 22. At ResearchOnline@Avondale.

McMullin, Ernan, (ed), *The Church and Galileo*, University of Notre Dame Press, 2005.

Methuen, Charlotte, *Maestlin's Teaching of Copernicus: The Evidence of His University Textbook and Disputations*, Isis, Vol. 87, No. 2, 1996, pp. 230-247.

Methuen, Charlotte, *Kepler's Tübingen: Stimulus to a Theological Mathematics*, Ashgate, 1998.

Meyer, Eric, *Galileo's Cosmogonical Calculations*, Isis, vol. 80, No. 3, 1989, pp. 456-468.

Miller, David Marshall, *The Thirty Years War and the Galileo Affair*, History of Science, 2008, pp. 49-74.

Moran, Bruce T., *Christoph Rothmann, The Copernican Theory, and Institutional and Technical Influences on the Criticism of Aristotelian Cosmology*, The Sixteenth Century Journal, Vol. 13, No. 3, 1982, pp. 85-108.

Morrison, Robert, *A Scholarly Intermediary between the Ottoman Empire and*

Renaissance Europe, Isis, Vol. 105, No. 1, Mar. 2014, pp. 32-57.

Mosley, Adam, *Bearing the Heavens: Tycho Brahe and the Astronomical Community of the Late Sixteenth Century*, Cambridge University Press, 2007.

Mueller, Paul R., S.J., *An Unblemished Success: Galileo's Sunspot Argument in the Dialogue*, Journal for the History of Astronomy, November, 2000.

Naylor, Ronald, *Galileo's Need for Precision: The "Point" of the Fourth Day Pendulum Experiment*, Isis, Vol. 68, No. 1, (Mar., 1977), pp. 97-103.

Neugebauer, O. *The Exact Sciences in Antiquity*, Dover, 1969.

Neugebauer, O, and Sachs, A. eds., *Mathematical Cuneiform Texts*, American Oriental Society, 1986.

Newton, Isaac, Sir, *Principia : Mathematical Principles of Natural Philosophy / Isaac Newton; A New Translation*, translators: I. Bernard Cohen and Anne Whitman, assisted by Julia Budenz, preceded by a guide to Newton's Principia by I. Bernard Cohen, University of California Press, 1999.

Norlind, Wihelm, *Copernicus and Luther: A Critical Study*, Isis, Vol. 44, No. 3, 1953, pp. 273-276.

North John, *The Norton History of Astronomy and Cosmology*, Norton, 1994.

Palmieri, Paolo, *Re-examining Galileo's Theory of Tides*, Archive for History of Exact Sciences, 53, 1998, pp. 223-375.

Palmieri, Paolo, *Science and Authority in Giacomo Zabarella*, History of Science, 2007, pp. 404-427.

Palmieri, Paolo, *Galileus Deceptus, Non Minime Decepit: A Re-Appraisal of a Counter-Argument in Dialogo to the Extrusion Effect of a Rotating Earth*, Journal for the History of Astronomy, 2008, pp. 425-452.

Peterson, Mark A., *Galileo's Muse: Renaissance Mathematics and the Arts*, Harvard University Press, 2011.

Phillips, William D. and Phillips, Carla Rahn, *The Worlds of Christopher Columbus*, Cambridge University Press, 1992.

Pohl, Frederick J., *Amerigo Vespucci: Pilot Major*, Columbia University Press, 1944.

Polanyi, Michael, *Personal Knowledge—Towards a Post-Critical Philosophy*, University of Chicago, 1958.

Ragep, F. Jamil, *Ali Qushji and Regiomontanus: Eccentric Transformations and Copernican Revolutions*, Journal for the History of Astronomy, 2005, pp. 359-371.

Raphael, Renée, *A Non-Astronomical Image in an Astronomical Text: Visualizing Motion in Riccioli's Almagestum Novum*, Journal for the History of Astronomy, 2011, pp. 73-90.

Rawlins, Dennis, *Eratosthenes' Geodesy Unraveled: Was There a High-Accuracy Hellenistic Astronomy?* Isis, Vol. 73, No 2. (Jun., 1982), pp. 259-265.

Redondi, Pietro, *Galileo: Heretic*, (trans: Raymond Rosenthal), Princeton University Press, 1987.

Reston, James Jr., *Galileo: A Life*, HarperCollins, 1994.

Robison, Wade L., *Galileo on the Moons of Jupiter*, Annals of Science, 1974, Vol. 31, No 2, pp. 165-169.

Robson, Eleanor, *Mesopotamian Mathematics, 2100-1600 BC: Technical Constants in Bureaucracy and Education*, Oxford University Press, 1999.

Roochnick, David, *Retrieving the Ancients*, Blackwell Publishing, 2004.

Rosen, Edward, *Three Copernican Treatises*, Dover, 1939/1959.

Rosen, Edward, *Copernicus Was Not a Priest*, Proceedings of the American Philosophical Society, Vol. 104, No. 6, December 1960, pp. 635-662.

Rosen, Edward, *Galileo and Kepler: Their First Two Contacts*, Isis, Vol. 57, No.2 (Summer 1966), pp. 262-264.

Rosen, Edward, *Copernicus and the Scientific Revolution*, An Anvil Original/Robert E. Krieger Publishing Company, 1984.

Rosen, Edward, *The Dissolution of the Solid Celestial Spheres*, Journal of the History of Ideas, Vol. 46, No. 1 (Jan-Mar, 1985), pp. 13-31.

Rubenstein, Richard E., *Aristotle's Children*, Harcourt, 2003.

Ruffner, J.A., *The Curved and the Straight: Cometary Theory from Kepler to Hevelius*, Journal for the History of Astronomy, 1971, pp. 178-194.

Russell, Jeffrey Burton, *Inventing the Flat Earth: Columbus and Modern Historians*, Praeger, 1997.

Russell, J.L., *Kepler's Laws of Planetary Motion: 1609-1666*, The British Journal for the History of Science, Vol. 2, 1964, pp. 1-24.

Russell, John L., *Catholic Astronomers and the Copernican system after the Condemnation of Galileo*, Annals of Science, 46, 1989, pp. 365-386.

Rutkin, H. Darrel, *Galileo Astrologer: Astrology and Mathematical Practice in the Late-Sixteenth and Early-seventeenth Centuries*, Galilaeana, II, 2005, pp. 107-143.

Sabra, A. I., *Arabic Science: Locality versus Essence*, Isis, Vol 87, No. 4 (Dec., 1996), pp. 654-670.

Sakamoto, Kuni, *The German Hercules's Heir: Pierre Gassendi's Reception of Keplerian Ideas*, Journal of the History of Ideas, 70 (2009): pp. 69-91.

Schmitt, Charles B., *On a Poem Misattributed to Galileo*, Isis, Vol. 63, No. 1 (Mar., 1972), pp. 95-97.

Schmitt, Charles B., *Aristotle and the Renaissance*, Harvard University Press, 1983.

Schofield, Christine Jones, *Tychonic and Semi-Tychonic World Systems*, Arno Press, 1981.

Segre, Michael, *Viviani's Life of Galileo*, Isis, Vol. 80, No. 2 (Jun., 1989), pp. 206-231.

Settle, Thomas B., *Experimental Sense in Galileo's Early Works and its Likely Sources*, pp. 831-850 in Largo Campo Di Filosofare, Eurosymposium Galileo 2001.

Settle, Thomas B., *Dante, the Inferno and Galileo*, in *Pictorial Means in Early Modern Engineering, 1400-1650*, Max Planck Institute for the History of Science, Wolfgang Lefèvre (ed), 2002, 139-157.

Shackelford, Jole, *Tycho Brahe, Laboratory Design, and the Aim of Science: Reading Plans in Context*, Isis, Vol 84, No. 2, 1993, pp. 211-230.

Shank, Michael H., *Regiomontanus and Homocentric Astronomy*, Journal for the History of Astronomy, 1998, pp. 157-166.

Shank, Michael H., *Regiomontanus on Ptolemy, Physical Orbs, and Astronomical Fictionalism: Goldsteinian Themes in the "Defense of Theon against George of Trebizond,"* Perspectives on Science, Vol. 10, No. 2, 2002, pp. 179-207.

Shank, Michael H., *Regiomontanus as a Physical Astronomer: Samplings from The Defence of Theon against George of Trebizond*, Journal for the History of Astronomy, 2007, pp. 325-349.

Shank, Michael H., *Setting up Copernicus? Astronomy and Natural Philosophy in Giambattista Capuano da Manfredonia's Expositio on the Sphere*, Early Science and Medicine,14, 2009, pp. 290-315.

Shapin, Steven, *The Scientific Revolution*, University of Chicago Press, 1996.

Sharratt, Michael, *Galileo: Decisive Innovator*, Blackwell, 1994.

Shea, W.R.J., *Galileo's Claim to Fame: The Proof that the Earth Moves from the Evidence of the Tides*, The British Journal for the History of Science, Vol 5, No. 18, 1970, pp. 111-127.

Shea, William R., *Galileo, Scheiner, and the Interpretation of Sunspots*, Isis, Vol. 61, No. 4 (Winter, 1970), pp. 498-519.

Shea, William R. and Artigas, Mariano, *Galileo in Rome: The Rise and Fall of a Troublesome Genius*, Oxford University Press, 2003.

Siebert, Harald, *The Early Search for Stellar Parallax: Galileo, Castelli, and Ramponi*, Journal for the History of Astronomy, (2005), pp. 251-271.

Smith, Alan G. R., *Science and Society in the Sixteenth and Seventeenth Centuries*. 1972.

Smith, George, "Isaac Newton", *The Stanford Encyclopedia of Philosophy (Fall 2008 Edition)*, Edward N. Zalta (ed.), URL = <http://plato.stanford.edu/archives/fall2008/entries/newton/>.

Smith, Logan Pearsall, *The Life and Letters of Sir Henry Wotton*, Oxford Clarendon Press, 1907.

Smith, Mark A., *Galileo's Proof for the Earth's Motion from the Movement of Sunspots*, Isis, Vol. 76, No. 4 (Dec., 1985), pp. 544-545.

Snelders, H. A. M., *Christian Huygens and Newton's Theory of Gravitation*, Notes Rec. R. Soc. Lond., 43, 1989, pp. 209-222.

Sobel, Dava, *Galileo's Daughter*, Walker, 1999.

Somerville, W.B., *The Description of Foucault's Pendulum*, Quarterly Journal of the Royal Astronomical Society, 1972, Vol. 13, pp. 40.

Stephenson, Bruce, *Kepler's Physical Astronomy*, Princeton University Press, 1994.

Stromgren, Elis, *Periodic Orbits in the Restricted Problem of Three Bodies in Their Relation to Hill's Work on the Motion of the Moon*, American Journal of Mathematics, Vol. 60, No. 4 (Oct., 1938), pp. 867-879.

Swerdlow, Noel M. *The Derivation and First Draft of Copernicus's Planetary*

Theory: A Translation of the Commentariolus with Commentary, Proceedings of the American Philosophical society, Vol 117, No. 6, December 1973, pp. 423-512.

Swerdlow, N. M. and Neugebauer, O. *Mathematical Astronomy in Copernicus's De Revolutionibus,* Springer-Verlag, 1984.

Swerdlow, N. M. *An Essay on Thomas Kuhn's First Scientific Revolution, The Copernican Revolution,* Proceedings of the American Philosophical Society, Vol 148, No. 1, March 2004, pp. 64-120.

Swerdlow, N. M. *Galileo's Horoscopes,* Journal for the History of Astronomy, 2004, pp. 135-141.

Swerdlow, N. M., *Copernicus and Astrology, with an Appendix of Translations of Primary Sources,* Perspectives on Science, 2012, vol. 20, no. 3, pp. 353-378.

Tarnas, Richard. *The Passion of the Western Mind,* Ballantine Books, 1991.

Taton, Reni; Wilson, Curtis; and Hoskin, Michael (eds.), *General History of Astronomy: Volume 2, Planetary Astronomy from the Renaissance to the Rise of Astrophysics (General History of Astronomy),* Cambridge University Press, 2003.

Taub, Liba. *Ptolemy's Universe,* Open Court, 1993.

Thoren, Victor. *The Lord of Uraniborg,* Cambridge University Press, 1990.

Toomer, G.J. *Hipparchus and Babylonian Astronomy,* from pp. 353-362 in *A Scientific Humanist: Studies in Memory of Abraham Sachs,* Erle Leichty, editor. 1988.

Topper, David, *Galileo, Sunspots, and the Motions of the Earth: Redux,* Isis, (1999), 90, pp. 757-767.

Topper, David, *Colluding with Galileo: On Mueller's Critique of My Analysis of Galileo's Sunspot Argument,* Journal for the History of Astronomy, February 2003, No 114, Vol. 34(1), pp. 75-76.

Tredwell, Katherine A., *Michael Maestlin and the Fate of the Narratio Prima,* Journal for the History of Astronomy, 2004, pp. 305-325.

Van De Mieroop, Marc, *A History of the Ancient Near East—ca. 3000-323 BC, 2nd Ed.,* Blackwell Publishing, 2007.

Van Helden, Albert, *The Telescope in the Seventeenth Century,* Isis, Vol. 65, No. 1 (Mar., 1974), pp. 38-58.

Van Helden, Albert, *The Invention of the Telescope,* Transactions of the American Philosophical Society, New Series, Vol. 67, No. 4 1977, pp. 1-67.

Van Helden, Albert, *Measuring the Universe,* University of Chicago Press, 1985.

Van Helden, Albert, *Telescopes and Authority from Galileo to Cassini,* Osiris, 1994, 9: pp. 9-29.

Vidmar, John, *The Catholic Church Through the Ages: A History,* Paulist Press, 2005.

Voelkel, James R., *Kepler and the New Astronomy,* Oxford Portraits in Science, Oxford University Press, 1999.

Voelkel, James R. and Gingerich, Owen, *Giovanni Antonio Magini's "Keplerian"*

Tables of 1614 and Their Implications for the Reception of Keplerian Astronomy in the Seventeenth Century, Journal for the History of Astronomy, 2001, Vol. 32, pp. 237-262.

Voelkel, James, *The Composition of Kepler's Astronomia Nova*, Princeton University Press, 2001.

von Erhardt, Rudolf and von Erhardt-Siebold, Erika, *Archimedes' Sand-Reckoner: Aristarchos and Copernicus*, Isis, Vol. 33, No. 5 (Mar., 1942), pp. 578-602.

Wallace, William A. O.P., *Galileo's Trial and the Proof of the Earth's Motion*, Catholic Dossier, 1.2 (1995), pp. 7-13.

Westfall, Richard S., *The Construction of Modern Science*, Cambridge University Press, 1971.

Westfall, Richard S., *Never at Rest: A Biography of Isaac Newton*, Cambridge University Press, 1983.

Westfall, Richard S., *Science and Patronage: Galileo and the Telescope*, Isis, Vol. 76, No. 1 (Mar., 1985), pp. 11-30.

Westfall, Richard S. *Essays on the Trial of Galileo*, Studi Galileiani, Vatican Observatory Publications, 1989.

Westfall, Richard S., *The Life of Isaac Newton*, Cambridge University Press, 1993.

Westman, Robert S., *The Melanchthon Circle, Rheticus, and the Wittenberg Interpretation of the Copernican Theory*, Isis, vol. 66, no. 2, 1975, pp. 164-193.

Westman, Robert S., *Introduction: The Copernican Achievement*, In *The Copernican Achievement*, ed. Robert S. Westman, University of California Press, 1975.

Westman, Robert S., *Three Responses to the Copernican Theory: Johannes Praetorius, Tycho Brahe, and Michael Maestlin*, ed. Robert S. Westman, University of California Press, 1975, pp. 285-345.

Westman, Robert S., *The Astronomer's Role in the Sixteenth Century: A Preliminary Study*, History of Science, 1980, pp. 105-147.

Westman, Robert S., *The Copernicans and the Churches*, From: "In God and Nature", Lindberg and Numbers eds., 1986, pp. 76-113.

Westman, Robert S., *The Copernican Question: Prognostication, Skepticism, and Celestial Order*, University of California Press, 2011.

Westman, Robert S., *The Copernican Question Revisited: A Reply to Noel Swerdlow and John Heilbron*, Perspectives on Science, 2013, pp. 100-136.

Wilken, Robert Louis, *The Spirit of Early Christian Thought*, Yale University Press, 2003.

Wilson, Curtis, *How Did Kepler Discover His First Two Laws?* Scientific American, 1972 (March), 226, pp. 93-106.

Wilson, Curtis, *Predictive Astronomy in the Century after Kepler*, in Planetary Astronomy from the Renaissance to the Rise of Astrophysics, Part A: Tycho Brahe to Newton, Cambridge University Press, 1989.

Wilson, Curtis, *Kepler's Laws, So Called*, The Newsletter of the Historical

Astronomy Division of the American Astronomical Society, No. 31, May 1994, pp. 1.

Winkler, Mary G. and Van Helden, Albert, *Representing the Heavens: Galileo and Visual Astronomy*, Isis, 1992, pp. 195-217.

Wisan, Winifred Lovell, *Galileo and God's Creation*, Isis, Vol. 77, No. 3 (Sep., 1986), pp. 473-486.

Wootton, David, *Galileo: Watcher of the Skies*, Yale University Press, 2010.

Wrightsman, Bruce, *Andreas Osiander's Contribution to the Copernican Achievement*, In *The Copernican Achievement*, ed. Robert S. Westman, University of California Press, 1975, pp. 213-243.

Zinner, E., *Regiomontanus: His Life and Work*, Studies in the History and Philosophy of Mathematics, Vol 1, Elesvier Science Publishing Company Inc, 1990.

CPSIA information can be obtained at www.ICGtesting.com
Printed in the USA
LVOW03s0821250815

451382LV00010B/128/P